OHIO PLACE NAMES

OHIO

PLACE

NAMES

LARRY L. MILLER

INDIANA UNIVERSITY PRESS   BLOOMINGTON AND INDIANAPOLIS

The paper used in this publication meets the minimum
requirements of American National Standard for Information
Sciences—Permanence of Paper for Printed Library
Materials, ANSI Z39.48-1984.

Manufactured in the United States of America

Library of Congress Cataloging-in-Publication Data

Miller, Larry L., date
Ohio place-names / Larry L. Miller.
p.   cm.
ISBN 0-253-32932-9 (alk. paper)
1. Names, Geographical—Ohio. 2. Ohio—History, Local.
I. Title.
F489.M55 1996
917.71'003—dc20   95-14555

1 2 3 4 5 01 00 99 98 97 96

To
Brody L. Nickol
and
N. J. Nickol

CONTENTS

Preface

This volume has been designed as an aid in historical or geographical research, as well as to satisfy the curiosity of general readers. Among those who may find it of interest or utility are librarians, library patrons, members of historical and genealogical societies, and laypersons.

While the book contains a certain amount of secondary or ancillary data, its primary purpose is to provide the "reasons" for naming Ohio's hamlets, towns, and cities. The compiler has striven diligently to meet this primary goal even when little else could be found regarding the place.

With any project of such an ambitious nature, it is necessary to circumscribe its bounds, designating what is within the purview of the work as well as distinguishing that which is outside the scope of the work. Not to do so is to blur the aims of the undertaking and allow it to get out of hand. When that occurs, a danger exists that the undertaking will become a lifelong, all-consuming task instead of a doable assignment with a reasonable expectation of culminating in a timely manner in a volume that will be made available to the public. For it is only by finally placing this work in the hands of readers and searchers that it can serve its purpose of answering questions and satisfying interest.

Notwithstanding that the book has been purposely designed to have distinct bounds and limitations, it may rightfully be claimed to possess by far the best and broadest coverage of any similar work on Ohio's populated places—not that there have been many books with the sole aim of addressing this niche; such compilations have been few and far between. In fact, the last substantive work to address a goal similar to that of this volume was published in the late 1950s. It contained fewer than 1,200 entries, and in many of them, disappointingly, the reasons for the names were not really explained. By contrast, the volume you are holding contains more than 2,500 place-name entries, and in virtually all of them the name rationale is set forth, albeit in a small percentage of cases the explanation is speculative, since no authoritative documentation exists or could be unearthed using reasonable investigative means.

Wherever possible, in addition to a reason for or explanation of the place-name, an attempt has been made to flesh out the entry with the year the place was founded, surveyed, settled, or platted. And, although current names are the primary focus, previous names are provided and discussed where such information was available. Where applicable and convenient to do so, incorporation dates are provided. In a great number of instances, the owner of the townsite upon inception is named.

The entries include Ohio cities, towns, villages, hamlets, and communities of every size and stature having their own distinct identities. No importance has been placed on the legal aspect of this terminology, and no fine distinctions have been attempted. Cities and villages, technically, have legal definitions. Even the word *hamlet* at one time was not generically applied—as I have taken the liberty to do here—to virtually any tiny community but instead had its own defined, legal application. Becoming overly concerned with geopolitical entity status was deemed a distraction from the primary goal of this compilation, so little attention should be paid to those terms as employed herein.

As a bonus, the names of Ohio's eighty-eight counties have been included, with brief meanings, in a separate listing.

Outside the parameters of this work are ghost towns and other places that no longer exist at their original location. Admittedly, one might have a difficult time discerning between some of the places included in this volume and those deemed ghost towns. The judgment to include places was often arbitrary; frequently it was based on being able to locate them on maps in current use. Township names have not been separately listed; very frequently the name of the township is duplicated in the name of a town within a township.

No neighborhoods or developments fall within the scope of the coverage. Developments are not in any sense towns or cities, and while neighborhoods often possess many of the distinctions that identify places as towns, they usually do not have defined boundaries, are unincorporated, and have never been laid out. In urban areas, neighborhoods may well be sections of cities or villages.

A high value has been placed on anecdotal material relating to the naming of towns. Consequently, wherever interesting stories regarding the naming process existed and could be located, a capsule account has been included for its human interest. In some instances, these accounts smack of being suspect. But they do add an element of humor to an often dry recitation, and so it was decided to incorporate them and let the reader make the judgment as to how much credence to place in them. No attempt was made to become the final arbiter between or among place-name explanations focusing on the same community. All accounts that were found are presented.

Nowadays, if a town were being founded and a name was required, no doubt it would be left to a computer to spit out unused possibilities, perhaps even to make the final selection. But few Ohio towns are being founded as the year 2000 approaches. Most were spawned from the late 1700s through the nineteenth century.

So what were the most common sources for town names in Ohio? Probably the surnames (in some cases the given names) of individuals—persons who were directly involved in founding the places or persons whom the namers desired to honor. Entries that fall into this category will be of special note to readers interested in onomastics.

In earlier years, the United States Post Office Department was tremendously influential in deciding on place-names. If a place wanted to obtain a post office, the department often dictated its name or a name change. The department preferred short names and ones that would not be confused with other Ohio post office names. In many instances, the name of the postmaster became the name of the place.

Names recycled from other states or countries now designate many Ohio places. Often the original name came from a city, region, state, or nation that the settlers had left behind.

The penetration of railroads through the state's countryside had a profound effect on the place-names. Equally influential was the Native American presence in Ohio: numerous towns were named after prominent Indians or carry names that trace back to Indian terms.

Canal building resulted in a stream of Ohio place-names, many of them beginning with or ending in *port,* since the coming of the canal automatically qualified a community on its banks as a shipping or receiving town.

Mining or minerals found locally, geophysical or aesthetic features, local flora, and battle sites were other frequent inspirations for Ohio place-names.

The compiler takes pride in the vital role that lay consultants played in bringing this volume to reality. In that respect, it is probably unique for books on this subject. These consultants are listed in an acknowledgments section at the end of the book.

Many letters were written to local newspaper editors around the state, who in turn published the compiler's plea for input from readers. Those who replied, gratifyingly, often had firsthand knowledge of the naming of a town in question; some were descendants of the founders and were able to furnish rich accounts of the town's formation.

Other letters went out to county historical and genealogical societies, some of which contributed information directly or disseminated the request for data to members who possessed such information. A few who received the plea passed it on to third parties in other states, resulting—ironically—in the receipt of information on the naming of tiny Ohio hamlets from states hundreds or even thousands of miles distant.

Thousands of hours of arduous library research also went into the volume, with the compiler tapping the holdings of at least a dozen libraries in several counties.

It should be emphasized that virtually nothing new is to be found in this volume; its main accomplishment is centralizing between two covers data that were widely scattered. Often the bits of information relevant to this work were subsumed within verbose, wide-ranging contexts and had to be diligently distilled out for presentation herein.

Credit and gratitude are owed to the chroniclers whose work made this one possible. Some place-names were discussed at length in early works, while others were accorded the briefest of mentions. But whether terse or detailed, such passages, when taken collectively, comprised a rich repository without which this volume would not have been possible.

Although William Overman's volume, *Ohio Town Names,* published in the 1950s, left many voids, it was still a landmark compilation whose value should not be understated. And Lindsey's place-name research, although more localized in nature, was equally significant. These were the pioneers of research into Ohio place-names.

In perusing this volume, readers may discover certain trends in the naming of Ohio towns. Early Mahoning and Trumbull countians seemed to have a proclivity for ending town designations with "Corners." The state's shortest town name is Ai, in Fulton County. Many others have three-letter names. The respect Americans had for the Marquis de Lafayette becomes apparent over the course of the book's contents. "Bloom," in some form, also occurs in numerous Ohio place-names.

Is the volume truly comprehensive? Not at all. While the reader will find more Ohio town and city names covered here than in any other extant work, there are still many places the names of which the compiler hoped to explain but whose rationales were not located despite assiduous sleuthing. If there is one consolation, it is that nothing brings forth corrections or additions so much as the publication of a book. The author encourages such criticism, since it could well prove the foundation for an expansion or updating of this volume.

To shed light on the early apportionment of Ohio's lands, a few key terms need to be explained briefly.

The Connecticut Western Reserve. Also known as the Western Reserve of Ohio, the Western Reserve of Connecticut, Ohio's Western Reserve, or simply the Western Reserve, this region reached westward 120 miles from Pennsylvania's western border. It encompassed much of northeast and north-central Ohio. Counties included in the Western Reserve (some only in part) were Ashtabula, Cuyahoga, Lake, Huron, Erie, Portage, Trumbull, Mahoning, Summit, Medina, Geauga, Lorain, Ottawa, and Ashland. All of the land included is north of the Forty-first Parallel. The Connecticut and New England influence is evident in many of the place-names found in this area of Ohio.

The Firelands. This area occupies Erie and Huron counties, at the western end of the Western Reserve. During the American Revolution, Tory (British) raiders set fire to many towns in Connecticut, causing the owners, or "sufferers," to lose their homes. In 1792, Connecticut granted approximately a half million acres in this western region to those whose property had been destroyed, and the area became known as the Firelands. About 1,870 former Connecticut inhabitants took advantage of this grant.

The Virginia Military District. Because soldiers from Virginia, at considerable expense to that state, had subdued a number of British forts in the future Ohio area during the Revolution, Virginia had the strongest claim to a portion of the Ohio lands. To make reparations to Virginia, it was granted an area bounded on the south by the Ohio River, on the east and north by the Scioto River, and on the west by the Little Miami River. That was done in 1784, and a number of former Virginia soldiers moved to this region and settled. Other terms applied to it include Virginia Military Tract and Virginia Military Reserve.

OHIO

PLACE

NAMES

Place-Names

Abanaka *Van Wert County.* This hamlet is thought to bear the name of an early Native American tribe or confederacy of tribes. The spelling of the place-name probably has undergone an evolution. The written form of the Native American name seems to have been Abenaki or Abnaki. These Indians allied with the French and intermarried with French missionaries. It is unclear why this name was applied here in northwestern Ohio, since the greatest Abnaki concentration seems to have been in the Northeast—particularly Maine—and in Ontario, Canada. There is a town in Vermont named Abnaki.

Abbeyville *Medina County.* Abbeyville dates to about 1832 and reportedly was so named out of respect for Abbey, the wife of Levi Janes.

Abbottsville *Darke County.* The community derives its name from the founder of the town, a Mr. Abbott.

Aberdeen *Brown County.* Laid out, 1816, by Nathan Ellis. Ellis named the site after his Scottish hometown, the city of Aberdeen.

Academia *Knox County.* Platted, 1893, as College Place. (This name may have been misspelled as "Collage Place" in some records.) College Place was created at the time Mount Vernon Academy was founded, so the name was a natural choice. Mount Vernon Academy was a high school for youths of the Seventh-Day Adventist faith.

Acme *Medina County.* This site was previously called Millersburg, for the pioneer family of Samuel Miller. It derives its current name from the prominence on which it is located.

Ada *Hardin County.* Laid out in 1853. Incorporated in 1861. According to local historians, at the time the question of a new name arose, the postmaster here had a daughter named Ada. As a consequence, Ada became the name of the village. The previous name, Johnstown, duplicated that of another Ohio community.

Adams Mills *Muskingum County.* A flouring mill was built on the Ohio Canal at this location by brothers having the surname Adams. They were former residents of Virginia.

Adamsville *Gallia County.* This Raccoon Township community was laid out in 1837 by Adam and William Rickabaugh and named for Adam.

Adamsville *Muskingum County.* It was 1832 when Mordecai Adams, the landowner, laid this place out into lots.

Addison *Gallia County.* This small community was named after Joseph Addison (1672–1719), the English poet and scholar who served his country as secretary of state and member of Parliament. A divergent opinion states that it was named after a New England town. The proprietors were William Watson, Robert Reynolds, and John Lanks. Reuben Rothgeb laid the site out for them.

Addyston *Hamilton County.* The site was populated as early as 1789. An industrial facility for the production of pipe was opened here in 1871 by Matthew Addy. The small community that arose around it was called Addyston. It was incorporated in 1891.

Adelphi *Ross County.* In Greek, this term means "brothers." The site was platted and surveyed in 1804 by General Nathaniel Massie for Reuben and Henry Abrams, who were brothers. In 1838, the place was incorporated.

Adena *Jefferson County.* John McLaughlin named Adena after Thomas Worthington's country estate, which he had visited on several occasions. McLaughlin represented this county in the state assembly for sixteen years, during which the group convened at Chillicothe, Zanesville, and finally Columbus. The estate named Adena was near Chillicothe, and when the legislative body was meeting but not in session, McLaughlin would visit his friend Worthington there.

Africa *Delaware County.* This location was first known as East Orange. Samuel Patterson was one of the first to settle the site, doing so about 1824 and taking title to a large portion of land. During and after the Civil War, the hamlet played a role in the underground railroad, since most residents were abolitionists and offered refuge to freed slaves, many of whom took up residence here. An antiabolitionist derisively referred to the community as Africa, because of the many blacks there, and the label caught on.

Afton *Clermont County.* The name may have been inspired by a reference in a popular Robert Burns song, "Flow gently sweet Afton." The Afton is a river in Scotland.

Ai *Fulton County.* Settled by 1837. The name was conferred in 1840 by Ami Richards. As the story is told, Mr. Richards found the name in the Bible, where Ai is a wicked town destroyed by the righteous Joshua. An alternative explanation for the village's name is that Richards had intended to name it Ami after himself, but when he placed it on the record, he omitted the "m," and it thus became Ai. In 1979, an elderly local farmer was quoted as saying, "That wicked village stuff was bunk. In those days, there was no post office. So the postal people at Toledo sent the mail to an early settler by the name of Ami Richards at Dutch Ridge, not knowing where else to send it. Then a post office was put in and the officials lopped off the name Richards, dropped the 'm' in Ami, and Ai was born, nice and short." Whichever tale is correct, Ai has the distinction of being the shortest place-name in Ohio.

Aid *Lawrence County.* Laid out in 1840. The town is said to have been named by a Mr. Haymaker. The only reason given is that a short name was desired.

Akron *Summit County (seat).* Laid out in 1825. The city's name traces to the Greek *akros,* for "high place" or "summit." Akron was incorporated in 1836. Simon Perkins is credited with founding it.

Albany *Athens County.* Albany was laid out in 1831 and named for the capital of New York.

Alexandria *Licking County.* Founded, 1830, by Alexander DeVilbis. The name comes from the founder's given name. DeVilbis had erected a mill at this locale in 1821.

Alexandria *Scioto County.* The hamlet takes its name from Alexandria, Virginia, although a man named Alexander established it. Alexander Parker founded the place for his brother, Colonel Thomas Parker. The year given for this act, 1787, seems implausibly early, so it may be in error.

Alexis *Monroe County.* This name possibly derives from that of the first postmaster (1891), John A. Alexander.

Alger *Hardin County.* This village was established in 1882 and dubbed Jagger for the founders, Elias and Marie (or Maria) Jagger. Later, the name was changed to honor a governor of Michigan (1885–1886) who was born in Ohio, Russell A. Alger. Alger also served as President William McKinley's secretary of war.

Alikanna *Jefferson County.* Alexander and Anna Beatty founded this village in 1814. Its name was composed by using portions of their given names.

Alledonia *Belmont County.* This hamlet was initially referred to as Caldwell, in honor of Alexander H. Caldwell. When a post office went into operation here, the name was changed (possibly in 1879) to Alledonia, thought to be from an Indian term translating as "high over." Ada Caldwell is credited with the renaming.

Allen Corners *Trumbull County.* This community is probably named, directly or indirectly, for one of the prominent Allens who lived in the vicinity in the formative years. Two of them, Dr. Dudley Allen and Albert Allen, were trustees of Kinsman Township.

Allen Junction *Lucas County.* The etymology of this label is vague. It may relate to early area resident Shadrack W. Allen (1838) or to L. W. Allen.

Allensburg *Highland County.* Laid out, 1839, on real estate owned by Charles Henderson and Robert Pugh. The name honors William Allen, a U.S. senator from Ohio.

Allensville *Vinton County.* Founded, 1837, by Henry Cozad. U.S. Senator William Allen of Ohio, later a governor of the state, gave his name to this village.

Allentown *Allen County.* Platted, 1835, by William Myers and George Povenmyre. One clue to this town's name is its location in Allen County. Another clue may be found in the roster of original members of the United Brethren Church at Allentown; it includes Amos, George W., Patience, Sarah, Catherine, and Joseph D. Allen.

Alliance *Stark County.* Several clustered towns formed an alliance in 1854 to constitute this city: Freedom, Mount Union, Mahoning, and Williamsport. Incorporation took place in 1889.

Alpha *Greene County.* As the county's initial settlement (1798), the site was labeled with the first letter in the Greek alphabet.

Alston's Mill *Butler County.* At times known as Graham's Mill, Fairplay, and Black Bottom, this place today honors Thomas Alston, who operated mills on the east side of the Great Miami River.

Alton *Franklin County.* Platted in 1836, the town was surveyed by Thomas Graham. It is said to have been named for Fred Althon, whose surname was common in the area at the time. Why the spellings fail to agree is uncertain.

Alvada *Seneca County.* Laid out, 1876, by William Smith on his farm. The surveyor was A. C. Turner. This village was named after Nettie Alvada Smith, the daughter of William and Sophia (or Annette) McClellan. William not only was a landowner but at various times ran sawmills and a grist mill, served as a trustee, operated stores, served in public offices, and was postmaster as well as ticket/freight/express agent. Nettie (1863–1895) became Alvada Smith Herbert.

Alvordton *Williams County.* Surveyed, 1881, by Emerson B. Opdyke. Henry D. Alvord, the land proprietor, founded the village, and it bears his name.

Amanda *Allen County.* The village was named for Fort Amanda, which Colonel James Poague had named for his wife, Amanda.

Amanda *Butler County.* Laid out, 1827, by Samuel Dickey and Robert Coddington. The name is said to honor Dickey's daughter.

Amberley *Hamilton County.* Chase Davies asked a Mr. French for a donation of property, apparently to establish this village. In return, Davies suggested that French be accorded the honor of naming the new village. Having toured England many times and convinced that the village's ultimate success would depend largely on the selection of a name that would add dignity and commemorate the rural atmosphere, French submitted a list of possibilities. Included were Edmunton, Moorlands, Connington, Surrey Village, Hawthorne, Amberley, High Meadows, Coverly, Cranleigh, Woodford, and Waverly. Although Edmunton could have had local significance (Edmund Buxton, or "Edmund the Pioneer," had settled the site), it did not make the final cut. Four people marked ballots, and only Connington and Amberley appeared on all four lists; Amberley was chosen. The place ultimately owes its name to the British town of Amberley, Gloucestershire. The Hamilton County village was incorporated in 1940.

Amelia *Clermont County.* The settlement was first known as Mill Town, which was corrupted to Milton. The post office was Amelia, complimenting Amelia Bowdoin, a highly respected local woman and the wife of Wesley Bowdoin.

Amesville *Athens County.* Laid out in 1837. The name of the site is thought to trace back to Sylvanus Ames, an early resident of Ames Township. The first meeting of the township board of trustees was held at Sylvanus's house in 1802. He also is known to have lived here in 1811, so in all probability he was a longtime citizen of the neighborhood.

Amherst *Lorain County.* The town was laid out in 1830 by Judge Josiah Harris. At some point, the place became known as North Amherst, after Amherst, New Hampshire. The name was bestowed by Jonas Stratton, a native of the New England state. In 1873, an adjacent town was chartered as Amherstville. In an apparent attempt to achieve some logic in the labels, in an unknown year North Amherst became known as Amherst and Amherstville became known as South Amherst. Both Amherst and South Amherst are in Amherst Township. (See the South Amherst entry.)

Amity *Knox County.* Laid out, 1832, by David Jackson. The original name of Emmettsville was changed to Amity ("friendship") about 1837. The post office was called Democracy, an appellation that was sometimes applied to the community.

Amity *Madison County.* Platted as New Canaan in 1831, the community is in Canaan Township. Some believe it was laid out in 1840 by William Towman, but one source credits Uri Beach and Dr. Lorenzo Beach with laying out the site nine years earlier. Amity became the name in 1834. Philosophical beliefs of the citizens may have influenced the current name, which implies harmony.

Amlin *Franklin County.* Founded, 1847, by Zeloria (or Zaloria) E. Amlin. Originally known as Amlin's Station, this hamlet is on the New York Central Railroad. At one time it was on the Columbus, Dublin & Maysville Railroad. Amlin's wife's name was Hester.

Amsden *Seneca County.* Ex-government surveyor and railroad agent Beman Amsden founded this village. It was he who decided to lay the tracks for a railroad in the vicinity. The place was populated sometime between the mid-1840s and mid-1850s.

Andersonville *Ross County.* Platted in 1851. Andersonville was named for the original landowner, Mahlon Anderson, by Lorenzi and Major Dunlap, who platted the town.

Andover *Ashtabula County.* Andover is in the township of the same name. Reportedly, Epaphas Lyman was responsible for a name change from Sharon to Andover, for Andover, Connecticut. Settled long previously, Andover was not incorporated until 1883. A second source describes the antecedent as a township in Tolland County, Connecticut, stating that the place was the birthplace of many settlers at this site. Some scholars of place-name etymology believe the "an" in Andover is a British reference to ash trees, with "dover" indicating the river. One source gives Lyman's first name as Epaphras and claims that he and Zadoc Steele settled the place sometime after 1798.

Angus *Seneca County.* The first resident here is thought to have been Jacob Flack. In 1883, a post office was established here by J. W. Angus, who had settled in 1862.

Ankenytown *Knox County.* This village was named for a settler from New England, George Ankeny.

Anna *Shelby County.* Probably settled before 1835 but after 1830. Surveyed, 1867, for John L. and Fletcher Thirkield. The place was first known as Carey's Station. Anna is said to have been the name of the wife of Fletcher Thirkield; she was the daughter of a Mr. Carey. Incorporation took place in 1877.

Annapolis *Crawford County.* First called Slifertown (Sulphur Springs Post Office), the place was laid out in 1833 by John Slifer, who, wishing to honor the capital of his native state of Maryland, changed the name to Annapolis.

Anthony *Athens County.* This hamlet retains the name of the first postmaster at the place (about 1884), Anthony Niggemeyer.

Antietam *Trumbull County.* The hamlet was apparently named in commemoration of the crucial Civil War battle waged at Antietam, Maryland, in 1862. The name, believed to be of Algonquian origin, may translate in part as "flow."

Antioch *Monroe County.* This biblical name traces back to a Syrian king of antiquity and a city about three hundred miles north of Jerusalem. The Monroe County place, laid out in 1837 by the Reverend William Jarvis, was initially called Jarvistown. Later Jarvis renamed it after the city where the disciples were first called "Christians." It was incorporated in 1895.

Antiquity *Meigs County.* This village is said to have been named by Nadok Cramer, who referred to a huge fallen rock formation at the site as "the Rock of Antiquity." The name stuck.

Antrim *Guernsey County.* Alexander Alexander laid out this site in Madison Township in 1830. Settlers had come from County Antrim, Ireland, and thus it was named to honor their ancestral home.

Antwerp *Paulding County.* This village bears the name of the Belgian port, thanks to the influence of German and Dutch settlers who came to this area in the 1800s.

Apple Creek *Wayne County.* Sometimes referred to as Apple Orchard Town. Johnny Appleseed (John Chapman) may have had a nursery here; he frequented this area. A stream named Apple Creek passes through the village.

Apple Grove *Meigs County.* The site where Apple Grove now reposes was part of the Ohio Company's Purchase. In 1817, William Jennings and S. B. Smith bought it from the company. Spencer H. Hayman surveyed it for them. In 1837, when the post office opened here, Mrs. Martha Padend (née Hayman) was given the honor of choosing a name. With numerous apple trees all about, she selected the name Apple Grove.

Appleton *Licking County.* Laid out, 1832, by Titus Knox and Carey Mead. The given name of a Zanesville attorney who owned a good deal of land in the township, Appleton Downer, inspired the name of this village.

Aquilla *Geauga County.* The village name was taken from adjacent Lake Aquilla, originally referred to as "the pond." In 1880, Judge Lester Taylor visualized the pond's outline as resembling an eagle's head, and that inspired him to name the pond Lake Aquilla, *aquila* being Latin for "eagle." (No reason was given for adding the second "l.") Early landowners here included John Ballard, Gaius Pease, Nathaniel Spencer, Reuben Hall, Alvin Allen, and Orrin Spencer. The village was incorporated in the late 1940s.

Arbaugh *Vinton County.* Although specifics are scarce, the town apparently was named for a person or persons with the surname of Arbaugh. Leah J. Arbaugh of Tupper's Plains, Ohio, writes: "I will tell you this about . . . Arbaugh. A post office and store were there. . . . They were my ancestors."

Arcadia *Hancock County.* One source states that this name honors the ancient Greek country and those who resided there. It is said the Arcadians were "praised for the simple life and [their] contentment," which "became known to both ancient and modern poets as the land of peace and quiet manners." The term thus implies a peaceful and romantic backdrop, a home of rural people and a picturesque, upland region. A Hancock County authority states that "apparently, the founders of Arcadia in Hancock County hoped life would be such in their community." The community was laid out in 1854 by Ambrose and David Peters. Incorporation took place in 1859.

Arcanum *Darke County.* This name may stem from *arcane,* denoting something mysterious, hidden, or obscure. It may imply that the place was in a remote area or was difficult to find. There also is an Arcanum, Virginia, but it is not known whether the Ohio community was named for it.

Archbold *Fulton County.* Settled, 1838, by George Ditto. The original village name, Archbald, is said to have been taken from the names (or nicknames) of two engineers on the railroad that came through town: "Arch" and "Bald." In the 1880s, the "a" was changed to "o," resulting in the current form. Incorporation took place in 1866.

Archer's Fork *Washington County.* Before the arrival of the first permanent settlers in this remote area, a squatter named Archer, it is said, eloped with the wife of another man and resided for a time at this location.

Arlington *Hancock County.* Arlington, Virginia, served as the inspiration in naming this Ohio place.

Armenia *Washington County.* A post office bearing this name opened here in 1887, with the surrounding settlement assuming the same name. In those days Armenia, the ancient country in western Asia, was mentioned prominently in the news as it struggled for national status.

Armitage *Athens County.* The surname of Hiram Armitage is commemorated at this site.

Armstrong *Wayne County.* In all probability, this name comes from one of several Armstrong families that settled the county. Thomas Armstrong resided in Clinton Township, John D. Armstrong in Salt Creek Township, and D. D. Armstrong in East Union Township.

Armstrong's Mills *Belmont County.* Thomas Armstrong settled this place in 1811. Alexander Armstrong and his brothers owned and ran the town's mills and a woolen factory here in 1846.

Arnheim *Brown County.* Laid out in 1837. The property was owned by Jacob Arn, who also resided here.

Artanna *Knox County.* This hamlet sprouted up around 1934, when a service station and store were opened. The store owners, Arthur and Anna Wolfe, purchased additional land in the vicinity, and others were attracted to the site. The name derives from a combination of Arthur and Anna.

Ash *Licking County.* Ash sprang up about 1879. As the story is told, Mrs. Thomas Carter conferred the name on the place after observing the abundance of ash timber nearby.

Ashland *Ashland County (seat).* Founded, 1815, by William Montgomery. Montgomery had come from Uniontown, Pennsylvania, and first called this place Uniontown. However, there being another Uniontown in Ohio, Congressman William Sloan submitted the name of Henry Clay's Kentucky estate, Ashland. (A second source states that the city was named for Ashland, Kentucky.) The name change came in 1822. Incorporation took place in 1830.

Ashley *Delaware County.* In earlier days, this village was known by the name of the township in which it lies, Oxford. The town was platted in 1849 by J. C. Avery and L. W. Ashley. Ashley is considered the founder of the community, and it was later renamed after him.

Ashtabula *Ashtabula County.* This city sits where the Ashtabula River flows into Lake Erie. "Place of many fish" is one translation of this Native American term. Incorporation was in 1828.

Ashville *Pickaway County.* The land proprietor here was Richard Stage. He sold off his holdings to Mahlon Ashbrook, merchant and businessman. The place probably takes the "Ash" in its name from Ashbrook. It was incorporated in 1880.

Assumption *Harrison County.* Formerly referred to as Caragher. Catholic settlers arrived here around 1850 and began the Church of Saint Mary's Assumption, accounting for the place-name. The church building was completed in 1869.

Astoria *Butler County.* It is not known why this spot was named Astoria, although most other places bearing this name trace it to John Jacob Astor. Astor, a fur trader, sponsored much exploration in western North America.

Athalia *Lawrence County.* According to accepted belief, Athalia was named in honor of a daughter of the founder.

Athens *Athens County (seat).* The name traces back to the great city of classical learning in Greece. It was so named in part because of the trend then current toward copying classical names but more because a seat of higher learning (Ohio University) was to be located here. The city was incorporated in 1811.

Attica *Seneca County.* The town of Attica, New York, inspired the name of this small community.

Atwater *Portage County.* An early settler here—perhaps the earliest—was Joshua Atwater in 1805, on property given to him by his father, Caleb Atwater, an original holder of land in Ohio's Western Reserve. Caleb named this town in 1799.

Atwater Center *Portage County.* Atwater Center sits near Atwater in the center of Atwater Township. (See the preceding entry.)

Auburn Center *Crawford County.* This hamlet is near the center of Auburn Township. The "Auburn" possibly comes from Auburn, New York, former home of at least two settlers, Daniel and Palmer Hulse, who influenced the name.

Auburn Center *Geauga County.* Auburn Center is at the center of Auburn Township; both take their name from Auburn, New York. The initial settler of the locale, in 1814, was Abner Colvin, from Auburn, New York.

Auburn Corners *Geauga County.* Situated at an intersection in Auburn Township, this community owes its name to Auburn, New York.

Augerburg *Portage County.* An auger-producing enterprise was located here near a fine source of timber suitable for auger handles.

Auglaize *Allen County.* "Fallen timbers" is said to be the meaning of this Shawnee term.

Aukerman *Wayne County.* An interurban railroad stop was located here at Aukerman's grocery store.

Aultman *Stark and Summit counties.* The name given to this place on the Stark-Summit county line is associated much more closely with Stark County than with Summit. A number of Aultmans became prominent in Stark County, and a medical center of long standing in Canton bears the Aultman name. Jacob Aultman came to the area in 1805. Cornelius Aultman was a highly successful manufacturer of agricultural equipment and machinery. By 1865, C. Aultman & Company was Canton's largest industry. John, Henry, and William were other well-known Aultman clan members.

Aurora *Portage County.* The future city of Aurora was settled around 1799 by the Harmon family, among others. A visitor in 1800, Major Amos Spafford, said that the name Aurora would have the twin distinction of representing the dawn of a new day and the name of his favorite daughter. Spafford apparently had been invited to suggest a name for the place by another early settler, Ebenezer Sheldon (or Shelton). Incorporation took place in 1928.

Austin *Ross County.* The name likely traces to James B. Austin, who preached on the Methodist Episcopal circuit in the 1800s. In nearby Jackson County, an H. F. Austin served on the board of directors of a railroad.

Austinburg *Ashtabula County.* Founded about 1800 by Judge Aliphalet (or Eliphalet) Austin, whose surname forms the prefix for the town name.

Austintown *Mahoning County.* Settled, 1798, by John McCollum and named after Judge Aliphalet (or Eliphalet) Austin (see also the entry for Austinburg, Ashtabula County). Austin served as a judge in Trumbull County at the turn of the century, and was an organizer of the Torrington Land Company.

Avery *Erie County.* The name may honor Rufus Avery or one of the seventeen other Averys listed in the name index of an early county biography.

Avon *Lorain County.* Originally known as Xeuma and later as Troy—probably for Troy, New York—Avon eventually assumed the name of its township, which was so named upon organization in 1824. Both township and town take their name from Avon, Massachusetts.

Avon Lake *Lorain County.* Avon Lake is on Lake Erie in Avon Township. The name probably traces to Avon, Massachusetts.

Axtel *Erie County.* The name may relate to William Axtel, Esquire, who in 1861 was a constable at Put-in-Bay.

Ayersville *Defiance County.* Never formally laid out. A post office was here by 1849, with Joseph Ayers as postmaster. Ayers, born in New Jersey in 1815, came to Ohio with his parents three years later.

Bachman *Montgomery County.* E. Bachman, a Clay Township landowner in 1851, is probably the person responsible for this designation on maps.

Bailey *Lucas County.* The name of this site may relate to local shipbuilders John E. and Daniel E. Bailey. They are believed to have been prominent in the area about 1874.

Bailey Lakes *Ashland County.* This relatively new village, in an area that includes a natural lake and several artificial ones, was incorporated in 1961. Lots were laid out by Don and J. E. Ringler. This Clearcreek Township area was entered by John Bailey in 1815, with land here remaining in the Bailey family for several generations. The predecessor to Bailey Lakes was Savannah Lake Park, formed in 1922 by James Edgar (Ed) Ringler. Years later, a letter was written to Miss Rae Bailey, James's granddaughter, who was working for the government in Washington, D.C., asking her permission to name the place Bailey Hills. She stated that the family would be honored. Because there was another Bailey Hills in Ohio, the name was altered to Bailey Lakes.

Bailey's Corners *Trumbull County.* Isaac Bailey, a carpenter, came to this locality in 1829. A native of Pennsylvania, he died in 1877. A son, Abram D. Bailey, was born in 1839.

Bailey's Mill *Belmont County.* About 1860, Jesse Bailey erected a mill at this locale, since known as Bailey's Mill.

Bainbridge *Geauga County.* Land here was bought in 1798 by Judson Canfield, Samuel Lord, and Rufus Pettibone. A man named David or Calvin Austin later purchased the property, and it was known as Austintown. Located in Bainbridge Township, which was named in honor of a hero of the Tripolitan War, Commander

William Bainbridge (1774–1833), the community also became Bainbridge. Commander Bainbridge captained the USS *Constitution* in the War of 1812.

Bainbridge *Ross County.* Founded, 1805, by Nathaniel Massie. The place obtained its name from the early nineteenth-century war hero Commander William Bainbridge.

Bairdstown *Wood County.* The hamlet was platted in 1874 for Josiah Baird. In 1881, it was incorporated.

Baker *Darke County.* This place took its name from a Mr. Baker who operated a store here. It is referred to by some as Baker's Store.

Bakersville *Coshocton County.* The place was named for John Baker, who begat the hamlet in 1848.

Baldwin's Corners *Mahoning County.* The place was named for a local Baldwin family. The name is sometimes styled Baldwin Corners.

Ballville *Sandusky County.* The site of this hamlet is also referred to locally as Ball's Battleground. In 1813, Colonel Ball and his men encountered a hostile contingent of Native Americans here; a fierce skirmish resulted in casualties on both sides.

Baltic *Tuscarawas County.* The ultimate antecedent name undoubtedly was the Baltic Sea. It is said that the early settlers favored a name that was terse and easy to pronounce.

Baltimore *Fairfield County.* This village was laid out by Henry Hildebrand in 1824. Hildebrand called it New Market, in honor of New Market, Virginia, his native town. Possibly spurred by the presence of many Maryland emigrants in this locality, the name evolved to Baltimore. A local historian tells a different story: that New Market and the adjacent communities of Rome and Basil (or Basel) arose in 1803 and later consolidated with their neighbors to create Baltimore, but not without a fight. Apparently the Ohio legislature decreed that Rome and New Market would be known as Baltimore, but Basil resisted the name for over a century and a quarter. In the 1950s, a judge ruled that both entities would be known as Baltimore.

Bangorville *Richland County.* William Moore had a foundry here as early as 1847. It is understood that a number of families from the Bangor, Maine, area came to this hamlet and settled, resulting in the name of Bangorville.

Bangs *Knox County.* In 1873, when a post office was established here, the superintendent of U.S. mail routes was George H. Bangs, and it is said that this community was named after him. One correspondent, however, reports that Bangs was the surname of the first resident.

Bannock *Belmont County.* Land for this place was donated on the condition that it be named in honor of the donor's son, Bruce. Unfortunately, that name was already in use elsewhere. Since the word *Bruce* was associated with Robert the Bruce and his victory at Bannockburn, Bannock became the second-choice name.

Barberton *Summit County.* Sometimes called the "Magic City," apparently because it grew so rapidly, Barberton was founded by O. C. (Ohio Columbus) Barber in 1891 and named for its founder. A noted center for the manufacture of matches, it was incorporated in 1893.

Barlow *Washington County.* This place-name traces to Joel Barlow (1754–1812), an American poet, diplomat, and agent for the Scioto Company, which encouraged French colonists to settle Gallipolis, Ohio, in 1790.

Barnesville *Belmont County.* This village was founded by its namesake, James Barnes, in 1808. Incorporation took place in 1835.

Barnhill *Tuscarawas County.* Judge J. Barnhill helped the hamlet obtain a post office in the early days. In return, the place was renamed for him. It formerly was known as Pike Run.

Barnsburg *Hamilton County.* The name probably traces to one or more of the seventeen Barneses who at one time resided in and around Colerain Township. Among the Barneses mentioned in vintage biographies are Sol, A. T., Stephen, Dan, M., and H. If the place-name is indeed connected to the family (or families), the "e" was dropped somewhere along the way.

Barrick *Carroll County.* George Barrick, born in 1838, became a highly respected farmer in Fox Township. It may have been for him or for a member of his family that this site was named. Another Barrick, Henry, resided in Orange Township. He was born in 1821.

Barr's Mills *Tuscarawas County.* The site was first known as Walter's Mill. After David Barr bought the grist mill in 1867, the name evolved to the current one. The community was settled during the middle decades of the nineteenth century by Germans, including Henry Froelich, Solomon Miller, John Reiser, Andrew Schrock, and Josiah Teters.

Bartlett *Washington County.* It is said that two Wesley Township villages, Plymouth and Pleasanton, grew into one. When questions arose as to which name to adopt, consensus could not be reached. The postmaster, Joel Bartlett, settled the matter by submitting his own name to the Post Office Department.

Barton *Belmont County.* The original owner of the land on which this town arose was Abner Barton. Annie P. Barton recorded the plat in 1905 and named it for Abner.

Bartramville *Lawrence County.* Bartramville sprang up about 1846, thanks to James Alexander Bartram (1795–1875), who came here from Pittsburgh.

Bascom *Seneca County.* Platted in 1837. One theory is that the village was named in honor of Scott & Bascom, publishers of the *Columbus State Journal.*

Basil *Fairfield County.* According to historians, this village was settled by persons of Swiss heritage, who named it for the city of Basel, Switzerland. Jonathan Flattery was the surveyor on the project, while Jacob Goss laid out the town.

Batavia *Clermont County (seat).* This name comes from the Latin term *Batavi,* which referred to an ancient German tribe. Much later, the name Batavian Republic was applied to what is now the Netherlands. Batavia, New York, was settled largely by Dutch immigrants, and it is possible that someone from that area influenced the naming of this Ohio town. Platted by George Ely and David C. Bryan in 1814, it was incorporated in 1836.

Batemantown *Knox County.* In 1815, a group of pioneers arrived here from Middlebury, Vermont. Mr. and Mrs. Alvin Bateman and Mr. and Mrs. Luther Bateman put down roots and continued to be prominent citizens of the community that bears their name.

Batesville *Noble County.* This village was first called Williamsburg, after William Finley, who settled here in Beaver Township about 1818. The place was platted about 1827 by Lebbeus Fordyce, surveyor. The Batesville designation arose after a post office was installed at Timothy Bates's mill. Bates was a Methodist minister as well as a mill owner.

Bath *Summit County.* Bath Township was surveyed in 1805, and this community was dubbed Wheatfield by the surveyor, Colonel Rial (or Riol) McArthur. About 1810, after Jason Hammond arrived from Bolton, Connecticut, the place became known as Hammondsburgh. Many fellow residents disliked Hammond, however, and some complained that the name was too long. When a selection of replacement names resulted in no consensus, Jonathan Hale is said to have fumed, "Oh, call it Jerusalem, Jericho, Bath—or anything but Hammondsburgh!" A motion to name it Bath was made and carried at a town meeting about 1818. Hale, who also came from Connecticut in 1810, is credited with being the first "legitimate" settler of Bath, Ohio.

Batson *Paulding County.* Eight Batsons appear in cemetery records for the area, including several laid to rest in Lehman Cemetery here in Benton Township. Among them are Andrew Batson, who was born in 1845, and Harry Batson, born in 1881.

Baude's Ferry *Brown County.* As early as 1800, a ferry operated at this location, taking passengers and goods across the Ohio River to Augusta, Kentucky. A ferry still existed here in 1992. The community is named for J. H. Baude, an early settler.

Bayard *Columbiana County.* Laid out, 1852, by landowners Cyrus Prentiss and James Farmer. The hamlet is probably named for Frederick Bayard, who arrived here in 1805.

Bay Bridge *Erie County.* This community is at the southeastern end of the Sandusky Bay Bridge.

Bay View *Erie County.* Located on the shore of Sandusky Bay, this town offers an exceptional view. Incorporation took place in 1951.

Bay Village *Cuyahoga County.* Incorporated in 1902, Bay Village is actually a city. Its name was inspired by its location on a bay of Lake Erie.

Bazetta *Trumbull County.* Settled, 1804, by John Budd, Moses Hampton, Edward Schofield, Henry Hulse, John Golden, and Joseph Pruden. It is said that at least one early citizen of the site searched diligently for the origin of the name, without success. Supposedly it is the only place in the world named Bazetta. Some speculate that the name is a hybrid, possibly from the names Bazaleel and Etta.

Beach City *Stark County.* Settled in 1816. At that time, Henry Willeard began a mill at this point, and the site was known as Willeard Mills. The Baltimore & Ohio Railroad came through in 1872, and some speculate that the current name honors the chief engineer of the railroad, Henry Beach. At some time this locale was also known as Barr's Mills, after Jonathan Barr. The town was incorporated in 1890.

Beallsville *Monroe County.* A man named Beall laid out the village in 1824, and the place was named in his honor. Not many years later, its name was changed to Elva. In 1841 it was incorporated, and about 1851 the name reverted to Beallsville.

Beamsville *Darke County.* This small community was laid out in 1837 by John Beam. It derives its name from him.

Bear's Mill *Darke County.* A mill was located at this site on the river in 1849 when a Mr. Bear purchased the facility and improved it. Subsequently the place took on the name Bear's Mill.

Beaumont *Athens County.* Because of large-scale salt manufacturing operations here, the site was initially known as Salina. That led to postal delivery confusion with Celina in Mercer County. In 1895, when the Hocking Valley Railroad sliced through the town, the community took the middle name of the line's chief engineer, Frederick Beaumont Sheldon.

Beaver *Pike County.* Laid out, 1839, by a man named Reynolds. For some time, this place was known as Reynoldstown. Later it was labeled Beaver or Beavertown, being located in the valley of Beaver Creek and in Beaver Township. Both the creek and the township were named because of the many beavers in local streams.

Beavercreek *Greene County.* The place takes its name from the adjacent Big Beaver Creek. In all probability, beaver colonies were present when the place was discovered. The village was not incorporated until 1980.

Beaver Dam *Allen County.* Locally, the name is sometimes styled Beaverdam. When the Indians first beheld this spot, they found two beaver dams. The town was laid out by Frederick Shull in 1853. Incorporation took place in 1878.

Beckett's *Washington County.* A post office went into operation here in 1888 in a store operated by Humphrey Beckett. The Beckett's label remains with the tiny community.

Beck's Mills *Holmes County.* In 1822, Michael Beck and his wife, Catherine Long Beck, arrived in this vicinity. Shortly thereafter they built a sawmill at this site. The ensuing hamlet prospered until the railroad came to nearby Millersburg, at which juncture activity here waned.

Bedford *Cuyahoga County.* This site was surveyed in 1810 and settled in 1813. Daniel Benedict was one of the earliest settlers. The place was named for Bedford, Connecticut, a place found on current maps as Bedford, New York. Apparently the eastern community was in an area of disputed boundary, with two states contending for it. Today a city, Bedford, Ohio, was incorporated in 1937.

Bedford Heights *Cuyahoga County.* Incorporated in 1951, Bedford Heights is now a city. It is contiguous with Bedford (see the preceding entry).

Beebe *Athens County.* Captain Hopson Beebe, a Revolutionary War officer who settled in Rome Township in 1804, is the person to whom this place-name traces. His son, Charles, also resided here. For a period, a Peter Beebe operated a mill in Rome Township.

Beebetown *Medina County.* In 1824, Daniel Coit sold fifty acres at this site to Adam Beebe, after whom it was named. Beebe was soon joined by Hollis Newton and Beebe's brothers, Benjamin and Roderick.

Beechwood *Stark County.* A third-generation Beechwood resident who grew up and went to school here writes that "they always said it got its name because of the beech trees that were on each side of what is called Beechwood Avenue."

Belden *Lorain County.* Bildad Beldin came to this area in 1816. The place-name is a misspelling of his surname.

Belfast *Highland County.* Belfast, Ireland, inspired the name of the town, which was established in 1834 on land belonging to Jonathan Weaver, Lancelot Brown, and James Storer. Because there was a Belfast in another county, the post office at this site went by the name Bell.

Belfort *Stark County.* Platted in 1849. A sizable contingent of settlers from France took up residence in this area. Their influence probably accounts for the naming of this hamlet for a city in eastern France.

Bellaire *Belmont County.* Part of this site was bought in 1802 by an early settler from Maryland, who named the future city after his home in that state. Bellaire was incorporated in 1857.

Bellbrook *Greene County.* This city was named in 1816 for Stephen Bell. Incorporation occurred in 1832.

Belle Center *Logan County.* Incorporated in 1867. The name derives from the place's location approximately midway between Kenton and Bellefontaine.

Bellefontaine *Logan County (seat).* Laid out in 1820. Blue Jacket's Town, a Native American settlement, once stood where Bellefontaine (French for "beautiful fountain") stands today. The present name was inspired by the limestone springs of high-quality water that are found at the site. Bellefontaine was incorporated in 1835 and today is a city.

Belle Valley *Noble County.* A train station was constructed here on the farm of Benton Thorland by the Cleveland & Marietta Railroad. A small village grew up and was called Belle Valley because of its bucolic setting. The town was platted in 1875.

Bellevue *Sandusky County.* This city was first known as Amsden's Corners. The place was settled by Mark Hopkins in 1815. Incorporation took place in 1851. Some claim that the name simply means "beautiful view," while others believe it was named for James H. Bell in 1839. Bell was a civil engineer who surveyed a route for the Mad River Railroad.

Bellpoint *Delaware County.* Laid out, 1835, by John Koopen. The *Columbus Dispatch* reports that the name stems from the town's situation on a bell-shaped segment of land where Mill Creek empties into the Scioto River. Thus locals admonish mapmakers to spell the name with a "Bell" instead of a "Belle." The bell shape of the promontory was more evident before construction of a nearby dam.

Bellville *Richland County.* James McClure lived here in 1809, when the place became known as McClure. He sold out to Robert Bell, a wealthy landholder, about 1824. In 1855, the community was laid out by Robert Bell, Sr.

Belmont *Belmont County.* Founded, 1808, by Joseph D. Wright and first known as Wrightstown. Later, in the hope (still unfulfilled) that the place might be designated as the county seat, it was changed to Belmont to coincide with the name of the county.

Beloit *Mahoning County.* In pioneer days, this location was known as Smithfield Station. In 1863, it was rechristened Beloit, apparently because the Republicans were in power at the time and the party's power base was in Beloit, Wisconsin.

Belpre *Washington County.* A broad river plain at this site was settled in 1789. It was given an Americanized version of the French term for "beautiful meadow," *belle pré.*

Bennett's Corners *Medina County.* Salathiel Bennett arrived here in the 1820s, thereby endowing the intersection with its name.

Bentleyville *Cuyahoga County.* Largely obscured today by nearby Chagrin Falls, Bentleyville was founded in 1831 by the Reverend Adamson Bentley.

Benton *Crawford County.* Laid out, 1841, by John Hazlett and George Bender. At one time this hamlet was known as Poplar. Later it was christened Benton, for Thomas Hart Benton (1782–1858), U.S. senator from Missouri. Hazlett was an enthusiastic admirer of Benton.

Benton Ridge *Hancock County.* Founded in 1835. Like a number of other places with "Benton" in their names, this location honors Senator Thomas Hart Benton, Democrat from Missouri. The senator was highly respected, even outside his home state. The "Ridge" aspect of the name refers to the topography.

Bentonville *Adams County.* Joseph Leedom laid out this town, which takes the name of Senator Thomas Hart Benton of Missouri. The platting took place in 1839.

Benwood *Monroe County.* Where the "Ben" aspect of the name comes from is uncertain, but the "wood" portion probably honors the first postmaster, William T. Wood. Wood ran the local general store.

Berea *Cuyahoga County.* John Baldwin, the Reverend James Gilruth, and the Reverend Harry O. Sheldon founded a religious colony at this site in 1836. Later, when permission to open a post office was obtained, the men were unable to agree on a name. Two of the men advocated biblical names, Sheldon favoring Berea and Gilruth preferring Tabor. Finally, to resolve the impasse, the two names were etched on a coin with one name on each side. Upon tossing the coin, it landed "Berea side up." Of the three founders, Baldwin was probably the most influential, arriving from Connecticut in 1827 and helping to organize what eventually became Baldwin-Wallace College here. The place had been settled much earlier, by Jared Hickox in 1809. The original Berea is mentioned in Acts 17:10 and may be spelled on maps as Veria. Today a city, Berea, Ohio, was incorporated in 1850.

Bergholz *Jefferson County.* Platted, 1883, by James Kelly, Christina Hess, and Morris J. Hess. The town, formed from the Allen, Hess, and Dorrance farms, was incorporated in 1906. A large mine was opened at this site and both the mine and the town were named for one of the owners, a Mrs. Bergholz. Much earlier, on the opposite side of the creek, a site known variously as Lick Skillet and Nebo was settled.

Berkey *Lucas County.* Also designated Berkey's Corners, the community gets its name from R. K. Berkeybile, a postmaster in early times. A post office operated nearby as early as 1835. The name was changed to Berkey in 1865.

Berkshire *Delaware County.* Platted in 1804. The inaugural name for the site was Berkshire Corners. Colonel Moses Byxbe settled the location. He hailed from Lenox, Berkshire County, Massachusetts.

Berlin *Erie County.* The community is in Berlin Township, which had been called Eldridge Township until 1832. A local citizen, Noah Hill, advanced the idea that since there was a town named Milan in the area, it would be logical to have a town and township named Berlin. One historical source attempted to support this explanation with a reference to a "Milan-Berlin Treaty." However, existence of such a document cannot be verified. Perhaps the inspiration came from the Berlin Decree (1806) or Napoleon's Milan Decree (1807).

Berlin *Holmes County.* Settled, 1811, by John Swigert, Samuel Knight, and their families, who came from Maryland. Originally from Germany, Swigert platted a town on his land and named it Berlin, after the city in his native land. Berlin is Holmes County's oldest village; platting took place in 1816. One source states that the site was settled, perhaps in 1812, by Amish, Germans, and Mennonites.

Berlin *Williams County.* This locality was settled by persons of German descent, accounting for the choice of name.

Berlin Center *Mahoning County.* Located near the center of Berlin Township, the place, like the township, owes its name to German influence. A German-born miller, Matthias Glass, ran a sawmill and grist mill here sometime after 1809. Another source spells Glass's given name with one "t," states that the place was founded in 1803, and claims that Glass named the site in remembrance of his fatherland.

Berlin Center Station *Mahoning County.* The "Station" aspect of the designation resulted from the location of this place on a railroad. It is a mile and a half from Berlin Center. (See the Berlin Center entry.)

Berne *Noble County.* This community dates to 1849 and takes its name from the Swiss city of Berne.

Bernice *Tuscarawas County.* This location was originally called Robinson. There being another town by that name in Ohio, the Post Office Department suggested that another name be chosen. A postal authority came to discuss the matter with the postmaster and while they were talking, the postmaster's daughter entered the room. When her father greeted her as Bernice, the postal inspector said, "There is the new name."

Berrysville *Highland County.* Platted, 1846, by Amos Sergeant. The Berrymans were a prominent early Highland County family, and this place was named after them.

Berwick *Seneca County.* Surveyed, 1844, by Thomas Heming. It is said that this Seneca County community was named by Joseph Campbell, who hailed from Berwick, Pennsylvania.

Best *Mahoning County.* An early county history lists in its biographical index the names of fifteen Bests. One or more of them resided in Smith Township, where this place is located. John Best was a citizen of Berlin Township, which adjoins Smith.

Bethany *Butler County.* A house is believed to have been constructed here as early as 1798 by David Williamson. The community was formally laid out in 1822 by Samuel Lowery. This place-name may stem from an identical place-name in Connecticut. Ultimately its inspiration was the town mentioned in the New Testament as the home of Lazarus.

Bethel *Clermont County.* Settled, 1798, by Obed Denham. (One source states that Denham laid out the town in 1797.) A native of Virginia who is said to have held strong views against slavery, Denham selected this Old Testament name. Bethel ("house of God") was a town about twelve miles from Jerusalem.

Bethesda *Belmont County.* A church in the vicinity gave its name to this community. The post office for the area was also known as Bethesda. The name refers to the spring-fed pool in Jerusalem mentioned in the Bible as having healing properties. A sawmill was operated here by Merrick S. Burr starting in 1852, and the railroad station was known as Burr. When Burr laid out a town, he named it Fairmont. But the Burr, Bethesda, and Fairmont names caused confusion, so in 1890 the railroad station became Bethesda; the town followed suit sometime afterward. Incorporation took place in 1910.

Bettsville *Seneca County.* John Betts surveyed and platted the community and named it after himself.

Beulah Beach *Erie County.* "Beulah" refers, according to *The New Westminster Dictionary of the Bible,* "to the once forsaken land of Palestine when it was restored to God's favor and repeopled after the captivity." The place-name was apparently imported to this spot from Cleveland, where a Beulah Park existed next to Euclid Beach. This Erie County locality has served since about 1921 as a religious campground administered by the Christian Missionary Alliance. "Beach" refers to the community's location on Lake Erie.

Bevan *Washington County.* In 1897, James A. Bevan operated the local post office here in his store, known as Bevan Bros. The hamlet that grew up around it retained the Bevan designation.

Beverly *Washington County.* Founded, 1831, by John Dodge, Jr. It is said that this place was settled as early as 1789, but a post office did not open until 1838. The belief is that Dodge had the site named for his ancestral homes—Beverly, Massachusetts, and Beverley, England.

Bevis *Hamilton County.* Sometime in the 1820s, Pennsylvania native Jess Bevis settled the township where this hamlet is located. The place takes its name from him.

Bexley *Franklin County.* It is generally accepted that this city, now surrounded by Columbus, took its name from the London borough of the same name. Incorporation occurred in 1908.

Bidwell *Gallia County.* Bidwell was named for an 1892 candidate for president, John Bidwell. An informant writes: "My grandfather, Wm. H. Fredrick, named the town after John Bidwell, a writer and strong prohibitionist. It [had been] called Heatley when they moved there. He was quite a reader and admired . . . Bidwell's writing and what he stood for. . . . I would assume it was changed [to Bidwell] around 1882." The names "Fredrick" and "Heatley" were transcribed from unfamiliar handwriting; thus it is possible that the accurate spellings may differ slightly.

Biggin Corners *Trumbull County.* In all probability, this place-name stems from Henry Biggins or other members of the Biggins clan who resided in this neighborhood. Henry was a member of the nearby Burg Hill (Burghill) Grange in 1875. Job Biggins was another local member of the clan.

Big Island *Marion County.* Platted, 1826, by Olson Norton. Big Island bears the name of the township in which it is located. The name comes from a prominent grove of trees that was situated in the middle of the prairie and looked like an island.

Big Plain *Madison County.* Early on, this location was known as California and as Big Plains. It is now found on maps as Big Plain. The town, laid out by Robert Thomas, William D. Pringle, and Thomas Chappel in 1849, was surrounded by spacious prairies known as the Big Plains.

Big Prairie *Holmes and Wayne counties.* The hamlet was founded by John Cannan and first called Cannansville. The area surrounding the community was largely flat and was referred to as "the big prairie." When a post office was established here in 1822, it was named Big Prairie and the town took on that identity. The locale was visited in 1802 by Johnny Appleseed (John Chapman, 1774–1845), who, true to his calling, planted apple orchards here. It was settled in 1811. In presettlement times, the site was considered impassable because of bogs and other wetlands considered "waste."

Big Run *Athens County.* A small settlement tracing to about 1840, Big Run takes its name from the largest creek in the area, which flows past here.

Big Springs *Logan County.* The name of this town traces to two springs at the site, one on the Henry Rosebrook farm and one on the Shepherd farm.

Bingham *Monroe County.* This place-name is a corruption of the name of Bingen, Germany. The community goes back to about 1868.

Bird's Run *Guernsey County.* Robert Atkinson entered this site at some unknown date and built a crude lodging near a stream. His only neighbor reportedly was a man named Bird. As the story is told, when Atkinson's wife died, Bird, along with some local Indians, assisted in burying her. To locate another woman to marry, Atkinson went back to Virginia, with the understanding that Bird would look after his property in his absence. Bird, however, piled Atkinson's household belongings into a boat, paddled downstream, entered the Muskingum River, and disappeared. Thus the community at this place on the stream became known as Bird's Run.

Birmingham *Erie County.* Located on a main artery between Chicago and Buffalo, Birmingham at one time was a thriving town, with a number of mills doing a good business. It is thought that the founder fancied it would become a major manufacturing hub, not unlike Birmingham, England.

Bishopville *Morgan County.* James Bishop, who laid out this village in 1859, also lent it his name.

Bismark *Huron County.* Originally labeled Paris, this hamlet probably changed names during or shortly after the Franco-Prussian War (1870–1871), which was deliberately provoked by the Prussian premier, Otto von Bismarck, who then became chancellor of the new German Empire. The "c" was omitted, but it is thought that this community was named for Bismarck (1815–1898). Some referred to this place as "the German settlement."

Blachleyville *Wayne County.* This name stems from William Blachley, who founded the community in 1833.

Blackfork Station *Jackson County.* About 1900, the D. D. Davis family persuaded some African Americans to come to southern Ohio to work in the family's coal mines. Blackfork Station took its name from these black workers and their families after some of them went to work in the Davis silica brick plant; the Baltimore & Ohio train would not go down the switch to pick up passengers, so a station was built on the main line. Blackfork Creek is the name of a local stream.

Blackhorse *Portage County.* The place-name apparently traces back to the Black Horse Tavern, which served as a way station for the stagecoach about 1850. The current Black Horse Tavern, a local landmark, is across the road and a stone's throw away from the site of the original establishment, now long gone.

Blacklick *Franklin County.* The community was situated on property owned by H. G. Black.

Bladen *Gallia County.* The hamlet takes its name from a Bladen family that settled it. A nearby cemetery is the burial site of the Bladens.

Bladensburg *Knox County.* Laid out, 1833, by John and Samuel Wheeler and Washington Houck. One correspondent from the area states that "it is common knowledge around here that our town was named after Bladensburg, Maryland, by early settlers who came from there." Another contributor mentioned that an historical battle had been fought in Bladensburg, England. Still another opines that "Bladensburg, Ohio, was named by one of my Davidson ancestors who fought in the Battle of Bladensburg, Maryland [in 1814] . . . and then moved to this area."

Blaine *Belmont County.* James G. Blaine, the Republican leader and 1884 presidential candidate, is the person after whom this hamlet is named.

Blaineville *Belmont County.* In 1903, the plat for this community was placed on the record by Matthew H. and Lucinda Coleman. It is said to have been named—perhaps for James G. Blaine—by a schoolteacher who taught here.

Blake *Medina County.* Blake was once known as Steamtown. Later the Honorable H. G. Blake was honored when the place was renamed. Blake was from nearby Medina.

Blakeslee *Williams County.* Surveyed, 1880, by A. T. Bement. The real estate here was owned by John Bowman, who began residing at the site in 1853. (One source spells his name Boman.) The name of the place honors Schuyler E. Blakeslee, who was a prominent attorney in Bryan. The barrister agreed to handle the incorporation papers free of charge if citizens would name the community after him. Bowman, or Boman, is said to have laid out the first lots in 1880.

Blanchard *Hardin County.* The hamlet is in Blanchard Township. It, the township, and the Blanchard River all derive their name from a Frenchman who settled in the area in an early year. It is said that he was a tailor by trade, so the Native Americans dubbed a stream in the area "Tailor's Creek." That waterway is now the Blanchard River.

Blanchester *Clinton County.* In 1832, this community was laid out by John and Joseph Blancett. The name is an adaptation of their surname.

Blissfield *Coshocton County.* A boy whose given name was Bliss is said to have been the inspiration for the place-name. The boy's grandfather, Abram Weatherwax, chose the name. The community was settled sometime before 1867, when the railroad arrived here.

Bloomdale *Hancock County.* Laid out in 1852. Located in Bloom Township, the town is said to fit the name. Thus the name is believed to fall into the descriptive category, but it was also thought to be harmonious to the ear.

Bloomfield *Morrow County.* Bloomfield is located in South Bloomfield Township, named in 1817. According to one account, when the subject of naming the village arose, several prominent citizens discussed the question as they stood in Roswell Clark's doorway. Clark suggested the appellation New Wabash. William Ayers, for some reason, favored Ayersville. Roger Blinn called their attention to the vista before them: a green field in summer dress, vibrantly adorned with clusters of wildflowers. It was then that Blinn suggested the name Bloomfield and all present agreed.

Bloomfield *Muskingum County.* Laid out, 1853, by Thomas Clegg. According to historical accounts, the place-name was inspired by orchards that were in bloom here at the time of the naming.

Bloomfield *Washington County.* The generally accepted version is that a family having the surname Flint came to this spot from Vermont and named it for Bloomfield, Essex County, Vermont. However, a check of current sources fails to disclose a Bloomfield, Vermont. There are various other Essexes and Bloomfields in the eastern states, so perhaps the Flints emigrated from one of them. A good candidate might be Bloomfield, Essex County, New Jersey.

Bloomingburg *Fayette County.* A newspaper covering the area reports that a Methodist Church circuit rider conferred the name on this place. Apparently he took note of the attractive gardens and flowered yards planted by the women of the church. The site previously bore the name New Lexington, but that duplicated the name of at least one other village, so a change was in order.

Blooming Grove *Morrow County.* The village earned its name by virtue of its picturesque situation. Laid out in 1835 by Salmon E. Harding, it was the birthplace of President Warren G. Harding (1865–1923).

Bloomville *Seneca County.* Termed a garden spot by some early residents, this community is in Bloom Township. The name may also have some relationship to a German patriot named Bloom. The site was settled in 1822.

Blue Ash *Hamilton County.* Settled before 1799. The community's first church or meetinghouse at nearby Carpenter's Run, as well as an eight-cornered building that provided schoolchildren with a refuge in the event of an attack by Native Americans, were constructed of blue ash logs, and this plentiful local timber inspired the name of the city.

Blue Ball *Butler and Warren counties.* This place had a post office as early as 1844. Its name is sometimes printed as Blueball. It was a stagecoach stop at an early date. Originally a tavern stand, the village took its name from the sign over the entrance of the Blue Ball Tavern. The sign bore a globe painted blue. Earlier the town went by the name Guilford.

Blue Row *Coshocton County.* The site may have acquired its name from the many Blues who lived in the vicinity. They included Peter and Mary, Adaline, Laura J., Clara, Daniel, and Harriet Blue.

Bluffton *Allen County.* Settled by Joseph Deford in 1833 and platted by him in 1837. Once called Shannon, the city was incorporated in 1861 as Bluffton, a name taken from a city in Indiana.

Boardman *Mahoning County.* The land was first owned by and the place was named for Elijah Boardman, a member of the Connecticut Land Company, who arrived in 1798 but did not settle here.

Boden *Guernsey County.* When a post office was established here, William E. Boden was Guernsey County's delegate to the Ohio legislature. The hamlet was named in his honor.

Bogart *Erie County.* This tiny spot may owe its name to a family or individual who resided here. D. D. Bogart was a Civil War veteran from Erie County, while Jay Bogart was mustered out in 1863.

Bolin's Mills *Vinton County.* William Bolen established mills here in 1845. The discrepancy in spelling is unaccounted for.

Bolivar *Tuscarawas County.* This community was settled in the late 1820s as Kellysville, named for one of the first canal commissioners, Alfred Kelly. But Kelly objected to the use of his name, so residents honored Simón Bolívar (1783–1830), "the George Washington of South America."

Bolton *Stark County.* This place-name is thought to trace back to Israel Bolton, a well-known figure here in 1842. Later, in 1884, another Bolton, Tom, was also well known in the area. It is not known whether the two were related.

Bond Hill *Hamilton County.* This Cincinnati suburb was founded by the Cooperative Land and Building Association in 1870 or 1871 on a spot known as Colonel Bond's Hill.

Boneta *Medina County.* This place is said to have been named by early settler Abraham Shontz in honor of his niece. The year he did so is uncertain. The niece's name was inspired by the Spanish word *bonita*, "beautiful."

Bonn *Washington County.* Described now as a virtual ghost town, Bonn was laid out in 1835 by the owner of the property, Nahum Ward. It took its name from the city of Bonn in Germany. Promising a major silk manufactory, Ward solicited German immigration. His mulberry trees failed to flourish, however, and the dream never materialized. There was a post office at Bonn from 1844 until 1901.

Booktown *Sandusky County.* Once the site of a stagecoach tavern and inn overlooking the Sandusky River, this junction may have taken its name from early settlers surnamed Bookmyer. It is known that settlers of that name lived in the vicinity. An alternate possibility comes from a correspondent: "As you approached Muskellunge Creek, you went down a small hill to cross a little iron and wood-plank bridge just above water level. Starting up the other side, you were confronted with a large billboard, constructed in the shape and picture of an open book. . . .

As I recall, the message was written in script. . . . Hence the name Booktown." The inn and tavern structures were torn down about 1956.

Boston *Belmont County.* The plat for this community was recorded in 1834. Mordecai Harper laid out the place, which was named for Boston, Massachusetts. The town has also been known as Atlas.

Boston Heights *Summit County.* This community is close to Boston Mills (see next entry).

Boston Mills *Summit County.* Even in the old days, citizens of Boston Mills could not agree on why the site took the name it did. Some believed it was so designated by a settler from Massachusetts, James Stanford. Others were convinced that Alfred Wolcott, Sr., the surveyor, named it.

Botkins *Shelby County.* In 1858, Russell Botkins laid out the lots for a town here, which came to be known by his surname. J. A. Wells did the surveying. Variations on the name have included Botkinsville, Bodkin, Bodkinsvill, Botkinsvill, and Stringtown.

Boughtonville *Huron County.* A family named Boughton came to this locality early on and is memorialized in the place-name. Boughtons mentioned in a history of the area include Darwin, E. G., and Theodore.

Bourneville *Ross County.* Laid out, 1832, by Isaac McCrackin and John Boswell. McCrackin and Boswell named the town for Colonel Alexander Bourne, who surveyed the area. (One source states that the place was laid out in 1852.)

Bowerston *Harrison County.* First known as Bowersville, this community was platted in 1852 by David and Nathaniel Bowers and Henry Hoover. Local burial records confirm that a raft of Bowerses—Ann, Anna, Barnhart, Caleb, David, Elias, Elizabeth, Esther, Jacob, John, Henry, Margaret, Margaret A., Susan, Thomas, and Samuel— were interred here.

Bowersville *Greene County.* Laid out, 1848, by Samuel T. Owens. The first settler and businessman of the town was Peter Bowermaster, and Owens is believed to have named the town in Bowermaster's honor. Christopher Hussey owned the site.

Bowling Green *Wood County (seat).* This city was once a clearing in the forest left from an army encampment in the War of 1812. When the town fathers sought a name for their community, Bowling Green was suggested by a veteran mail carrier who, in the first decade of the nineteenth century, had delivered mail in Kentucky and Tennessee and was fond of Bowling Green, Kentucky. The recommendation was favorably received by the citizens of this Ohio place. Incorporation took place in 1855.

Bowlusville *Clark and Champaign counties.* Bowlusville's name traces back to Samuel H. Bowlus, who operated a grain dealership at this location.

Bowman *Mahoning County.* In the 1874 atlas of the county, no fewer than twenty-seven Bowmans are mentioned in the index. At this place, Josiah Bowman and C. C. Bowman held adjoining parcels. Immediately to the north, Andrew P. Bowman owned land, and just north of him, John J. Bowman added to the Bowman holdings.

Boyd's Corners *Mahoning County.* Five Boyds appear in the 1874 county atlas. This place-name may be traceable to James W. Boyd or his family.

Braceville *Trumbull County.* This spot was first referred to as Millantown, for a squatter named Millan. Ralph Freeman and others settled here about 1803. At the organization of the township, in 1811, the place was named for one of the proprietors, Jonathan Brace.

Bradford *Darke and Miami counties.* First known as Richmond—it was on the Richmond & Covington Railroad—the community later became the home of a railroad roundhouse on the Pennsylvania Railroad. Located between Indianapolis and Columbus, it became known as Bradford Junction, in recognition of a railway mail clerk named Thomas Bradford.

Bradley *Jefferson County.* This place-name probably traces back to one of several Bradleys who resided in the vicinity. Before 1886, the Reverend Dan F. Bradley preached in nearby Steubenville. Charles Bradley resided near Wellsville, while W. H. Bradley operated a mill at Mingo. Eight Bradleys appear in the biographical index of a county history.

Bradner *Wood County.* Surveyed, 1875, by John Bradner and Ross Crocker. Bradner left his surname as his legacy to this place. It was incorporated in 1889.

Bradrick *Lawrence County.* Bradrick's heyday began about 1877. The name traces back to the Reverend T. H. Bradrick of the Kingsley Chapel of the Methodist Episcopal Church.

Brady Lake *Portage County.* The village takes its name from Captain Sam Brady, who eluded hostile Native Americans here in 1790 when he leapt the Cuyahoga River and concealed himself under a log in a nearby lake until the Indians gave up searching for him. Brady's vault across the torrent was estimated at twenty-one feet. The pursuing Indians were forced to take a longer route around to the spot before trying to pick up his trail. Captain Brady was a noted Indian fighter from Pennsylvania. Brady Lake was incorporated in 1927.

Bradysville *Adams County.* This community was named for its founder, Van S. Brady, who laid it out in 1839.

Braffettsville *Darke County.* The spelling of this place-name may have taken a turn over the years. It is believed to trace back to members of a Broffett family who were prominent at this locality, starting with James Broffett, who married in 1794. Silas and Alfred Broffett were also identified with this place.

Brailey *Fulton County.* Moses R. Brailey settled in this vicinity in 1857. The hamlet's name probably commemorates him, his family, or another member of the Brailey family. Moses is believed to have been a farmer.

Brandt *Miami County.* Once the site of a plow factory, Brandt was founded in 1839. Some Brandts in this vicinity spelled their surnames Brant, dropping the "d." Joseph B. Brandt, born 1859, farmed locally. Alfred M. Brandt, born 1882, was an attorney. David Brant and Melchi Brandt were their ancestors.

Bratenahl *Cuyahoga County.* Settling in the mid-nineteenth century, Charles Bratenahl became a prominent landowner here on Lake Erie's shore. Incorporation occurred in 1904.

Brecksville *Cuyahoga County.* Settled in 1811. This city was named in recognition of two early arrivals at the place, Robert and John Breck. Brecksville was incorporated in 1921.

Brecon *Hamilton County.* The origin of this place-name is unclear. The best guess is that since a D. Brecount and an S. Brecount were living in this area (Sycamore Township) about 1869, the place-name is an adaptation of their surname, possibly resulting from the way the name sounded when pronounced.

Bremen *Fairfield County.* Settled, 1834, by George Berry. Bremen is named for the German city.

Brennersville *Preble County.* It is said that at one time this place was known as Sniffletown. About 1835, John Brenner laid out a town here.

Brewster *Stark County.* This village may have been named after Calvin Brewster, the first justice of the peace in this township (Sugar Creek) in 1816. Brewster was incorporated in 1910.

Briarwood Beach *Medina County.* This community was founded in the 1950s, a lakefront neighborhood. Speculation is that the name was chosen because it sounded good to the developers. It was incorporated in 1955.

Brice *Franklin County.* Joseph B. Powell founded the town in 1879. He desired to bestow the family surname on the community but learned that a town called Powell already existed in Ohio. As an alternative he selected Brice, in gratitude to an attorney, Calvin Brice, who had been influential in enticing a railroad to come through the town. Brice later became a U.S. senator. The community was incorporated in 1960.

Briceton *Paulding County.* Several Brices are found in county records. In 1876, Patrick Joseph Brice married Anna Gilreon. In 1891, James Brice married Florence Glawson. Laura Brice and Mary Brice are also in the records. This place-name probably relates to one or more of these Brices.

Bridgeport *Belmont County.* Platted in 1806. This town, initially known as North Canton, took the Bridgeport name upon incorporation in 1836. There was a bridge over the Ohio River here, and the town was a river port, so the name fit.

Bridges *Highland County.* When this place was searching for a name, someone noted that four bridges crossed Hardin Creek to speed traffic into and out of the community.

Bridgewater Center *Williams County.* Surveyed, 1867, by A. T. Bement on the land of Joseph Diebely. The name bespeaks the central position of the village in Bridgewater Township.

Brier Hill *Mahoning County.* Two accounts are advanced as the possible rationale behind this name. One holds that brier thickets abounded on an elevation here. Another claims that the place may have been named in honor of the Brierly family, whose home was a stagecoach stop.

Brighton *Lorain County.* Variations exist as to the genesis of this place-name. One source holds that it traces to Brighton, New York, since immigrants to this area came from that state. Another suggests that a person named Abner Loveland named it in 1820 because he deemed the site a "bright spot." A third suggests that the name traces directly to the English seaside resort of the same name.

Brilliant *Jefferson County.* This place has been characterized by a succession of names. First it was Phillipsburg, followed by LaGrange. There being another La-Grange in Ohio, the mail was often misdirected. A man named W. H. Rogers is said to have advocated the change to Brilliant, justifying it by the presence in town of a glassmaking firm. The company was either named Brilliant or its products were considered lustrous (or both).

Brimfield *Portage County.* John Wyles was a proprietor of the real estate at this location, and the current name, which went into effect in 1830, traces back to Brimfield, Massachusetts, from which Wyles had come. The first permanent residents arrived earlier, in 1816, and the area was known for several years as Thorndike. Among the earliest settlers were John Boosinger and Henry and Israel Augustus Thorndike.

Brimfield Station *Portage County.* The "Station" aspect of the designation comes from the location on a railroad. The old stationhouse still stands not far from Brimfield but is used for other purposes. (See also the Brimfield entry.)

Brinker's Corners *Pickaway County.* An implement store at this locality was operated by Jonathan Brinker. The site probably owes its name to him.

Brinkhaven *Knox County.* Technically, Brinkhaven is the name of the post office here, but it appears on some maps as though it were a village. The village is actually named Gann (or Village of Gann), after John Gann, who donated land for a railroad right-of-way (see the Gann entry). Still earlier names included Mount Holly and Non-Peril (or Nonpareil), the latter an apparent reference to the flat location above the Mohican River. It is said that the contractor for the railroad was a man from Scotland and Mount Holly reminded him of his Scottish hometown, Brinkhaven. The contractor asked that the town be renamed Brinkhaven. Instead, the post office was so named. The place is said to have been the setting for James Fenimore Cooper's novel *The Last of the Mohicans.* A correspondent says that Brinkhaven was platted in 1828 as Port Jackson.

Bristol *Morgan County.* Founded, 1831, by Thomas Stevens. Bristol takes its name from the English city of the same name. The village is often known locally as Muttonburg. In Charles Robertson's 1886 *History of Morgan County*, this passage appears: "Some envious and evil-disposed person, full of expedients to blast the good name, fame, and prospects of the embryo village, and being moved in his hatred and ill will by that evil spirit that seems to have control over the human heart, put into circulation a report that some of its inhabitants had a taste for mutton, and mutton they would have, whether in a legitimate way or not. These outside barbarians who had lost their mutton, instead of leaving their ninety and nine unlost sheep and going forth in a friendly way in search of the lost one, in their hatred and contempt of the villagers gave the town just blooming into importance and notice, the contemptible name of Muttonburg, by which name it is now known far and near and will so continue to be known and called, it is feared, until the Angel Gabriel sounds his last trumpet."

Bristolville *Trumbull County.* Settled in 1801 by Alfred Wolcott, the place is in Bristol Township. The town proper came into being in 1807 and was named for Wolcott's former home, Bristol, Connecticut. Wolcott was the surveyor of the tract.

Broadview Heights *Cuyahoga County.* The rolling wooded hills of Broadview Heights afforded a broad view from one of the highest elevations in the county. Broadview Heights is today a city, having been incorporated in 1926.

Broadway *Union County.* The first resident here was Peleg Cranston. A petition to plat a village was presented in 1865 by Leonard Richey and L. C. Pooler. One version of the name rationale, handed down verbally, goes like this: "The AG&W Railway is not standard track gauge; it is about one foot wider and is referred to as broad gauge. The road that crosses the track here is the only stone road in the township and is referred to as the highway. Why not take the 'broad' from broad gauge and the 'way' from highway and have Broadway?"

Broadwell *Athens County.* The land here was owned by Ann E. Broadwell, and the hamlet was named for her. She laid out the site in 1886.

Brockway *Trumbull County.* The community derives its name from one of its original settlers, Edward Brockway.

Brokaw *Morgan County.* Members of the Brokaw family were present in Morgan County in 1828. The land where the Big Bottom Massacre took place was owned by Obediah Brokaw. This hamlet is named for the Brokaws. On January 2, 1791, a party made up of Delaware and Wyandot Indians raided a small settlement outpost here, killing twelve and taking five prisoners, one of whom died shortly afterward. Two of the settlers escaped to warn others.

Broken Sword *Crawford County.* According to a newspaper article, the village and creek here were given this name after Colonel William Crawford jammed his sword into the creek bank and broke it off at the hilt to prevent Native Americans from killing him with his own weapon. They then burned him at the stake. The place-name is sometimes styled as one word: Brokensword.

Brooklyn *Cuyahoga County.* Laid out, 1830, by Moses Fish. The community nearly became known as Egypt when one of the first settlers, Oziah Brainerd, suggested that name because of the abundance of corn grown here. It eventually was dubbed Brooklyn simply because the sound of it appealed to the town fathers. Brooklyn was incorporated in 1867.

Brooklyn Heights *Cuyahoga County.* Located at the outskirts of Brooklyn, this village was incorporated in 1903. (See Brooklyn entry.)

Brook Park *Cuyahoga County.* Categorized as descriptive and promotional, this name was applied to the city in 1914, the year of incorporation, by W. J. Sifleet, who was inspired by the streams and brooks that meandered through the parklike site on their way to Rocky River. Sifleet served as the first mayor of the community.

Brookside *Belmont County.* Brookside arose about 1900, the year of its incorporation. The name comes from its situation overlooking Wheeling Creek.

Brookville *Montgomery County.* Laid out, 1850, by Jacob Frees, who also surveyed the site for proprietor Jacob Flory. The headwaters of Wolf Creek flow here, forming a brook that inspired the name.

Brownhelm *Lorain County.* Area citizens offered the opportunity to name the place to Colonel Henry Brown. He dubbed the site Brownhelm, causing some consternation among certain local citizens. Those who didn't care for the name interpreted it as implying that Brown was at the helm, or steering their ship. In reality, it is thought, he was looking for a euphonious ending for his surname, and used the Saxon *ham* or *hem* (home), softened by adding an "l." Thus his intent was "Brown's home." At one time a petition was circulated to change the name to Freedom, but the move failed. Brownhelm was settled about 1818.

Brown's Corners *Trumbull County.* The 1874 county atlas reveals that James Brown held real estate at this location.

Brown's Mills *Washington County.* In 1815, Samuel Brown II erected a mill on Wolf Creek at this location. When a post office opened in 1819, Brown became postmaster.

Brownstown *Wyandot County.* The site was formerly known as Brown's Corners. It was named after a Mr. Brown, the first settler at the location, who is said to have stayed about three years in the late 1830s.

Brownsville *Licking County.* The founder, Adam Brown, assigned his surname to this place.

Brownsville *Monroe County.* Brownsville was founded in 1834 by Israel Brown. An early post office at this site was known as Jolly.

Brunersburg *Defiance County.* Two of the earliest residents at this location on Bean Creek (the Tiffin River) were Joseph Partee and John Perkins, a surveyor. The first settler in Noble Township, Perkins built a sawmill and a dam here, later adding a grist mill at the opposite end of the dam. In 1833 or 1839, he sold the mill operation to Daniel Bruner, for whom the town was named.

Brunswick *Medina County.* Founded in 1815. Incorporated in 1960. Two versions of the name rationale for this city exist. One holds that the name was selected simply because it was pleasing to the ear. An alternative explanation is that early settlers put name possibilities into a hat and drew out Brunswick.

Bryan *Williams County (seat).* A prominent state officeholder, the Honorable John A. Bryan, is credited with developing a good portion of northwest Ohio. The city of Bryan is named for him. Incorporation took place in 1941.

Buchanan *Pike County.* The fifteenth president of the United States, James Buchanan, is the individual for whom this village is named. The community took root during Buchanan's administration (1857–1861).

Buchtel *Athens County.* Buchtel was laid out in 1876 by John R. Buchtel of Akron, acting on behalf of the Akron Iron Company, which had purchased large tracts of mineral-laden land in Athens and Hocking counties.

Buckland *Auglaize County.* The label on this place likely results from one or more Buck families that resided in the area in its formative years. Ebenezer Buck held land here in 1835, while one township south, Enoch Buck resided. Another possibility is that there is some connection to General Buckland of Fremont, Ohio, who advocated laying a railroad through the area.

Bucyrus *Crawford County (seat).* Colonel Kilbourne, said to have been an admirer of the ancient Persian ruler Cyrus the Great, founded this city. Historians speculate that the name was formed by placing the initial syllable of the word *beautiful* before Cyrus's name. Incorporation took place in 1822.

Buena Vista *Fayette County.* This name translates from the Spanish as "good view." The community was named for a like-named place in Virginia.

Buena Vista *Scioto County.* Located near the Ohio River, the community takes its name from the *buena vista* (Spanish for "good view") obtained from its vantage point.

Buford *Highland County.* The hamlet dates to 1834. Robert Lindsey was the landowner and platted the town. Lindsey's wife was a member of the Buford family from Kentucky. A Revolutionary War soldier, Colonel Abraham Buford, owned several surveys in the county. The community is named for the colonel.

Bulah *Ashtabula County.* This place-name is a short version of *ashtabula,* a Native American term that translates roughly as "place of many fish."

Bundysburg *Geauga County.* Thirteen Bundys are mentioned in an early pioneer and general history of the county. Two of them, Ephraim and Moses, arrived by ox team from Southampton, Massachusetts, in 1816, walking on ice near the shore of the Great Lakes a good portion of the way. Upon arrival at this site, they discovered, by sheer happenstance, their brother Elisha, among others, and christened the location Bundysburg (or Bundysburgh).

Burbank *Wayne and Medina counties.* The first settler recalled by name was David Baker, who arrived in 1830. However, the place was probably settled prior to that. It was first called Bridgeport because of the number of bridges and streams here. This name remained until 1868, when it was changed to Burbank owing to confusion with the Bridgeport located on the Ohio River. Why Burbank? The answer is not known with certainty. One theory is that "bank" came from its location on the banks of Killbuck Creek and "bur" was inspired by a large burdock growth along the stream or from chestnut burrs that were abundant in the area. Another possibility involves the old Naftzger mill, in early days a significant industry here. This theory holds that the name combines the "burr" used in the mill with the "bank" of the Killbuck. Burbank was incorporated in 1868 or 1869.

Burghill *Trumbull County.* Founded in 1798 or 1799. This burg supposedly was named by William Bushnell, a pioneer, to denote its location at the highest point in Vernon Township. At a later date, the business district was moved downhill and closer to the railroad, but the name survived the move.

Burgoon *Sandusky County.* The locale first was known as Warner, for Peter Warner, who laid out a portion of the village. The town eventually was called by the name of the post office, Burgoon, reportedly as a compliment to the superintendent of the new railroad.

Burkettsville *Mercer and Darke counties.* A pioneer settler of the area, a Mr. Burkett, is the person to whom this place-name leads.

Burkhart *Monroe County.* A German-born settler, Martin Burkhart, is the person to whom this place-name traces. Among the early property owners in this locality were J. A., David, A. B., A., and J. M. Burkhart.

Burlingham *Meigs County.* The first postmaster here bore the surname Burlingham, and the community assumed his name.

Burnett's Corners *Wayne County.* A family having the Burnett surname operated a grocery store at this location.

Burton *Geauga County.* It is thought that the son of founder Titus Street was named Burton and this village was named after him. Incorporation was in 1908.

Burton City *Wayne County.* Surveyed, 1850, by John Brinkerhoff and initially named Fairview. The name was changed to recognize a man named Burton who operated coal mines at this place.

Burtonville *Clinton County.* About 1844, a grist mill was constructed at this site by Peyton Burton. The location continues to bear his name.

Bushnell *Ashtabula County.* In the early 1830s, one of Monroe Township's original trustees was Sedgwick Bushnell. The name of this place honors him.

Busy Corners *Sandusky County.* Apparently a number of accidents occurred here where Route 51, carrying Toledo traffic, and Route 20, carrying Fremont traffic, intersect. Add to that a nearby railroad crossing, and all the elements were present for Busy Corners.

Butler *Richland County.* Laid out, 1848, by Daniel Spohn but settled as early as 1820. At one time, the place was casually referred to as Spohntown. At still another time it was called Independence. Ultimately the name was changed to agree with that of the post office, Butler, named in honor of General William O. Butler of Kentucky (1791–1880). A hero of the Mexican War, Butler was the Democratic vice presidential running mate of Lewis Cass in 1848.

Butler Mill *Hancock County.* A. Butler, J. Butler, and E. Butler owned property adjoining this site at one time. Located on Beaver Creek, it probably was the site of a sawmill or grist mill.

Butlerville *Warren County.* Little is known about the founding of this village except that it was laid out in 1838 by the proprietor, Abraham (or Abram) B. Butler.

Byer *Jackson County.* Before the Civil War, this hamlet was known as Ellsworth. It was changed to Byer in recognition of the Byers family, which owned land that reached to Main Street. Cemetery records reveal that at least twenty-nine persons having the Byers surname were laid to rest in the vicinity of this hamlet.

Byesville *Guernsey County.* Early in the nineteenth century, the first flour mill to be established in this vicinity was set in motion by Jonathan Bye. The village took on Bye's name. It was incorporated in 1882.

Byhalia *Union County.* There is no accord on the meaning or origin of this town's name. One source claims (via verbal history) that the designation means "place of the oaks" in a Native American language. Another claims that it is biblical in origin. There is said to be a Byhalia in a southern state, but the origin of its name is equally unclear. This place was first called Pennyville, but since Horace Pinney, along with Matt Lingrel, was one of the first settlers, the correct version was probably Pinneyville. Settlers were in this vicinity by 1830.

Cable *Champaign County.* This community was platted by James B. Armstrong in 1851, 1852, or 1853 for Philander S. Cable. One source, however, credits Cable with laying out the town and claims the year was 1853. The first residents were Mr. and Mrs. Henry Nincehelser.

Cadiz *Harrison County (seat).* During the 1808–1814 War of the Spanish Peninsula, the Spanish city of Cádiz was mentioned prominently in American newspapers, inspiring the name of this city. Incorporation was accomplished in 1831.

Cadiz Junction *Harrison County.* This place is on a rail line not far from Cadiz. (See Cadiz entry.)

Cadmus *Gallia County.* This hamlet was known until 1886 as Sprinkle's Mill, after a Mr. Sprinkle. One source states that its current name refers to a character in a Greek play. A second source claims that after Sprinkle's death, local citizens gathered to choose a new name. Joe Worthington, manager of the Smith Store, suggested Cadmus, for the legendary founder of the ancient Greek city of Thebes.

Cairo *Allen County*. The great city in Egypt is said to have inspired the name of this place, which came into being as a village in 1875.

Calcutta *Columbiana County*. At one time this site was given the biblical place-name Ninevah. At still another juncture it was known as Foulkstown, in honor of early settler William Foulks (or, more likely, Foulkes). Foulks and Michael Shertz laid it out in 1810 as West Union. The current name of Calcutta refers to the city in India.

Caldersburg *Coshocton County*. James Calder founded this place in 1816.

Caldwell *Noble County (seat)*. Although this community was settled as early as 1814, it was not organized until 1857. The name honors Joseph Caldwell, who drilled the first oil well in Ohio in 1814. The town was incorporated in 1870.

Caledonia *Marion County*. Surveyed and platted by Samuel Holmes in 1834, this place was once known as Van Buskirk, after Lawrence E. Van Buskirk, postmaster from 1832 to 1842. According to legend, the village's current name was proposed by a Scotsman and the change was made in 1835. Caledonia was the Roman name for what is now Scotland.

Calla *Mahoning County*. Calla lilies are said to have been grown in abundance at this place by members of the Templin family of settlers.

Camba *Jackson County*. This name may be Welsh, since some settlers in these environs were of Welsh extraction. It may be an adaptation of the term *Cambria* or *Cambrian* (Wales or Welsh).

Cambridge *Guernsey County (seat)*. Laid out, 1806, by Zacheus Beatty and Jacob Gomber. Many of this city's settlers came from the Cambridge, Maryland area, and it was named for that place. Incorporation was accomplished in 1837.

Camden *Lorain County*. The property owner, Gideon Waugh, suggested the Camden name in remembrance of his upstate New York home. Waugh purchased the property in the 1820s from absentee owners. The "Cam" being a river in England and "den" meaning a dell or glen, it seemed an appropriate choice, since the Vermilion River meanders through a glen here.

Camden *Preble County*. Founded in 1818. William Moore laid out this hamlet, at first calling it Dover. Later it was renamed Newcomb in honor of a state senator from Montgomery County, George Newcomb. The current name stems from the city of Camden, South Carolina. It took on this third and final name the same year the village was incorporated, 1832.

Cameron *Monroe County.* Dating to 1860, this place-name honors Simon Cameron, U.S. senator from 1857 to 1861.

Camp *Pike County.* This diminutive collection of structures is in Camp Creek Township. Camp Creek is the primary waterway in the township, and Camp is situated on its banks.

Campbell *Mahoning County.* This site was known earlier as East Youngstown. Its current name recognizes James Campbell, who was president of Youngstown Sheet & Tube in 1926. Now a city, it was incorporated in 1909.

Campbellsport *Portage County.* A pioneer, John Campbell, came here in 1805, acting as land agent for Samuel Hinckley, the proprietor. Initially known as Campbell's Port, the place was an important trading center on the canal. Campbell's title (or rank) is found variously as captain, colonel, and general. A woolen factory went into operation here in 1848. Information on Campbellsport is found in *Portage Heritage*.

Campbellstown *Preble County.* An astonishing 115 Campbells appear in the biographical index of an early county history. One of the most prominent was William Campbell (1793–1860), who settled in Gasper Township.

Canaan *Wayne County.* Founded in 1828. This name is biblical, being the ancient name of Palestine. One reference source gives the literal meaning as "belonging to the land of red-purple," perhaps a reference to a colorant traded in the biblical Canaan.

Canaanville *Athens County.* The name of this "ville," situated in Canaan Township, was suggested by the Canaan (later Palestine) of the Bible, said to be a land flowing with milk and honey. There was a Canaan, Connecticut, as early as 1738.

Canal Fulton *Stark County.* This village was formerly known as Milan. At about the time a canal was put through, the name was changed to honor the inventor of the steamboat, Robert Fulton. Canal Fulton was incorporated in 1840.

Canal Lewisville *Coshocton County.* T. Butler Lewis and Solomon Vail founded this village in 1832, and it assumed Lewis's name.

Canal Winchester *Franklin and Fairfield counties.* The "Canal" portion of the designation may have been added after the building of a canal put the village on the waterway. The "Winchester" aspect is attributable to the city in Virginia.

Canfield *Mahoning County.* Judson Canfield, after whom the community was named, arrived at this locality as early as 1798. He held deed to 6,171 acres here. The township (Canfield) was named in 1800 and the town assumed the same label. Samuel Canfield (relationship to Judson uncertain) owned 437 acres at the site. Other prominent early Canfields here included Henry J., a son of Judson, and

Edward G., who served one term as prosecuting attorney for Mahoning County. Incorporation dates to 1849.

Cannelville *Muskingum County.* Cannel coal was discovered here in 1885 by Jacob Ballou. The following year the village was incorporated.

Cannonsburg *Hancock County.* The genesis of this name is vague. Longtime area residents recently stated that accounts passed down from their parents attributed the name to the location of a military post nearby. However, the existence of a post in the area could not be confirmed by a search of historical records. A source speculates that this account may be "an apocryphal story that evolved in the local folklore." No person with the surname of Cannon could be tied to this location.

Cannon's Mills *Columbiana County.* In 1812, John Cannon erected a grist mill here, using the energy of the Middle Beaver Creek. The place came to be known by his name. Cannon operated the mill until the building of a canal cut off his energy supply.

Canton *Stark County (seat).* Bazaleel Wells, an international trader, founded and named the city. Historians are unsure which of two theories explains the name. One theory holds that Wells was influenced by a Baltimore citizen who named his estate after the Chinese city of Canton. The other holds that Wells adopted the French term *canton,* "district," which designates a sovereign state in the Swiss confederation. Settlement here is thought to have begun in 1805. Wells and James Leonard platted the community in 1806, and incorporation came in 1822.

Captina *Belmont County.* The hamlet takes its name from Captina Creek. *Captina* is said to be a Native American word seen spelled in a variety of ways and thought to mean "captain." The site was referred to by locals as Capteen. The name has a long history. George Washington refers to Captina Creek in a journal entry dated October 1770, where he also states that the stream was alternately known as Fox Grapevine Creek, for wild grapes that grew eight miles upstream from the Ohio River. An Indian encampment called Grapevine Town was situated there.

Carbon Hill *Hocking County.* Laid out, 1873, by the Honorable Thomas Ewing and the landowner, Isom Finley. There were extensive coal deposits here, resulting in the name Carbon Hill.

Carbondale *Athens County.* A coal works went into operation here in 1867, resulting in this name.

Cardington *Morrow County.* This is also the name of the surrounding township. A carding mill once operated in the village.

Carey *Ross County.* This map designation may lead back to the Reverend Nathan Carey, the first Baptist preacher in his township; he also ministered to a congregation in Deerfield Township sometime after 1820, sharing the duties with other clergymen. Or, the name may trace to Alonzo Carey, who resided in this county at an early date. He was the son of William Carey, an early settler in adjoining Highland County.

Carey *Wyandot County.* R. M. Shuler and W. M. Buell laid out the town in 1843. It was named for Judge John Carey, president of a railroad that ran through the village.

Careytown *Highland County.* The post office at this site opened in 1889. The Carey family owned the land nearby, and the location assumed the family's name.

Carlisle Station *Warren County.* This place dates from 1813, according to one source. On some maps it appears as Carlisle. The name stems from a land purchase here by the Honorable George Carlisle of Cincinnati. A second source states that the place was settled by William Barkalow and Arthur Vanderveer of Freehold, New Jersey, in 1804 and was referred to as the Jersey Settlement. The current name, sometimes shortened to Carlisle, came into use in 1850.

Carltonville *Meigs County.* Carlton College, founded by a Mr. Carlton, lent its name to this site.

Carman *Harrison County.* This place designation is thought to trace back to a German Township farmer, L. N. Carman, or his family.

Caroline *Seneca County.* Surveyed, 1828, for Hector and Byron Kilbourne and Cornelius Gilmore by James Kilbourne. Caroline is said to have been the name of Cornelius Gilmore's daughter.

Carpenter *Meigs County.* In an era when railroads and railroad stations were much sought after as town assets, State Senator J. L. Carpenter facilitated both for this hamlet. He reportedly signed over some rights-of-way for the railroad, then donated a site for the depot. A second source casts a vote not for J. L. but for Amos Carpenter, Sr., as the town namesake. This source also mentions a Jesse C. Carpenter.

Carroll *Fairfield County.* The Ohio and Hocking canals came together here at an angle, affecting the manner in which the town's streets were laid out by brothers Oliver and William Tong. They named the community in honor of Charles Carroll of Carrollton, Maryland, the last surviving signer of the Declaration of Independence, who died in Baltimore in 1832 at age ninety-six. William Tong was one of the early contractors on the Ohio Canal.

Carrollton *Carroll County (seat).* Laid out in 1815. First known as Centerville, this village was renamed Carrollton in 1833 in honor of a signer of the Declaration of Independence, Charles Carroll, who had died the preceding year. The community was incorporated in 1834.

Carrothers *Seneca County*. John Newman laid out this place in 1837 for John Carrothers.

Carter *Washington County*. The Carter Oil Company operated here when a post office was established in 1899 along Wingett Run in Ludlow Township.

Carthagena *Mercer County*. Augustus Wattles and a contingent of black freedmen took up residence here in 1835. The name comes from the ancient city of Carthage in northern Africa. The town is said to have been laid out in 1840 by Charles Moore, an African American.

Carysville *Champaign County*. First known as Trenton, the hamlet was laid out in 1833 by Calvin Carey.

Cassella *Mercer County*. According to one source, this place-name is the result of a misprint of the German word for chapel, *cappella*. (*Cappella* is an Italian word, however.) A second source gives the German term as *kappella* (correct spelling: *Kappelle*), and traces the name back to a Convent of the Precious Blood. In 1860, the site was known as Marysville; other temporary labels included Frogtown and Dogtown.

Casstown *Miami County*. Laid out, 1832, by Luke Daney and Rankin Westfall. It was formerly called Trimmensburgh. The current name honors Lewis Cass (1782–1866), a Zanesville, Ohio, lawyer who became a U.S. senator from Michigan and Democratic candidate for president in 1848.

Castalia *Erie County*. The Blue Hole spring is located here, and the village is said to have taken its name from the legendary spring of Castalia that issued from the foot of Mount Parnassus in Greece. The waters of the Blue Hole are known for their depth and clarity. The village was incorporated in 1946.

Castine *Darke County*. Castine's name traces back to a French trapper, M. Decastin (possibly DeCastin), who annually made this spot a stopover on his trips from Canada to Kentucky. The village was incorporated in 1909.

Catawba *Clark County*. Settled, 1838, by George Dawson and Israel Marsh of Vermont. The place-name was suggested, it is said, when Marsh planted a cutting from a Catawba grapevine near his cabin. *Catawba* is the name of Native American people who once inhabited the Eastern Seaboard. The word is said to mean "cut-off."

Catawba Junction *Champaign County*. A railroad ran through this site. For "Catawba," see the preceding entry.

Cavett *Van Wert County*. In 1836, Joseph H. Cavett took possession of eighty-eight acres in Washington Township, and the hamlet of Cavett probably takes its name from him. William Cavett was the patriarch of a family residing in Ridge Township about 1839 to 1861. Ira Cavett was another local member of the Cavett clan. The community was mapped in 1879 by Homer J. Loudenback.

Cecil *Paulding County*. An elderly resident tells this anecdote: "A young man used to get on the train [near here]. When asked where he was going, [he] answered, 'To see Sal.' Thus, the town of Cecil, Ohio was named." Another current resident, ninety years old, provides this version, passed along verbally from his elders: "After the railroad was built—when the first train came through—the place was still without a name. The conductor's given name was Cecil, so he called the town Cecil." The burg was incorporated in 1882.

Cedarhill *Fairfield County*. The site takes its name from the tall, stately cedar trees that once encircled the church here. At one time it was a thriving rest point for travelers between Lancaster and Circleville.

Cedar Mills *Adams County*. This settlement is on Cedar Run, and mills probably operated here in the early days.

Cedarville *Greene County*. Laid out, 1816, by William and Jesse Newport. Incorporated in 1843. The profusion of cedar trees here prompted the naming of the place. It was formerly known as Milford, but since Ohio had at least one other Milford, the need for a change was recognized.

Celeryville *Huron County*. Founded in 1904. Persons from Holland via Kalamazoo, Michigan, settled this site, growing celery and onions in the rich soil they found here.

Celina *Mercer County (seat)*. Settled in 1834. The city took its name from Salina, New York. Incorporation came in 1861.

Centerburg *Knox County*. Centerburg was named as a result of its location in the center of Ohio.

Centerfield *Highland County*. Platted, 1831, by John M. Combs. The place was laid out on the land of William Crawford, and the settlement's center lay in a large field—or so the story goes.

Center-of-the-World *Trumbull County*. This unusual sobriquet was conferred upon the site by Randall Wilmot, who arrived from Pennsylvania in the 1840s following business setbacks. An ardent opponent of slavery, Wilmot operated a stagecoach stop here on the Akron-to-Pittsburgh route. Hoping to recoup his business losses, he also stabled horses and kept a combination bar and lunchstand. He was doing all right at Center-of-the-World until the Cleveland & Mahoning Railroad siphoned off much of his trade. He eventually relocated to Cortland, where he dubbed his home End-of-the-World. His son, David, became a U.S. senator from Pennsylvania; he also served in the House of Representatives, presided over the Thirteenth Pennsylvania Court District, and served as a judge of the U.S. Court of Claims. As a congressman, he submitted the Wilmot Proviso to prohibit slavery in U.S. territories, but the measure failed in 1847. The place-name also appears in print as Center-World and Center-of-World.

Centerpoint *Gallia County*. This town, also called Wales, served as a central point for Welsh pioneers who arrived in the 1840s.

Centerton. *Huron County*. This community occupies the geographical center of Norwich Township.

Center Village. *Delaware County*. Laid out in 1848. The community, formerly known as Centerville, is at the center of Harlem Township.

Centerville *Belmont County*. Laid out, 1828, by Thomas Jackson. The site is near the center of Smith Township.

Centerville *Clinton County*. Laid out in 1816 (or 1815). Timothy Jones of Virginia was the landowner. The name probably comes from the village's location near the center of Wayne Township.

Centerville *Gallia County*. Reuben Rambo and John Roof were the first settlers here. Rambo and Timothy Jones laid the place out in 1853, with William Preston doing the surveying. It was named because of its location midway between Jackson and Gallipolis. The name is also seen written as Centreville. It was settled largely by Welshmen. Thurman Post Office, named for George Thurman, was here.

Centerville *Montgomery County*. Not only is Centerville situated at the center of Washington Township, but, as one chronicler observed, "it was centrally located among roughly a dozen similar pioneer villages" (*A Sense of Time*). The name was originally spelled Centreville. Incorporated in 1830, Centerville is now a city. Settlement may have taken place as early as 1800.

Centerville *Wayne County*. Centerville was named for its position, about halfway between Big Prairie and Shreve. It was founded in 1850.

Central College *Franklin County*. This minuscule community was originally called Amalthea. Amalthea was the given name of the fiancée of Timothy Lee, who founded the town; she died before the two could be married. In 1842, Lee donated land for the establishment of an institution of higher learning to be called the Central College of Ohio. Eventually the name of the college was adopted as that of the community. The name Amalthea then faded away, although local historians still call their group the Amalthea Historical Society.

Ceylon Junction *Erie County*. Arising about 1853, this hamlet took its name from the Indian Ocean island of Ceylon (now Sri Lanka). The name was applied for an unknown reason by an unknown person.

Chagrin Falls *Cuyahoga County*. Incorporated in 1844. At least three theories attempt to account for this place-name. One holds that early explorers and surveyors in Moses Cleaveland's party were chagrined when they learned that the river they had reached (now called the Chagrin) was not the Cuyahoga, as they had assumed. A second suggests that *shagrin* (or *shaguin*), an Indian word for "clear water," evoked the name. Still a third advances the possibility that the place takes the name of Sieur de Saguin, an early French trader.

Chalfant *Perry County*. The hamlet, also known as Chalfant Station, takes its name from Robert Chalfant. A current resident describes the town as a thriving place before the 1930s, doing a lot of shipping via rail. It had a number of merchants and a school with the first eight grades, now long since closed. This resident, who lives in a house Chalfant built before 1850, states that of eight homes remaining in the community, seven are on land once owned by Chalfant.

Chambersburg *Gallia County*. The birth of this town traces to 1852, when John C. Chambers laid it out.

Champion Center *Trumbull County*. Located in Champion Township, this community bears the name of Henry Champion of Connecticut, who was the land agent for this sector of the county and owned much of the property himself. Sometimes the site is known simply as Champion. Settlement in this area began about 1806.

Champion Heights *Trumbull County*. This site derives its name from Henry Champion of Connecticut. It is just south of Champion Center in Champion Township (see the preceding entry).

Champion Station *Trumbull County*. Like Champion Center and Champion Heights, Champion Station takes its label from Henry Champion (see the two preceding entries). The "Station" aspect probably relates to the location on a rail-road line.

Chandlersville *Muskingum County*. In about 1799, John Chandler, a Connecticut native and former resident of Vermont, moved to this site and operated a grist mill. The place bears his name. The town was platted in 1842 by John Stevens.

Chapel *Ashtabula County*. Many years ago, a landmark church was located here between Jefferson and Austinburg. It was from this church that Chapel derived its name.

Chapel Hill *Perry County*. Founded in 1849. Irish settlers erected a Catholic church here in 1850, and the name resulted from the presence of the church.

Chardon *Geauga County (seat).* The first settler here was Norman Canfield in 1812. Peter Chardon Brooks, a Bostonian, agreed to donate land for the town seat if town fathers would give it his name. Chardon was incorporated in 1851.

Charity Rotch *Stark County.* Charity Rotch was also the name of the charitable wife of an enterprising farmer and industrialist, Thomas Rotch (1767–1823). The site that assumed her name has been absorbed into the city of Massillon. Thomas laid out Kendal in 1811 and in 1822 owned the Kendal Woolen Factory. (Kendal too is now part of Massillon.) The Rotches were members of the Society of Friends (Quakers), and Charity was admired as a noble person who shared her material wealth with the less fortunate. She died in 1824 after having established the Kendal Charity School. Thomas is credited with having introduced Spanish merino sheep into the area.

Charlestown *Portage County.* This tiny hamlet was named for an early settler, Charles Curtiss.

Charloe *Paulding County.* Laid out in 1839. The land proprietor was John Hudson. Earlier this place was the site of the Oquanoxa Reservation. The Native Americans who lived here were mostly of the Ottawa tribe. In 1820, they sold the reservation back to the government and most moved west to a spot near the mouth of the Kansas River. A few remained at this location with their last chief, Charloe Peter, until the 1840s. The place took Charloe's name.

Charm *Holmes County.* As the story goes, the initial designation for this tiny community was Stevenson, adapted from the name of an Amish man, Stephan Yoder, who worked the land here with his son. It may have been named Stevenson by the early 1860s. About twenty-five years later, when residents applied for a post office, they were given a list of names by the Post Office Department and asked to choose one. They chose Charm. Some think the naming had a connection to local jeweler and watch repairman Joni J. Yoder, because in those days it was popular to wear a cumbersome watch chain with an ornament—called a charm—attached. Before the name Stevenson came into use, the site was known locally as Pootchtown. Supposedly an early German visitor, taking a gander at the hamlet, remarked, "*Ed is yust ein gleiner pootcha*" (which translates, some people say, as "It is just a little bunch"). And Pootchtown it became. But an Amish woman contended that the name was inspired by a local pipe smoker who, when he blew out the smoke, always went "pootsch."

Chase *Athens County.* In 1866, one of the township trustees was Homer Chase, and the place-name is probably attributable to him or one of his ancestors. John M. Chase arrived in this township (Alexander) in 1817 from Maine, settled in Alexander Township, and died in 1860. His son Gardiner F. Chase had been born in Maine in 1811. Circa 1905, the Edwin Chase family resided in Carthage Township, Athens County.

Chase *Hancock County.* This spot appears to coincide with property once owned by J. Chase and may have been a railroad stop.

Chaseville *Noble County*. Chaseville's name honors an Ohio senator, Salmon P. Chase (1808–1873), who served as President Lincoln's secretary of the treasury and was appointed chief justice of the United States by Lincoln in 1864.

Chatfield *Crawford County*. The village of Chatfield took its name from the township in which it is located. The township was named for Oliver and Silas Chatfield, who were early settlers (1827). When the town was laid out here in 1840, it was called Richville, for the land proprietor, Nathan Rich. Later, at the urging of postal authorities, the name was changed.

Chatham *Medina County*. This community was named after the township in which it is located. The township was named for Chatham, England. One source claims, however, that the original settlers brought the name with them from the Chatham, New York area. In any case, the town was founded after 1833.

Chauncey *Athens County*. In 1839, this village was named in recognition of a Philadelphia entrepreneur, Elihue Chauncey. With Thomas Ewing, Roswell Colt, and Samuel F. Vinton, Chauncey controlled thousands of acres of prime Hocking Valley land. Here the men laid out this town and established salt and coal works.

Chautauqua *Montgomery and Warren counties*. This name probably was brought to this area from the lake or county of the same name in southwestern New York. It is an Iroquoian term with many speculative translations. Among them, according to the *Illustrated Dictionary of Place-Names,* are "where the fish was taken out," "bag tied in the middle," "foggy place," "place where a child was washed away," "place where one was lost," and "place of easy death."

Chenoweth *Madison County*. John Chenoweth settled the site in 1820.

Cherokee *Logan County*. Settled in 1832 and laid out by Robert Edminston, Dr. Samuel A. Morton, and Alexander Thompson with surveyor James W. Marmon. Cherokee takes its name from a nearby stream, Cherokee Man's Run. The Cherokee people were once prevalent in this vicinity.

Cherry Valley *Ashtabula County*. This name is shared by the hamlet and the township in which it is located. According to one source, "the name is said to have come from the fact that cherry trees were growing along the bank of a creek in the northern part of the township." Josiah Creery, a settler who arrived in 1823 from Richfield, New York, suggested the name.

Chesapeake *Lawrence County*. Nothing is recorded about how this place received its name, and experts do not agree on the meaning. The *Illustrated Dictionary of Place-Names* states that it may be Algonquian for "on the big day."

Cheshire *Gallia County*. A county in England or a town in New England may have inspired this place-name.

Chester Center *Geauga County.* Chester Center occupies the approximate center of Chester Township. (For more details, see the Chesterland entry.)

Chesterhill *Morgan County.* Dempsey Boswell, Elijah Hiatt, and Exum Bundy purchased one hundred acres here in 1834, paying one dollar per acre. The purchase was made from General Rufus Putnam of the Ohio Company. None of the founders wanted his name used in the town name, and the men somehow decided upon Chester. However, there was another Ohio town called Chester, so they altered it to Chesterfield. But there was also another Chesterfield, and in 1838, when a post office was sought, the name was changed to Chester Hill. In 1895, the capital "H" was dropped, and the style became Chesterhill. One source states that the name Chester traces back to Quaker settlers who came from Chester, Pennsylvania.

Chesterland *Geauga County.* The community's name is taken from its surrounding entity, Chester Township. Why the township was so named has long been open to speculation. The ancient Romans used the word *castra* to label strategically situated towns with strong defenses, and the Saxons modified that term to *chester.* It is not known whether these terms had any influence on the place-name here. It may simply have been adopted from one of the eastern Chesters in New York, Pennsylvania, Connecticut, or elsewhere.

Chesterville *Morrow County.* Laid out in 1829. A man named Miles owned a local tavern and at first the site was dubbed Miles' Cross Roads. In 1833, the label was changed to Chesterville, many of the early settlers having come from Chester, Pennsylvania.

Cheviot *Hamilton County.* This locality derives its name from a range of hills on the Scottish-English border. The city of Cheviot was incorporated in 1818.

Chicago Junction *Huron County.* This community arose in 1874–1875 when the Chicago division of the Baltimore & Ohio Railroad joined with the Mansfield-Columbus division. The extension was known as the Baltimore, Pittsburgh, & Chicago Railway. The community was incorporated in 1882.

Chickasaw *Mercer County.* This locale owes its name to the Chickasaw, a Native American tribe that once frequented the area. The town was incorporated in 1891.

Chillicothe *Ross County (seat).* Nathaniel Massie founded this city in 1796. "Principal town" is how the Shawnee word *chillicothe* translates, according to one source, but a second opinion claims that it means "town at the leaning bank." Chillicothe, according to this alternate source, was the name of one of the major tribes of the Shawnee people. The city of Chillicothe was incorporated in 1804.

Chippewa *Wayne County.* Surveyed, 1816, for Stephen Ford by Daniel L. McClure. It is assumed that all the Chippewa names in this region trace back to the

Chippewa Indians. The first house here was built by Captain John Routson of the Chippewa Rangers.

Chippewa Lake *Medina County.* Laid out and platted in 1873. The name comes from the Chippewa tribe and the natural lake here.

Chippewa-on-the-Lake *Medina County.* This village, a resort community on the shore of Chippewa Lake, was incorporated in 1929 (see the preceding entry).

Chittenden Corners *Summit County.* This diminutive collection of homes arose on what had been the John Chittenden and Charles G. Chittenden farms.

Christiansburg *Champaign County.* Platted, 1817, by Joshua Howell, who settled the site. Like other early settlers at the place, Howell came from the Christiansburg, Virginia, area and brought the name with him.

Churchill *Trumbull County.* Located in Liberty Township, the site was once known as Liberty. The Post Office Department urged a name change in 1833 while a Presbyterian church was being constructed here on a small rise. That combination prompted the Church Hill name, which eventually became one word.

Churchtown *Washington County.* In 1866, Saint John the Baptist Catholic Church was completed at this place, once called Uniontown. The post office first adopted the Churchtown name. The spire of the edifice could be seen for miles.

Cincinnati *Hamilton County (seat).* The city's name first was Losantiville, a term thought to have diverse origins—Greek, Latin, and French. It is thought to have indicated the "city opposite the mouth," which may have referred to the Licking River in Kentucky. The Cincinnati name, according to historians, was conferred in 1790 by General Arthur St. Clair, the first governor of the Northwest Territory, who had his headquarters here. The immediate antecedent for this label was the Society of the Cincinnati, which had just been formed and named for a heroic early Roman military figure and farmer, Cincinnatus.

Circleville *Pickaway County (seat).* The local historical society states that this community was originally constructed within a prehistoric circular earthwork. Early settlers discovered the concentric rings upon their arrival, about 1810. The town was planned with this framework in mind and named Circleville accordingly. The circular enclosure was circumscribed by a high embankment. Jacob Zieger became the proprietor of the portion within the circle. Other features discovered here included what were described as a square fort, a round fort, and a mound. Incorporation of Circleville took place in 1814; today it is a city.

Claibourne *Union County.* The plat was surveyed in 1881 by Frederick J. Sager. The town was probably named by or for Richard Claibourne, the original proprietor of much of the land in the township.

Clarington *Monroe County.* This farmsite was eventually purchased by David Pierson, who in 1822 laid out a town here. He named it in honor of his daughter, Clarinda.

Clark *Coshocton County.* Surveyed, 1828, but never platted. Located in Clark Township, Clark takes its name from the founder, Samuel Clark.

Clarksburg *Ross County.* George Clark laid out Clarksburg in 1817 and named it for himself.

Clarksfield *Huron County.* This village was established in 1820, taking its name from James Clark of Connecticut. During the Revolutionary War, Clark had sustained losses from British raids totaling over a thousand pounds sterling. After the Revolution and subsequent treaty, Clark and other Connecticut "sufferers" had been given land grants in northern Ohio, west of the Connecticut Land Company properties, to make up for their losses. Curtis Clark also became a landowner here.

Clarksville *Clinton County.* Laid out, 1837, by William Hadley. Sarah Clark Hadley, William's wife, was honored when her husband named the town for her. A second source agrees with those details but states that the year was 1816.

Clarksville *Perry County.* The community was founded in 1850 or 1854. The name was the brainchild of Daniel Clark, a merchant and native of Jackson Township.

Clay Center *Ottawa County.* The name is believed to honor Henry Clay but may have been influenced by nearby clay deposits. The site is near the center of Clay Township. One of the earliest settlers was William Clark, who is credited with naming the place. He leased land here in 1863, purchasing it in 1869. Clay Center was incorporated in 1947.

Claysville *Guernsey County.* Claysville takes its name not from Henry Clay, who did traverse the area, but from the nearby Clay Pike, so named because its surface consisted of clay instead of stone or other material. Herdsmen preferred the Pike because it was easier on animals' hooves than stone.

Clayton *Montgomery County.* A soldier in the War of 1812, John Clayton, is the person for whom this community was named.

Clearport *Fairfield County.* The hamlet takes its name from its location on Clear Creek. Mills and other water-dependent industries operated in this vicinity. Clearport was established in 1853.

Cleveland *Cuyahoga County (seat).* The city was founded in 1796 by General Moses Cleaveland on the shores of Lake Erie. Sometime in the first twenty years of its existence, the first "a" in the general's name got dropped in the place designation.

Incorporation as a village took place in 1814, while incorporation as a city occurred in 1836.

Cleveland Heights *Cuyahoga County.* Cleveland Heights takes its name from its situation on an Appalachian plateau a few miles east of Cleveland on Lake Erie. It became a village in 1903 and a city in 1921. (Also see preceding entry.)

Cleves *Hamilton County.* Laid out in 1818 by General William Henry Harrison and originally known as Clevestown. The place was named for the maternal branch of the Symmes family. John Cleves Symmes was a prominent early landowner in this area. Incorporation took place in 1875.

Clifton *Clark and Greene counties.* Prominent cliffs along the Little Miami River at this location prompted the village's name ("Cliff Town").

Clifton *Hamilton County.* Clifton was founded by attorney Flamer Ball in 1850 and incorporated the same year. Once within the current territory of this town was the Clifton farm, from which the town takes its name.

Cline *Monroe County.* A number of Clines were associated with this vicinity. In 1894, I. P. Cline and Oliver Cline helped build a stone school nearby. Joseph Cline settled in the area in 1804. John Cline and Isaac M. Cline were other family members identified with this locality in Washington Township. George Cline, Sr., and Susannah Cline had nine children, some of whom located in the next township west, Benton Township.

Clinton *Clinton County.* This tiny hamlet takes its name from the same source as Clinton County: George Clinton, vice president of the county's organizing group (1810), who had been a delegate to the second Continental Congress. The community was never platted.

Clinton *Summit County.* About 1816, William Harvey laid out this town on the canal. It was named for Governor DeWitt Clinton of New York.

Cloverdale *Putnam County.* Platted, 1891 or 1892, by E. W. Dimock. (One source gives his name as Dimmick.) He is said to have performed the survey for W. H. and E. M. Mozier, although proprietors are listed as Tunis and Nora Truax and Austin and Mary Combs. Former names for this location included Evansport, Evansville, and Drucilla. The Cloverleaf Railroad penetrated the area in 1877 and joined with the Tangent Railroad at this location. Both lines were part of the Findlay, Fort Wayne, & Western system. Incorporation took place in 1902.

Clyde *Sandusky County.* Formerly Centreville, the community was laid out by William Hamer and Philip Beery; it was incorporated in 1866. The current name was selected over Centreville and Hamerville. It was proposed by a Dr. Treadway, a popular citizen, "for beauty and brevity."

Coalburg *Trumbull County*. With a large Welsh population, Coalburg is said to have been quite a busy place when coal was plentiful in Hubbard Township.

Coal Gate *Hocking County*. Coal Gate takes its name from the fuel. The name is often misspelled as Colgate.

Coal Ridge *Noble County*. This once-booming coal-mining site sat on a ridge.

Coal Run *Washington County*. A town arose here between 1836 and 1841, when improvements were made to the Muskingum River course. A pocket of coal was exposed at the foot of the hills, and coal was even obtained from the riverbed during periods of low water levels.

Coalton *Jackson County*. German and Welsh miners who constituted the early population here named the place Eurekaville. However, located as it is in Coal Township in a coal-mining locale, the community eventually assumed the name Coalton.

Coats *Monroe County*. A family named Coates owned the land at this location, which, minus the "e," continues to use the name. One family member was George W. Coates. It is unclear whether he was the family patriarch. Another, William E. Coates, lived from 1895 to 1973.

Cochransville *Monroe County*. In 1846, Thomas Cochran laid out a town at this location.

Coddingville *Medina County*. The hamlet of Coddingville traces its name back to the several Codding families who put down roots in the vicinity. Burt Codding came in 1818 from Bristol, New York, to settle land near Granger.

Coffee Corners *Trumbull County*. Several persons with the Coffee surname lived in this locale during its settlement years, including Isaac E. Coffee and Truman Coffee. Identified more closely with the Canfield area, Isaac became an attorney. It is uncertain whether he was the same Coffee who, in 1880, became a principal in the Niles-area firm of Church & Coffee (dry goods and groceries).

Coitsville Center *Mahoning County*. This community is at the center of Coitsville Township, which derives its name from Daniel Coit of Connecticut. Sometime before 1798, Coit bought the township land from the Connecticut Land Company. The Reverend William Wick was an early settler at this place (1801).

Colby *Sandusky County*. A Colby native, born in 1915, writes that "there was an engineer on the Road by the name of Walter Colpy, whom I presume was working when the Nickel Plate was just new, about 1885. I was told by my father that Colby was named after this man. I . . . remember that [agent/operator] Jim Griffin told me that Walter Colpy was known for blowing the whistle so loud." The spelling discrepancy between the man's name and the town's name is not accounted for. Providing a somewhat similar explanation was another Colby native, whose family resided here for over a hundred years. "From the notes my father left me," he states, "Colby was named from Collipy, the man who was the railroad dispatcher. From [Nickel Plate headquarters in] Fort Wayne, they asked the name of [our] place. [Collipy] said, 'as yet it has no name.' Headquarters then asked what *his* name was, and he replied Collipy. And they shortened it to Colby."

Cold Springs *Clark County*. A number of high-quality freshwater springs were present in the township, and one of them was at this site.

Coldwater *Mercer County*. This is one of the towns in Ohio that were, in earlier times, called Buzzards' Glory. This one, however, would more correctly have been styled "Buzzard's Glory," as it was so called for David Buzzard, who ran a general store at the location. Later, the name became Franktown, after a number of families with the Frank surname who populated the locality. In 1883, the name was changed to its current form in honor of the clear, cold water that feeds the creek east of town. Coldwater was incorporated in 1883.

Colebrook *Ashtabula County*. In 1808, after Oliver Phelps acquired land at this location, the place was called Phelps. Three years later a village was born, and the name was changed to Colebrook. Some families who pioneered this place had come from Colebrook, Connecticut.

Colerain *Belmont County*. Early Scotch-Irish immigrants dubbed this place in remembrance of a town named Coleraine in northern Ireland from which some had come. But first it was called Concord. The name was changed to Colerain to coincide with the name of the township.

Coletown *Darke County*. In 1818, Samuel Cole, Sr., came to this area from New Jersey. The place likely owes its name to him.

Colfax *Fairfield County*. When citizens of the area desired a post office in 1869, they submitted the Colfax name to Washington for consideration, and approval was granted. It honors President Ulysses S. Grant's vice president, Schuyler Colfax (1823–1885) of Indiana.

College Corner *Butler and Preble counties*. This village took its name from its proximity to Miami University in nearby Oxford. In addition, it is tucked into the northwest corner of Butler County and the southwest corner of Preble County. Incorporation occurred in 1900.

College Hill *Hamilton County*. Located at one of the highest elevations in the county, this site also was the home of the Ohio Female College. The land was sold in 1796 by Judge Symmes to Nehemiah Tunis, who in turn conveyed title to Jabez C. Tunis. College Hill also was the home of Cary's Academy (also known as Farmer's College).

Collins *Huron County.* One theory is that the town's name was borrowed from an official of the Lake Shore, Michigan, & Southern Railroad, which had a track running through Collins. Another possibility is that the name stems from Collinsville, Connecticut. One of Collins's early arrivals reportedly came from that village, now a subdivision of Canton, Connecticut.

Collinsville *Butler County.* Charles Collins, an English wagonmaker, purchased the first lot here from Matthew Richardson. A post office was established in 1836.

Columbia *Williams County.* Surveyed, 1854, by Seth B. Hyatt. The land was owned by William Rannels, J. R. McConnell, and Alfred Gambell. It has been speculated that the song "Columbia, the Gem of the Ocean" evoked this name; but no documentation can be found, and historians put little credence in the theory.

Columbia Hills Corners *Lorain County.* When George Williams built a golf course and country club not far from this spot, then called Copopa, he used his influence to give the place a more marketable name.

Columbiana *Columbiana County.* The city was named for the county. The county's name is said to combine the names Columbus and Anne. It took on this name in 1805, after first being dubbed Dixonville for an early settler, John Dixon, a Quaker. Dixon had arrived on the scene in 1802. The county was created in 1803. Columbiana was incorporated in 1837.

Columbia Station *Lorain County.* This site in Columbia Township takes its name from the township. The "Station" part is a result of the place's location on a railroad. The township was named in 1811 by Sally Twitchell Bronson Adams, the widow of an early settler, for her hometown, Columbia, Connecticut. Her husband had been Levi Bronson, one of the township's earliest settlers, and Sally was given the honor of naming the township in 1811, when it was formed. Later a postmaster, Thomas G. Bronson, tried to name the post office Copokah after the Indian word for Rocky River. But the Post Office Department in Washington miswrote it as Copopa, a term still used by some residents.

Columbus *Franklin County (seat).* Founded in 1812 and named for Christopher Columbus, this metropolis is the state's capital. A senator from Franklin County, Joseph Foos, suggested the name in 1816.

Columbus Grove *Putnam County.* Laid out, 1842, by Captain Frederick Fruchey. Fruchey and most of the other early settlers at this place came from the Columbus, Ohio, area. The spot was formerly the location of an Indian sugar grove.

Comargo *Warren County.* This name is thought to be related in some way to the Native American presence in the locality.

Commercial Point *Pickaway County.* In 1841, this village was laid out by Wiley H. Beckett, who dubbed it Genoa. In 1843, an adjoining community was established by James H. Burnley and called Rome. In 1851, the more-or-less merged entities incorporated as Genoa. The name Commercial Point came about in 1872, reportedly at the suggestion of Eli Harsh but formalized by a special act of the Ohio legislature. Commercial Point had railroad service and was a bustling mercantile center.

Condit *Delaware County.* L. S. Condit, who migrated here from New Jersey, gave his name to the site. The Condit name also graces Condit Station, North Condit, and South Condit. The train station was on the Pennsylvania Railroad. L. S. Condit is credited with being one of the first persons to bottle milk; he was engaged in the creamery business. Forty-one Condits appear in the index of an early county biographical directory, including E. J., E. W., and E. M. All of them farmed in this township (Trenton) and near this locality.

Conesville *Coshocton County.* A collection of houses sprang up, possibly not entirely by coincidence, around a distillery established in 1847 by Beebe S. Cone and associates. Cone became the first postmaster here. (One source states that the distillery was erected in 1851.) In 1857, fire destroyed the distillery; later the rebuilt facility met the same fate. Cone then moved to Iowa and gave his name to a town there as well.

Congo *Perry County.* This settlement was named for "Congo" Mooney, who came here with a contingent of African Americans from Alabama in the late 1880s to lay rail tracks. The blacks dubbed their encampment "The Congo," and Mooney, a popular and interesting figure on the local scene, was nicknamed "Congo." Coal mining was the primary occupation here, and the coal was of the finest quality. Other residents were of Hungarian, Irish, or Slavic descent. The place was known for its outstanding baseball teams.

Congress *Wayne County.* The community, in Congress Township, was named for the United States Congress.

Conneaut *Ashtabula County.* Sources differ on the meaning of this Indian word. Some believe it means "place of many fish" (it is located on Lake Erie), while others translate it as "there is an increase." The latter, they feel, refers to the rising of Lake Erie's waters. It may stem from an Onondaga Iroquois term, *wa-koano/hote*. Still another source claims that the word is a Seneca term meaning "a place where snow stays late in the spring." Now a city, Conneaut was incorporated in 1834.

Conotton *Harrison County.* The best guess is that this name stems from an Indian word, *kannoten*. In Carroll County, just north of here, there is a stream called Kannoten, and it crosses into this area. The Conotton Valley Railroad is a local line.

Conover *Miami County.* Founded and laid out, 1856, by Solomon G. Brecount. Brecount named the town for A. G. Conover, the surveyor of the site.

Constitution *Washington County.* Settled, 1806, by Ephraim Cutler. The place was first called Noggletown after Isaac Noggle, who took up residence here about 1808.

Cutler was one of the last survivors and most prominent members of the convention that framed the state constitution, and when a post office was established here in 1842, the site was called Constitution.

Continental *Putnam County.* Although this place was also known between 1886 and 1899 as Marice City, it was known as Continental before, during, and after that period. The name derives from the Continental Railway Company, which was planning to lay a line through the area in the late nineteenth century. Among the first settlers were the Luke Ducatt family, in 1886. Marice City was laid out by George Skinner that year for the proprietor, General A. V. Rice, and his daughter, Mary, after whom he named the town. Continental was incorporated in 1888.

Contreras *Butler County.* The Battle of Contreras, which took place in August 1847 during the Mexican War, inspired the designation for this community.

Converse *Van Wert County.* Sometime after 1883, when the Chicago & Atlantic Railroad went through nearby Elgin, a man named Cal Converse served as station agent there. This place-name probably honors Converse or his relatives. Previous names and nicknames included Centerville, Five Points, and Lick Skillet.

Convoy *Van Wert County.* The founder, Robert Nesbit, hailed from Conmbaugh (Convoy), Ireland. This is the only town named Convoy in the United States.

Cook *Fayette County.* A right-of-way here was yielded to the Baltimore & Ohio Railroad by Matthew S. Cook, resulting in the Cook place-name.

Coolville *Athens County.* A pioneer who arrived at this location in 1814 either named or had a hand in naming the place for his father, Simeon Cooley. The community was laid out in 1818 and incorporated in 1855.

Coolville Station *Athens County.* Coolville Station was a stop on the railroad just north of Coolville (see Coolville entry).

Cooney *Williams County.* This locality was known as Northwest Center when, so the tale goes, a group of locals who passed the time at the community store decided that it needed a different name. One of the men looked at another named Fox, who worked in the store, and suggested that Fox would make a good name for the village. Fox, however, is said to have objected and instead submitted Coon, perhaps in jest. Taking the form Cooney, the name persisted.

Cooperdale *Coshocton County.* This site was settled in 1815 by Noah Cooper. The name is undoubtedly in recognition of him or his family. Much later, in 1866, a David Cooper purchased land and operated a sawmill here.

Coopersville *Pike County.* About 1857, a trading boat on the canal was operated by a man named Cooper. The site became known by his name.

Copley *Summit County.* When land at this site was distributed, much of it accrued to a Bostonian named Gardner Green, and the place was first called Greenfield. Green later changed the name to Copley, reportedly after his wife's maiden name. Mrs. Green was said to have been a linear descendant of Lord Copley of England.

Corner *Washington County.* A post office opened in Tolson's store here in 1890. It gained its label by virtue of its location at the intersection of five roads in Belpre Township.

Cornersburg *Mahoning County.* Situated at the intersection of Canfield and Tippecanoe roads, this hamlet remains small and out of the way.

Cortland *Trumbull County.* In 1829, Enos (or Samuel) Bacon operated a store here, resulting in the site's designation as Baconsburgh. The current name probably was applied when the the Erie Railroad came through, perhaps evoked by Cortland, New York. Another theory is that the name refers to an Erie Railroad agent.

Cortsville *Clark County.* Cortsville bears the name of Robert Cort, who is said to have settled in this township (Green) in 1830. Cort undertook the construction of a carpenter shop and residence for William Marshall and in 1835 became partners with Marshall. They built a storehouse at this location.

Corwin *Warren County.* Laid out, 1844, by John and Joel W. Johnson, proprietors. The town may have been named for Robert G. Corwin, an early attorney in this area, or for an Ohio governor and U.S. congressman, Thomas Corwin (1794–1865). A number of Corwins resided in this county during its early years. Ichabod Corwin came from Kentucky in 1796.

Coshocton *Coshocton County (seat).* The city's name comes from an Algonquian word that translates roughly as "ferry" or "river crossing." First called Tuscarawas, Coshocton was laid out by John Matthews and Ebenezer Buckingham in 1802. It was incorporated in 1833.

Coulter *Richland County.* In a joint history of the Richland-Ashland counties area, forty-one Coulters are mentioned. The name of this hamlet probably goes back to Christopher Columbus Coulter or his father, the Reverend John Coulter. John and his wife, Almina Thomas, resided in this township (Monroe). So did John's brother, Melzer.

Cove *Jackson County.* Located on Cove Road north of the Appalachian Highway, this community is nestled in a valley with a high rocky hill overlooking it. The site fits the definition of a cove: "a sheltered nook or recess, as in cliffs," or "a strip of open land extending into the woods." The community is thought to have been founded in the 1830s by settlers from Pennsylvania.

Covington *Miami County.* Laid out, 1816, for Jacob Ullery and Daniel Wright by Benjamin Cox. An earlier village at the location was known as Friendship, and other superseded names include Stillwater and Newberry. Incorporation took place in 1835, with the name honoring General Leonard Wales Covington (1768–1813) of the War of 1812.

Cowlesville *Miami County*. The community was started around 1842 by Samuel Y. Pearson. The place takes its name from the Cowles family, which operated a grist mill, still house, and grain warehouse at the location.

Cozaddale *Warren County*. The town was laid out in 1871 by John J. Cozad, proprietor of the site. Before that it was known as Dallasburg, after Vice President George M. Dallas (1792–1864).

Crabtree *Scioto County*. One assumes that the presence of Crabtree families in this township (Morgan) is the reason for this place-name. Persons named Crabtree lived here from the early days. One was a storekeeper, another a township trustee.

Craig Beach *Mahoning County*. A popular swimming spot in recent times, this site was the home of an early (1803–1804) Milton Township family named Craig. Craig Beach was incorporated in 1932.

Craigton *Wayne County*. Although attribution for this place-name cannot be made with certainty, Craigs living in the area were probably responsible. John Craig, justice of the peace two townships north of this site in 1843, fought in the Mexican War. In nearby Wooster, Arthur Craig was marshal in 1857.

Cranberry Prairie *Mercer County*. The location acquired its name from the area's wild cranberry bogs in the early years. The site was settled by German families in the mid-1800s.

Crawford *Wyandot County*. At one time referred to as Crawfordsville, this community is named for Colonel William Crawford, who was killed in 1782 by Delaware Indians. This town had a number of inhabitants prior to 1845.

Creola *Vinton County*. This place was laid out in 1830 by Cornelius Karns, who hailed from Greenbrier, Virginia. In earlier times, it was known as Karns City and Karns Grove. The Post Office Department complained of confusion, so citizens were open to a new name. It is said that a local resident named Doretta Steele, who was reading a book that frequently referred to the Creole Indians, suggested Creola, and the name, being unique, was found acceptable.

Crescent *Belmont County*. Crescent probably derives its name from its location on a section of land formed by an abrupt bend in Wheeling Creek.

Crestline *Crawford County*. At the time of its platting, this site was believed to be Ohio's highest point. Once known as North Livingston, it was laid out in 1851 and incorporated in 1858.

Creston *Wayne County*. Creston perches near the Chippewa River along the crest of hills, thus being a town at the crest. It is said to date to 1860 and was once referred to as Pike's Station.

Cridersville *Auglaize County*. Settled about 1858. One of the first to settle here was John Murdock, who opened a dry goods store. The village was platted in 1859 by Ephraim Crider and subsequently named after him.

Crissey *Lucas County*. This place-name may trace back to Josiah Cressy, an early township clerk, with the current spelling being a corruption of the original.

Crooked Tree *Noble County*. For decades a tree provided a landmark at this hamlet. It has been gone for many years.

Crossenville *Perry County*. The town was laid out in 1817 by William Crossen.

Crosskeys *Monroe County*. Dating to 1893, the community may have been named to commemorate a Civil War battle.

Crown City *Gallia County*. Tradition has it that Crown City was originally known as the Point, the Crown, or Crown Point. Local politicians worked to bring about a compromise and decided upon Crown Point. When the Post Office Department told them that name was in use, they settled for Crown City. Laid out by Hiram Rankins, Crown City was incorporated in 1874.

Cuba *Clinton County*. At the time this community arose (1913), the practice of naming places for Spanish-American War sites and other exotic locales was in vogue. This name doubtlessly stems from the Cuba in the Caribbean Sea.

Cumberland *Guernsey County*. Platted, 1828, by James Bay. The name is said to have been submitted by his wife. The Bays hailed from Washington, Pennsylvania, on the National (or Cumberland) Road, which was being extended through Ohio.

Cummings *Wood County*. This settlement may have arisen around a sawmill established by Giddings & Cummings in 1880 in the midst of a heavily timbered area.

Curtice *Ottawa County*. Sometime past the midpoint of the nineteenth century, Joshua E. Curtice arrived at this Allen Township place and established the town that bears his name.

Custar *Wood County*. This community was originally called Lewisburg. A duplication of names necessitated a change at the time of incorporation. The Battle of the Little Bighorn was in the news, so it was decided to name the town for the slain General George Custer (1839–1876), a native of New Rumley, Ohio. However, when railroad workers made the sign for the station, they misspelled the name as Custar.

Cutler *Washington County.* When, in 1855, a post office opened at this Cutler Township site, it was called Olds. In 1863 the name was changed to Cutler in gratitude to William Parker Cutler, who was instrumental in bringing a railroad through the area.

Cuyahoga Falls *Summit County.* The city of Cuyahoga Falls gets its name quite naturally, being situated on a stretch of rapids of the Cuyahoga River, with small waterfalls nearby. *Cuyahoga* is an Indian word meaning "crooked river." Incorporation took place in 1836.

Cuyahoga Heights *Cuyahoga County.* This suburb of Cleveland is near the Cuyahoga River and commands a higher elevation than the city. The village was incorporated in 1918.

Cynthiana *Pike County.* Laid out, 1835–1840, by David Eubanks. Having a wife named Anna and a daughter named Cynthia, Eubanks combined their names to create the euphonious Cynthiana.

Dairy *Monroe County.* The hamlet, never platted, took on this name as a result of a large dairy operation nearby.

Dale *Washington County.* This place bore the names of Hebron and Fairview before the opening of a post office at the site. Then it was named for Theodore Dana Dale, who was responsible for the completion in 1884 of a Toledo & Ohio Railroad extension connecting Washington County with points north and west.

Dalton *Wayne County.* An area newspaper's files reveal that Dalton is a product of the consolidation of three small clustered communities: Sharon, Middletown (founded 1828), and Dover (founded 1817). Curt Freet, inspired by his hometown of Dalton, Georgia, is said to have suggested the current name. One source claims that the name was coined from the three former names. The town was incorporated in 1855.

Damascus *Columbiana and Mahoning counties.* Settled in 1806. Laid out, 1807 or 1808, by Horton Howard. The site is said to have been named by a Quaker settler. According to William Overman, the hamlet's two streams reminded citizens of a passage from 2 Kings 5:12: "Are not Abana and Pharpar, rivers of Damascus, better than all the waters of Israel?" Damascus, the ancient city that is mentioned in both the Old and the New Testaments, sits in a fertile valley; it is now the capital of Syria.

Danbury *Ottawa County.* Settlers named this place in 1803 for Danbury, Connecticut, their former home.

Danville *Highland County.* Platted in 1835. This village likely takes its name from the early proprietor of the site, Daniel P. March.

Danville *Knox County.* This community was founded sometime between 1813 and 1818 by Jonathan Sapp. It was named for Daniel Sapp, a soldier in the War of 1812. Today's Danville is a product of the consolidation, around 1920, of the original Danville and two other closely clustered entities, Buckeye and Rossville.

Darbydale *Franklin County.* The village is on Darby Creek. Both village and stream take their name from the Wyandot Indian leader, Chief Darby.

Darbyville *Pickaway County.* Platted in 1826. The village and nearby Little Darby Creek were named after Chief Darby, the Wyandot leader. Incorporation took place in 1835.

Darlington *Richland County.* The place-name is undoubtedly connected to the Darlington family, many branches of which resided in Richland and Ashland counties. (These counties once formed a single entity.) Forty-one Darlingtons are listed in the index of an early biographical atlas, and Marion M. Darlington (born 1859), Robert Darlington, John M. Darlington (born 1829), and John Darlington (born 1819) appear in the index of an old county history. All of these Darlingtons seem to be linked to townships other than the one in which this community is located, however, so the hamlet's name must trace back to some other Darlington. The town was once named Hagerstown for Christopher Hager, who settled the place, and later Hagersville, which was suggested by the postmaster at the time.

Darnell *Champaign County.* This place was laid out in 1893 by a man named Darnell.

Darrowville *Summit County.* A newspaper report states that one of the county's first settlers, Joseph (or George) Darrow, purchased land here in 1799. Darrow had been a surveyor with David Hudson, for whom the next town north of Darrowville is named (see Hudson entry).

Darrtown *Butler County.* In 1803, Conrad Darr began planning the village, which he platted eleven years later and named for himself. The first resident was Abraham Darr, who also became the first postmaster.

Dawes *Washington County.* This Grandview Township place, also known as Beavertown, honors General Rufus R. Dawes. Dawes was in charge of an Ohio Valley Railroad enterprise with ambitions of building a rail link up from Marietta along the Ohio

River to Bellaire. A post office named Dawes went into service in 1882. The projected railroad failed, however, when funds were depleted.

Dayton *Montgomery County (seat)*. This major city owes its name to the Honorable Jonathan Dayton (1760–1824), an early landowner who plotted the town in 1795. He and three others owned the majority of the real estate at the site. At various times, Dayton was a resident of New Jersey, a soldier in the Revolution, a member of Congress, and a delegate to the Constitutional Convention. Incorporation took place in 1805.

Deavertown *Morgan County*. First known as New Market, this community was laid out in 1815 by Reuben and Levi Deaver, previously of Maryland.

Deep Cut *Auglaize County*. Where the Miami & Erie Canal crosses Salem Township, the angles and curves of the waterway were surveyed with the goal of negotiating the divide at the most accessible point. This juncture became known as the Deep Cut. During the height of canal activity, the place attained a post office and a couple of stores.

Deer Park *Hamilton County*. This promotional or descriptive name may have been inspired by deer roaming the parklike setting in the early years of the place's development.

Deerfield *Portage County*. Settled, about 1799. An early arrival hailed from Deerfield, Massachusetts, and applied the label to this community.

Deering *Lawrence County*. James M. and John Deering were settlers in this township in 1830. This place-name may be related to them.

Defiance *Defiance County (seat)*. Laid out in 1822. Both city and county take their name from Fort Defiance, which was erected here in 1794 by General Anthony Wayne. Wayne touted the fort as "strong enough to defy hell and all her emissaries" to capture it. Such defiance is thought to have inspired the name.

DeForest *Trumbull County*. In the county during its formative years were Emery and Abram DeForest. Although it is uncertain that either ever lived at this location, it is likely that the place was named after one of them or the DeForest family.

DeGraff *Logan County*. Laid out, 1850, by William Boggs. Incorporated in 1864. A civil engineer named DeGraff came to this locale, elected to make it a railroad stop on the route between Springhill and Logansville, and named the site DeGraff.

Delano *Ross County*. At least one Delano family resided locally, as Mrs. L. G. (Martha) Delano is mentioned in an account of township activities.

Delaware *Delaware County (seat).* Founded, 1808, by Moses Byxbe. Settled, 1807, by Joseph Barber. The name was inspired by the Delaware Indians, whose cornfields bordered the village. Delaware is the birthplace of Rutherford B. Hayes, the nation's nineteenth president. Formerly named Millville, the city was incorporated in 1816.

Delightful *Trumbull County.* The name of this place is also seen with an additional "l" at the end. The only explanation advanced by historical sources for the name of the community is that the first arrivals were delighted with their new home.

Delisle *Darke County.* Mrs. Fairchild is said to have laid out this community about 1850 in anticipation of the coming of the Greenville & Miami Railroad. A resident named Delilah is believed to have inspired the name.

Dell *Washington County.* Dell was selected as a descriptive and euphonious name for this place in Newport Township at Eight Mile when a post office was opened in 1884.

Dellroy *Carroll County.* Platted, 1849, by Philip Crabbs. Dellroy was first known as Canonsburg, after the southwestern Pennsylvania city from which many early settlers came. The post office here was named Leavitt, for a Dr. Leavitt. By 1878, many of the miners had moved on and residents wanted to change Canonsburg's name. As the story is told, a traveling man, after staying overnight at the local hotel, went out onto the porch, surveyed the scene, and remarked, "This is really a royal dell!" Someone thought it would make a fine name for the village, so it was called Dell Royal. Someone else decided the "al" was superfluous, and it was shortened to Dell Roy. Later the U.S. Post Office Department dropped the Leavitt name and adopted Dell Roy. There was some uncertainty, however, about whether the form should be Dell Roy or Dellroy. President Grover Cleveland's new bride was asked to decide, and she voted for Dellroy.

Delmont *Fairfield County.* This diminutive community is said to have been named for a housemaid named Della who worked at the home of Frederick Shaeffer.

Delphi *Huron County.* Many early settlers in this locale came from upstate New York, where there is a Delphi as well as several other communities using classical names. Delphi was the ancient Greek seat of the Delphic oracle.

Delphos *Allen and Van Wert counties.* Ferdinand Bredeick, who arrived at this site in 1845, platted the original community. Later an addition was platted by the Reverend John Bredeick. The various entities became known as East Bredeick, West Bredeick, and Howard Town. A meeting was eventually convened to decide on a name for a unified entity. According to one source, Father Bredeick submitted the name Delphos, and it was agreed to. This source contends that the word denoted "from nothing to a great city." A second source assigned the translation "brother" to the Greek word and speculated that the label was conferred by early Greek settlers. However, a scholar contends that it is unlikely that anyone of Greek descent settled here during the town's formative period and that the name probably was assigned by someone with a classical education. Today a city, Delphos was incorporated in 1851 or 1854.

Delta *Fulton County.* Delta had a number of cognomens in earlier days, among them Tadmore, Tadpole, Greensprings, Fingerville, and Slab Shanty. One theory holds that the name Delta resulted when some observant soul noted that Bad Creek formed the Greek letter delta on its path through town. Locals thought the word meant "fertile valley"; this is some of the richest farmland in Ohio. The village was incorporated in 1863. The Delta post office, first located on the property of William Meeker, was moved into town.

Denmark *Ashtabula County.* This place was settled in 1809 by David Knapp, John Dibble, and Peter Knapp, not long after the British bombarded Copenhagen, Denmark. It may have been named out of sympathy for the Danes. A second possibility is that early inhabitants arrived from Denmark, New York.

Dennison *Tuscarawas County.* Although settled earlier, Dennison was not laid out as a town until 1865. It was named for the Honorable William Dennison, described by one source as "Ohio's famous war governor."

Depew *Shelby County.* The name is believed to honor a pre-1900 candidate for Ohio's General Assembly named Depew. The previous name of this site is said to have been Heckleburney.

Derthick *Athens County.* This name stems from the Derthick coal mine here. It traces back to about 1888.

Deserted Camp *Clinton County.* A historical marker near this hamlet gives the story behind its name: "Near this site in October 1780, General Benjamin Logan with an army of 700 Kentucky volunteers camped on their way to destroy seven Indian towns in the Mad River Valley. During the night, a renegade deserted the camp to warn the Indians. The army burned 200 cabins and 15,000 bushels of corn before returning. Later, this site became an important survey point. Indians scalped the deserter."

Deshler *Henry County.* Incorporated in 1876. This village name honors John W. Deshler, the owner of a large amount of land in the vicinity.

Deucher *Washington County.* The community and post office designated Deucher were named for a Scottish family that settled at this Independence Township location in 1852. The post office opened in 1885.

Deunquat *Wyandot County.* It is difficult to pin a birth date on this community, which at one time was quite a lively place. In earlier times, possibly prior to 1863, it was known as Petersburg. It is thought that around 1881—possibly a few years earlier—Tilghman Zellner learned that postal authorities desired a name change. Zellner reportedly returned from a trip to Upper Sandusky with the suggestion of

Deunquat as the name, in honor of a Wyandot Indian chief. Another spelling of the chief's name is Doanquod.

Devil Town *Wayne County.* An essay by Bonnie Knox states that Devil Town (or Deviltown) was originally known as Tannerville, owing to the presence of a tannery. Most of the tannery workers resided outside the area and roomed in town during the week. In the evenings, with time on their hands, they drank whiskey, played cards, and got overly boisterous. Fights often ensued. People started calling the place Devil Town, and eventually the name was changed. One of the earliest landowners here was J. Miller, in 1827.

Devola *Washington County.* The name of this community traces back to an early settler, Captain Jonathan Devol, Jr. (See the next entry.)

Devol's Dam *Washington County.* Captain Jonathan Devol, Jr., arrived here in 1796 and built a wing dam for the efficient operation of a mill. Devol was a Revolutionary War soldier, shipwright, poet, and skilled mechanic. This place was also known as Union Mills Village.

Deweyville *Hancock County.* Platted in 1881 by John B. Williams, the place was named in recognition of a man named Dewey. It was never incorporated.

Dexter *Meigs County.* The reason for the name is unclear, but it was possibly in honor of Timothy Dexter, who arrived in Meigs County in 1801.

Dexter City *Noble County.* Platted in 1870; incorporated in 1881. The first building here was constructed by Dexter W. Sullivan, after whom the town is named.

Dialton *Clark County.* A post office was established here in 1865. The village owes its name to a Judge Dial of Springfield, Ohio.

Diamond *Portage County.* Diamond was founded by O. B. Mason in 1880. Mason was born in northern Stark County in 1838. Moving to this locality, he became postmaster and operated the train depot and restaurant, while his wife did the accounting and bookkeeping. Many Welsh persons came to Diamond and worked in the four coal mines operating here in 1880. A leading mine owner was the Black Diamond Coal Company, and this hamlet takes its name from that firm.

Digby *Wood County.* The name may have been inspired by John E. Digby or his family. Digby was a trustee in this township (Liberty) in 1881–1884.

Dille's Bottom *Belmont County.* In 1793 or 1794, John and Samuel Dille settled bottomland at this location. The name is often spelled without the apostrophe.

Dillonvale *Jefferson County.* A plat of this place was made in 1816 by Nathan Updegraff, but it languished. In 1889, when a new plat was drawn up, the place was called Dillon (later expanded with the addition of "vale"). The village was incorporated in 1902. It is not known whether the name is connected with John J. Dillon, who was born in Ireland, moved to Pittsburgh, and became president of the city council in Steubenville in the late nineteenth century. A glassworker, Dillon married Elizabeth Fleming in 1888.

Doanville *Athens County.* This locale may have taken its name from William S. Doan or one of his descendants. William can be placed in a township at the opposite end of the county about 1820.

Dobbstown *Lawrence County.* John Dobbs, Jr., came here from Pennsylvania in 1850. He was born in 1821.

Dodd's *Warren County.* In a book on Deerfield Township, twenty-seven persons with the Dodd surname are mentioned. Benjamin Dodd walked to this southwestern Ohio area from Lancaster, Pennsylvania, at age nineteen. By 1808, he had a farm here. He and his wife, Martha, had eleven children. This place-name probably traces back to his family—or one of the other Dodd families nearby.

Dodgeville *Ashtabula County.* Dodgeville was named for Jeremiah Dodge, an early merchant doing business at the locale.

Dodsonville *Highland County.* Platted, 1839, by Daniel Shaffer. In 1797, substantial tracts of land in this region were surveyed by Joshua Dodson from Virginia. The township, the community, and Dodson Creek perpetuate his memory.

Doherty *Monroe County.* Franklin Doherty resided here in 1883. He was born in Pennsylvania about 1823.

Dola *Hardin County.* The name of this community once was North Washington. However, many other places in Ohio also used Washington in their names, causing confusion for the post office. It was Mrs. Clevenger, wife of the town's doctor, who renamed the place Dola, after her hometown in Ireland. This change occurred about 1900.

Dolly Varden *Clark County.* Laid out, 1872, by Simington Buffenbarger. This community takes its name from a character in a Charles Dickens novel. Dolly Varden was the daughter of locksmith Gabriel Varden in *Barnaby Rudge*.

Donnelsville *Clark County.* Among the first prominent citizens of Bethel Township was Jonathan Donnel, and Donnel became a well-known name in Clark County. Donnel's Creek, a stream watering the land of David Lowry, was named by Lowry for his friend.

Donnelsville Station *Clark County.* For the "Donnelsville" aspect of this place-name, see the preceding entry. The "Station" aspect probably refers to the site's location on the railroad, not far from Donnelsville.

Dorset *Ashtabula County.* This site was known as Millsford as late as 1828. A townsman, Lyman Larabee, persuaded his fellow citizens to rename it after his Vermont hometown, Dorset.

Douglass *Putnam County.* This place-name may relate to J. Douglass, who was an early landowner in nearby Union Township.

Dover *Tuscarawas County.* Founded by Christian Deardorff and Jesse Slingluff. The proprietor was Colonel James Morrison. Slingluff and Deardorff, both from Baltimore, Maryland, visited the site in 1802 and took a liking to the fertile region. In 1805, they came back and purchased the plot from Colonel Morrison. In 1807, they laid out the community that was to become the city of Dover. The name may honor an early family in the area. Incorporation took place in 1842.

Downingville *Carroll and Stark counties.* Downingville was named in honor of James Downing, son-in-law of Isaac Miller, who laid out the site.

Doylestown *Wayne County.* This place was surveyed in 1827 by Charles Christmas. The town was laid out by and named after William Doyle. It was incorporated in 1867.

Drake's *Perry County.* This site takes its name from a family of Drakes who owned a hotel here.

Drakesburg *Portage County.* Located in Freedom Township, this place owes its name to Orsamus Drake, who built the Freedom House Tavern here in 1836. Drake had arrived from Massachusetts in 1829.

Drinkle *Fairfield County.* The town was known as Mechanicsburg before it became Drinkle, in recognition of Clay Drinkle, who later became postmaster at Lancaster in this county. One source gives the individual's name as H. C. Drinkle and adds that his son, Charles H. Drinkle, Sr., died in 1991 at the age of 100.

Dublin *Franklin and Delaware counties.* The city was laid out in 1818 by John Sells and incorporated in 1845. The surveyor was John Shields, who was accorded the privilege of naming it after his former home in Ireland. One source also spells his name Sheilds.

Duboisville *Belmont County.* The plat for this small settlement was recorded in 1913 by John Dubois.

Ducat *Wood County.* This village was surveyed in 1890 by D. D. Ames for Exea Ducat, Thomas J. Ducat, and Quincy A. Mercer. It owes its name to the Ducats.

Dudley *Noble County.* One county history lists sixteen Dudleys in its biographical index. This place-name probably traces back to one or more of them.

Duffy *Monroe County.* This circa-1890 community owes its name to John Duffy, born in New York around 1817.

Dull *Van Wert County.* This name is honorific, not descriptive. The community was formerly the village of McKee. In 1879, it was laid out by J. M. Dull, Martin Lintermoot, and Nicholas Fry and subsequently came to be known as Dull.

Dumontsville *Fairfield County.* This community owes its name to a Frenchman, Jacob Dumont.

Dunbridge *Wood County.* Surveyed, 1882, by Ferdinand Wenz for Robert Dunn. One historical source states that "the *Sentinel* suggested the name Dunn-der-berg, but the owner adopted the first three letters of his own name and the last six from Trowbridge and joined them" to form Dunbridge. A partially dissenting source claims that two men, surnamed Dunn and Strawbridge, were influential in obtaining a railroad station for the community.

Duncan Falls *Muskingum County.* The local explanation is that the place was named for a local trapper residing in the vicinity before 1800.

Dundas *Vinton County.* The community was settled and named by Scottish immigrants in the 1800s. *Dundas* is said to mean "town" in a Scottish dialect. The community probably grew up around the mining industry in the 1870s.

Dundee *Tuscarawas County.* The first settlers here were of Scotch-Irish heritage and named the place after Dundee, Scotland. Michael Wallick laid out the first lots in 1847, although the area was settled well before that.

Dungannon *Columbiana County.* Laid out, 1838 (one source says 1836), by George Sloan. Dungannon was named in honor of Sloan's native area in Ireland.

Dungannon *Noble County.* A post office (with a different name) was here as early as 1867. The community takes its name from Dungannon, Ireland.

Dunham *Washington County.* Located in Dunham Township, this community takes its name from Jonathan Dunham, who farmed here starting in 1804. There was a Dunham post office from 1857 to 1902.

Dunkinsville *Adams County.* Laid out in 1841. James Dunkin was mentioned in deed records from 1805–1806 and probably is the person after whom the place was named. The post office here was also called Dunkinsville.

Dunkirk *Hardin County.* Dunkirk had its beginnings about 1852. It was probably named for the city of Dunkirk, New York.

Dunlap *Hamilton County.* The site formerly answered to Georgetown and Dunlap's Station. It was laid out as Georgetown in 1829. The current name likely leads back to John Dunlap, the first settler in Colerain Township. An Irishman from Coleraine in northern Ireland, Dunlap came to the area around 1790. Other Dunlaps identified with this locale were Andrew A., George, William H., and Robert E.

Dupont *Putnam County.* Platted, 1877, by E. W. Dimock. The town was named in honor of Rear Admiral S. F. DuPont (1803–1865), a commander of Union naval forces during the Civil War. The village was incorporated in 1888.

Durbin *Mercer County.* George P. Durbin, a farmer, was the postmaster here, accounting for the place-name. His ancestors had arrived in America in 1638 with others sent by Cecilius Calvert, Lord Baltimore, and had settled near what is now Baltimore, Maryland.

Duvall *Noble County.* The name of this village may relate to Richard Duvall, who helped the county organize in 1849.

Duvall *Pickaway County.* In 1890–1902, W. R. Duvall was a prominent journalist in the county. This place-name is probably traceable to him or his forebears.

Dyesville *Meigs County.* In 1883, Seldon and Margaret Dye donated land here for a church. As a consequence, the hamlet became known as Dyesville. Another Meigs County Dye, Martin, once of Pagetown, was probably a relative of Seldon and Margaret.

Eagleport *Morgan County.* Platted, 1883, by Semet Ramey. In the Muskingum River was an island; on this island was a large sycamore tree; and for several years, there was an eagle's nest in the tree. Thus the island was called Eagle Island, and when a town grew up on the river's bank, residents called it Eagleport.

Eagleville *Ashtabula County.* It is believed locally that a family of early settlers gave the place its name, after observing a nest of eagles in the area. It was said that one of the eagles made a habit of perching on the mill roof. This may be given credence, since this and other counties bordering Lake Erie still possess eagle populations.

East Batavia Heights *Clermont County.* This community is due east of Batavia (see Batavia entry).

East Boyer *Mahoning County.* Fifteen Boyers were listed in the county atlas of 1874. Norman J. Boyer held land in Milton Township and may be the person to whom this name is attributable.

East Brookfield *Stark County.* This site was settled largely by pioneers from the village of Brookfield in Clinton County, New York. The "East" prefix distinguishes it from West Brookfield, also in Stark County.

East Cadiz *Harrison County.* East Cadiz in reality is northeast of Cadiz. For the "Cadiz" portion of the name, see the Cadiz entry.

East Canton *Stark County.* Formerly called Osnaburg, East Canton comes by its name quite naturally, being just a few miles due east of Canton. It was founded in 1805 and incorporated in 1880.

East Cleveland *Cuyahoga County.* As the name suggests, East Cleveland is just east of the city of Cleveland (see Cleveland entry). East Cleveland is a city, incorporated in 1873.

East Danville *Highland County.* East Danville in actuality is just southeast of Danville. The post office was called Winkle, after a prominent local family, so this site also was sometimes referred to as Winkle. Earlier still, it was referred to as Straight Out; when locals gave directions to it from Danville, they would point and say, "It's one mile, straight out." (See Danville entry.)

East Farmington *Trumbull County.* This burg's name makes sense. The place is in Farmington Township and is east of the communities of Farmington and West Farmington. The names all relate to Farmington, Connecticut, prior home of some of the area's earliest settlers.

East Fultonham *Muskingum County.* Laid out, 1815, by Henry Hummel and John Porter. The initial name of this community was Uniontown. However, there was another Uniontown in Ohio, and after application was made for a post office in 1828, it was considered necessary to settle upon a new name. The postmaster general appointed Lyle Fulton as postmaster, and the post office took on the name of East Fultonham. It is just east of a site known as Fultonham. East Fultonham began to grow after the railroad came through, missing Fultonham. (See Fultonham entry.)

East Goshen *Mahoning County.* Situated in Goshen Township, East Goshen is east of Goshen Center. (See Goshen Center entry.)

Eastlake *Lake County.* The city is east of Cleveland and fronts on Lake Erie. It was incorporated in 1948.

East Lewistown *Mahoning County.* Founded, 1830, by George Houck, Henry Thoman, Peter Goder, and John Nold. When the site was laid out, three families living at the crossroads had the Lewis surname.

East Liverpool *Columbiana County*. Settlers arrived here as early as 1795, and the city was founded by a Quaker, Thomas Fawcett, in 1798. First known as Saint Clair and later as Fawcettstown, it was incorporated in 1834. The name was changed to East Liverpool after a number of English potters settled here.

East Monroe *Highland County*. Platted, 1816, by Robert Worthington. The town was established adjacent to David Rees's community of Monroe, which no longer appears on maps. The "Monroe" aspect of the name probably refers to President James Monroe.

East Norwalk *Huron County*. East Norwalk is a short distance northeast of Norwalk. (See Norwalk entry.)

East Palestine *Columbiana County*. Settled by Quakers, this community employs a biblical name. The "East" aspect may relate to its position in the extreme eastern side of the county. In the Bible, Palestine referred to an area north of the Sinai Peninsula with the Mediterranean Sea on its west. Before 1832, East Palestine, Ohio, was called Mechanicsburg. Now a city, it was incorporated in 1876.

East Richland *Belmont County*. "East" was placed before the name of the township to form this town's name. William Carman is thought to have named it when he laid out the place in 1832. The township's name was a natural choice, since the area was blessed with a limestone soil rich in nutrients and highly conducive to growing crops.

East Sparta *Stark County*. Amos Janney laid out the village in 1815 and reportedly named it for ancient Athens's rival, Sparta. Historical accounts suggest that Janney hoped that the name would inspire the village's citizens to make it into a vibrant metropolis like the Greek city.

East Springfield *Jefferson County*. The name of this site is probably the result of its location, slightly east of the Springfield Township boundary. John Gillis, Jr., laid out the community in 1803.

East Townsend *Huron County*. See the Townsend entry.

East Trumbull *Ashtabula County*. Located in the eastern sector of Trumbull Township, the community is also east of the hamlet of Trumbull. (See Trumbull entry.)

East Union *Wayne County*. Settled in 1809–1810. The initial name of this community was Crosskeys (or Cross Keys). Simon Chaffin, Sr., a former resident of Union, Maine, is credited with naming East Union.

Eaton *Preble County (seat)*. Founded by William Bruce in 1805 or 1806. Named by the proprietor when the town was laid out, Eaton honors Captain William Eaton (1764–1811), who distinguished himself in the Tripolitan War. Incorporation was in 1826.

Echo *Belmont County.* The community was named for the Troll Brothers' Echo Mine here.

Eckley *Carroll County.* Eckley takes its name from General Ephraim R. Eckley (1811–1908), who was a member of Congress from this district when a post office was installed here. He served from 1863 to 1869.

Eckley *Fulton County.* The family of Jacob and Magdalena Eckley resided here in German Township from at least 1851 to 1900.

Eckmansville *Adams County.* Henry Eckman, a blacksmith, arrived here in 1824 and is given credit for forging this town out of the countryside.

Edenton *Clermont County.* William Slone, a bugler in General Anthony Wayne's army at the Battle of Fallen Timbers (1794), gave this place its first name: Sloneville. Later a settler or settlers arrived from Edenton, North Carolina, and changed the designation.

Edgefield *Fayette County.* This place takes its name from the proprietor, a former Lynchburg, Virginia, resident named Obadiah Edge.

Edgerton *Williams County.* Alfred P. Edgerton, a prominent area land developer, inspired the name of this village.

Edgewater Beach *Licking County.* This community reposes on the shores of Buckeye Lake.

Edinburg *Portage County.* When William McFate purchased the first lot here, he was given the privilege of naming the place. He chose Edinburgh, after the metropolis in his native Scotland. One source tells a different story: that Crawford White, after laying out the town, thought it resembled the Garden of Eden and named it Edenburg, with the spelling eventually evolving to the current form.

Edison *Morrow County.* The earlier names of this site near Mount Gilead were Gilead Station and Levering. The current name was conferred out of admiration for the famed inventor Thomas Edison, who was born in Ohio.

Edmunds *Scioto County.* The name of this hamlet probably relates to an early citizen, George Edmunds, who was superintendent of the Webster Firebrick Company. In the early 1870s, a siding called the Edmunds Switch was built to facilitate the loading of clay for the brickyard.

Edon *Williams County.* A resident of Edon saved a newspaper clipping stating that "this was Weston until the Postal Service . . . pointed out another Weston . . . in Wood County. . . . So . . . this town became Edon. No one remembers why. But the . . . townsfolk know it was once called Mudsock because of what happened every spring before the streets were paved. The best theory is that the rich farmland surrounding Edon led to people thinking of it as the Garden of Eden and some long-ago recorder was a poor speller. Indeed, the highway signs announcing Edon across the border in Indiana spell it Eden. But not here." Edon was incorporated in 1868.

Edwardsville *Warren County.* One source states that Edward Thomas laid out this town in 1824, and it became known by his given name. A second source states that George W. Edwards and John Rayle platted the community in 1863.

Egypt *Belmont County.* Early farmers are said to have affixed this name, observing that it appeared to be good corn country, according to a volume entitled *Names for a New Land*.

Eifort *Scioto County.* This name reminds historians of two Civil War–era soldiers, Colonel Sebastian Eifort and his son, Lieutenant Colonel William H. Eifort. The elder Eifort, born in Germany in 1817, was described as "a born leader and manager." The Harrison Foundry in this county was built in 1853 by Henry Spellman and Boston Eifort. But Boston's relationship to the other two Eiforts is unknown, and so is the relationship of the Eiforts to the name of this place.

Eldorado *Preble County.* Of Spanish origin, this label means "golden" or "gilding," and suggests riches. It is speculated that the namers thought they had struck it rich upon settling here.

Elgin *Van Wert County.* Founded in 1845. The earliest settler was Jonathan Van Eman. Property was being purchased here by Van Eman and others in the 1830s. The former name of this place was Yorktown. In 1882, after the Erie Railroad came through town, it was called to the attention of the town fathers that there was a Yorktown Post Office on the Erie Railroad in Pennsylvania, and they were persuaded to rename the community. For reasons that remain uncertain, they selected Elgin. Incorporation took place in 1897.

Elida *Allen County.* This community was platted in 1852 by Griffith John, who named it for his brother Elijah. Verbal evolution led to the current form. Elijah John never lived at this locality. Griffith John was of Welsh stock and arrived here from Pennsylvania in 1831. Eventually he became proprietor of 1,640 acres locally and had twelve children. He operated a maple sugar camp here in the 1840s. Elida was incorporated in 1876 or 1878.

Elizabethtown *Hamilton County.* Elizabethtown is said to be named for the wife of Isaac Mills, who in 1817 platted the town. The site was probably first settled by Micajah Dunn in 1795. The town is said to have been founded in 1806.

Elk *Noble County.* Many elk once roamed these environs. The community dates to 1873. Its name duplicates the name of the township in which it is located.

Elk Fork *Vinton County.* Situated in Elk Township, the community was named for the abundance of elk that once roamed the area. The stream that drains the area is also named Elk.

Ellet *Summit County.* The name of this place probably traces to King J. Ellet, son of John and Elizabeth Ellet, who settled in Springfield Township in 1810. King was born there in 1831 and served as a county commissioner.

Elliott's Cross Roads *Morgan County.* This name traces to 1850, when a post office was established in the Elliott family's general store. A tiny hamlet sprang up around it here where two roads intersected.

Ellis *Muskingum County.* The first settler here may have been Elias E. Ellis, around 1805. Among the pioneer families of Muskingum Township were Edward Ellis and George Ellis, and the Ellis families were large.

Elliston *Ottawa County.* This name may originally have been Ellis Town. An L. Ellis appears on the survey at this location in an 1874 atlas of the county. Ellis was a landowner at this Benton Township site.

Ellsworth *Mahoning County.* The initial settler at this site may have been Captain Joseph Coit, in 1804. The place-name derives from the owner of a large tract of Western Reserve real estate, the respected Connecticut citizen Oliver Ellsworth (1745–1807), a framer of the U.S. Constitution. It was Ellsworth who was responsible for the term *United States* in the Constitution.

Elmwood *Highland County.* A stately grove of elms grew here in the 1800s, inspiring the name.

Elyria *Lorain County (seat).* Heman Ely donated the money and land for the seat of county government, and the city was named for him. Ely settled nearby at what became known as Ely's Mills. The year of incorporation was 1833.

Empire *Jefferson County.* Empire was first called Stumptown, after a notable stand of trees was cut down here. Next it was known as Shanghai, after Captain James Young brought the first Shanghai chickens to this region in 1850. Later still the site was dubbed Olive City, after the youngest daughter of Lewis K. McCoy, who in 1857 laid out the village. After 1885, the Empire sewer pipe plant brought marked growth, and the firm offered the village enough bricks for a public building on the condition that the name be changed to Empire City. This condition was accepted. Truth apparently prevailed in 1897 when the village was incorporated and the "City" was dropped.

England *Ashland County.* Also known as England Station, this hamlet owes its name to a Reverend England who owned a large tract of land here and was pastor of the Dickey Church. After Tidewater Oil bought a parcel of land for a pumping station, it was named England Station.

Englewood *Montgomery County.* Platted in 1841. The current name came about in 1915 as the result of a local contest. It is said that Englewood was a name in a book being read by Elmer Smith, who liked it, nominated it as the new name, and won the contest. The place had been known as Harrisburgh from about 1841 to 1871. In the latter year, Postmaster Harvey Iames renamed the location Iamton. Post Office Department printers in Washington, certain that "Iamton" was a typographical error, set it up as Jamtown. So Jamtown it was, until the contest was held to select a more dignified name. Now a city, Englewood was incorporated in 1914.

Eno *Gallia County.* Eno derives its designation from a post office once maintained here by Peola Eno.

Enterprise *Preble County.* The community began with the building of several stores, or enterprises, so that may have evoked the name.

Equity *Washington County.* The farmers and Grange members in this Adams Township settlement considered themselves equals and chose Fairplay as the name for the place. But in 1888, the Post Office Department forced them to change the name because there was a Fairplay Post Office in Jefferson County. They settled for Equity.

Erastus *Mercer County.* There once was a mill here run by a Mr. Murphy, and the location was known as Murphysburg. When a post office was installed here later in a store owned by a Mrs. Walker, the widow's son, Erastus, sent his own name in to the Post Office Department, accounting for the label which the place retains to this day.

Erhart *Medina County.* The name of the hamlet probably traces back to Joseph Erhart, an Ohio native who resided here after 1840 and operated a large lumber yard. The place was identified as Erhart about 1874.

Essex *Union County.* The name probably traces back ultimately to Essex County, England. However, there are places named Essex in New Jersey, New York, Massachusetts, and other states. Settlers from one of those places may have conveyed the name to this locality.

Euclid *Cuyahoga County.* Both the city and township in which it is located owe their name to the Greek mathematician Euclid. The naming is attributed to surveyors in Moses Cleaveland's party (circa 1796 and after), who had been educated in mathematics and sought to honor the founder of the discipline. By 1810, Euclid was the recognized name of the township. The city was incorporated in 1930.

Euphemia *Preble County.* Laid out by John Muma, the hamlet is named after Muma's wife.

Eureka *Mahoning County.* A Greek word meaning "I have found it," Eureka was applied to an early Mennonite settlement and school here. Mennonite communities customarily adopted the name of the school as the name of the community.

Evansburg *Coshocton County.* This site was laid out in 1830 by Isaac Evans.

Evansport *Defiance County.* The town, founded in 1835 by Jacob Cay and Albert G. and Amos Evans, took the name of the Evanses.

Evendale *Hamilton County.* A 1990s village councilperson explained the place's name: "As with so many towns and cities of that time, our school district was named by describing the location; using the old English name for a valley ("dale") and combining that with a word which meant level, flat, or smooth ("even")—giving us the name Evendale." The label was employed as early as 1885 for the Evendale School District 10. The first Evendale school had been built in 1840 by Jesse Cunningham and a few other early settlers. Jesse's parents, James and Janet Cunningham, were the first settlers of the site. Citizens did not vote for incorporation until 1950, and it became an incorporated village in 1951.

Everett *Summit County.* Elijah Everett, a war casualty (presumably the Civil War), went into service from the same township in which this place is located (Boston). His or his family's relationship to the place-name is unknown. An earlier name for this site was Johnny Cake Lock.

Evergreen *Gallia County.* Evergreen trees that grew in profusion near here gave the place its name.

Ewington *Gallia County.* In 1810, Abraham M. Ewing of Bath County, Virginia, pioneered this area, and the site was laid out in 1852 by George Ewing. One source states that it was named for William Ewing, who was born in Virginia in 1756, became an Indian fighter with the militia in Ohio, and died in 1822. He was known as "Swago Bill" after a creek that he lived near for a time in West Virginia. Still another source, writing from the Ewington area, states that "Ewington . . . was headquarters of Dr. Ewing and we assume it was named in his honor."

Excello *Butler County.* Harding, Erwin, & Company erected a paper mill here in 1865, naming it the Excello Paper Company. The place-name stems from this business. A post office operated here in 1870 on a site that around 1795 was called Morrell's Station.

Fairborn *Greene County.* In 1950, two adjacent, rival towns, Fairfield and Osborn, merged to form Fairborn. Incorporation took place the same year.

Fairfax *Highland County.* Platted, 1845, by Benjamin F. Pulliam. The community bears the name of Pulliam's birthplace, Fairfax Courthouse, Virginia.

Fair Haven *Preble County.* Laid out by Jonathan Caldwell in 1832, this place was dubbed Fair Haven by a Captain Bonny of Hamilton because of its lovely situation in the agriculturally rich Four-Mile Valley.

Fairlawn *Summit County.* This community began as a suburb of Akron. Its first houses were in a development known as Fairlawn Heights Estates, a name chosen for its commercial appeal. In 1959, the name Fairlawn Village came into use, thanks largely to Charles M. Lambe.The village was incorporated the following year, and today Fairlawn is a city.

Fairpoint *Belmont County.* The attractiveness of this site and the vantage point it offered inspired the name.

Fairport Harbor *Lake County.* Founded in 1812. The community was initially called Grandon, a name derived from the nearby Grand River. The current name is descriptive, inspired by the suitability of the site as a port. Ohio's third governor, Samuel Huntington, incorporated the town in 1836. It is thought to have been laid out by Samuel and Abraham Skinner to furnish the area with port facilities.

Fairview *Belmont County.* This village, part of which extends into Guernsey County, takes its name from its picturesque location.

Fairview Park *Cuyahoga County.* This site was settled in 1817 by Asahel Mastick and his brother, Colonel Benjamin Mastick, from Massachusetts. It gained village status in 1910 and became a city in 1950, when the name was changed from Fairview Village to Fairview Park. It does indeed provide a fair view from its location in the area known as the "emerald necklace" of the metropolitan Cleveland parks system, and it has been aggressive in acquiring parkland: Bain Park in 1929, Bohlken Park in 1952. It absorbed Parkview Village in 1967.

Farley *Morgan County.* This tiny community traces its name to a Farley family that resided nearby in the early days of settlement.

Farmdale *Trumbull County.* This spot is the hub of a rich dairy farming area, and its location suggested the name to its early settlers.

Farmer *Defiance County.* Platted by John Norway. This village, located in Farmer Township and known to many as Farmer Center, was named for Nathan Farmer, who arrived in the township about 1833.

Farmersville *Montgomery County.* Platted, 1832, by Oliver Dalrymple. Some say that Farmersville was named in the expectation that farmers would constitute the majority of those seeking to purchase lots.

Farmington *Trumbull County.* In close proximity in Farmington Township are Farmington, East Farmington, and West Farmington. They were named for Farmington, Connecticut, by E. P. Wolcott. Wolcott and his wife had lived in the Connecticut town. The first settlers here were Captain Lewis Wolcott and David Curtis in 1806. Joel and Ira Hyde settled East Farmington in 1818, while the westward sojourn of Joel and Eliza Peck concluded at West Farmington.

Fathermac *Belmont County.* Laid out in 1905, this hamlet is said to have been named after a Father McEachen.

Fay *Washington County.* Beginning in 1844, the Reverend Levi Lankton Fay was instrumental in establishing Congregational churches in Lawrence Township. There was a Fay post office from 1887 to 1936.

Fayette *Fulton County.* It is thought that the village is one of many in the United States named in honor of the Marquis de Lafayette, the French soldier who served with distinction under General George Washington during the American Revolution.

Fayetteville *Brown County.* Settled in 1811. Incorporated in 1868. Persons of French descent who settled this location named it after the Marquis de Lafayette.

Fearing *Washington County.* The post office and the small community take their name from a prominent early settler, the Honorable Paul Fearing, who arrived about 1788. The township, established in 1808, was also named Fearing. In 1878, the name of the post office was changed to Stanleyville.

Federal *Athens County.* Now seen on most maps simply as Federal, the complete name of this place was Federal Creek. The creek derived its name from its thirteen branches, which were seen to correspond to the thirteen original colonies that formed the federal system.

Feesburg *Brown County.* Thomas J. Fee laid out this town in 1835. It is named after him.

Felicity *Clermont County.* Laid out, 1817, by Peter Hastings and William Fee. One of the earliest proprietors was Thomas Fee, who obtained land here in 1805. In 1806, William Fee purchased even more, eventually becoming the largest landowner in this part of the county. Both the earlier name, Feestown, and the eventual name of Felicity are believed traceable to William.

Fernald *Hamilton County.* A librarian in the area states that "unfortunately, I was unable to locate the origins of the [Fernald] name, but evidently its naming precedes the location of the . . . Fernald Feed Materials Production Center to the area." The same source provided an excerpt from Stanley W. McClure's *History of Crosby Township,* which states: "Although a number of sources have been consulted, the origin of the [Fernald] name has not been found. It seems probable, however, that the name originated from a member of the Fernald family, who may have been an official of the Chesapeake & Ohio Railroad engaged in the construction of the railroad . . . from 1903 and later."

Ferry *Greene County.* The site, also known as Clio, had its beginnings in 1796, when it became the first settlement in the county. A ferry operated here over a stream called Middle Run.

Fields *Lorain County.* Formerly Fields Corners, this site was settled at an early date by members of the Fields family.

Fifteen *Washington County.* This settlement along Fifteenmile Creek measured fifteen miles from the county courthouse in Marietta. It is sometimes known as Fifteen-Mile. The post office here was opened in 1872.

Fillmore *Washington County.* The community of Fillmore was established at what was known as the Lower Settlement, in Decatur Township. The year was 1851. At that time, Millard Fillmore was president, so the place took his name.

Fincastle *Brown County.* Laid out, 1835, by John Alexander, Sr. A Colonel Stivers christened the community after a town in Virginia.

Findlay *Hancock County (seat).* Established, 1829, on the site of Fort Findlay. The name refers to Colonel James Findlay, who achieved fame in the War of 1812. The year of incorporation was 1838.

Firebrick *Lawrence County.* This tiny community arose about 1911 to serve as home to an iron furnace works. The furnaces were lined with firebricks.

Fisher *Athens County.* A shoemaker named Thomas Fisher came to this vicinity from Maryland about 1835. His name remains.

Fitch *Mahoning County.* A leading Youngstown-area businessman, John H. Fitch, gave this community its name. Fitch came to prominence in the first decade of the 1900s.

Fitch's Corner *Mahoning County.* In 1900, Charles William Fitch purchased two hundred acres here and built a house on the southwest corner of the intersection. The place became known as Fitch's Corner. It appears on some maps as Fitch.

Fitchville *Huron County.* It is thought that an early settler in Sherman Township was Burwell Fitch (approximately 1812). It is also believed that a Connecticut resident with the last name of Fitch owned a good deal of land in the township.

Fivemile *Brown County.* Fivemile is slightly south of Upper Fivemile and is named for Fivemile Creek. (See Upper Fivemile entry.)

Five Points *Ashland County.* Five roads meet here.

Five Points *Pickaway County.* Five roads meet here.

Five Points *Warren County.* This Clear Creek Township site is at the junction of five roads. In the early days, it had a school, a blacksmith shop, and a few homes.

Fleming *Washington County.* The railroad station, post office, and surrounding neighborhood at this site bear the name of John Fleming, a Scotsman who arrived here in 1822. The post office went into operation in 1866.

Fletcher *Miami County.* Long before there was a town here, the site was settled by Joseph Beck. In 1830, J. T. Mallory laid out a community, naming it for the second merchant at the place, Samuel Fletcher. The town was incorporated in 1848.

Flint *Franklin County.* Although it is possible that the community was named for Flint, Michigan, a researcher with the local genealogical society offers another explanation: this area was cut by deep ravines in which could be found extensive deposits of flint, which probably provided a ready supply of material for the arrowheads and spears of early Native Americans who frequented this locale.

Flora *Meigs County.* A postmaster at this place around 1820 who had a daughter named Flora named the site in her honor.

Florence *Erie County.* Surveyed, 1807, by Jabez Wright. The first farm here was that of Ezra Sprague in 1809. Before 1817, the place was known as Jessup for one of the landowners, Ebenezer Jessup. Jessup fell into disfavor because of his high prices and general avarice, however, and when the township was formed, both it and the community were labeled Florence. It has been conjectured that this name belonged to the wife of one of the early settlers.

Florence *Madison County.* When a railroad station was established here, it was named Florence Station in honor of Robinson Florence, who owned five hundred acres where the town was later situated. Robinson was born on Christmas Day, 1809, the son of Judge William Florence of Pickaway County. The elder Florence (or Flourance) had come to Ohio from Virginia (now West Virginia).

Florida *Henry County.* This name, a Spanish term meaning "flowery," was probably suggested by the flora of the state.

Flushing *Belmont County.* Laid out, 1813, by Jesse Foulke. Flushing is the English spelling of Vlissingen, the seaport in Holland for which this Ohio community was named.

Fly *Monroe County.* Early residents here desired a terse name for their settlement, and somehow Fly caught on. That is the short explanation for this unusual moniker. But numerous other anecdotes address the town's name. Strung out as it was along the Ohio River, the town first became known as Stringtown; but even then the post office was known as Fly. One story is that a fly lit on a map while citizens were debating names and thus became immortalized. A similar story says that a fly landed on the chin of one of the town fathers as they were discussing place-names, and he exclaimed, "Dang that fly!" Another story claims that a wayfarer beholding the community from a high ridge asked another, "How do we get down there, fly?" Others endorse an explanation that has a postal official becoming irate at citizens and a local congressman who were lobbying for a post office. The official termed the site "just a flyspeck on the map" and suggested Flyspeck as a name. When the congressman threatened to take up the matter on the floor of the House, the postal authority deleted "speck" and left "Fly." One source points out that the first postmaster here, Francis Marion Cain, desired to call the place Cainsville. "Too much like Gainsville," the Post Office Department replied. Cain then submitted several other labels, all of which were rejected, before suggesting Fly, adding, "It's just a fly town, anyway." Yet another story has a postal personage visiting the burg to establish the post office and dismissing the name Stringtown as too long. Male citizens were convened at the livery stable attempting to arrive at a suitable substitute name when a fly came to rest on Jimmy Bradfield's face, prompting him to suggest Fly.

Folsom *Highland County.* When residents of this hamlet petitioned for a post office, it was granted in the maiden name of President Grover Cleveland's wife, Frances Folsom Cleveland, whom he married in 1886 in the White House.

Footville *Ashtabula County.* According to historical documents, there was once a sawmill operating locally which went by the name of the partners, Grant & Foote. This place-name, according to one source, preserves the name of one of the mill's partners. A second source states that the site bears the name of an individual who erected a schoolhouse at the site in 1847, Lauren B. Foot.

Foraker *Hardin County.* The community was laid out in 1886 by Henry Price and first named Oakland. Its current name honors a governor of Ohio, J. B. Foraker (1846–1917).

Forest *Hardin County.* An impressive stand of timber that covered the locality is thought to have inspired this name. The community was laid out and platted by John A. Gormley and surveyed by J. Harvey David in 1855. It was incorporated ten years later.

Forestville *Hamilton County.* This place sits in a forested section of the county, and it was the home of Henry Forest, one of the area's original settlers. Either or both factors may account for the place-name.

Forgy *Clark County.* The site, a whistle stop on the Big Four Railroad, took its name from a railroad employee, C. S. Forgy.

Fort Jennings *Putnam County.* About 1812, a Colonel Jennings terrorized and subdued Ottawa Indians in these environs. Fort Jennings perpetuates his name. Incorporation was in 1882.

Fort Loramie *Shelby County.* The name derives from Peter Loramie, a French-Canadian trader who established an early trading post at this site. The community was incorporated in 1837.

Fort Recovery *Mercer County.* General Anthony Wayne built a fort here in 1793 after recovering territory lost by General Arthur St. Clair two years earlier. The community of Fort Recovery was incorporated in 1858.

Fort Shawnee *Allen County.* The site takes its name from the Shawnee Indians. The village was incorporated in 1960.

Foster *Warren County.* James H. Foster operated a store here on the Little Miami River from 1842 to 1865. His father, Henry, maintained a store at a place that became known as Foster's Crossing.

Fostoria *Seneca County.* The towns of Risdon and Rome consolidated under the label Fostoria, which honored a popular storekeeper, C. W. Foster. The name dates to 1854. Today a city, the community was incorporated in 1851.

Fowler *Trumbull County.* The place was first dubbed Westfield, the name of the proprietor's Massachusetts hometown. When the township was organized in 1807, it took the name of proprietor Samuel Fowler, and the community also took that name. Samuel's brother, Abner F. Fowler, was the first settler at this place, in 1799.

Fowler Ridge *Trumbull County.* This site is just west of Fowler in Fowler Township. (See Fowler entry.)

Fowler's Mills *Geauga County.* This Chagrin River location had a sawmill, grist mill, and mill house that were erected and operated by Hiram, Edwin (one source says Edward), and Milo Fowler sometime between 1820 and 1830. Their surname has clung to the location (sometimes styled Fowler's Mill).

Foxtown *Monroe County.* Isaac, Mack, Thomas, and William Fox were among the initial settlers at this locality.

Frampton *Licking County.* A magistrate in this township, John Frampton, is the source of this place-name. Garrison Frampton operated a mill in this county.

Franconia *Putnam County.* First known as Sugar Grove, the town was renamed Franconia after the village in New Hampshire. It was laid out by Dr. Jacob DeWeese in 1837.

Frankfort *Ross County.* In 1816, John McNeil laid out this community on his farm and labeled it Oldtown. When it was incorporated in 1827, the state legislature decreed that the name would be Frankfort. Why it was changed is uncertain.

Franklin Furnace *Scioto County.* The Franklin Furnace iron works was built in 1826 by settlers from New Hampshire, and a community grew up around it. Both were named for Benjamin Franklin.

Franklin Square *Columbiana County.* Local residents conjecture that many early settlers came here from Franklin, Pennsylvania, and named this place after their former home. There is, however, a Franklin Square, New York. Others believe the name honors Benjamin Franklin. It was laid out by Frederick Best in 1828.

Frazeysburg *Muskingum County.* Laid out, about 1822, by John Roberts or Clark Hollenback, the founder. The surveyor is said to have been Charles Roberts. The place was first known as Knoxville. Hollenback sold the site in 1828 to Samuel Frazey, who changed the name. Frazey, a commissioner appointed by the state, helped lay out roads here. The village was incorporated in 1868.

Frazier *Muskingum County.* This place-name may trace back to J. W. Frazier of Frazeysburg, who was born into a large family in 1835. David Frazier, his great-great-grandfather, is said to be the patriarch of the Frazier family in America.

Frederick *Miami and Montgomery counties.* Laid out, 1828, by Leonard Eller. The name is sometimes spelled without the second "e." The village's original name, Fredericktown, probably honored Frederick Yount, an aged resident in the early days. Joseph Bowman was reportedly the first citizen of the place about 1820.

Fredericksburg *Wayne County.* In 1824, an associate judge of Wayne County, Jacob Frederick, laid out this community, and his name became attached to it.

Fredericktown *Columbiana County.* In 1833, George Frederick laid off lots for this town and named the place after himself.

Fredericktown *Knox County.* Laid out, 1807, by John Kerr. The surveyor, W. Y. Farquhar, named the place after his Maryland hometown of Frederick. Incorporation came in 1850.

Freedom *Portage County.* Some accounts say that the name Freedom was suggested by the wife of an early settler, Charles Paine, who founded the place in 1818; one fellow settler supposed that Mrs. Paine was thus expressing her ardent love of liberty. Other accounts say that the name may be attributed to the fact that many of the early settlers had escaped debts in their previous hometowns. Freedom was known at an earlier time as North Rootstown, for landowner Ephraim Root.

Freedom Station *Portage County.* Freedom Station was a stop on the railroad near Freedom (see the preceding entry).

Fremont *Sandusky County (seat).* Two earlier names of this city were Croghanville and Lower Sandusky. The place was surveyed and laid out by a Lieutenant Wormley in 1816 (but one source states that the community was founded in 1813). Opposition to one of the name changes came from a Judge Howland, who wrote a poem opposing it. In 1849, the name Lower Sandusky was changed to Fremont, honoring Colonel John Charles Frémont (1813–1890), the noted explorer who became a presidential candidate in 1856. Incorporation occurred in 1866.

Frenchtown *Darke County.* Many early settlers here were French, including J. P. Berge, who arrived in 1838.

Fresno *Coshocton County.* The name of the community was changed from Boyd's Mills to Avondale in 1875. But there was another Avondale near Cincinnati, and to lessen confusion at the post office, in 1905 the Coshocton Avondale was changed to Fresno. Dr. Harry Wallace is said to have suggested the new name; a former resident, he had moved to Fresno, California, and was so fond of it that he urged the renaming in letters written back to his former hometown.

Friendship *Scioto County.* According to the Nile Township historian, local settlers and Shawnee Indians who met here along Turkey Creek for an annual feast lasting two or three days stressed friendship, and that became the name of the community.

Friendsville *Medina County.* Settled, 1817, by Mr. and Mrs. Joseph S. Winston. Mr. Winston became postmaster here, and the site became identified as Winston's Corners. Later the post office was removed from this place, creating considerable animosity. Much later, in 1868, a post office was returned to the area, encompassing not only Winston's Corners but also Morse's Corners. The combined site was called Friendsville, possibly because the owners of an inn in the area wanted to make people feel welcome.

Fulda *Noble County.* Founded in 1861; surveyed by Charles Burlingame the same year. The proprietor was John Brahler. The village was settled predominantly by Germans and was given the name of a city in Germany.

Fullertown *Geauga County.* Thomas Fuller opened a flour mill here on the Chagrin River in 1822 and lent his name to the place.

Fulton *Morrow County.* An early tannery was established on or near the Fulton farm in this township, and it is likely that the name of the site relates to that farm family. Samuel Fulton was born here in 1825; he and his wife had eight children.

Fultonham *Muskingum County.* Laid out in 1815. The name traces back to Lyle Fulton, who became postmaster about 1828. The place had been called Uniontown, but that designation duplicated another place-name in Ohio and had to be changed.

Funk *Wayne County.* This place was once known as Kauffman Corners. In 1894, when a village was platted for John and Sarah Austen, the name became Austen. It was discovered later the name duplicated another Ohio place, so it was changed to Funk. Zenas Funk was born in this township in 1842, while Hugh Funk (b. 1802) emigrated to this township. Historians believe the name honors a prominent early citizen, grocer W. D. Funk (better known as "D."). But because many of his relatives also called the community home, the name may be said to honor any or all of them. One local Funk—Michael—helped Elmer Yocum build the first house in nearby Congress.

Furmandale *Butler County.* Earlier names for the town were Snaptown, Snopstown, and Schnapstown—all thought to be corruptions of Schnappstown, since a distillery and the Butler Tavern were located here. A post office called Furmandale did business here for a short while, beginning in 1857. The name goes back to Nathaniel Furman, who purchased the Butler Tavern and turned it into a boarding school for girls.

Gageville *Ashtabula County.* Three settlers here were John, Stephen, and Joshua Gage. They arrived in 1815.

Gahanna *Franklin County.* This town's name originally applied to a stream and may stem from *hanna,* said to be the Algonquian word for "stream."

Galena *Delaware County.* Gilbert Carpenter founded a village named Zoar here in 1809. William Carpenter finished laying it out in 1813. In 1816, it was platted. A post office was desired in 1834, but there was a Zoar in Tuscarawas County, so it was necessary to choose a new name. Three individuals were appointed as a committee to come up with a suitable name. They decided to place the nominations into a hat and allow the first passerby to draw out the winning name. Galena was the name drawn. The place is said to have been named by Nathan Dustin, but it is unclear whether he was the person who drew out the name or the one who submitted it. Galena was incorporated in 1924.

Galion *Crawford County.* This city was once known as Goshen, a label that caused postal delivery confusion with more than one other entity in Ohio. The postmaster general suggested the name Galion, although his reasoning remains the subject of conjecture. Galion was incorporated in 1842. Other early appellations for the site included Moccasin, Hosfords, Spangtown, Horseshoe, The Corners, and Hardscrabble.

Gallia *Gallia County.* The town, like the county, takes its name from the Latin word for France, *Gallia*. The French settled this county.

Gallipolis *Gallia County (seat).* One of the oldest cities in the state, Gallipolis was settled in 1790. Only four years later, a post office opened here. The name, a combination of French (*Galli*) and Greek (*polis*), means "city of the Gauls." It was settled by members of the French Five Hundred.

Galloway *Franklin County.* The property where Galloway reposes was owned in turn by several persons. Samuel and Joan Galloway purchased a portion of it in 1861 or before. Over the years, they added to their real estate holdings, then sold off some and even repurchased a parcel. One source states, "For a time, there was indecision about the naming of the town. It was finally decided to call it Galloway, after S. Galloway." Whitehead Coleman was originally given one thousand acres here, in 1798, by the U.S. government, in consideration of military services. Shortly thereafter, the Colemans sold to John P. Pleasant. Later owners included Clark Higgins, Samuel Kell, M. A. Platt, Rosline Smith, Spicer L. Smith, George W. McDowell, and D. B. Peters. The Columbus, Springfield, & Cincinnati Railroad was also given a narrow passage.

Gambier *Knox County.* The town dates to at least 1824 and is the home of Kenyon College. Lord James Gambier of England is the person to whom the town owes its name. It is said that founder Philander Chase journeyed to England to raise money for a theological seminary and college, obtaining $30,000 from three prominent donors, including Gambier. The college was named for Lord Kenyon and the seminary for Lord Bexley.

Ganges *Richland County.* For an unknown reason the town was given the name of the river in India. This place formerly bore the name Trucksville.

Gann *Knox County.* Laid out, 1838, by John Hibbitts. This hamlet was known earlier—among other names—as Mount Holly. According to one source, the president of the Cleveland, Mount Vernon, & Columbus Railroad changed the name to honor George Gann of Union Township. It is unclear what role Gann played in the early history of this place. A second source states that the place took its name from John Gann, who, it says, donated the land for the railroad. (See Brinkhaven entry.)

Gano *Butler County.* The community was platted in 1873 by Charles Gano following entry of the railroad into the area.

Gardner *Crawford County.* In 1821, James Gardner acted as an overseer of the poor and a bondsman. The name of this place may be connected to him or his family.

Garfield *Mahoning County.* This hamlet gained its name early in the 1870s from an Ohio native son, congressman, and future president, James A. Garfield (1831–1881).

Garfield Heights *Cuyahoga County.* One of the initial settlers at this site was Abram Garfield, the father of James A. Garfield, who became the twentieth president of the United States in 1881 and was killed by an assassin a few months later. The year of incorporation was 1904. Garfield Heights is now a city.

Garrettsville *Portage County.* Founded in 1804. The township's first settler was Colonel John Garrett, after whom Garrettsville was named. Incorporation took place in 1864.

Gasville *Washington County.* A large gas well operation existed here about 1888, the year the place earned a post office (which closed in 1908).

Gates Mills *Cuyahoga County.* In 1812, Halsey Gates settled at this place. He purchased property and in 1826 built a mill on it. Gates Mills was incorporated in 1924.

Gaver's *Columbiana County.* In 1804, Gedeon Gaver settled on a farmsite that later was occupied by the Gaver's Post Office. The first Methodist Episcopal service in Wayne Township is said to have taken place at Gedeon Gaver's house.

Gaysport *Muskingum County.* Laid out, 1836, by Asa Gay. Locks and dams were being built on the Muskingum River nearby, giving the site the "port" aspect of its name.

Geeburg *Mahoning County.* One theory holds that this Ellsworth Township site owes its name to local land proprietor Josh Gee. A second advances the belief that the name leads back to the Reverend Nicholas Gee, a Methodist preacher, who came to these parts from New York State in 1823. Three other Gees were in the index of the county's 1874 atlas.

Gem *Noble County.* The Post Office Department requested that a short name be chosen, and Gem was the result. The town was born about 1895.

Gem Beach *Ottawa County.* Platted in 1944. This community is in Catawba Island Township, Catawba Island itself being a peninsula, not an island. It is believed that the moniker Gem Beach was given to the place by developers who hoped to make it sound attractive. It has Lake Erie frontage.

Geneva *Ashtabula County.* Two theories exist regarding Geneva's name rationale. One centers on the fact that a number of the early settlers came from Geneva, New York. Those who subscribe to this explanation believe that the name was suggested by Levi Gaylord. The second theory speculates that Gideon Granger, the proprietor, put forth the name to honor the Swiss home of his associate, Albert Gallatin, who was a member of President Thomas Jefferson's cabinet. Arriving from upstate New York, the initial band of settlers here included James Morrison, Elisha Ward, Levi Gaylord, and Theobalt Barthalomew. Now a city, Geneva was incorporated in 1866. The surrounding township—also named Geneva—was organized in 1816, and the community took on its separate identity the same year.

Geneva *Fairfield County.* Geneva is probably named for Geneva, Switzerland. Many of the early settlers in this county were of German-Swiss heritage, and several other county communities carry names of places in Switzerland.

Geneva-on-the-Lake *Ashtabula County.* This is a resort community on Lake Erie. The "Geneva" segment of the designation refers either to Geneva, New York, or Geneva, Switzerland. (See Geneva entry.) The village was incorporated in 1927.

Genntown *Warren County.* Lying in Turtle Creek Township, Genntown takes its name from Colonel Jethro Genn, who located a short distance northeast of Lebanon, Ohio, in this county.

Genoa *Ottawa County.* Platted in 1857. The accepted belief is that this community takes its name from Genoa, Italy.

Georgetown *Brown County (seat).* Surveyed in 1819. The proprietors were Henry Newkirk and Alan Woods. Georgetown, Kentucky, inspired the name for this village.

Georgetown *Harrison County.* Platted in 1814. It is presumed that this name traces to the man who laid out the town, George Riggle. Although it is relatively unusual for the given name to be lent to a town, possibly it seemed preferable to Riggletown.

Georgetown *Knox County.* The proprietor here was David Ewers, from Loudoun County, Virginia. The hamlet probably takes its name from George Gibson, later a landowner on the west side of the road, and George Ewers (David's son), on the east. David Ewers arrived here in 1810.

Georgetown *Miami County.* Laid out in 1840. Apparently the place bears the given name of George Hatfield. It is not clear what if any role Hatfield played in the birth of the town.

Gephart *Scioto County.* Gephart takes its designation from the surname of the first postmaster at the place, Lewis Gephart (1856). Gephart named the post office Lilly.

Gerald *Henry County.* In 1892, a son, Gerald, was born to Mike Donnelly and his wife. It was for the boy that this town was named. Mike Donnelly was a judge in the county.

Germano *Harrison County.* Situated in German Township, this hamlet was founded in 1815 by Frederick Zollers, a German.

Germantown *Mahoning County.* The name was probably applied because of a Mennonite settlement at this locality. The Mennonites were of Swiss origin, but many had been driven into Germany.

Germantown *Montgomery County.* Laid out, 1814, by Philip Gunkel. Germantown takes its name from a town of the same designation in Pennsylvania. It is in German Township.

Gettysburg *Darke County.* Laid out about 1830. Gettysburg was founded by John Hershey and named for the town in Pennsylvania that today is best known for its Civil War battlefield and President Abraham Lincoln's address. Darke County's Gettysburg was incorporated in 1866.

Gettysburg *Preble County.* Laid out, 1832, by John Curry. Curry was from Pennsylvania and at first named the site Harrisburg, for the capital of the Keystone State. However, there being another town of that name in Ohio, the name was changed to that of the site of the famous Civil War battleground, also in Pennsylvania. In Preble County, both Harrisburg and Gettysburg originally had an "h" at the end when written.

Geyer *Auglaize County.* In 1892, with increased railroad service nearby, George Geyer laid out this place on his farm. It soon began to thrive and was incorporated a few years later. He did the platting in 1893. It has been variously known as Geyer, Geyer Village, and Geyer City. Mr. Geyer entered the future townsite in 1840.

Ghent *Summit County.* The Treaty of Ghent was signed in 1814 in Ghent, Belgium, concluding the War of 1812 between the United States and England. At about the time of the signing, a hamlet was founded here, probably taking the name of the Belgian city.

Gibisonville *Hocking County.* Laid out, 1840, by Samuel and William Gibison. The town derives its name from the men who laid it out. Later a Joel Gibison was postmaster at this location.

Gibson *Guernsey County.* According to one source, the site was named for James Gibson, said to have erected a warehouse near the railroad here. The place is sometimes known as Gibson Station. One of the earliest and most prominent pioneer families was a Gibson clan that settled in Liberty Township, Guernsey County. However, this hamlet is located well to the south of Liberty Township, so it is not known if James was a member of this contingent. Sixty-two Gibsons are listed in the biographical index of a single Guernsey County tome.

Gibsonburg *Sandusky County.* Founded by William H. Gibson, this village was surveyed in 1871. J. F. Yeasting and T. D. Stevenson assisted him in laying it out.

Giddings *Ashtabula County.* Joshua R. Giddings (1795–1864), who represented the Western Reserve in the U.S. Congress and helped found the Republican party in the mid-1800s, is the person for whom this junction was named. Giddings was a noted opponent of slavery.

Gilboa *Putnam County.* Laid out by Elisha Stout about 1830. Stout built the first grist mill and sawmill at this location. The name of the place is derived from Mount Gilboa, mentioned in the Bible (1 Chronicles 10:1 and elsewhere).

Gilmore *Tuscarawas County.* Founded, 1848, by Walter M. Blake. This hamlet is named in recognition of Nathaniel Gilmore, a well-to-do Irish farmer who resided in the vicinity.

Ginghamsburg *Miami County.* Oddly, this community was so named because a storekeeper here, Silas Wells, always wore a gingham coat. So consistent was he in this habit that he was nicknamed Gingham.

Girard *Trumbull County.* Settled about 1800. Stephen Girard, a philanthropist from Philadelphia, is the person for whom the city was named. The community became an entity in the 1830s.

Girton *Sandusky County.* In 1844, David Girton arrived in Ashland County, Ohio, from Columbia County, Pennsylvania. Subsequently he married and had ten children. The fifth offspring was named David Kinney Girton. In 1860, the Girtons moved to Wood County, Ohio, purchasing another farm, and eventually David Kinney Girton bought one at this site in Sandusky County. Eventually (perhaps in the 1880s) a railroad desired to build through the farm, and in exchange for the right-of-way grant, D. K. Girton required the line to erect a station there and name it Girton. Before long, additional houses, stores, and a church were built at the site. The railroad may have been an interurban; it does not show up on today's map. These data were provided by an elderly scion of the Girton family who also has the Girton surname.

Givens *Pike County.* In 1858, one of the township trustees was a man named James Givens. It is believed that this place bears his name.

Glade *Jackson County.* Glade probably was named simply because it fit the dictionary definition: an open space in a wood or forest. The hamlet is situated in an open valley, and at the time the name was applied, the rest of the description probably fit better.

Glandorf *Putnam County.* John F. Kahle, Professor William Horstmann, and others came to this place from Glandorf, Germany, in 1833, purchased land, colonized, and built churches. They were followed shortly by others from Germany. The place was incorporated as a village in 1891.

Glasgow *Columbiana County.* Presbyterians of Scottish heritage were the initial settlers at this place. Early records put their arrival between 1805 and 1815. The name is that of the city in Scotland.

Glasgow *Tuscarawas County.* The Glasgow and Port Washington Iron & Coal Company was established here in 1874 by Scottish industrialists. A blast furnace operated here for one or two years. The place takes its name from Glasgow, Scotland.

Glass *Washington County.* The site probably takes the name of a Revolutionary War soldier who arrived in this county in 1825, Henry Glass.

Glass Rock *Perry County.* Glass Rock owes its name to the "glass sand" that is quarried locally and refined by the Central Silica Company, now a branch of Ogleby Norton Company. Operations began in the early 1900s.

Glencoe *Belmont County.* Laid out in 1855. Two theories exist regarding the naming of the site. It may have been so named for a valley family named Coe, or it could have been named for a Scottish community called Glencoe.

Glendale *Hamilton County.* Laid out in 1852. Originally a series of fine cultivated farms belonging to Edmund R. Glenn, John M. Cochran, John Riddle, Robert Watson, and others, this community is probably traceable in name to Glenn. Incorporation took place in 1947.

Glen Este *Clermont County.* An official of the Cincinnati, Georgetown, & Portsmouth Railroad, David K. Este, is the person after whom this community was named. Este was with the railroad in 1885.

Glenmore *Van Wert County.* This place-name cannot be explained in detail. Originally it was Gilmore. Why it was changed is uncertain, but the change apparently took place in 1889. Some say it was laid out in 1890, while others say 1893.

Glenn Summit *Gallia County.* A family bearing the surname Glenn operated a general store here for years, after the Hocking Valley Railroad penetrated the area. (One source spells the family name Glen.)

Glen Roy *Jackson County.* The founder of the town was Andrew Roy, whose surname remains with the community. Roy served as Ohio's chief inspector of mines when the position was created. The "glen" portion alludes to a Scottish mountain valley.

Glenwillow *Cuyahoga County.* Originally the name of this locale was Falls Junction. During the administration of the first mayor, named Avery, the name was changed to Willow Glen, inspired by a glen of willow trees west of Cochran Road near Pettibone Road. Citizens later decided they preferred a one-word name, and it was changed to Glenwillow. The village was incorporated in 1914.

Gloria Glens *Medina County.* Of relatively recent vintage, this community's name is likely a combination inspired by the glenlike topography and the given name of the wife of one of the developers. Incorporation took place in 1931.

Glouster *Athens County.* The place was laid out in 1882 and named Sedalia for the lilt of the word. The post office, however, would not approve the name, since there was another town of that name in Madison County. Gloucester was selected by a native of the English city and county of Gloucester, Mrs. William Bowkley. In transmitting the name choice to postal authorities in the nation's capital, the spelling came out Glouster.

Glynwood *Auglaize County.* John Glynn, a native of Ireland who settled near the village site in 1857, inspired the name for this community, which was laid out in 1876.

Gnadenhutten *Tuscarawas County.* German Moravian missionaries gave this village its name in 1772. A probable translation of the German word is "tabernacle of grace."

Goe's Station *Greene County.* This hamlet traces back to 1846. It arose around a water station of the Little Miami Railroad. The land here was owned by the Goe family.

Golden Corners *Wayne County.* Founded in the early 1800s, this site was so named because of its initial appearance, featuring fields on all four corners that were covered with goldenrod.

Golf Manor *Hamilton County.* The area's first family, named Pieper, arrived from Germany in the 1880s. Golf Manor was incorporated as a village in 1947, the name resulting from the fact that three golf courses—Crest Hills, Stoneybrook, and Losantiville—then bordered the tiny municipality.

Gomer *Allen County.* This community has a rich Welsh heritage: Welsh settlers arrived here in 1833. The name is biblical for Noah's grandson Gomer, said to be "father of the Celts, Gauls, Irish, Scots, Welsh." James Nicholas and Samuel Ramsay laid out the site in 1850.

Good Hope *Fayette County.* James Sargent and Robert Harper laid out this community in 1849. The accepted story is that many early settlers here came from a place called Good Hope in Pennsylvania.

Goodwin *Paulding County.* Many Goodwins are listed in the marriage and cemetery records of this county. Noah Goodwin married Hannah Sullivan in 1852. Ten other Goodwins are mentioned in the marriage records, while cemetery records mention this surname thirteen times.

Gordon *Darke County.* The ancestors of the Gordon family for whom this town is named lived in France originally and spelled their name Gourdon. They fled local troubles in the twelfth century and moved to Scotland, becoming known as the Gordons. John, Robert, Charles, George, and Thomas Gordon came to America in 1684. Thomas's family settled in Perth Amboy, New Jersey. Philip Gordon, son of Thomas Gordon III, came to this area in Ohio in 1839, and he and his family are buried in this town. It was incorporated in 1900.

Gore *Hocking County.* The explanation of this hamlet's name is that it was "neatly inserted" into a corner of Hocking County, much as a dressmaker fits a small piece of cloth (a gore) into a larger one. *Gore* also means "a small usually triangular piece of land."

Goshen *Clermont County.* A town named Goshen in an eastern state may have been recalled when this community was named, or the name may have been biblically inspired. Goshen was the district in ancient Egypt where the descendants of Jacob lived until the Exodus. The name implies rich soil.

Goshen *Tuscarawas County.* The hamlet is in Goshen Township. (See the name explanation in the preceding entry.)

Goshen Center *Mahoning County.* Settled in 1804. Organized in 1810. The name is said to have been borrowed from a Goshen in Connecticut. Goshen Township, which surrounds this place, was also organized in 1810.

Gosline *Perry County.* A coal-mining town, this place once went by the name Goston. W. A. Gosline & Company founded it. Its biggest boom was from about 1902 to the 1920s. William A. Gosline was a coal operator based in Toledo. His firm worked this area after operating mines in the Shawnee area for many years.

Gould *Ashtabula County.* The first postmaster at this locality, Archibald Gould, gave his name to the community.

Gracey *Washington County.* The name traces to the first postmaster here, William S. Gracey, in 1882.

Grafton *Lorain County.* This name was adopted when the Big Four Railroad was pushed through the area. It may echo Grafton, Massachusetts. The community was incorporated in 1882 but the neighborhood was settled much earlier.

Graham *Monroe County.* James Graham of Malaga Township, born in Pennsylvania about 1778, is the person after whom this place took its name, according to one source. Another claims it was landowner Robert Graham, about 1832. The two Grahams may have been related.

Graham Corners *Coshocton County.* One settlement history lists six Grahams prominent in the county early on, although none in this township (Washington). Still, only a mile or so to the west lies Pike Township, which John C. Graham and Alex Graham called home.

Grahamsville *Jackson County.* The property here was owned by John Graham, who laid out the community, probably in the early 1850s. The family of James Graham also resided here.

Grand Rapids *Wood County.* Surveyed in 1833 by Ambrose Rice for John N. Graham and located in Grand Rapids Township. The area was settled in the 1820s. The town, formerly known as Weston and Gilead, is adjacent to an area of the Maumee River referred to as "the head of the rapids."

Grand River *Lake County.* The village reposes on the shores of the Grand River, stretches of which are officially designated as scenic, affording a measure of protection. The river was once called Geauga, a Native American word that some persons believe means "great" or "grand." They claim that Geauga is an English corruption of *chogage, cherage,* or *chocago.* The publisher of *Ohio County Maps,* however, gives the meaning of Geauga as "raccoon" (*sheauga shipe* = raccoon river). Still others hold that Geauga is the equivalent of Cuyahoga, or "crooked."

Grandview *Washington County.* Grandview's name was suggested by its situation overlooking the picturesque Ohio River, against a backdrop of wooded hills. The village, township (established 1802), and post office (established 1831) all use the Grandview name.

Grandview Heights *Franklin County.* The name of this Columbus suburb began in 1890 with an exclamation by Mrs. George Cambridge Urlin when she beheld the vista from the tower of the family's just-finished mansion: "What a grand view!" Her husband, trained in photography, founded the Columbus Bicycle Company and the Laminated Tube Company. He also dealt in real estate and development. The "Heights" aspect of the city's name comes from the location of an early part of the community, having been built on high ground overlooking the road leading to Columbus.

Grangerburg *Medina County.* The town was named for its township, Granger. The name traces back to absentee land proprietor Gideon Granger of Connecticut.

(One source says New York.) Land here was purchased from Granger by four farmers from Bristol, Ontario County, New York, in 1817. Later they had to default on their mortgages, and the land reverted to Granger's ownership. Grangerburg is sometimes referred to simply as Granger.

Grant *Hardin County.* The community was named Grant because the post office at the site opened during the presidential term (1869–1877) of Ulysses S. Grant.

Granville *Licking County.* Welsh persons from East Granville, Massachusetts, founded the community in 1805. Members of the Scioto Company, they purchased 28,000 acres in the vicinity. Incorporation was in 1832.

Grape Grove *Greene County.* William Lewis and Andrew Fogg purchased this property in 1830 and planted an eight-acre vineyard. It soon became known as Grape Grove.

Grassy Point *Hardin County.* Grassy Point was a popular spot before white settlement. It is a high point of land resembling a prairie, and Native Americans favored it as a campsite. The place offered a good view of the surrounding area and was readily defensible.

Gratiot *Licking County.* Laid out in 1829. When the United States Army Corps of Engineers supervised the building of the National Road (now U.S. 40) between Columbus and Zanesville, the chief of the corps was General Charles Gratiot. This village was named in recognition of him. It was incorporated in 1940.

Gratis *Preble County.* An account of this name is recorded in the *History of Preble County.* The publisher, H. Z. Williams & Brother, states that early citizens from the southern portion of the county resented having to travel far north to Lanier Township in order to vote. A group composed mainly of Society of Friends members petitioned a commissioners' meeting for a new, southerly township. The commissioners at first refused. Then Samuel Stubbs spoke up for the Quakers, not only reiterating their points but also arguing that the new township should be granted to them "gratis." His speech was persuasive, and his recommendations carried. The county clerk, A. C. Lanier, even took action to name the new township Gratis. The same name was adopted by the town.

Gravel Bank *Washington County.* When the Bate post office name was changed in 1891, James F. Briggs, postmaster, dubbed it Gravel Bank. This name was suggested by the abundance of gravel in the area, which boasted several operating gravel pits.

Graysville *Monroe County.* This place assumed its name after it was laid out in 1835 by Daniel Gray.

Graytown *Ottawa County.* Probably never surveyed and dating to an unknown year, Graytown apparently got its name from the color of the limestone deposits in the locality.

Great Bend *Meigs County.* This village lies just above a major bend in the Ohio River.

Greenbrier *Monroe County.* A longtime resident of this area writes: "I assume Greenbrier was named for the viney green briers that grew [there]. They were a real problem when Dad first farmed this land." The Greenbrier Methodist Church dates to 1873, but how far back the place-name goes is not clear.

Greenbush *Brown County.* Laid out, 1838, by Joseph Kratzer. At the time the town was platted off into lots, the site was overgrown with luxuriant green foliage. This situation begat the name Greenbush. The town is in Green Township.

Green Camp *Marion County.* The encampment of Captain David Green was located near this village during the War of 1812. The place was laid out in 1838 (one source says 1836) by David Beach. In 1843, John G. Bradshaw became a permanent resident. In 1875, the town was incorporated as Green Camp. It was formerly called Berwick.

Greencastle *Fairfield County.* John Hamilton was the surveyor for the community, which was laid out in 1810 (or 1815) by Jesse D. Courtright. After mentioning both these men, an early account goes on to say, "He lived where his daughter and Mrs. Sarah Green now reside," but since the pronoun reference is unclear, it is not known whether the writer means Hamilton or Courtright. In any case, the place-name may relate in some fashion to the Green family, of which Sarah apparently was a member by marriage. The name was popularly styled Green Castle at first.

Greene Center *Trumbull County.* This community lies at the center of Greene Township. The designation is attributable to Gardner Greene of Massachusetts, who is said to have secured what is now the township of Howland and then exchanged parcels with Joseph Howland, who had secured what is now Greene Township.

Greenesburg *Sandusky County.* The place was laid out by John L. Greene, who opened a store here in 1836.

Greenfield *Highland County.* General Duncan McArthur, perhaps in 1796, came upon this lush setting of rolling uplands where Native Americans had pastured their mounts, and he may have named it. One early observer described this locale as "a level green plain" with an Indian encampment on it. McArthur and his surveyors platted the town in 1802. (Other sources say it was "platted" in 1799, "laid out" in 1796, and "surveyed" in 1791 or 1796.) McArthur is said to have spent his boyhood years in Greenfield, Erie County, Pennsylvania, and that may also have influenced the name here. Incorporation was accomplished in 1841.

Greenford *Mahoning County.* Located in Green Township, this community may have been named in honor of Connecticut Land Company member Gardiner Green (or Greene).

Greenhills *Hamilton County.* Greenhills is one of three experimental communities developed across the country by the Works Progress Administration (WPA) in the Great Depression era. (The others are Greenbelt, Maryland, and Greendale, Wisconsin.) The site was the highest elevation in Hamilton County. The initial construction phase began in 1935; the first residents moved in in 1938. Emphasis was placed on "greenbelt zoning." Parks and public areas were deeded to the village government, and 1,800 acres surrounding the town were deeded to the county park district to form an area known as Winton Woods. The Civilian Conservation Corps reforested the area, planting thousands of trees. The zoning allows no tree removal within the greenbelt. Greenhills, incorporated in 1938, received a "Tree City USA" designation eight years running.

Greensburg *Summit County.* Founded, 1828, by David Blair. This community derives its name from Green Township, within which it is located. The township was named in honor of Gardner Green, who held an interest in the Connecticut Land Company. Green's surname is seen variously as Green and Greene, and his given name as Gardner or Gardiner.

Green Spring *Sandusky County* (with a portion in Seneca County). Settled by M. B. Adams about 1834. Green Spring received its name because of a mineral spring situated nearby. It is in Green Creek Township.

Green's Store *Jackson County.* A man named Green once operated a store at this location.

Greentown *Stark County.* Laid out, 1816, by Henry Wise and Peter Dickerhoof, the proprietors. This community may have been named for Thomas Green, described in one source as a "renegade."

Greenville *Darke County* (*seat*). In October 1793, General Anthony Wayne and two thousand men arrived at this spot and built a fifty-acre fort. The following month, Wayne named it Fort Greene Ville, in honor of his Revolutionary War compatriot General Nathanael Greene (1742–1786). From here, Wayne took his army to Fallen Timbers, where he defeated the Native American tribes of the territory northwest of the Ohio River. He then invited the defeated chiefs to Fort Greene Ville to sign a peace treaty, now known as the Treaty of Greene Ville. When the town was platted in 1808, it was named Greenville. It was incorporated in 1832.

Greenwich *Huron County.* The name of Greenwich, Fairfield County, Connecticut, was transported west with emigrants and conferred upon this spot. The first settler, Henry Carpenter, arrived in 1817. The township bears the same name. The community was incorporated as a village in 1879.

Greer *Knox County.* This north-central Ohio site was settled in 1827 by the R. Greer family. In 1836, Robert Greer purchased the land, laid out the town, and named it after himself. At one time there were at least seven Greer families living at or near this site. It was known as Greersville for a time.

Grelton *Henry County.* Laid out, 1881, by Eli C. Clay. The name, formerly spelled Grellton, honors Alexander Grelle.

Griffith *Monroe County.* A number of Griffiths have been identified in this area. Benjamin Griffith was here in 1847. William Griffith, Eliaz Griffith, and five others with this surname are listed in the biographical index of a county history.

Griggs' Corners *Ashtabula County.* Solomon Griggs, an early settler, had his domicile here. The "Corners" aspect of the name may refer to intersecting thoroughfares or to the coming together here of four townships.

Groesbeck *Hamilton County.* This community bears the surname of a prominent early Cincinnati-area family.

Grosvenor *Athens County.* The label on this community probably traces back to the family of an Athens-area attorney, the Honorable Charles H. Grosvenor (circa 1880).

Grove City *Franklin County.* In 1851 or 1852, landowner William Foster Breck platted the village with the assistance of William Sibray, George Weygandt, and Jeremiah Smith. Breck named the place for a nearby grove of trees. (One account states that it was named for "the large groves of trees the settlers left as they cleared the land for homes and farms.") William Breck was the son-in-law of John Smith, the original landowner at the site. In 1852, Breck opened the first post office here. The village was incorporated in 1866. The land on which Grove City stands was once part of two Virginia Military District land grants. The warrants for them were issued to Colonel William Washington (George's nephew) and General Daniel Morgan.

Groveport *Franklin County.* The place was formerly called Wert's Grove, for Jacob B. Wert, who laid it out in 1843. In 1844, William H. Rarey laid out Rarey's Port immediately east of Wert's Grove. Eventually, all agreed that a common name would be desirable. The parties compromised in 1846 by dropping the personal-name portion of each designation, leaving "grove" and "port." The town is on an old canal. Incorporation came in 1847.

Grover Hill *Paulding County.* Laid out in 1887. The community was named in honor of President Grover Cleveland (1837–1908). One source gives the place-name as Grove Hill. The town was incorporated in 1891.

Guerne *Wayne County.* This village arose in the 1920s. It is said that at a neighborhood picnic in the 1930s, a resident, Louise Merillat, advanced Guerne as a name for the place; her late husband had been a member of the Guerne family and numerous descendants of the family remained in the area. They were originally from Switzerland.

Guernsey *Guernsey County.* Like the county in which it is located, the community is so named because many early residents emigrated from the Isle of Guernsey. It was platted in 1872 by John Fordyce, J. W. Robins, and Madison Robins.

Guilford *Columbiana County.* Platted in 1835. The village takes its name from the canal's engineer, William Gill. Originally it was spelled Gillford.

Gurneyville *Clinton County.* Platted, 1847, for proprietor David McMillan. McMillan named the place in honor of a noted member of the Society of Friends, Joseph John Gurney.

Gustavus Center *Trumbull County.* Both the place and the township in which it is located were named in recognition of Gustavus Storrs. Lemuel Storrs, his father, surveyed a substantial portion of this area.

Gutman *Auglaize County.* A dry goods and general store was kept here by Mary E. and John N. Gutman. The Gutman brothers ran the grain elevator. John's mother, Nellie E. Gutman, assisted in operating the store. One source states that the town is named for Nellie.

Guysville *Athens County.* Chauncey Carpenter laid out this hamlet in 1861. About three years later, a post office was obtained, largely through the efforts of Guy Barrows, who was appointed the first postmaster. The town carries Barrows's given name. It was also known as Savannah.

Gypsum *Ottawa County.* The name was conferred because of the presence here of gypsum beds adjacent to the shoreline of Sandusky Bay and Lake Erie. The beds were extensively mined for many years.

Hackney *Morgan County.* Laid out in 1847. First called Elizabeth, this town has been known as Hackney since 1855, when, according to one source, an inebriated gentleman passed through the village shouting, "Hurrah for Hackney!" Another authority states that an Irishman, Patrick Sherlock, went to England and brought back to his Center Township farm several fine horses of the Hackney breed. A post office bearing the Hackney name opened in 1872 in Chester Wilson's store.

Hageman *Warren County.* This name traces back to Henry Hageman, father of the Reverend R. S. Hageman. In 1879, the post office here was known as Camp Hageman, and the area itself was at one time referred to as Hageman Station. It was situated on the C.L.&N. Railroad.

Hagler *Fayette County.* The right-of-way through the townsite for the Detroit, Toledo, & Ironton Railroad was donated by William and Jesse Hagler, and the village name recognizes their good deed.

Hake's Corners *Trumbull County.* This intersection probably took its name from one of the Hakes or Hake families, who resided in the area. William D. Hake was a Civil War survivor and farmer, born in Howland Township in 1837. His parents were George and Catherine Hake. A Trumbull-Mahoning counties history mentions nine Hakes in its biographical index. In a record of early Trumbull County marriages, fourteen women and twenty men having the Hake surname are listed.

Hale's Creek *Scioto County.* The place "is named for the creek, which was named for the first settler on its banks," according to an elderly resident of the area.

Hallsville *Ross County.* Founded in 1837. The hamlet was known originally as Economy. When a post office opened, the name was changed to Hallsville, after William Hall, the postmaster. James Hall, probably a relative, was once mayor of nearby Adelphi (about 1838).

Hambden *Geauga County.* Hambden was named for Hamden, Connecticut, the "b" being added to set it apart from a town in southern Ohio named Hamden. A divergent view holds that the town was named for Hampden, Massachusetts. Before 1820 the place was known as Bondstown, for Dr. Solomon Bond, who purchased the site in 1801 and named it after himself. Oliver Phelps was an even earlier proprietor. The community was laid out in 1819.

Hamburg *Fairfield County.* Laid out, sometime after 1812, by William Medill. (One source credits John Roland, in 1817.) The name probably echoes Hamburg, Germany, given the German-Swiss influence in this area.

Hamer *Williams County.* Surveyed, 1851, by James Thompson. The land proprietor was Theron Landon. It is believed that the village was named in honor of General Thomas Hamer, who gained fame in the Mexican War. General Hamer, a popular Ohio politician, died in Monterrey, Mexico, in 1846.

Hamersville *Brown County.* When residents here petitioned for a post office, Thomas L. Hamer, a member of Congress, was helpful in getting one for them, so they named the village after him.

Hametown *Wayne and Summit counties.* A firm that manufactured hames existed here in 1850. Hames are the rigid pieces of material along the two sides of a horse's collar to which the traces are attached. A small community that arose around the factory took the name Hametown from the product.

Hamilton *Butler County (seat).* General Arthur St. Clair, the first governor of the Northwest Territory, and his men established Fort Hamilton here in 1791. Both the fort and the subsequent city were named for Alexander Hamilton (1755–1804), who was secretary of the treasury under President George Washington. The land proprietor here was Israel Ludlow, who sold the parcel to Jonathan Dayton, founder of Dayton, Ohio. One source also calls him the founder of Hamilton and credits Ludlow with laying out this city. Some of its earliest settlers were soldiers who remained when General Anthony Wayne's army disbanded. Hamilton was incorporated in 1810.

Hamler *Henry County.* Platted in 1875. Earlier this place was known as Belton. The name it now sports traces back to John Hamler.

Hamlet *Clermont County.* The site was initially referred to as Brown's Farm, since the land here was owned by a Farmer Brown. The burg arose about 1830. The current name has no Shakespearean roots; it is merely the old term for "small village."

Hammansburg *Wood County.* This town was surveyed in 1873 by W. H. Wood for William Hammond and Jacob Ackerman. Samuel Hamman was a member of the Board of Trade in this township in 1892, but it is uncertain whether the town name traces back to Hamman (or perhaps even to Hammond).

Hammond's Corners *Summit County.* The place-name is believed to refer to Jason Hammond, from Connecticut, who settled nearby Bath. (Bath was initially known as Hammondsburgh.) An attorney, Rolland O. Hammond (born 1826), practiced at Bath and served for four years as postmaster at Akron. Whether Rolland and Jason were related is not known.

Hammondsville *Jefferson County.* Charles Hammond owned the property on which this town was laid out in 1852.

Hancock *Hancock County.* Like the county, this diminutive community owes its name to John Hancock (1737–1793), the first signer of the Declaration of Independence and president of the Continental Congress.

Handwork's Corners *Mahoning County.* The surname Handwork belonged to at least five individuals residing in the county during its early years, and the place-name is probably tied to one of them or to a Handwork family.

Hanging Rock *Lawrence County.* A prominent sandstone cliff, four hundred feet high, inspired the name of this community. John Means is credited with founding it in 1820. Means operated an iron furnace here.

Hanover *Licking County.* A large number of Germans settled here, and Hanover was named for the city of Hannover, Germany. The village was incorporated in 1874.

Hanoverton *Columbiana County.* This community was platted by James Craig in 1813 and dubbed Hanover, perhaps because some of the original residents came from Hanover, Pennsylvania. The post office closed in 1815, and when residents reapplied for one in 1828, the Post Office Department added "ton" at the end of the name to distinguish it from the Hanover in Licking County.

Harbor Hills *Licking County.* Harbor Hills overlooks an inlet of Buckeye Lake, hence the name.

Harbor View *Lucas County.* Harbor View is so named because of its location on Maumee Bay. It was incorporated in 1910.

Hardin *Seneca County.* Platted in 1816. The proprietors were James Lenox, Thomas McClish, and Joseph Steinberger. The name was submitted by Colonel John Johnson to honor Colonel John Hardin of Kentucky (1753–1792), who had led many expeditions against Native Americans and was assassinated on this site by Shawnees.

Hardscrabble *Medina County.* Hardscrabble was first labeled Marysville, after the wife of Henry H. Coit, the owner of the property here. Later, it is said, there was a scramble (or scrabble) by immigrants to purchase land in this vicinity, and the name was changed to commemorate that period. The word *hardscrabble* also refers to getting a meager living on poor soil. The village was platted in 1837.

Harlem *Delaware County.* Laid out in 1849. Formerly known as Buddtown, the village adopted the name of a city in the Netherlands (now usually spelled Haarlem).

Harlem Springs *Carroll County.* Isaac Wiggins laid off lots in or before 1840. The "Harlem" aspect of the name has its roots in the Netherlands (see the preceding entry). Visitors were drawn to this spot by chalybeate (iron-rich) springs that were thought to have a beneficial effect.

Harley's *Fairfield County.* It is not known who or what "Harley" was named for, but a post office that opened here in 1889 was named Yelrah. That is Harley spelled backwards.

Harmar *Washington County.* When a post office opened here in 1813 on a point at the mouth of the Muskingum River, it was dubbed Point Harmar after nearby Fort Harmar. The fort had been named in honor of General Josiah Harmar in 1785. In 1841, the name of the post office was shortened to Harmar, and the hamlet took on the same truncated label.

Harper *Logan County.* Founded, 1851, by John Q. Williams. Several Harpers are mentioned in the history of the county, but one can only speculate on how this place-name may relate to them.

Harper *Ross County.* In 1798, Alexander Harper moved into this area, eventually locating on six hundred acres in Buckskin Township, in which this hamlet is situated. James and Robert Harper also settled here.

Harpersfield *Ashtabula County.* A number of the early residents arrived from Harpersfield, New York, and they decided to confer the same name on this place. The New York community was named for Joseph Harper, who moved there in 1771 from Connecticut. One of the first settlers to erect a dwelling near the Ohio Harpersfield was Joseph's son, Alex, in 1798. A separate source refers to the son as Captain Alexander C. Harper and credits him rather than his father with founding Harpersfield, New York, in 1770.

Harpster *Wyandot County.* Once known as Fowler (for C. R. Fowler, whose land abutted the town at the east), the village now bears the name of David Harpster. With John Wood, Harpster founded the town in 1876 on land they owned. Harpster also opened the first store here.

Harrietsville *Noble County.* Laid out, 1839, by Moses Spencer. The village name honors Spencer's daughter, Harriet, who became the town's first postmistress.

Harrisburg *Franklin County.* Founded, 1836, by Joseph Chenoweth. Chenoweth arrived here that year from the Pennsylvania capital, Harrisburg, and conferred the same name upon his new home.

Harrisburg *Stark County.* Jacob Matthias platted Harrisburg in 1827. The capital city of Pennsylvania was the inspiration for its name.

Harrison *Hamilton County.* Founded, 1810, by Jonas Crane. The ninth president of the United States, General William Henry Harrison (1773–1841), is the person for whom the town was named. Harrison lived in this region of Ohio, although never in this community. It is said that the earliest settlers arrived here before 1800, and that the town was laid out in 1813.

Harrisonville *Meigs County.* Laid out in 1840. The plotting of this village occurred during the Harrison-Tyler presidential campaign, and the place was named for General (later President) William Henry Harrison.

Harris Station *Ross County.* This place-name may relate to John Harris or his progeny. John had a large parcel of land surveyed in nearby Scioto Township in 1799. The "Station" segment of the name probably refers to a stop on the railroad that bisected the hamlet. The place is also known simply as Harris. Three Harrises, including John and Ira, dot the biographical roster in an early tome on the county's history. An archivist with the local historical society states that the place was "named for the postmaster."

Harrod *Allen County.* Platted, 1882, by J. Condant Smith. In the 1870s, when railroads were being built in the county, a station named Harrod was established. It was so named in tribute to William Harrod and his son, James, who operated a sawmill in the area and provided timber to the railroad for construction of the stationhouse. A small village sprang up around it, also taking the name Harrod. Incorporation occurred in 1889. Other early Harrods were Abram and, in the 1870s, Bert.

Harshaville *Adams County.* The history of this town parallels that of the Harsha Flouring Mills, around which the town grew. A post office was established here in 1864. Twenty-two Harshas appear in the biographical index of an early county history.

Hartford *Licking County.* The place was platted in 1824 by Elijah Durfey and Ezekiel Wells. The township's early settlers came from Connecticut and the place-name was taken from the city in that state. The township, too, was named Hartford.

Hartford *Trumbull County.* This town is located in Hartford Township, which was organized in 1811, taking its name from Hartford, Connecticut, the hometown of the first area settler, Edward Brockway (1799). The site was purchased in 1798 by Ephraim Root and Urial Holmes.

Hartleyville *Athens County.* William Hartley came here from Pennsylvania in the early 1800s.

Hartsgrove *Ashtabula County.* The community was originally called Matherstown, for Samuel Mather, who claimed to own the plot. Records showed, however, that William Hart of Connecticut was the proprietor. Following litigation, the village was organized in 1822 and named in honor of Hart.

Hartshorn *Monroe County.* David Hartshorn operated a general store here. The place-name probably came from his surname. Joseph P. Hartshorn was another family member associated with this locality. Samuel M. Hartshorn was born in Wayne Township, this county, the son of Samuel Hartshorn (1811–1891).

Hartville *Stark County.* Lots in this town were laid out in 1850 by Joseph Shollen-berger, George Held, and John Whitacre. The name may be a combination of part of the name of an early settler, John Morehart, and the Pennsylvania Dutch translation of "Willis" ("ville"). Incorporation took place in 1951.

Harveysburg *Warren County.* This village was founded in 1815 by William Harvey, who later (1827) purchased the site. The place is named for George Harvey, whose relationship to William is unknown.

Haselton *Mahoning County.* This name is thought to trace back to a person named John Haselton.

Haskins *Wood County.* The town takes its name from Whitcomb Haskins, one of sixteen children of twice-married Henry Haskins of Massachusetts. Whitcomb was born in Massachusetts in 1805 and from 1846 to 1860 owned the land where the village reposes. Henry's mother, Eunice Pierce Haskins, was a cousin of President Franklin Pierce.

Hatfield *Perry County.* Information about the origin of this place-name is scanty. A Hatfield family once resided here.

Hatton *Wood County.* The place was first known as East Millgrove Station. A post office was established here in 1882, and the name of the place was changed to Hatton in honor of the postmaster general.

Havana *Huron County.* A warehouse and store were constructed at this location by Horatio N. Owen, who dubbed the place Havana. At the time, there was a high level of American interest in Cuba, possibly accounting for Owen's choice of a name.

Havens *Sandusky County.* The community was named for Henry Havens. Henry's father, William, was born in New Jersey in 1775, and moved to Franklin County, Ohio, about 1815. Henry moved here to Jackson Township after marrying in 1831. He purchased 160 acres from the government for $1.25 an acre. During the ensuing years, portions of this acreage were passed on to various family members. Grain and other commodities were shipped by rail from Havens Station.

Havensport *Fairfield County.* Located on the Ohio Canal, this village, according to one source, was platted in 1831 by Isaac Havens. Another source states that the community was laid out by George Havens. Perhaps the two Havenses shared the founding duties. Another possibility is that one source provided the wrong given name.

Haverhill *Scioto County.* Aaron Burr was the first namesake of the community, when it was called Burrsburg by Jean G. Gervais, the first settler, in 1797. Emigrants from New England who arrived later renamed it for their native New Hampshire town.

Haviland *Paulding County.* Three Havilands are listed in a volume of county marriage records: Margaret in 1860, Mary Ann in 1860, and Martha in 1861. The place-name may relate to one or more of these individuals or their families.

Hawk *Vinton County.* An early settler, Wes Hawk, is said to be the person for whom the place was named.

Haydenville *Hocking County.* The community was founded in 1852 by Peter Hayden, an industrialist from Columbus, who viewed it as "the ideal town." Hayden is credited with recognizing the economic potential of the clay and coal deposits that existed here, and he constructed a facility for the manufacture of sewer pipe.

Hayesville *Ashland County.* Laid out in 1830 by Linus Hayes and John Cox. Its name honors Hayes.

Haynes *Hocking County.* The site is probably named for Jacob S. Haynes, a native of this township (Salt Creek), who farmed land here and served in the Civil War. His parents were Christopher and Annie, and Jacob was born in 1842.

Haynesville *Union County.* Jonathan Haynes laid out this town in 1838. It is not known who named the place for him.

Heath *Licking County.* In 1947, the Pure Oil Company established its Heath Refinery here on the outskirts of Newark. The place was incorporated as a village in 1952, and in 1965 it became a city.

Hebbardsville *Athens County.* This place-name traces back to P. G. Hebbard, born in this township (Alexander) in 1830, or to his forebears. P. G. was a farmer; his father, Alanson H., was an Athens County pioneer.

Hebron *Licking County.* This place-name probably comes from the Bible. The ancient city of Hebron is mentioned in Genesis, and it still stands, some twenty miles south of Jerusalem. It is one of the world's oldest inhabited communities.

Hector *Putnam County.* Laid out in 1882. The place was named in honor of Hector Havemeyer of the Hector Stave Company. The firm was a major industry in the town. E. W. Dimmock (or Dimmick) did the platting.

Hedges *Paulding County.* When the Continental Railroad was being constructed through this area, W. C. Hedges, a Tiffin resident, laid out several communities, including this one, which retained his name.

Heiser's Corners *Mahoning County.* This southern Milton Township place probably owes its name to Charles Heiser, listed in an 1874 county atlas as holding land at this spot.

Helena *Sandusky County.* In 1885, a general vote was cast and the name of this place was officially changed from Elkhorn to Helena. That was the name of the youngest daughter of Joseph Garn, who settled here about 1832. Incorporation took place in 1905. There was once quite an oil boom at Helena.

Helmick *Coshocton County.* The hamlet's name honors William Helmick, a member of Congress who represented this district.

Hemlock *Perry County.* This town name memorializes the formidable hemlock trees that stood at the site when it was being laid out.

Hendrysburg *Belmont County.* The town was laid out in 1828 by Charles Hendry. "Burg" was affixed to Hendry's name two years later, making both the post office and town Hendrysburg.

Henning's Mills *Clermont County.* The place was settled as early as 1836. The name was conferred as a compliment to J. N. Henning about the time he became the first postmaster, in 1858. Henning also is credited with being the founder of the village.

Hepburn *Hardin County.* Founded in 1882, this community honors Ohio native and Iowa congressman William Hepburn (1833–1916), joint author of the Pure Food and Drugs Act of 1906.

Herbert's Corners *Mahoning County.* This name may relate to Rees Herbert, born in Wales in 1804, who settled in the Youngstown area in 1842.

Herner's Corners *Trumbull County.* The Lewis Herner land parcels were located here, according to the 1874 county atlas. This fact probably accounts for the place-name.

Heslop *Washington County.* Heslops resided here in Lawrence Township as early as 1844. The place was named for the family.

Hessville *Sandusky County.* Sometime prior to 1835, this town was founded by Henry Bowman and Levi Hess. Levi was the son of David Hess, a proprietor of land in the vicinity at that time.

Hestoria *Brown County.* Laid out in 1860. This community took its name from a combination of the names of the wife (Hester) and daughter (Victoria) of Nicholas F. Devore.

Hickoryville *Warren County.* The town derived its name from a hickory grove at the site.

Hicks *Warren County.* This Wayne Township locale took its name from a Quaker, Elias Hicks.

Hicksville *Defiance County.* Founded in 1836 by Henry Hicks, Isaac Smith, and John Bryan, this community derived its name from Hicks. Incorporation came about in 1875.

Hiett *Brown County.* Young's Mill, located here on Eagle Creek, was owned by John Hiett, who also donated about half the money for construction of Hiett Chapel and was one of its first deacons. John and William Hiett settled near here in 1806, William having obtained three hundred acres. Other Hietts here included Eliza and Arbelus, and Samuel and Sarah. The site was known to some as Fizzleville.

Higby *Ross County.* It is believed that this place-name traces ultimately to Dexter Higbey, who arrived in the county in 1812. The spelling discrepancy is unaccounted for. Dexter's son Judah was a prominent farmer and wagonmaker. The Norfolk & Western Railroad located a station on a parcel of farmland he owned. Soon a post office was opened here as well. Both went by the name Higby.

Higginsport *Brown County.* One source claims that Robert Higgins settled at this spot in 1894 and the town was named for him—perhaps by him, too. The county's historical society, however, points to Colonel Robert Higgins as the namesake, saying that the colonel replatted the site in 1816. In 1804, according to the society, the place was referred to as White Haven.

High Hill *Muskingum County.* This tiny hamlet is at one of the highest elevations in this portion of the county. It is uncertain whether High Hill is the same as Gilbaut's

Hill, which was settled around 1825 by the Gillogly family. Charles Gilbaut was the patriarch of the family.

Highland *Highland County.* The village takes its name from the county, which was so named because it is on high land between the Little Miami and Scioto rivers. After being platted by John Connor in 1816, it was called Lexington. That name caused confusion with other like-named places, however, so the change was effected.

Highland Station *Highland County.* The hamlet takes its name from nearby Highland (see the preceding entry). "Station" was added because it was a stop on the Baltimore & Ohio Railroad.

Highlandtown *Columbiana County.* The name, recalling the Highlands of Scotland, stems from the considerable Scotch Presbyterian influence of early settlers in the county. It was first known as Inverness; some of its settlers came from that county in the Highlands. There are several other Scottish place-names in this county.

Hilliard *Franklin County.* This community was laid out in 1853 by John R. Hilliard and bears his name.

Hills and Dales *Stark County.* Developers probably applied this name to promote the Canton suburb. It was incorporated in 1929.

Hillsboro *Highland County (seat).* Laid out in 1807. The owner of the site was Benjamin Ellicott from Baltimore. The city is set on a hill, some seven hundred feet above a river. For most people, that explains the name. But one source offers another possibility, stating that a colorful character named Captain Billy Hill once resided here.

Hinckley *Medina County.* Known as the place to which the buzzards return annually (on or about March 15), Hinckley took its name from a Massachusetts judge, Samuel Hinckley. As a member of the Connecticut Land Company, Hinckley held the deed to land at this site.

Hiram *Portage County.* In 1804, Christopher Redding became the first permanent settler here. (One source states, however, that William Williams settled the place in 1799.) Colonel Daniel Tilden, proprietor of land in the township, reportedly suggested naming the site for Hiram (969–936 B.C.), the king of Tyre mentioned in the Old Testament, and it is said that his recommendation was endorsed unanimously. Hiram and his workman (also named Hiram) helped Solomon build the great temple, and one flowery source claims that Tilden and his fellow masons desired to honor "the widow's son, the Illustrious Ancient Master Workman on Solomon's Temple, and patron saint of the masons." Hiram was incorporated in 1893.

Hiram Rapids *Portage County.* This site near Hiram is on a stretch of the Cuyahoga River popular with enthusiasts of canoeing. (See the preceding entry.)

Hiramsburgh *Noble County.* The village takes its name from its founder, Hiram Calvert, and dates to about 1836. These days, it is often spelled without the concluding "h." A man named Talley settled the site.

Hitchcock *Jackson County.* Hitchcock, which dates to about 1903, is said to have been named for a Hitchcock brick plant that was located here. The plant is thought to have been built by William E. Dee of Chicago and later sold to a Hitchcock from Portsmouth, Ohio.

Hoagland *Highland County.* An early family named Hoagland resided here. At one time the place was commonly referred to as Hoagland's Crossing, possibly because the Baltimore & Ohio Railroad tracks crossed a creek here.

Hocking *Athens County.* See the next entry for an explanation of the name of this place.

Hockingport *Athens County.* "Hocking" comes from the Native American term *hockhocking,* which means "bottle." The village takes its name from the Hocking River; it reposes at the point where the Ohio and Hocking rivers merge. This waterway was navigable to Hockingport.

Holgate *Henry County.* In 1874, a group acquired land here. The purchasers were headed by William C. Holgate. Holgate was incorporated in 1881.

Holland *Lucas County.* An early settler here, given name uncertain, was a Mr. Hall. Desiring to christen the place after himself, he applied to the appropriate local authorities, requesting that the designation be Halland ("Hall-land"). It is thought that the name was misspelled by a clerk, resulting in Holland. The community was incorporated in 1924.

Holloway *Belmont County.* The Holloway family moved to this place from Virginia in 1827. In 1883, one member of the family, Isaac Holloway, platted this town, and his name was conferred upon it.

Hollowtown *Highland County.* This place was never platted but became somewhat of a trade center. Anthony Hollow is the person for whom it was named. Early in the 1800s, he operated a store at this location. The post office here was known as Ridings, the name of a local tradesman.

Holmesville *Holmes County.* At about this spot, Jonathan Grant and his son arrived on foot from Pennsylvania in 1809 and erected a cabin nearby. In 1817, the first white male and first white female born in Holmes County saw the light of day near Holmesville. The community takes it name from the county, which in turn is named for Major Andrew Holmes, a young officer in the War of 1812. Major Holmes was killed in August 1814.

Homer *Licking County.* Founded, 1816, by John Chonner. When the local post office opened, it took the name of Homer, the Greek poet, and the town followed suit. Prior to that, the community was known as Burlington.

Homer *Medina County.* Homer Township was organized in 1833. Its name and that of the hamlet honor the Greek poet Homer. The name is said to have been submitted by a preacher who rode a circuit in this area.

Homerville *Medina County.* This burg sprang up about 1839 and is in Homer Township. Both take their names from the Greek poet Homer.

Homeworth *Columbiana County.* As early as 1851, this community was known as Winchester (Middle Sandy Post Office). Because of the existence of another Winchester in Ohio, the names of the post office and village were changed to Homeworth in 1869. It is believed this choice was made simply because it was a pleasant place to live, or one "worthy of making your home." Prior to 1880, the H. Thomas Manufacturing Company made agricultural tools here in great quantity. It was important to Mr. Thomas that the place not be confused with other towns. He is thought to have been influential in getting the name changed to Homeworth.

Hooker *Fairfield County.* Once known as Hooker Station, this community was a stop on the Hocking Valley Railroad. An early owner of the property here was a Revolutionary War veteran named James Welk (or Wells), who obtained it around 1805, selling it to the Hookers who settled here in 1810: the Samuel Hooker, Sr., family and Samuel's bachelor brother, Richard. The latter served four terms as a state representative and twice as a state senator.

Hooksburgh *Morgan County.* Henry Hook arrived in Windsor Township in 1836. It is to him that the village owes its name. It is often spelled without the "h" on the end.

Hooven *Hamilton County.* This community was initially known as Berea. There is another Berea in Ohio, but it is not known if that is why this one was renamed. The current designation traces to a Colonel Hooven of Hamilton, Ohio, who bankrolled the Cincinnati Horseshoe & Iron Company.

Hopkinsville *Warren County.* This hamlet dates back to 1808. Three of the early merchants here were Boss Erwin, Matthias Rapp, and Colonel John Hopkins. The name of the latter was chosen for the site.

Horn's Mill *Fairfield County.* The first mill at this hamlet was the Ream Mill, later purchased by the Eckerts and known as Eckert Mill. Later still, the Horn family operated the facility, resulting in the current name. Fred Horn operated the mill, but it is uncertain whether his father, John George, did so. John George came to this county from Bavaria. The mill, first powered by the waters of the Hocking River, later got its power from a canal.

Hoskinsville *Noble County.* Platted, 1839, by John F. Talley. The name traces back to a Colonel Erastus Hoskins, who about 1825 started a church and school at this place. Hoskins did so in his capacity as one of the original members of a Methodist Episcopal congregation. Hoskins was also the first postmaster in the village.

Houcktown *Hancock County.* Laid out, 1853, by J. F. Houck. When founded, this hamlet was named North Liberty. A later addition (there were several) was made by A. M. Houck, presumably a relative of J. F. In 1856, when a post office was established, it was called Houcktown for the founder, so the town also took on that moniker.

Houston *Shelby County.* Platted in 1838. The site was settled about 1814 by Robert Houston. It was platted for Harvey Houston. The relationship between the two Houstons in not known. The survey was performed in 1838 by Jonathan Counts.

Howenstine *Stark County.* The place-name probably traces in some manner to George Howenstine, a farmer in this area. He was born in Pennsylvania in 1807.

Howland *Trumbull County.* The first settlers here were John Earl, Captain John Adgate, James Ward, Michael Pelts, John Reeves, and John Daily. The place is also known as Howland Corners. The township land was purchased in 1812 by James Howland.

Hoytville *Wood County.* William Hoyt and G. B. Mills had this place surveyed in 1873. Hoyt's surname lives on in the town's designation.

Hubbard *Trumbull County.* Nehemiah Hubbard purchased all or most of the surrounding township land in 1801. The city bears his name. Incorporation occurred in 1868.

Huber *Hancock County.* Several Hubers resided in the general area at an early time, but it has not been possible to attribute this place-name to any one of them with certainty. Benjamin Huber was a prominent grist mill operator on Eagle Creek from 1846 until 1865. He also served several terms as county treasurer. His sons, Jacob and Samuel, were pharmacists in Findlay. A Huber School was built in 1889 in southwest Findlay.

Huber Heights *Montgomery County.* Developer-builder Charles Huber is the person from whom the community took its name. Another Huber, Peter F., born in 1844, also became prominent in this locality. H. Loran Huber was born in 1863. Huber Heights was incorporated in 1981.

Hudson *Summit County.* Town founder David Hudson came here from Goshen, Connecticut. At the time of founding, in 1800, there were no other communities in Summit County. Incorporation took place in 1837.

Hue *Vinton County.* A source within Vinton County speculates that this site is so named because of the colorful autumn scenery at the locale. It is on the side of a hill in extremely hilly country "and the trees are just beautiful in the spring and fall." This explanation seems somewhat dubious, but it is the only one available.

Hulington *Clermont County.* At the point where Ulrey's Run intersected the path of the Cincinnati & Portsmouth Railroad, Albert J. Huling laid out a town in 1877. It became known, aptly, as Hulington.

Hull *Athens County.* This tiny site owes its name to S. T. Hull, Wakeman Hull, or the Hull family. S. T. arrived in this township (Lodi) in 1839; his son, Hiram, was born in 1848. Wakeman was a trustee in the township in 1840, 1843, and 1846–1848.

Hull Prairie *Wood County.* Surveyed in 1861 for John H. Weller, C. W. Carpenter, and Joseph H. Gardner. The land here was once owned by David Hull, who settled in 1822. The prairie takes its name from David Hull.

Hume *Allen County.* The place-name honors Alex F. Hume, who at one time held a state Supreme Court judgeship.

Hunchbarger's Corners *Darke County.* Sometimes seen spelled as Hunchberger's, this hamlet owes its identity to an early merchant and blacksmith, Jacob Hunchbarger.

Hunt *Knox County.* The site was sometimes referred to as Hunt's Station, which was actually a short distance west on the Baltimore & Ohio Railroad. The name is thought to recognize a Revolutionary War veteran, Jonathan Hunt, who built an inn at the corner of Newark and Sycamore roads.

Hunter *Belmont County.* Laid out, 1849, by Nathaniel Anderson. W. F. Hunter of Monroe County was the inspiration for the name of this town. At the time, he was a congressman representing this district.

Huntersville *Hardin County.* Laid out and platted by Thomas Hitchcock in 1836. Huntersville was named out of respect for Hitchcock's friend, Jabez Hunter.

Huntington *Lorain County.* Located in a township of the same name, this place takes its name from Huntington, Connecticut. Several immigrants to this place came from the Connecticut village. Huntington, Ohio, was incorporated in 1822.

Hunting Valley *Cuyahoga County.* This entity in the Chagrin Valley was named for the bucolic nature of the setting. It was incorporated in 1924.

Huntsburg *Geauga County.* The land here was purchased in 1803 by John Breck and Eben Hunt of Connecticut. Hunt's name became attached to the community.

Hunt's Corners *Huron County.* Hiel Hunt, for whom this site was named, settled initially in Venice, Ohio, in 1816. At some later date, he moved here. He is said to have passed away at the age of 100.

Huntsville *Butler County.* The hamlet was founded by Thomas Hunt about 1800. Hunt died in 1814 at age sixty-five.

Huntsville *Logan County.* Laid out and surveyed, 1846, by Alex Harbison. Aaron L. Hunt, who toiled as a surveyor in this county, is the person for whom Huntsville was named.

Hurford *Harrison County.* Twenty-five Hurfords are listed in a county history index. John Hurford lived in Green Township, just a mile or so south of the township where the hamlet designated Hurford is situated. John died in 1846. Joseph Hurford, of this county, was born in 1809. Both were prominent early settlers of British lineage. The families reportedly were linear descendants of Lord John Hurford.

Huron *Erie County.* The city is named for the township it is in, which in turn is named for the Huron River. The place was the site of a trading post run by the French in 1749. Huron Township was established in 1817. French-Canadian in origin, the word *huron* is said to translate generally as "rough person." Canada's French used the term in reference to the Native Americans who became known as the Hurons. When they moved into the northern United States, they changed their tribal name to Wyandot. In 1804, Jean Baptiste Flammond founded this city. The first Yankee here was probably Jared Ward, who came in 1808. Huron was incorporated in 1835.

Hustead *Clark County.* Early area settlers having the Hustead surname left that mark on the hamlet.

Hyatt's *Delaware County.* Henry A. Hyatt mapped this community in 1876, when it was dubbed Hyattsville. A year later, when the post office opened with Hyatt as postmaster, the name was shortened.

Iberia *Morrow County.* Founded in 1827. Platted, 1832, by landowners Frederick Meyers and Samuel Foster. Robert Rowland, a young man who was visiting relatives here, suggested the name. Rowland apparently had traveled extensively and had encountered the name Iberia (which refers to the homeland of the Spanish and Portuguese) labeling a town in South America. The name impressed him with its beauty, and when he submitted it as a possible cognomen for this Morrow County place, townspeople accepted it at once.

Iler *Seneca County.* Possibly the first settler here was Henry Huffman, in 1827. Jacob Iler, a native of Pennsylvania, arrived in 1832, and the village was named for him. It was not until 1885 that the community obtained a post office, which was incorporated into a general store.

Ilesboro *Hocking County.* In 1835, Henry Iles, the property owner, laid out a town here. For a time it was spelled Ilesborough.

Independence *Cuyahoga County.* Founded, 1830, by L. Strong. This city is in Independence Township. A newspaper article states that New Englanders who settled the locality desired to be "independent" of nearby Cleveland. Another theory holds that the community was named in honor of Independence Day. Incorporation took place in 1914.

Indian Camp *Guernsey County.* Indian Camp is on Indian Camp Run, at a site that had indeed seen Native American encampments. Later, five mills operated on the stream.

Indian Hill *Hamilton County.* Incorporated in 1941, this city traces back its name to a legend passed down through the generations. According to the story, Native Americans were accused of stealing three horses from the Nelson's Station (Madisonville) settlement. Settlers pursued them and shot one who had been unfortunate enough to select a lame horse. Years later, his body was discovered on a farm on a hill above Madisonville, giving birth to the name Indian Hill as a designation for this place. Early owners of the land in this section were Judge John Symmes, followed by Major Benjamin Stites. The Shawnee, Miami, and Delaware tribes had frequented the area.

Ink *Seneca County.* It is possible this hamlet was named for Morgan Ink, an early secretary of the Seneca County Agricultural Society.

Irondale *Jefferson County.* Originally the site wore the label Pottsdale, for Samuel Potts. Later it was Huntersville, for John Hunter, manager of the coal company that breathed new life into the town in 1816. The current name relates to the Pioneer Iron Company and was assigned in 1869. Pioneer mined ore and established a rolling mill at this location. The community arose about 1806 around a salt well operated by Potts. In 1949, Irondale was incorporated.

Iron Spot *Muskingum County.* John H. Beem laid out the community, which became known as Beem City. Later, owing to heavy mineral deposits in the township, the place-name was changed.

Ironton *Lawrence County (seat)*. At the hub of southern Ohio's "Hanging Rock" iron region, Ironton undoubtedly owes its name to the pig iron industry that flourished here during more prosperous years. In 1851, Ironton incorporated.

Irville *Muskingum County*. The story is told locally of John Irvine, who had a wooden leg. This handicap tended to keep him close to home, so he founded a town in order to attract residents who could keep him company. The place-name derives from Irvine.

Irwin *Union County*. One source states that Irwin was also known as Irwin Station, a site that was platted but never recorded. It was laid out in honor of an early settler, a Mr. Irwin, but never flourished. A second account comes from a 1976 centennial booklet, which contains an 1876 plat map reflecting what seems to have been a busy little village: "Irwin was so named in honor of one of the early settlers, William B. Irwin, a son of John Irwin, who in 1806 settled on a farm in the southwest corner of Union Township, present site of the Village of Irwin." John Irwin was born in 1770 in York County, Pennsylvania, while William Brisbane Irwin was born in Ohio County, Virginia, in 1795. William became a brigadier general in the militia and served the county as both a commissioner and county surveyor.

Island Creek *Jefferson County*. Island Creek is also the name of the township. The hamlet takes its name from a stream emptying into the Ohio River opposite Brown's Island at Costonia. The creek runs west to east.

Isleta *Coshocton County*. Locals spin a tale of the town's label being the name of an attractive young woman. It is said she was the heartthrob of the railroad's chief engineer when a rail line was being constructed through the area.

Ithaca *Darke County*. The city of Ithaca, New York, is the place for which this community was named. The Darke County site was laid out in 1832 and incorporated in 1840.

Ivorydale *Hamilton County*. Ivory soap was once manufactured in this town by Procter & Gamble, which has its headquarters in nearby Cincinnati.

Jackson *Crawford County*. It is likely this place-name relates to Phares Jackson, a judge in about 1845, or to a justice of the peace named Thomas Jackson.

Jackson *Jackson County (seat).* Platted in 1816 and 1819. The name honors the hero of the War of 1812 and president (1829–1837) of the United States, Andrew Jackson. Incorporation of the place, now a city, was in 1842.

Jacksonburg *Butler County.* Laid out, 1816, by John Baird, John Craig, and Henry Weaver. In 1818, a post office was established here, which went by the name Jacksonboro (later Jacksonborough). The place is thought to have been named for the hero of the Battle of New Orleans and president, Andrew Jackson. Incorporation took place in 1835. The post office was discontinued in 1903.

Jackson Ridge *Monroe County.* This ridge was settled in 1816 by Abraham Jackson, his wife, and their young son, Robert. They arrived from Fayette County, Pennsylvania.

Jacksontown *Licking County.* The proprietor, Thomas Harris, laid out this town. It is named for the hero of New Orleans, Andrew Jackson. The town dates to circa 1826.

Jacksonville *Adams County.* Laid out, 1815, by William Thomas. The community was named out of respect for "Old Hickory," Andrew Jackson.

Jacksonville *Athens County.* Oliver D. Jackson laid out the place, which bears his name, in 1882. That same year, he opened a coal mine not far away. Jackson was the proprietor of coal-rich land in the valley.

Jacobsburg *Belmont County.* The hamlet bears the name of Jacob Calvert, who, in 1815, laid out the place.

Jacobsburg *Monroe County.* The label may refer to the first postmaster (1858) at the site, Jacob H. Hamilton. However, fifteen persons with the Jacobs surname are listed in an early county biographical index.

Jacobsport *Coshocton County.* Jacob Waggoner laid the village out in 1836.

Jamestown *Greene County.* Surveyed, 1815, by Thomas P. Mooreman and a Mr. Thomas. Martin Mendenhall and Thomas Browder were the original proprietors. The name stems from Jamestown, Virginia. Browder, who was born in the Virginia city, suggested that the name be adopted for this site. The incorporation process was consummated in 1842.

Jasper *Pike County.* Laid out in 1833 by Ohio Governor Robert Lucas, the place is said to be named for a Sergeant Jasper, a hero of the Revolutionary War.

Jasper Mills *Fayette County.* William Jasper is the person after whom this hamlet was named.

Jaysville *Darke County.* An early settler here was Isaac Jay, who owned the land where Jaysville eventually arose.

Jefferson *Ashtabula County (seat).* In 1805, owner Gideon Granger surveyed this locale into lots suitable for families to build upon. It was named out of admiration for President Thomas Jefferson (1743–1826).

Jefferson *Pickaway County.* Laid out, 1803, by Henry Nevill. It is said that the founder of the town built a tavern here. On the tavern's front was a sign that bore the likeness of Thomas Jefferson, and thus the place came to be known as Jefferson.

Jeffersonville *Fayette County.* Jeffersonville is in Jefferson Township. Thomas Jefferson, the nation's third president, is the person from whom both town and township take their name.

Jelloway *Knox County.* Laid out, 1840, by Freeman Pipher and originally called Brownsville. The current name memorializes Tom Jelloway, a Native American chief whose tribe often camped near this site, on the banks of Big Jelloway Creek or Little Jelloway Creek.

Jenera *Hancock County.* Platted in 1883. The first physician to serve the town, A. B. Jener, is the person to whom the name traces back. The town was incorporated in 1892. It was settled well before formalization as a village.

Jericho *Butler County.* The early community was built mostly by Squire McLean. David Lee's was the first house; it was constructed in 1841. The name comes, perhaps, from Jericho, New York, but eventually traces back to the prehistoric town of Jericho. That place, which is mentioned in both the Old and New Testaments, is regarded as the oldest city in the world. It is in the Jordan River Valley, five miles from the northern terminus of the Dead Sea and seventeen miles from Jerusalem. A Bible dictionary speculates that the name means "moon city" or "place of fragrance."

Jerles *Monroe County.* The first postmaster at this location, in 1884, was Thomas F. Jerles. The place likely adopted his name.

Jeromeville *Ashland County.* Laid out, 1815, by Christian Deardorff and William Vaughn. This place was named in recognition of the French trader John (or Jean) Baptiste Jerome, the original proprietor of the land. A white scouting party visited this place as early as 1761.

Jerry City *Wood County.* John Smith had this town site surveyed in 1861 by J. Hastings. The town is named for a businessman in Fostoria, Jerry Nesslerode. It had originally been called Stulltown, after an early settler at the site, and later Shiloh, which duplicated the name of another Ohio place. Jerry City was incorporated in 1876.

Jersey *Licking County.* Laid out, 1832, by Lewis Headley, Edward Beecher, Wickliffe Condit, and Andrew Pierson. The village and township name (Jersey) is a consequence of Headley's having hailed from New Jersey. Emigrants were coming to the area prior to 1820; a post office opened in 1830.

Jerusalem *Monroe County.* This village was never platted. In 1825, it was settled by James Vernon and William Kennard. Subsequently a group of Orthodox Friends built a church in the northeast sector of the town, while the Hixites established one in another sector. The story is that the community got its name when John Powell referred to the one as Jerusalem and the other as Jericho.

Jewell *Defiance County.* A former postmaster general, Marshall Jewell, is the person honored in the naming of this community.

Jewett *Harrison County.* The place-name may trace back to Thomas L. Jewett or his family. Jewett served as a prosecutor in the county from 1844 to 1848 and as a judge from 1852 to 1854. One source states that the name is in recognition of a one-time president of the Pittsburgh, Cincinnati, & St. Louis Railroad, T. M. Jewett. Whether Thomas L. and T. M. were related is not known. An earlier name for this site was Fairview.

Job's *Hocking County.* One account states that the place took the name of an enthusiastic and skilled coal miner or mining company official named Job.

Jobtown *Belmont County.* Jobtown was named in honor of an early resident, P. H. Job, in about 1888.

Joetown *Morgan County.* At an early date, the community boasted only three houses, all owned by men named Joe: J. Risen, J. Newlon, and J. Morin.

Johnson *Fayette County.* According to a newspaper item, this hamlet took its name from Jesse Johnson.

Johnson's Island *Ottawa County.* This place was originally named Bull's Island, after its first owner. But when L. B. Johnson bought it in 1852, it became Johnson's Island. "It had been an Indian torturing ground for both whites and Indians," one historical source notes. However, it was best known as a Union prison for Confederate officers.

Johnston *Trumbull County.* Located in Johnston Township, this place bears the name of Captain James Johnston of Salisbury, Connecticut, who purchased the tract of land from the Connecticut Land Company.

Johnston Corners *Trumbull County.* Located near Johnston in Johnston Township, this intersection takes its name from Captain James Johnston of Salisbury, Connecticut, who purchased the land here from the Connecticut Land Company.

Johnstown *Licking County.* An early landowner, James Johnston, gives his name to this community; the discrepancy in spelling is not accounted for. An alternative source claims that Dr. Oliver Bigelow of New York State laid out the town in 1813, probably naming it for the city of Johnstown, New York.

Johnsville *Morrow County.* John Ely and William H. Shauck laid out the town in 1834. It was named for Ely by adding "ville" to the possessive of his first name.

Jones City *Putnam County.* Platted in 1890. The community was set off for R. W. and Ella Jones by the surveyor, Evan Jones.

Jonestown *Van Wert County.* Founded in 1886 and platted in 1887. The first grain elevator at this site was erected by Evan B. Jones, with the community retaining his surname. Jones died in 1891.

Joy *Morgan County.* An oil well drilled here on a Mr. Joy's farm to a depth of less than two hundred feet nonetheless produced as much as 1,400 barrels per day, according to a 1902 book compiled by the state geologist.

Judson *Athens County.* William Judson was the first postmaster here in 1889.

Jumbo *Hardin County.* This place-name came as a result of residents' desire for a post office. The storekeeper who sought the office in 1885 was required to submit a name. Having just read that Jumbo, promoted by P. T. Barnum as the largest elephant in the world, had been struck by a train and killed in Canada, the storekeeper nominated Jumbo as the name.

Junction City *Perry County.* The settlement developed as a railroad junction town, resulting in the name.

Junior Furnace *Scioto County.* The builders who in 1826 had erected the Franklin Furnace iron works in this county (see the Franklin Furnace entry) in 1828 constructed the Junior Furnace iron works, which, as the name implies, was smaller. Like the larger furnace, the newer one supported a surrounding community that took on its name.

Justus *Stark County.* A farmer, Andrew Putnam, and a flour mill partner, William H. Justus, laid out and recorded the initial plat plan for the town in 1874. One of the miller's descendants, Fred W. Justus, later became the postmaster at nearby Massillon.

Kalida *Putnam County.* The village was platted in 1834 and incorporated in 1839. The name reportedly means "beautiful."

Kanauga *Gallia County.* A native of this community states that its first name was Fair Haven and that it was part of the Ohio Land Grant. Kanauga was laid out for the French Five Hundred, whose settlement was moved four miles downriver in 1790. When the question of a post office name for this hamlet arose, it was observed that there were two Fair Havens in Ohio, and the one in Gallia County was selected for re-naming. The first postmaster, reportedly a Mr. Pausley, christened the town Kanauga from two Indian names, *Kanau*, from the Kanawha River, which intersects the Ohio here, and *Auga*, from the Chickamauga Creek, just beyond the hills behind the town.

Kansas *Seneca County.* *American Place-Names* states that this place was named for the Kansas Territory in 1855, "when the name was much in the news because of the slavery question." According to the same source, a tribe of Native Americans was referred to by the French as *Kansa*, while the Spaniards termed them *Escansaque*.

Keene *Coshocton County.* This burg was laid out in 1820 by Jesse Beals, who came from Keene, New Hampshire.

Keith *Noble County.* Among the earliest settlers here were Mary Keith, year uncertain, and Peter and Benjamin Keith from Pennsylvania. Blacksmiths and bellmakers, Peter and Benjamin made bells for many customers in and out of the county. James Farley and Peter Keith opened a store here. P. W. Keith operated a grist mill nearby in 1861. In 1870, Adam Keith was a charter member of the Oddfellows Lodge. And in 1881, the Keith & Cunningham store was a popular place to meet.

Kelley's Island *Erie County.* The island in Lake Erie was purchased from its Connecticut owner in 1833 by two brothers, Irad and Datus Kelley of Cleveland. A third brother, Alfred, was the mastermind behind the Ohio Canal. Kelley's Island once bore the name Cunningham's Island, after a squatter named Cunningham who is said to have been the island's only resident, sometime before the War of 1812.

Kelloggsville *Ashtabula County.* Settled in 1799 by Colonel Stephen Moulten, this place was purchased by three Ferguson brothers and became known as Ferguson's Settlement. Later the brothers divested themselves of the site and Amos and Martin Kellogg became the new owners, but the Ferguson's Settlement name persisted until 1814. The name transition probably took place after Amos Kellogg became the first postmaster. The post office was located in his home.

Kelsey *Belmont County.* When the railroad passed through these environs, one farm that it cut through was owned by William J. Kelsey. When a minuscule hamlet arose around the train station, the place became known as Kelsey.

Kendal *Stark County.* Thomas Rotch named this community, now a ward of Massillon, for a manufacturing town in northern England.

Kent *Portage County.* Settled, 1805, by John Haymaker and his wife. This place was originally known as Franklin Mills, and an adjoining sector of it was known as Carthage. Aaron Olmsted of Hartford, Connecticut, owned the land here and decreed the name to be Franklin, after his son. In 1832, Zenas Kent purchased property here. The current place-name honors him. A relative, Marvin Kent, became governor of Ohio. Kent today is Portage County's most populous municipality. Incorporation took place in 1920.

Kenton *Hardin County (seat).* Platted in 1833. Kenton is the namesake of Indian fighter Simon Kenton. Now a city, it was incorporated in 1845.

Kerr *Gallia County.* Right-of-way for a railroad through this place was deeded by John N. Kerr, who owned a thousand acres here and, in 1874, served on a commission to plan a narrow-gauge rail line to serve the area. In return, the railroad was to establish a station at the site. Kerr's son was installed as station agent. In 1875, a post office was opened, with C. W. Kerr as first postmaster. He held this position until he sold his business to his son, R. S. Kerr. Sometimes the place is referred to as Kerr Station. Another Kerr—George—farmed land just west of Woodsfield. His relationship to John, if any, is unknown.

Kerr *Monroe County.* This place-name probably leads back to George Kerr, who farmed just west of Woodsfield. In 1874, John Kerr served on a commission to plan a narrow-gauge rail line to serve the area.

Kessler *Miami County.* A number of Kesslers resided and worked near this place outside West Milton. W. S. Kessler practiced law in this locale starting about 1886. He was born in Union Township, Miami County. Wirt Kessler was involved in real estate and insurance, taught, and farmed. He was a son of William B. and Mary A. Kessler. A. H. Kessler was a railway postal clerk. One of the Kesslers was postmaster at West Milton beginning in 1898.

Kettering *Montgomery County.* Charles F. ("Boss") Kettering, inventor of the cash register and the automotive self-starter, is the person for whom this city was named. Kettering resided here, according to a newspaper account. By 1951, Kettering took up virtually the entire township, and the township government could not supply its needs. Voters asked for the name and incorporation in their petition and got their wishes in 1952.

Kettlersville *Shelby County.* Platted in 1873, this village was established on land owned by Christopher Kettler.

Keystone Station *Jackson County.* The nearby Keystone Furnace hauled pig iron to its switch here on the Baltimore & Ohio Railroad, a site known as Keystone Station. The Keystone State is the nickname of Pennsylvania, but it is unclear whether there was a Pennsylvania connection to the furnace operation here.

Kidron *Holmes County.* Two naming accounts are set forth in the book *Sonnenberg—Haven and Heritage* by James O. Lehman. One states that George Ross, who resided east of Jericho, named this place Kidron when he sought to open a post office. Although other names were submitted, residents seemed to like Kidron. "Brook Kidron" ran through Ross's farm, "so it must have reminded him of the romantic scenery of Palestine and its streams, valleys, and hills, as well as its well-known villages and cities." The second explanation holds that when community leaders met to settle on a name and thus obtain a post office, W. H. Lehman suggested the name Cheese Factory Town, owing to the presence here of a cheese factory. But Nicholas and Cleophas Amstutz instead insisted upon a biblical name. "Cleophas was blindfolded, then opened the Bible at random, rested his finger upon an open page, removed the blindfold, and found that the nearest place-name to his finger was 'the brook Kidron.'" In the Bible, Kidron is a usually waterless valley east of Jerusalem that divides the eastern parts of the city from the Mount of Olives.

Kidron Station *Wayne County.* Kidron Station served as a rail stop for the Kidron area. It is thought to date to 1828. See the preceding entry for an explanation of the naming.

Kiefer *Coshocton County.* Initially this site was dubbed Ridgeway. The postmaster general suggested that the name be changed to avoid confusion with another place. The current name honors a General Kiefer.

Kieferville *Putnam County.* Platted, 1870, by Lewis E. Holtz. The town's name honors D. A. Kiefer.

Kilbourne *Delaware County.* First known as Eden, this community was platted in 1835 by Isaac Leonard and Daniel G. Thurston. It was named Eden because of its lush vegetation and multiplicity of animals. In 1837, the name was changed to the given name of the first postmaster, Kilbourne M. Thrall. (Postal records in one instance refer to Coton Thrall; however, historians seem in agreement that the first name of Kilbourne Thrall was used for the place-name.)

Kilesville *Madison County.* Nine Kiles are listed in the biographical index of an early county history. It is thought that this hamlet owes its name to James A. Kile, born in 1834, who farmed near Plain City in this township (Darby). The town may also be found listed as Kileville or simply Kile. One source states that the place "was named for the Kile family" and was "probably founded sometime between 1875 and 1900." The same source says that the Kile family owned and operated the town grain elevator for three generations. The second-generation owner, Elton M. Kile, graduated in 1912 from law school at Ohio State University.

Kilgore *Carroll County.* This name recognizes Daniel Kilgore, a representative to the U.S. Congress from Cadiz, Ohio. John Abel laid out the community.

Killbuck *Holmes County.* Settled in 1811. This village was named for a Native American known as Killbuck, who played a prominent role in events of the region. The place was first known as Shrimplin's Settlement, after the earliest white settler,

Abraham Shrimplin. A less likely version claims a settlement date of 1882 and theorizes that the village was named when an Indian hunter killed a buck and shouted, "Kill 'em buck!"

Kilvert *Athens County.* Samuel Kilvert, once involved in the coal business locally, is the person for whom the place was named.

Kimbolton *Guernsey County.* Located in Liberty Township, this village too was once called Liberty. The current name is said to come from a town in England. It was recommended to the citizens by a man they all respected, Naphtali Luccock. Luccock was journeying westward when he stopped in the hamlet, which was not flourishing. Townspeople convinced him to stay and open a store. Luccock became prominent in the community, and it eventually grew. He suggested the name in 1850 when a post office was obtained. Kimbolton was incorporated in 1885.

Kinderhook *Pickaway County.* In an earlier day, this community, situated on the C&MV Railroad, was known variously as Yellow Bud Station and Yellow Bird. Postal officials often confused it with Yellowbud, Ross County. The name was changed to Kinderhook by a railroad official, probably in honor of "Old Kinderhook," President Martin Van Buren (1782–1862).

Kingsbury *Meigs County.* Kingsbury Creek was probably named for an early Bedford Township settler named Harland Kingsbury. The hamlet also is probably named for Harland.

King's Corners *Trumbull County.* A Connecticut native, ironworker Barber King, moved here to Howland Township in 1806. At least four generations of the family farmed here, including James Franklin King. Other local Kings included William and Sarah McConnell King and their son, J. M. King, the latter born in Kinsman Township in 1825. Robert King served as a justice of the peace in the area.

King's Mills *Warren County.* This place-name leads back to the King Powder Company, founded in 1878 by J. W. and A. King. The "Mills" aspect of the name referred to the Great Western Powder Mills. The community had formerly been Gainsboro, laid out by Ralph Hunt in 1815.

Kingston *Ross County.* Founded in 1805 by Thomas Ing. Ing dubbed the village Ingston. Some locals objected, and the designation became Kingston.

Kingsville *Ashtabula County.* Established in 1810. From Forbesville, the name of this town evolved, through common usage, to Forbestail and Forbesdale. An Ohio historian, J. H. Galbreath, states that the name was changed to Kingsville after a man named King promised to furnish two dollars' worth of liquor to the residents if they would take his name for the name of the town. Since they desired a name-change for the place, they happily accepted his offer. In a variant account, the claim is made that Kingsville was initially known as Fobes Dale, in honor of the first permanent settler, Captain Walter Fobes. This version goes on to state that the name did not sit well with certain citizens, and eventually the designation was changed to Norwich, for Norwich, Connecticut. However, since Fobes had been born in that town, some residents felt it was still unnecessarily deferential to Fobes. Here the account dovetails more or less with the Galbreath version by averring that a Conneaut man named King offered four gallons of whiskey if the townspeople would adopt his own surname as the place-name. And the rest, as they say, is history.

Kingsville *Tuscarawas County.* John King platted the village in 1831.

Kingsville *Union County.* Levi Phelps surveyed this venue in 1834 for Samuel King. The place adopted Samuel's surname.

Kingsway *Sandusky County.* This site took its name from an early postmaster here, George W. King. King was also a director and stockholder of the Kingsway Grain and Elevator Company. A native of Fairfield County, born in 1840, he spent nearly his entire life in Sandusky County. He also served as the local justice of the peace. Kingsway is on the Wheeling & Lake Erie Railroad.

Kinnikinnick *Ross County.* This place is on Kinnikinnick Creek. The name is a Native American word that is said to translate as "a mixture of tobacco with red willow."

Kinsey *Montgomery County.* The name of this community undoubtedly traces back to early settler David Kinsey (circa 1806).

Kinsman *Trumbull County.* Both this place and Kinsman Township take their name from John Kinsman. One source claims that he arrived in 1799 and originally owned the site as well as other extensive tracts in this region. Other settlers began arriving in 1802.

Kipling *Guernsey County.* The place was formerly called Rigby, then Klondyke. When the Post Office Department rejected both names, a committee submitted to postal authorities a list of names of famous living men, including Gladstone, Dewey, and McKinley. These too were rejected. Kipling, for the British author of *The Jungle Book* and *Captains Courageous,* Rudyard Kipling (1865–1936), was then suggested and subsequently accepted.

Kipton *Lorain County.* This name is said to trace back to a prominent Railway Express employee from Buffalo named Kip. Postal history reveals that a post office opened here in 1837 was called Ponoislise. Shortly thereafter the name was changed to North Camden (it is in Camden Township). But after the railroad station was erected in 1852, the place became known as Camden Station. The following year, when lots were laid off by proprietor William H. Whitney for a town, the intent was to name it after Whitney's hometown, Binghamton, New York. Somehow that plan never materialized, and the last name utilized, Kipton, remains the designation.

Kirby *Wyandot County.* Laid out in 1854. The village was surveyed by Dr. J. H. Williams for M. H. Kirby.

Kirkersville *Licking County.* Dr. William C. Kirker in 1832 laid out this village, which came to be known by his name. It was incorporated in 1910.

Kirkpatrick *Marion County.* Formerly Letimberville, this place was laid out in 1833 by Marturen Letimbra. Later the name was changed to that of a blacksmith who operated a shop in this community.

Kirkwood *Belmont County.* This community was laid out by Joseph Kirkwood, son of Captain Robert Kirkwood, in 1834.

Kirkwood *Shelby County.* The original name of this place was Pontiac, a word that has Native American connections. Owing to the existence of another place named Pontiac, the village was renamed Kirkwood in 1879 in honor of D. Kirkwood Gillespie, who operated a grain elevator here.

Kirtland *Lake County.* The village was founded in 1817. The name came from the resident-general of the Connecticut Land Company, Turhand Kirtland, an eminent figure in the history of this area. His eldest son, Dr. Jared Potter Kirtland, was founder of the Cleveland Medical College.

Kirtland Hills *Lake County.* This village near Kirtland was named in honor of Dr. Jared Potter Kirtland, a noted naturalist who taught at Willoughby College and founded the Cleveland Medical College. (See also the preceding entry.) The village was incorporated in 1926.

Kitchen *Jackson County.* Cemetery inscriptions in this township attest to a former concentration of persons named Kitchen. Kitchens commemorated on local gravestones include B. Frederick, Benjamin F., Mildred M., R. Franklin, David M., Donald, Lora M., John R., Mary Jane, and Orson S. One source speculates that a rural store and post office were named for a country physician practicing here when the Cincinnati, Hamilton, & Dayton Railroad came through.

Kitts' Hill *Lawrence County.* A number of folks with the surname Kitts lived in this vicinity. No doubt this place-name is traceable to one or more of these families. The Kittses included Edward F., born 1843; his wife, Mary, born the same year; Emma Willis, born 1877; Rose, born 1870; Normal D., born 1897; Ella Jenkins, born 1874; Bessie, born 1895; George, birth year not clear; and Madie, died 1895.

Kline's Corners *Trumbull County.* The most extensive early landholder in this township (Liberty) was Peter Kline. His family was from Pennsylvania.

Knaufville *Mahoning County.* Shortly after 1802, an individual or family with the Knauf surname came to this area. The community probably is named after that person or family.

Knockemstiff *Ross County.* One source reports a possible explanation for this place-name: "Supposedly a preacher came into the village on horseback. He saw a man and woman physically fighting. The minister asked what the name of the town was. 'I'll answer you as soon as I knock him stiff,' she is said to have replied." But an archivist for the area historical society reports that the place "allegedly received its name from the moonshiners and roughnecks who lived there. The liquor of the former and fisticuffs of the latter would 'knock 'em stiff.'" A local historian states that *knockemstiff* was a slang term for a homemade brew produced in the area in earlier days. The fact that nearby New Straitsville holds a Moonshine Festival each May lends credibility to the latter explanation.

Knoxville *Jefferson County.* Henry Knox (1750–1806), the first U.S. secretary of war, is the person for whom this community was named. The site is in Knox Township.

Kossuth *Auglaize County.* The name honors the Hungarian revolutionary hero Louis Kossuth (1802–1894), who visited the United States in 1851–1852. In 1848 he served as his country's finance minister.

Kuhn *Monroe County.* Peter Kuhn came to this township (Malaga) about 1847 from Germany. Elias Kuhn and John Kuhn appear as landowners on an early plat map of the area.

Kunklesville *Williams County.* Henry S. Kunkle, one in a succession of storekeepers at the location, is said to have laid out the town. His grandfather, also Henry S., served as a county commissioner. The community, known variously as Kunkle, Kunkle's Corners, and Kunklesville, sprang up around 1855.

Kyle *Butler County.* Also referred to as Kyle's Station, this village was settled by Thomas Kyle in 1803. He emigrated to this county from Fayette County, Pennsylvania.

LaCarne *Ottawa County.* This name is a vestige of the French-Canadian influence exerted upon the area before Ohio attained statehood (during the late 1700s and after). There was once a community called Frenchtown in the county, and the Toussaint River is nearby.

Lafayette *Allen County.* Platted by William B. Weyer. The name is indicative of the esteem in which the American revolutionary hero from France, the Marquis de Lafayette, was held. An early historical reference states that the name was "selected to perpetuate a great and useful name in the midst of the wilderness" and offers the opinion that "the very name is an index to the character of its [the town's] people."

Lafayette *Madison County.* This village undoubtedly was named—like many other places—for the Frenchman Marquis de Lafayette. William Minter laid off lots in 1837, although the locality was settled considerably earlier.

Lafayette *Medina County.* This Lafayette, one of several communities so named in the state, is in Lafayette Township. The name honors the French general the Marquis de Lafayette (1757–1834).

Laferty *Belmont County.* This hamlet arose in 1880 and was named for Dr. Joseph Laferty. His significance to the place is unclear.

Lagrange *Lorain County.* The Marquis de Lafayette's rural French estate was named Lagrange, and respect for the revolutionary hero ran so high that local residents selected that name for their town.

Laing's *Monroe County.* This hamlet assumed its present name when a post office was maintained in a house here belonging to Randolph Laing. The place, initially known as New Castle, was founded in 1836 by Frederick and William Myers.

Lake Fork *Ashland County.* Two roads forked at this location on the brink of the Mohicanville Reservoir. The name is sometimes printed as Lake Fort.

Lakeline *Lake County.* This name results from the location of the place along the lake line of Lake Erie. Incorporated in 1929, it was recognized as a political subdivision by the county commissioners in 1951.

Lake Milton *Mahoning County.* The earliest settlers here included Samuel Bowles, John Vanetten, Amos Porter, and Samuel Linton. On a lake, the place probably took its name from the city of Milton, Connecticut.

Lakemore Village *Summit County.* A small lake within the confines gives the place its name. Incorporation was in 1921.

Lakeside *Fairfield County.* Lakeside overlooks Buckeye Lake.

Lakeside *Ottawa County.* The name derives from the place's situation on the shore of Lake Erie. A Methodist Church group purchased the site in 1869, named it, and continues to use it for church retreats. Summer camp meetings were started, perhaps as early as 1870, by a Methodist minister from Port Clinton named Duval. The location also evolved into a recreational and vacation resort.

Lakeview *Logan County.* Settled by William H. Hover (or Hoover), this village sprang up between 1875 and 1883. Its name is a result of its situation on Indian Lake.

Lakeview *Noble County.* Lakeview overlooks Senecaville Lake.

Lakeville *Holmes County.* Lakeville was founded about 1849 in an area dotted with several natural glacial lakes (Odell's Lake, Round Lake, Long Lake, Mud Lake). Also nearby are Bonnett Lake and Lake Fork, the latter being a creek. About 1900, the town's name was changed from Lakeville to Plimpton. A state representative and judge, Henry Curtis, owned a good deal of local land, and his daughter's married name was Plimpton. But the new name lasted only five or ten years before it was changed back to Lakeville.

Lakewood *Cuyahoga County.* Until 1889 this spot bore the name East Rockport. Its current name is descriptive of the wooded shoreline and its situation on Lake Erie. Lakewood became a city in 1911.

Lancaster *Fairfield County (seat).* Ebenezer Zane, who held deed to the land here, laid it off into lots in 1800. It was initially known as New Lancaster. Many of its earliest citizens had arrived from the Lancaster, Pennsylvania, area, and they transplanted the name. Lancaster, now a city, was incorporated in 1805.

Landeck *Allen County.* Surveyed in 1872; laid out in 1872 or 1873; village status achieved in 1873. The first settler was Sebastian Ley, in the late 1850s. The third in a series of resident pastors in this village was a Father Brem, from Austria. It was he who picked the name Landeck, which translates roughly as "corner land." There is a village in Austria by that name, and the Allen County Landeck is in a corner of the county. The land belonged to the church. The two resident pastors preceding Father Brem were Fathers Maesfranc and Seltzer, and for a time the place was known as Seltzerville.

Landis *Darke County.* This hamlet probably traces back its name to Christian Landis, born in 1822. Other Landises in the vicinity included John, a farmer born in 1818, and David.

Lansing *Belmont County.* This hamlet may have been named for Lansing, Michigan—if in fact that city predated this place. Or it may have been named for Judge John Lansing (1754–circa 1829). A town in New York State was named for this judge. It is also conceivable that Lansing, Ohio, was named for the town in the Empire State, perhaps by someone from that place who settled here. The naming was said to have been done by a political candidate sometime between 1898 and 1903, who selected it from a list of proposed names. It was once known as Soaptown, due to the fact that a local firm produced soap and dried it outdoors on boards.

LaRue *Marion County.* The genesis of this village traces back to about 1845. It takes its name from a militia officer who owned land here, Major LaRue. The year of incorporation was 1851.

Lashley *Noble County.* The name is thought to trace back to one of the Lashleys who lived in the area. Philip Lashley was a Civil War veteran from this county, while in nearby Kennonsburg, Leonard Lashley was a merchant in the early 1900s.

Lattasburg *Wayne County.* Known as West Union until 1855, the village was surveyed by J. W. Hoegner for Jacob Grose in 1851. It was later renamed for Ephraim Latta, a manufacturer of hand sickles. An explanation to which some subscribe is that the place takes the name of Jacob Latta, a blacksmith.

Lattaville *Ross County.* This village takes its name from William and Morris Latta, who arrived here early in the 1800s (before 1812). Sometimes the town name is given as Lattasville.

Latty *Paulding County.* A large landholder in this vicinity, Judge A. S. Latty, is the person for whom the hamlet was named.

Laura *Miami County.* Laid out, 1840, by Riley McCool and Wesley Sharp. The place acquired this name in 1852 from the name of the daughter of a Mr. Yount, the first postmaster.

Laurelville *Hocking County.* Laid out, 1871, by John Albin, W. S. Albin, and Solomon Riegel. The village took its name from nearby Laurel Creek, which was so named because of the profusion of laurel bushes growing in the vicinity.

Lawrence *Stark County.* Laid out in 1852 by the Honorable Arnold Lynch and Philip McCune, Esquire, Lawrence—sometimes called North Lawrence—is in Lawrence Township, a place named for Captain James Lawrence (1781–1830) of the U.S. Navy. Captain Lawrence is said to have uttered the now-famous words "Don't give up the ship!" during the War of 1812.

Lawrence *Washington County.* This hamlet and the township in which it is located derive their name from Captain James Lawrence, a U.S. Navy hero (see the preceding entry).

Lawrenceville *Clark County.* Platted, 1843, by Emanuel and Margaret Circle. First known as Noblesville, this community was renamed, upon acquiring a post office, in honor of Judge Lawrence, a member of the U.S. Congress.

Layhigh *Butler County.* It is presumed that Layhigh is so named because of its situation on high ground that is drained by a number of streams.

Layland *Coshocton County.* Founded in 1887. The original owner of the site was James Layland. After James donated the property, his son, Ephraim, laid out a town here.

Layman *Washington County.* The first successful Democratic newspaper in Washington County, called the *Marietta Republican,* was published by Amos Layman. This locality takes its name from him.

Layton *Auglaize County.* In all probability, the designation traces back to one of several Laytons who were once prominent in the area. Colonel W. M. V. Layton resided and was employed in Wapakoneta. He married Sarah Whitney and they had six children. Colonel Layton died in 1879. Judge F. C. Layton was a respected community member in 1915.

Leavittsburg *Trumbull County.* The community is named for the family of John L. Leavitt. One of the original proprietors, John L. Leavitt, Jr., came to the area about 1800. The family's roots were in Suffield, Connecticut.

Leavittsville *Carroll County.* First called Monroe after President James Monroe, this community bears the name of a Dr. Leavitt who was once prominent in this area. At the time the Dellroy post office was being renamed, it was also decided to rename this small, unincorporated hamlet three miles south of Dellroy. The new name of Leavittsville is believed to have been conferred by Thomas James in 1850. (See also the Dellroy entry.)

Lebanon *Warren County (seat).* Settled, 1796, by Henry Taylor and Ichabod Corwin. Platted, 1802, by Ichabod Corwin, Silas Hurin, Ephraim Hathaway, and Samuel Manning. Because this town site had so many cedar trees, it was named for the biblical mountain of Lebanon, known for its cedars. Now a city, Lebanon was incorporated in 1810.

Leesville *Carroll County.* The community was founded and settled in 1812 by Thomas Price and Peter Saunders. Price, from the Baltimore, Maryland, area, named the site Leesburg, for Leesburg, Virginia. A town was platted about 1820. At some point, and for an unknown reason, the "burg" was changed to "ville," and it became Leesville. Incorporation took place in 1836.

Leesville *Crawford County.* The village, laid out by the Reverend Robert Lee in 1829, assumed the Lee family's name.

Leetonia *Columbiana County.* Platted in 1867. William Lee once operated a coal and iron enterprise here. The year of incorporation was 1869.

Leipsic *Putnam County.* Leipzig (also spelled Leipsic) in Germany is the namesake of this place. Many early residents had come from the Old World city. Leipsic, Ohio, was laid out and platted in 1857; incorporation took place in 1874.

Leistville *Pickaway County.* The place-name probably had its origin with an early settler in the area, clergyman Jacob Leist, a Lutheran. In 1860, Philip Leist was a deacon at a church in the county, but his relationship to Jacob is not known. Andrew Leist also lived in this area early on.

Leith *Washington County.* The first family to settle in this general area, about 1800, bore the surname Leith. A post office called Leith or Leith Run did business here from 1891 to 1942.

Lemert *Crawford County.* Elsewhere in this county (Texas Township), about 1826, there lived a Lewis Lemert. It is probable that he was connected to this place-name.

Lemoyne *Wood County.* This place-name is the result of French-Canadian influence in this area before statehood.

Lenox *Ashtabula County.* The place was once called Millerstown, for local land proprietor Asmun Miller. In 1818, the label was changed to Lenox by emigrants from Massachusetts who wished to commemorate their hometown in the Berkshire Hills. Ohio's Lenox was settled by 1807 by Gideon Granger.

Leo *Jackson County.* This community was laid out in 1844 by Samuel Swift, who dubbed it Swiftsville. When G. H. Greene was named postmaster (1874–1875), he renamed the place in honor of a pope named Leo, perhaps Leo XIII (1810–1903).

Leonardsburg *Delaware County.* S. G. Caulkins laid out the town in 1852, naming it for the first merchant here, A. Leonard.

LeSourdsville *Butler County.* Sometime in the mid-1800s, Benjamin LeSourd bought ninety-five acres here from Abraham Freeman and founded a town. His stated intent was to build "a great city," a goal not yet achieved.

Lester *Medina County.* The accepted version has it that the settlement was named by a man named Cook—probably Zimri Cook—who owned a great deal of land in the vicinity. Cook arrived here in 1841. The name Lester is said to be an Americanization of Leicester, Cook's home county in England.

Letart Falls *Meigs County.* According to a story handed down through generations, a Frenchman who was found drowned in the falls at this location on the Ohio River had the word *Letart* tattooed on his arm. Since then the town, the township, and the post office have included Letart in their names.

Lewisburg *Preble County.* The name of this community was originally spelled with an "h" at the end. Its namesake was Lewisburg, Virginia (now in West Virginia). Incorporation was in 1816.

Lewis Center *Delaware County.* The first settler at or near this site was John Johnson, in 1823. The village dates to about 1850, when a railroad came through. The name was assigned by William L. Lewis, whose family donated land for the train depot.

Lewistown *Logan County.* Founded about 1832, Lewistown is said to have been named after "Captain" John Lewis, a Shawnee village chief.

Lexington *Richland County.* Named for Lexington, Massachusetts, site of a historic battle against the British in 1775, this community was laid out in 1812. Amariah Watson, who emigrated from the Massachusetts village, is said to have owned land here and founded this town, which was incorporated in 1841.

Lexington *Stark County.* The community, in Lexington Township, was named in remembrance of the first battle of the American Revolution at Lexington, Massachusetts. It was surveyed in 1807.

Leyda *Carroll County.* Platted in 1837 by Henry Leyda, the hamlet bears his name.

Liberty *Montgomery County.* Laid out, 1815, by the landowner, Peter Becher, but settled earlier. It has been speculated that the place-name commemorates the pioneers' love of freedom. In the words of one historian, the name "expressed to the pioneers a sentiment most dear."

Liberty Hill *Washington County.* This hilltop site in Aurelius Township had a post office from 1855 to 1865. How it got the "Liberty" aspect of its name is unclear.

Lightsville *Darke County.* When the hamlet was laid out in 1874 by William B. Light, Lightsville was born, thereby bringing light to Darke County.

Lilly Chapel *Madison County.* When a Methodist church was erected here in 1850, Wesley Lilly was the proprietor of the land on which it sat, and the house of worship became known as Lilly Chapel. The town, laid out in 1874 by Henry Gilroy and Henry Lilly, was known to some as Gilroy. However, the established Lilly Chapel name prevailed.

Lima *Allen County (seat).* Now a city, Lima (pronounced LIE-muh) was laid out as a town in 1831. Patrick G. Goode proposed the name, which was evoked by Lima, Peru, though the Peruvian city's name is pronounced differently (LEE-muh). Lima, Ohio, was incorporated in 1842.

Lime City *Wood County.* With a flourishing lime-quarrying industry, Lime City came by its name quite naturally. Established in 1883 or 1884 by C. H. Sawyer, the lime works was the principal employer in the community. The town was surveyed in 1887 by C. H. Judson. Citizens petitioned to the Post Office Department for the name.

Limerick *Jackson County.* The ethnic joke handed down to explain Limerick's name is that a drunken Irishman "came riding along one of the five roads which entered the village. He took off his hat and shouted 'Hooray for Limerick!' Since that day, the little village has been called Limerick." That legend appears in the *History of Jackson County Sesquicentennial Edition.*

Limestone *Ottawa County.* This entity, never platted, dates to an unknown period. Limestone occurring near the surface here gave the place-name.

Lincoln *Richland County.* The sixteenth president of the United States, Abraham Lincoln, was the inspiration for this place-name.

Lincoln Heights *Hamilton County.* This locale was settled primarily by African Americans. In naming the site, a number of considerations came into play, including whether the proposed name was in use anywhere else in Ohio. Residents wanted a name to "symbolize the historic struggles of black people and promote feelings of racial pride and solidarity among members of the community." They finally agreed on Lincoln Heights. According to one source, "This name was selected because of the important role . . . Abraham Lincoln played in the emancipation of the slaves. . . . Some people wanted to call it Grandview Heights Subdivision; some had one name and some had others. We wanted a name that would symbolize what the community stood for. . . . We got to discussing freedom and what it meant. . . . The Negro achieved freedom under the Lincoln administration. . . . Freedom . . . meant that we had a chance to better our conditions, a chance to make something out of ourselves. Now, we were free to build a city that was Negro-owned and controlled. So the majority felt that Lincoln Heights was the name that exemplified what the community stood for. . . . This is why we chose that name." Incorporation came in 1946.

Lindale *Clermont County.* When a post office was established here in 1869, for unknown reasons it was labeled Lyndon. At some later date, it was renamed Lindale, probably adapting the "Lyn" and adding the word for a gently undulating space between hills ("dale"). Those familiar with the site confirm that the name aptly describes the locale.

Lindentree *Carroll County.* A contributor states that before a community existed at this site, there was a small hill on top of which was a level area punctuated with several beautiful linden trees. Excellent shade trees, the lindens also flowered and perfumed the air on warm summer nights. Area residents in search of a home for a United Brethren Church, a cemetery, and a schoolhouse selected this pleasant place and christened it Lindentree. The schoolhouse and church are gone now, the hillside has been strip-mined for coal up close to the cemetery, and the lindens are gone, but the cemetery has been well kept.

Lindenville *Ashtabula County.* A wealth of linden trees arrayed at this location provided the place with a natural name.

Lindsey *Sandusky County.* Surveyed, 1868, by Isaiah Overmyer and C. A. Monk. (One source claims that Lindsey was originally platted by E. B. Phillips and B. F. Roberts in 1853.) Charles Loose is said to have been the first settler. The etymology of the name is unclear. It may trace back to Byron, Frank, Herman, Eluther, or A. B. Lindsey; all of them were prominent in the county during the early years.

Linndale *Cuyahoga County.* About 1872 Robert Linn bought three hundred acres in this locality, and a town was laid out. Linndale was incorporated in 1902.

Linnville *Licking County.* The village was laid out by Samuel Parr in 1829. Parr named the place for Adam Linn, the first merchant in town. Other Licking County Linns included the families of James and John Linn, of Irish descent, who had come from Pennsylvania.

Linton Mills *Coshocton County.* This Linton Township place is said to have been named by James Miskimen, a county commissioner in 1812, after the township in Virginia from which he had come. However, in an attempt to verify this account using current sources, no town, township, or county named Linton could be located in Virginia, West Virginia, or Maryland. Interestingly, there was a person named Amelia Linton in Coshocton County sometime in the 1800s. J. V. Heslip laid out Linton Mills in 1849.

Linwood *Hamilton County.* A correspondent describes Linwood as "a once-stately Cincinnati suburb with tree-lined streets, some of which may have been basswood or linden trees." This probably accounts for the name.

Linworth *Franklin County.* The community gained this name as a result of its location, about midway between Dublin and Worthington. Earlier it had been called Elmwood.

Lipkey's Corners *Mahoning County.* Lipkey's Corners derives its name from a Lipkey family that settled here in the formative years.

Lisbon *Columbiana County (seat).* Laid out, 1803, by Lewis Kinney. Today a city, the site was incorporated as a village in 1814. Until 1898, the community was New Lisbon, settled by Quakers and named in commemoration of Christopher Columbus's residence in Lisbon, Portugal.

Litchfield *Medina County.* This region was wholly owned by Judge Holmes of Litchfield, Connecticut, who had it surveyed. While under his ownership, it was best known as Holmestown.

Lithopolous *Fairfield County.* Laid out, 1814 or 1815, by Frederick Baugher. The initial name of the site was Centreville (or Centerville). When rock known as "freestone" was found in both quantity and quality here and began to be quarried, the name of the community was changed to Lithopolous. The term translates as "stone city" from the Greek. Incorporation was accomplished in 1836.

Little Hocking *Washington County.* This name is an abbreviation of the original Little Hockhocking, taken from the name conferred upon a nearby river by the Delaware Indians. *Hockhocking* means "bottle" or "bottlenecks" and refers to the river's numerous narrow passages. A post office opened here in 1824; the Post Office Department shortened the name for convenience in 1879. George Washington is said to have camped here in 1770.

Little Sandusky *Wyandot County.* Platted, 1831, by Stephen Fowler and John Wilson. The men dubbed the community Little Sandusky because of its location, a short distance south of where Little Sandusky Creek flowed into the Sandusky River. (See also the Sandusky entry.)

Lock *Knox County.* Founded in 1836. Laid out, 1837, by Isham Abbott, who is thought to have named the place as well. Lock sits on the boundary with Licking County. It is possible that this name was created by combining the "L" from Licking and the "ock" sound from Knox. No canal locks were nearby, and apparently no one having the Lock surname lived here. However, a Mr. Lockwood was involved with the founding of Brandon, one township away. Perhaps he was involved in some way with Lock as well.

Lockbourne *Franklin County.* This canal-front village was laid out in 1831 by Colonel James Kilbourne. The "Lock" portion of the name comes from the canal locks, and the suffix traces back to the surname Kilbourne. The town was incorporated in 1902.

Lockington *Shelby County.* An item in a 1950 edition of the *Ohio Engineer* states that this site is adjacent to a confluence of the Erie & Miami Canal with Loramie Creek, involving the use of an aqueduct. A series of five locks stepped the water level to the elevation of the village, which arose around the lockmaster's residence and the turning basin. Lockington was incorporated in 1850.

Lockland *Hamilton County.* Nicholas Longworth and Lewis Howell laid out this village in 1829. It owes its name to the Miami Canal locks located here. It was incorporated in 1849.

Lockport *Williams County.* Surveyed, 1836, by Miller Arrowsmith. John Evans was proprietor of the land. Some claim this village was named for a set of locks constructed at or near the site. This, however, is based on hearsay, not documentation.

Lockville *Fairfield County.* Laid out before 1845 by Francis Cunningham. Located on the Ohio Canal, Lockville takes its name from the several locks placed strategically along this stretch of the waterway.

Lockville Station *Fairfield County.* The "Station" portion of the name probably stems from its location on a railroad. (Also see the preceding entry.)

Lockwood *Trumbull County.* Until 1905, this site was referred to as Huckleberry. Huckleberry bushes, as well as other varieties of berries, grew in profusion nearby. One explanation for the current name is that it honors Belva Lockwood, once a Canfield resident, who in 1884 ran for president of the United States after being nominated by the National Equal Rights party.

Locust Grove *Adams County.* This community was laid out and named by Urban W. Cannon in 1835. He built a hotel and planted a grove of locust trees, and by the latter the place was known.

Locust Ridge *Brown County.* Buildings were probably first erected at this site about 1835. The entire township (Pike) lies on an elevated ridge that divides the East Fork of the Little Miami River from White Oak Creek. The ridge was heavily timbered with both black locust and red locust trees.

Lodi *Medina County.* Founded by Judge Joseph Harris. The community's name echoes that of the Italian place where Napoleon won a victory in 1796. The year of incorporation was 1891.

Logan *Hocking County (seat).* This city was established in 1816 by Colonel Thomas Worthington. Said to have been named for the Mingo Indian chief James John Logan, it was incorporated in 1839.

Logansville *Logan County.* While the county takes its name from General Benjamin Logan, a soldier in the Indian Wars, the community is named for the Mingo Indian chief James John Logan. William Dickson and a Mr. Thompson platted the town in 1827.

London *Madison County (seat).* The public library in this city reports that "the assumption is that it was named for London, England, because so many people from the British Isles settled here. [But] the London Company surveyed this area, so that could be another possibility." London was incorporated in 1831.

Londonderry *Guernsey County.* Platted in 1815 by Robert Wilkins. Located in the township of the same name, the village was named for the birthplace in Ireland of Wilkins's father.

Londonderry *Ross County.* Laid out, 1831, by Nathan Cox and Adam Stewart. The village takes its name from Londonderry, Ireland, Stewart's former home. Sometimes this place was referred to as Gillespie Post Office, owing to the existence of another Londonderry in Ohio.

Long Beach *Ottawa County.* Platted in 1923. This name appears to be an accurate designation for this elongated strip fronting Lake Erie.

Long Bottom *Meigs County.* Laid out, 1866, by Daniel McKee. An entire stretch of land extending north along the Ohio River from this site bore the Long Bottom designation. Its configuration inspired the name of this bottomland. The locale was probably settled prior to 1800.

Lorain *Lorain County.* Incorporated in 1837, the city at first was referred to as Black River Settlement, later Charleston. It was eventually named Lorain after the

Alsace-Lorraine region of France by a local judge, Heman Ely. (Ely's name forms part of the name of the nearby county seat, Elyria.) The judge had traveled in France and had been impressed by Lorraine.

Lordstown *Trumbull County.* Samuel P. Lord is the person after whom this town was named. Lordstown was incorporated in 1975.

Lottridge *Athens County.* In 1805, Bernardus B. Lottridge settled in Carthage Township, site of this village, and farmed. His son Isaac served in the state legislature while another son, Simon, was a justice of the peace. A second source discloses that, at some point, landholders very near this site included J. D. Lottridge and S. H. Lottridge. One of them was probably the postmaster. It is not readily evident whether Simon Lottridge and S. H. Lottridge were one and the same.

Loudon *Adams County.* Settled in 1839. E. G. Lovett was the first merchant in the town. The earliest settlers here made the trek from Loudon County, Virginia.

Loudonville *Ashland County.* Sources relate that Loudonville was given its name by James Loudon Priest, an area farmer, who wished to honor his mother, Nancy Loudon. Priest and Stephen Butler laid out the village in 1814. The year of incorporation was 1850.

Louisville *Stark County.* Originally this community's name was spelled Lewisville. It was changed because of a duplication within Ohio. An early settler and landowner, Henry Lautzenheiser, labeled the place with the given name of his son, Lewis. (One source spells Henry's name Loutzenheiser.) Henry and Frederick Faint were land proprietors who started the town in 1834. The change in the spelling of the place-name was suggested by the Post Office Department. In 1872, the city was incorporated.

Loveland *Clermont, Hamilton, and Warren counties.* A military figure, Colonel Loveland, is the individual for whom this community was named. Now a city, it was incorporated in 1876.

Lovell *Morgan County.* This hamlet was named after the Lovells—Captain Thomas, Oliver M., and Russell.

Lovell *Wyandot County.* Two years after completion of the CHV&T Railroad, Lovell B. Harris laid out this hamlet near the station site, and it bears his given name.

Lowell *Seneca County.* Founded in 1822. The town earned its name thanks largely to the woolen mills once located here. It was named for an important New England textile center, Lowell, Massachusetts.

Lowellville *Mahoning County.* Founded in 1840. This name may stem from the Lowell Coal Mining Company, which began operations here. One historian speculates, however, that the name was inspired by a "low spot" between hills and along the river.

Lower Newport *Washington County.* The place is in the southern portion of Newport Township.

Lower Salem *Washington County.* Salem Township was formed in 1797 and named for Salem, Massachusetts. When the post office opened in 1828, it was designated Lower Salem to distinguish it from other places in Ohio known as Salem.

Loyal Oak *Summit County.* Loyal Oak was first known as Bates' Corners. Lyman and Nathan Bates came to this place in 1817 or 1818. The rationale behind the name has been the subject of considerable speculation. In *Ohio's Western Reserve,* Lindsey advances the unlikely theory that "pioneers (perhaps) wanted to commemorate the Charter Oak, in which Connecticut's charter was once hidden to prevent seizure by the King's agents in the late 1600's."

Loydsville *Belmont County.* This name is sometimes styled Loydville. Joshua Loyd gave it his name upon laying out the community in 1831.

Lucas *Richland County.* The first person to clear land here, in 1807 or 1808, was Jacob Stoner, who was staying nearby with his father-in-law, Archibald Gardner. In 1819, David Tucker filed claim for the land, but didn't receive title until 1824. It was not until 1836 that a village was laid out; it was platted by the county surveyor, a Mr. Steward. David Tucker's brother, John, had come to the county from New Hampshire in 1818. Later, when David returned to New Hampshire to get married, John had power of attorney to sell lot deeds. According to one source, the village takes its name from the Tuckers' mother, Elizabeth Lucas, the daughter of a former New Hampshire governor. According to a second source, it was named in honor of Robert Lucas, Ohio governor from 1832 to 1836. Still another authority credits John Tucker with laying out the village. David Tucker returned to Lucas in 1849 and remained until his death.

Lucasville *Scioto County.* Lucasville was founded in 1819 by John Lucas, whose son Robert was Ohio's governor from 1832 until 1836. John's father, William, served in the Revolutionary War.

Luckey *Wood County.* Surveyed, 1881, by George Kirk. George Luckey became the first postmaster at the place, also in 1881.

Ludington *Perry County.* Founded in 1883 by Mary A. Corcoran and Catherine Kelly, Ludington was a mining town, like many other places in this area. It was sited on eight acres bought from Benjamin Sanders. In 1880, Benjamin Ludington was one of a party of three who purchased the land of a major coal company nearby, during bankruptcy proceedings.

Ludlow Falls *Miami County.* The village acquired its name because of falls on nearby Ludlow's Creek. The creek was named after one of the original surveyors of the area. Incorporation was in 1910.

Luhrig *Athens County.* This community in a once-thriving coal-mining locale was given the name of a German who developed an important piece of coal-washing machinery.

Luke Chute *Washington County.* Sometime before 1815, Luke Emerson constructed a mill here on the Muskingum River and built a wing dam out from the Waterford Township side. That made the water flow faster for more efficient mill operation, but it also created a dangerous place for flatboatmen passing downriver. The boatmen dubbed the site Luke's Chute, and the name was adopted for the post office and hamlet as well.

Lumberton *Clinton County.* Settled in 1820; platted in 1853. Lumberton acquired its name from a town of the same name in New Jersey.

Lykens *Crawford County.* This community is in Lykens Township. The place was once known derisively as Buljo and later as Santa Fe. Several citizens had come from Lykens, Pennsylvania, and one of them, Jacob Lintner, strongly advocated adopting that name for this place. Others agreed. J. F. Feighner, the surveyor, and H. W. McDonald are credited with founding the town in 1870.

Lynchburg *Highland County.* A man named Botts, from Lynchburg, Virginia, owned the land where this Lynchburg now stands. Others settled the place in 1806. It was laid out as a town in 1832.

Lyndhurst *Cuyahoga County.* Three years after incorporation, in 1920, the designation for this location was changed from Euclidville to Lyndhurst. The earlier name caused confusion with Euclid. Accounts state that when citizens decided the name had to be changed, the council held a contest among school students. Spotting the name Lyndhurst on a New Jersey map, Bill Emshoff submitted it as an entry and won.

Lyndon *Ross County.* John Higgins laid out this place in 1853. It was first known as Zora. Samuel Langdon, the first postmaster in the town, purchased the land and renamed the place after his hometown in Massachusetts. (One source refers to the town father as John N. Huggins.)

Lynx *Adams County.* A post office was established here in 1879. The name stems from the prevalence of wildcats in the neighborhood.

Lyra *Scioto County.* This hamlet was named for the constellation Lyra by the first postmaster, George W. Thompson, in 1850.

Lysander *Athens County.* The first postmaster at this location was Lysander K. Davis. Apparently the chance for duplication or confusion of names was minimized by using his given name as the place-name instead of Davis.

Lytle *Warren County.* At one time, this site was called Raysville. A co-owner was M. Mills. Literature of the local historical society explains the place-name thusly: "Tradition has it [that] when the post office was established, a number of names were submitted to the department in Washington and all were rejected. The name Lytle, caught at a glance on the label of a shoebox, was then submitted and accepted." It might also be noted that several Lytles are found in local annals. Andrew Lytle paid taxes in Deerfield Township in 1810, while William Lytle, Jr., purchased a lot in 1825. In 1811, Esther Lytle married David Cox.

Mabee *Jackson County.* The name derives from the first postmaster at this place, a Mabee or Mabees, whose years of service are uncertain. The place, on or near Mabee's Pike, has also been known as Mabee's Corner.

Macedonia *Summit County.* Early settlers at this place are thought to have come from Macedon, New York, but historians are not certain whether this place was named for the New York site. A second possibility is that it bears the name of the ancient political state of Macedonia in southeastern Europe. Ohio's Macedonia was incorporated in 1921 and now holds city status.

Mack *Hamilton County.* This place-name may trace back to Alexander Mack (born 1842), his son, Charles W. Mack (born 1866), or their families.

Macksburg *Washington County.* The name was changed from Regnier's Mills to Macksburg in 1873. William Whiting McIntosh operated the first store here, starting about 1827. Local folks got in the habit of referring to the site as Mack's Store, which eventually evolved into Macksburg.

Madeira *Hamilton County.* Laid out, 1871, by J. D. Moore and J. L. Holbrook. The name was taken from the owner of a large neighborhood tract, John Madeira, who was treasurer of the Marietta & Cincinnati Railroad.

Madison *Lake County.* This Madison Township community is named for President James Madison. It was incorporated in 1867.

Magnetic Springs *Union County.* This community owes its existence to several free-gushing mineral springs in the neighborhood. Said to have highly medicinal or curative properties, the springs drew invalids and persons suffering a variety of maladies. Many of them remained here, forming the nucleus of a busy village. In 1879, F. A. Gartner surveyed the settlement, although residents had been there for some years. In 1883, incorporation took place.

Magnolia *Stark and Carroll counties.* Founded, 1834, by Richard Elson. Elson reportedly was a Virginian who had traveled the American South and taken a liking to the magnolia trees of the region. When he began a business here, he called it the Magnolia Mills, and the brand of flour he produced carried the "Magnolia" label. The village was incorporated in 1846.

Mahoning *Portage County.* This place on Mahoning Creek is said to bear a French name meaning "at the lick."

Maineville *Warren County.* Platted and incorporated in 1850. The proprietors were Seth G. Tufts and Silas Dudley. Many early residents had emigrated from Maine about 1815. Moses Dudley is considered the first permanent settler. Yankeetown was an earlier name.

Malaga *Monroe County.* The town was laid out in 1818 by John Henderson in the township of the same name. Many places named Malaga trace the name to the Spanish city Málaga. In the West and Southwest, such a place-name is usually traceable to the variety of grapes called Malaga, according to *American Place-Names*. This reference work also attributes one application of Malaga to an Algonquian word translating as "cedar."

Mallet Creek *Medina County.* Mallet Creek takes its name from Henry Mallett, an early settler (1819). The second "t" was dropped.

Malta *Morgan County.* Founded, 1816, by the owners of the site, Simon Pool and John Bell. The village was named for the Mediterranean island which Pool had visited as a youth. One source states that Pool's given name was Simeon and that he had served as a sailor.

Malvern *Carroll County.* Lewis Vail and Joseph Tidbald, the proprietors, acquired the land here in 1829 and named the place for Malvern, Pennsylvania. It is thought to have been platted in 1834 by William Hardesty. An alternative explanation for the name is that it may trace back to a College of Malvern in Worcestershire, England. Adherents of this theory point to the fact that Hardesty is a common name in that British county. Malvern was incorporated in 1869. At one time it may have been referred to as Troy.

Manchester *Adams County.* This town, founded by Nathaniel Massie in 1791, was the first settlement in the Virginia Military District. Massie's ancestors were from Manchester, England.

Mann *Ashtabula County.* The name of this hamlet leads back to the Mann family, early settlers in the area.

Mansfield *Richland County (seat).* The city was established under the direction of the surveyor general of the United States, Jared Mansfield, in 1808.

Mantua *Portage County.* Settled, 1798, by Abraham L. Honey, William Crooks, John Leavitt, Rufus Edwards, and Elias Harmon. David Abbott performed the survey. It was John Leavitt who dubbed this village after the ancient town in northern Italy that had been captured in 1797 by Napoleon. Incorporation took place in 1898.

Mantua Corners *Portage County.* This hamlet is thought to predate the nearby larger village of Mantua (see the preceding entry). Two state routes intersect at Mantua Corners.

Mantua Station *Portage County.* Like Mantua Corners, Mantua Station might be referred to as a "suburb" of Mantua (see the Mantua entry). Mantua Station was a stop on the railroad.

Maple Heights *Cuyahoga County.* With maple trees lining numerous streets in this city, the name Maple Heights must have seemed a natural choice to town fathers. Incorporation took place in 1932.

Maplewood *Shelby County.* Platted in 1872. The place was first called Tileton because a tile-making plant operated in the village. But another county also had a Tileton, and mail was being misdirected. The name Maplewood is said to have been suggested by a woman who was impressed by the many beautiful maple trees in the neighborhood. The conversion of the name from Tileton to Maplewood apparently was gradual, perhaps beginning in the 1880s and culminating in the early 1900s.

Marblecliff *Franklin County.* This Columbus suburb sprang up around the Marble Cliff Mills, which opened about 1858. Earlier, the Bachus, McCoy's, and Matere's mills operated at or near this site. It is said that the rocky cliffs near the mills provided refuge for rattlesnakes.

Marble Furnace *Adams County.* Founded, 1812, by Thomas James and Duncan McArthur. The name was evoked by the marblelike appearance of the limestone quarried at this location.

Marblehead *Ottawa County.* One source states that early immigrants to this place came from Marblehead, Massachusetts, and noted the similarity of the cape here to the one there; thus the name. At one time, thanks to copious amounts of limestone quarried nearby, it was called Plasterbed. Settled in 1809, it is best known for the Marblehead Lighthouse on a peninsula jutting into Lake Erie. A second source says that an early settler dubbed this place Marble Headland, mistaking the white limestone he beheld for marble.

Marchand *Stark County.* The name probably relates to Clarence Marchand, who taught school not far distant, at Belfort. A Charles E. Marchand purchased the Alliance Opera House in this county in 1877. Always suspect, the poorly constructed building collapsed in 1886, somehow with no fatalities or injuries. The building manager was Florian C. Marchand.

Marengo *Morrow County.* The name is thought to commemorate Napoleon's defeat of the Austrians in 1800 at Marengo, Italy. Isaac P. Freeman erected the first building in this town in 1843.

Maria Stein *Mercer County.* This village takes its name from a Swiss Benedictine convent that, in 1846, dispatched members of the Sisters of the Precious Blood to settle two hundred acres here. The name means, "Mary of the Rock" or, as some say, "Our Lady of the Rock."

Mariemont *Hamilton County.* A local philanthropist, Mrs. Emery, spent the summers at her Newport, Rhode Island, estate called Mariemont. When this town began to arise, she obtained regular updates on its progress from Thomas Hogan, Jr., who made frequent forays between the two Mariemonts. This Ohio village, incorporated in 1941, is named for the estate in Rhode Island. The "Marie" portion of the name is pronounced "Mary." Additional details may be found in *The Mariemont Story.*

Marietta *Washington County* (seat). In 1788, this became the first permanent settlement in the Northwest Territory. It was initially called Adelphi, but the name soon was changed to Marietta. The name was taken from the name of Marie Antoinette, a sign of the respect Revolutionary War veterans had for the French queen for her assistance during the war. Marietta was incorporated in 1825.

Marion *Marion County (seat).* The city was known in earlier times as Jacob's Well. In 1822, it was dubbed Marion in honor of "the Swamp Fox," Francis Marion (circa 1732–1795), a Revolutionary War officer.

Mark Center *Defiance County.* Laid out, 1875, by Frederick Harmening. Another portion was laid out later by Josiah Kyle and A. M. Anderson. Even before 1875, a community stood at this site near the center of Mark Township. The town was originally to be named Kenton, for Mark Kenton, who made the first improvements in the area, sometime before 1852. However, because there was another Kenton in Ohio, the place became known by his given name instead.

Marlboro *Stark County.* The Duke of Marlboro is thought to have inspired the name of this place. Quakers laid off the townsite.

Marquand Mills *Muskingum County.* Charles Marquand arrived here from the Isle of Guernsey in 1810, starting a salt works and operating grain, saw, and carding mills.

Marquis *Mahoning County.* The first name of this hamlet was Loveland, for David Loveland, an early settler. When this name caused confusion with another site in

Ohio, it was changed to Marquis in honor of Sam Marquis, longtime conductor on the Erie Railroad, Niles & Lisbon Branch.

Marr *Monroe County.* A Maryland native, Daniel Marr, born about 1783, gave his name to this settlement, which dates to 1880.

Marseilles *Wyandot County.* Marseilles Township was laid out in 1824. Both it and the community here were named for the seaport in France.

Marshall *Highland County.* First platted in 1817 as West Liberty, then in 1837 as Marshall. In 1836, a few months after the death of Chief Justice John Marshall, residents petitioned to change the name to Marshall.

Marshallville *Wayne County.* A post office was opened here in 1819, at which time the name was changed from Bristol to Marshallville. A Dalton, Ohio, citizen named James Marshall founded the community two years before the post office was established.

Martin *Ottawa County.* This place is in Clay Township and takes its name, according to one source, from the family of an early resident, Franklin H. Martin. Several other Martins lived in the vicinity, including Eugene, a native of France born in 1867; Leo (born 1906) and family; and August, born 1898.

Martin's Ferry *Belmont County.* Absalom Martin settled the site in 1787 after arriving from New Jersey and named it Jefferson in 1795. His hope was that it would become the county seat, but it failed to prosper. His son, Ebenezer Martin, revived the place, rechristening it Martinsville. The Post Office Department later requested a different name, and since Ebenezer had begun operating a ferry service across the Ohio River here, the name became Martin's Ferry. Today it is a city of modest size; it was incorporated in 1865.

Martinstown *Hancock County.* Martin Hollobaugh laid out a town here in 1836.

Marysville *Union County (seat).* Settled, 1816, by Jonathan Summers; established in 1820. The founder of the city was Samuel W. Cuthbertson, who named it after his daughter, Mary. The place previously was called Shady City, owing to its numerous maple trees. Incorporation was in 1838.

Mason *Warren County.* Laid out, 1815, by Major William Mason. He originally called it Palmyra, but that duplicated the name of another Ohio town, so a committee (1839–1840) was appointed to select a new name.

Massieville *Ross County.* Settled before 1805; laid out as Hopetown by Henry Musselman in 1819. In 1852, Waller Massie moved here and established a steam sawmill. The place became known as Massie; later it acquired the "ville."

Massillon *Stark County.* Founded in 1826. The city was laid out by James Duncan and Ferdinand Hurxthal. It was named in honor of Jean Baptiste Massillon (1663–1742), a French clergyman whose sermons were Mrs. Duncan's favorite reading. Incorporation occurred in 1838.

Masury *Trumbull County.* It is believed that Masury borrowed its name from a Polish family that lived in the vicinity.

Mather's Mill *Warren County.* In 1807, Richard Mather bought the mill at this site from Lewis Rees. Mather also kept a store and smith shop. A dam was built for Mather by George Zentmire.

Maumee *Lucas County.* Laid out, 1817, by Major William Oliver on the Maumee River. *Maumee* derives from a Miami Indian word. Some authorities say that *maumee* and *miami* are the same word, meaning "mother." According to *The History of Maumee*, "The first of the tribes in the region was known as *Tweetwees*; another *Twigtwee*; and another *Omee* and *Aumiami* . . . by contraction, *Omee*. The word 'Miami' is said to signify Mother in the Attowa language. . . . The word 'Maumee' is then a corruption of *Omee-Aumiami*." The place now occupied by Maumee (the name was shortened from Maumee City in 1887) was a beehive of activity as early as the 1700s, when an Indian village stood here. British, French, and Americans later plied the area along with the Native Americans. Maumee was incorporated in 1838 (as Maumee City).

Maximo *Stark County.* A descendant of Daniel Kropf, a telegrapher with the Pennsylvania Railroad at Maximo, states that Kropf was told by railroad officials that they named the place Maximo because "it was the maximum highest point [on the railroad] between Pittsburgh and Fort Wayne, Indiana." Kropf, born in 1874, was killed by lightning in 1905 at the dispatch office in Maximo.

Maxon *Washington County.* This place takes its name from a post office that was open briefly in 1901. It was named for the Maxon family. Henry Maxon was one of the original forty-eight settlers of Marietta, Ohio, in 1788.

Maxville *Perry County.* Laid out in 1850 by William McCormick. The place was first referred to as Mc'sville, then Maxville.

May Hill *Adams County.* The designation likely stems from a May family residing nearby. About 1865, a Miss Myrtle May lived near here with her parents.

Maynard *Belmont County.* Laid out in 1874. It is thought that this settlement took its name from Horace Maynard, who in 1880 was Postmaster General of the United States.

Maysville *Hardin County.* This site is believed to have acquired its name from a local farm family named May.

McArthur *Vinton County (seat).* This place was named for an early governor of Ohio, Duncan McArthur (1772–1839). It was incorporated in 1851.

McAvan *Washington County.* A hamlet surrounding a station on the M&C Railroad, this place took the name of John McAvan, an Irishman who farmed nearby.

McCartyville *Shelby County.* Laid out, 1876, by J. A. Wells. Patrick McCarty, although not the first settler, came to the site in 1868 and assumed a position as the town's first postmaster. The town is said to have been settled primarily by persons of Irish descent.

McClimansville *Madison County.* McClimans was a common name around here. The McClimans brothers built a hotel in nearby Danville, while Solomon McClimans farmed in the Range area, just west of this hamlet. Solomon was born in 1835, the son of Isaac and Mary McClimans. In the 1890s and early 1900s, the James McClimans family resided here.

McClure *Henry County.* Laid out, 1880, using farmland belonging to John McClure. The town was incorporated in 1886.

McClure *Shelby County.* This tiny hamlet may owe its name to area resident and businessman B. C. McClure or his forebears. McClure was prominent around the turn of the century, running a grocery store in Pasco. Local relatives at that time included Harry McClure, Clara McClure, Pearl McClure Wheeler, Gertrude Simes McClure, and Elizabeth McClure.

McComb *Hancock County.* Laid out, 1847, by Benjamin Todd. This town's first name was Pleasantville, probably after Pleasant Township, a name that celebrates the general pleasantness of the surrounding area. After subsequent additions, the community was incorporated (1858) and renamed, according to one source, for the village's first physician, Dr. Samuel McComb Turner. A conflicting source, the McComb Centennial booklet, states that an early settler, Elisha Fout, who had been a soldier at Plattsburgh, New York, in the War of 1812 under the command of General Alexander Macomb (1782–1841), suggested the name.

McConnelsville *Morgan County (seat).* Dating to 1817, the village was known as Old Town for a while. It was platted by General Robert McConnell and took its current name from him. In 1836, the village was incorporated.

McCuneville *Perry County.* Earlier names included Salt Works and Tallyho. The village was founded in 1829 but not platted until 1873, by the McCunes. It is said that a Mr. McCune, of Newark, Ohio, built a salt manufacturing facility here when a branch of the Baltimore & Ohio Railroad was thrust through to Shawnee.

McCutchenville *Seneca and Wyandot counties.* Two of the earliest residents at this location were Joseph and Hannah McCutchen. It is believed the place takes its name from them. Joseph was a prominent pioneer and attained the rank of colonel during the Civil War. The village was platted in 1829 by Dr. G. W. Sampson.

McDermott *Scioto County.* The hamlet derives its name from the McDermott Stone Company which, along with James Barker and Honor Barker, had it platted in 1898.

McDonald *Muskingum County.* Many pioneer McDonalds came to this county. The place-name probably traces back to E. McDonald (born 1846), who was the postmaster here. He was also a merchant and justice of the peace.

McDonald *Trumbull County.* A pioneer family named McDonald left its mark on this place.

McDonaldsville *Stark County.* Laid out and platted in 1829. The proprietors were Abraham Routan and John Clapper, while Henry Beard performed the surveying. When queried about a name for the village, Beard submitted McDonaldsville to honor a Revolutionary War officer, General Marion McDonald. Beard, a student of the war, apparently was impressed by accounts of McDonald's exploits and decisions. McDonald fought under General Francis Marion, the "Swamp Fox."

McGill *Paulding County.* Although the source of the place-name cannot be pinpointed to one McGill or another, several called the area home during the mid-1800s. John McGill married Mary Shelly in this county in 1865, while in 1843, Julia Ann Hurley became the wife of Daniel McGill.

McGonigle *Butler County.* James McGonigle was the first postmaster here, but the village is said to be named for Phillip McGonigle. Phillip contracted to lay a mile of railroad track, and his house served as the railroad station. About 1830, a still and a mill operated at this locality.

McGuffey *Hardin County.* The descendants of early landowner John McGuffey named this community for him in 1833.

McKay's Corners *Mahoning County.* The president of Home Savings & Loan Company in Youngstown, James McKay, operated a farm at this site about 1900. It was from him that this hamlet got its name.

McKay's Station *Clinton County.* Never platted, McKay's Station sprang up as a result of local railway activity. The name recognizes Alfred McKay, who is said to have given most of the lots away to those wishing to reside in the community.

McKinley Heights *Trumbull County.* Nine years after President William McKinley's 1901 assassination, attorney Lulu Mackey Wess had his birth home transported from nearby Niles to this place. She opened it to the public after restoring it. Neighborhood residents took pride in it and chose to name their community McKinley Heights.

McLean *Fayette County.* The Cincinnati, Hamilton, & Dayton Railroad was given a right-of-way here by landowner James McLean. As a consequence, the place was named for him.

McLeish *Athens County.* The McLeish Coal Mining Company conducted operations here about 1900; the name remains.

McLuney *Perry County.* Organized in 1855. The name is that of a creek on which the town is situated. The creek almost certainly was named for a person or family, but no data could be located. McLuney had a post office as early as 1850.

McMorran *Logan County.* John and Grant McMorran purchased land at this place and founded the town in 1909.

Meacham *Trumbull County.* This community derives its name from a local family named Meacham. About 1828, Lucretia Meacham taught school in this township, using the cellar of her home as a classroom.

Mecca *Trumbull County.* The name undoubtedly was inspired by the city of Mecca (now in Saudi Arabia), the birthplace of Muhammad and the goal of Muslim pilgrimages. Town fathers probably aspired to create a "mecca" for the area, to which many would come to do business. The hamlet is in Mecca Township, settled as early as 1811 but not formally organized until 1821.

Mechanicsburg *Champaign County.* Apparently a Captain Culver was held in high regard by town fathers, as it was for Culver's occupation—mechanical engineer—that the village was named. The "burg" suffix was added upon incorporation in 1834.

Mechanicsburg *Crawford County.* Between 1845 and 1850, several blacksmiths and other craftsmen opened shops here. Included were Israel H. Irwin and Samuel Hilborn, both blacksmiths, a trade labeled "mechanic" in those days. A cooper, a cabinetmaker, a carpenter, and an individual who started a grist mill operation also populated this place during its earliest days as a town.

Medill *Athens County.* An 1856 Democratic candidate for Congress from Ohio named Medill is the person to whom this place-name leads.

Medina *Medina County (seat).* Settled, 1814, by Zenas Hamilton; platted in 1818; incorporated as a village in 1835. Two accounts of the naming of this city survive. One holds that it was named for a community of the same name in New York State. The second claims that a prominent local property owner, Elijah Boardman, being a well-read man, first named the township Mecca, after the Muslim pilgrimage site. In doing so, he foresaw that this area would be "the end of the trail" for Yankees heading west. However, there being a Mecca in Trumbull County, a new label was chosen, that of Medina, a reference to the burial site of Muhammad and thus like Mecca a place of pilgrimage.

Medway *Clark County.* Settled, 1807, by the Reverend Archibald Steele, who ran a grist mill. In 1816, he platted the town. The name apparently came about as a result of its location, "medway" between Dayton and Springfield.

Meeker *Darke County.* The name probably traces back to David L. Meeker, born 1827, who became a lawyer and judge in this area. He was elected county prosecutor in 1856 and 1858.

Meeker *Marion County.* Settled about 1823 by Samuel Franklin. The community was first known as Cochranton, for Colonel William Cochran. Scott Town became the name in 1844, apparently remaining so for many years. In 1908, the label became Meeker, for G. W. Meeker. Meeker was expected to be instrumental in bringing an electric interurban route to this place; however, the interurban never materialized.

Meigs *Morgan County.* Ohio's governor in 1810, Return J. Meigs (1764–1825?), was honored with the naming of this community. Meigs County, also named after Governor Meigs, was created later, in 1819.

Meigsville *Muskingum County.* The village was known early on as Lytlesburg, for George Lytle. It is in Meigs Township, which, like this community, traces back its name to Governor Return J. Meigs, of Marietta. Gilbert Bishop laid out the town in 1840.

Melmore *Seneca County.* Laid out in 1824. It is said that this cognomen was created by James Kilbourne when he was surveying roads in the area. Kilbourne is believed to have joined *mel* from the Latin (meaning "honey") to the English word "more" to identify this spot where Honey Creek crossed the road that Kilbourne was surveying.

Melrose *Paulding County.* It is said that Melrose was platted by two unnamed Scotsmen about 1845 and named by them in honor of Melrose Abbey in Scotland. However, records reveal that the formal laying out of the village took place in 1855. In 1888, the town was incorporated.

Memphis *Clinton County.* Founded in 1849. Although it cannot be said with certainty whether Memphis, Tennessee, influenced the naming of this tiny hamlet, one source claims that "many settlers came from Tennessee." The antecedent of both, no doubt, was the ancient city of Memphis on the Nile River in Egypt.

Mentor *Lake County.* This name, according to one source, was intended to memorialize the individual who tutored Ulysses' son in Greek mythology. Another claims that the community took the name from an early citizen named Hiram Mentor. The town was incorporated in 1855.

Mentor-on-the-Lake *Lake County.* This community spun off from Mentor (see preceding entry) and possesses Lake Erie frontage. It is located just west-northwest of Mentor. Now a city, Mentor-on-the-Lake was incorporated in 1924.

Mercer *Mercer County.* Laid out by Bernard Brewster in 1833, the village is the namesake of General Hugh Mercer (circa 1725–1777), a Virginian who served and died in the American Revolution.

Mercerville *Gallia County.* Mercerville was named for its founder, Mercer Hall.

Merriam *Muskingum County.* Also referred to as Merriam Station, this location owes its name to Cyrus Merriam, who helped conceal slaves here.

Mesopotamia *Trumbull County.* Doubling as the name of the township, Mesopotamia translates as "two rivers." One historian observed that the town name "never has seemed appropriate" and went on to call it "a pity."

Metamora *Fulton County.* The plat for the village was filed in 1851, and incorporation took place in 1893. According to a reference source, Metamora was a deeply respected loyal warrior of the Wampanoag tribe. His father was Chief Massasoit. When the colonists took over Massachusetts, Metamora tried to be friends with them, to no avail. He was later killed by his own people. A contemporary source close to the town adds, "I like to think the men who gave the name to our small town did so in the hope that the settlers here would be people who exemplified the virtues of the original Metamora: bravery and courage; staunch friendship; love and loyalty to home and family." A second, less plausible, humorous version of how the village got its name goes like this: One of the first settlers in Metamora was named Morey Potter. An Indian child went home after a visit with the settler and when asked where he had been, answered, "I met-a-morey today." And hence the name, Metamora!

Metham *Coshocton County.* This place-name likely traces to a prominent early figure in the area, Colonel Pren Metham, who held a great deal of agricultural land in the vicinity. Colonel Metham was born in 1830.

Meyers Lake *Stark County.* A mecca during the big band era of the 1930s and 1940s, this place bears the name of Andrew Meyer, who came to this locale in 1814. Meyers Lake was incorporated in 1928.

Miamisburg *Montgomery County.* Laid out in 1818. This locale first was referred to as Hole's Station, in deference to Zachariah Hole, who is said to have erected an abode in 1800. "Miami" is believed to mean "mother" in an Indian tongue. "Burg," of course, indicates a settlement of one stature or another. Miamisburg was incorporated in 1832 and today is a city.

Miamitown *Hamilton County.* A post office operated at what was then Miami, Ohio, from 1807 to 1904. Upon the reopening of a post office at the location in 1931, the name Miamitown was installed. The Chesapeake & Ohio Railroad maintained a depot east of town, calling it Miami, and apparently that caused confusion between it and the village, so the village was labeled Miamitown. It lies on the banks of the Great Miami River and had been inhabited by the Miami Indians. The original town of Miami was founded by Arthur Henrie in 1816, when he laid out lots. He was believed to be a nephew of Patrick Henry. "Miami" is said to translate from an Indian language as "mother."

Miamiville *Clermont County.* The community is near the Little Miami River. (See the preceding entry.)

Middlebourne *Guernsey County.* The village derives its name from its location, about halfway between Zanesville, Ohio, and Wheeling, West Virginia.

Middlebranch *Stark County.* Surveyed and platted, 1881, by John Pontius. Pontius was the owner of the site, which may have been occupied as early as 1811. It takes its name from its position on the middle branch of Nimishillen Creek.

Middleburg *Noble County.* Dating to 1845, Middleburg sits at about the center of Elk Township.

Middleburg Heights *Cuyahoga County.* An early settler in this locale was Jared Hickox, in 1809. Some of the families migrating to the site began their treks in Middleburg, New York, importing the name along with them. Middleburg Heights was incorporated as a city in 1961.

Middlebury *Van Wert County.* Middlebury gains its name, according to one account, by virtue of its position halfway between Decatur, Indiana, and Van Wert, Ohio. A second version states that a salesman, inquiring in the village, asked how far it was to the next town. He was informed that it was nine miles to Van Wert, Decatur, or Willshire. The inquirer then remarked that the community seemed to be in the "middle" of all of them. The previous name was Daisie.

Middlefield *Geauga County.* Isaac and Jane Thompson and their children became the earliest permanent settlers at this place in 1799. It gained its name because of its situation at the midpoint of an early path between Painesville and Warren. The year 1908 marked Middlefield's incorporation.

Middle Point *Van Wert County.* L. B. and H. N. Sykes laid out this village in 1852. It was incorporated in 1874 or 1875. It was so named because of its situation halfway between Van Wert and Delphos. The name is sometimes written Middlepoint.

Middleport *Meigs County.* Located in Salisbury Township, the town originally bore the same label. The change was probably a result of the orientation of the site, at the approximate halfway point, by water, between Pittsburgh and Cincinnati.

Middleton *Columbiana County.* Platted by a Quaker surveyor and elder, William Heald, Middleton was established about 1803 by Society of Friends members. Their first meeting, termed for some reason the Middle Meeting, in turn suggested the place-name.

Middleton *Jackson County.* Laid out, 1827, by Oliver Tison. Halfway between Wilkesville and Jackson, this place was once called Middle Town.

Middletown *Butler County.* Laid out, 1802, by Steven Vail. The name is a function of the city's location, midway between Dayton and Cincinnati. Incorporation occurred in 1833.

Middletown *Champaign County.* This name was applied by virtue of the community's placement in the center of Wayne Township. It was 1833 when John Miller laid it out.

Middletown *Crawford County.* Laid out, 1835, by Henry Hershner. The site was owned by Hershner, the Snyders, and the Ashcrofts. It seems likely that the name is the result of the place's location, midway between Bucyrus and Mansfield.

Middletown *Perry County.* Laid out in 1853. This village was so named because of its location, midway between Logan and Somerset.

Midvale *Tuscarawas County.* Although the village was settled somewhat earlier, John M. Rutledge platted it in 1888. It is midway between the county seat (New Philadelphia) and Uhrichsville. The "vale" may have started out as "ville." Incorporation was in 1927.

Midway *Belmont County.* Recorded, 1903, by Ida M. and Frank Gamble. The place was so named because it was equidistant from Fairpoint and Blaineville.

Midway *Madison County.* Platted in 1833. The landowners were Lockhart Biggs, William Morris, and Frank Thompson. This place was considered a central point on the trip between Philadelphia and Chicago. It is also midway across the southern tier of the county, east to west, and is about equidistant to other local towns of importance. Midway was incorporated in 1845.

Mifflin *Ashland County.* This place-name leads back to a corresponding place in Pennsylvania—possibly the Pittsburgh suburb of West Mifflin. In any event, the ultimate source is an early Pennsylvania governor, Thomas Mifflin (1744–1800).

Mifflinville *Franklin County.* Founded in 1840. Mifflinville is in Mifflin Township. See the preceding entry for the explanation of the name.

Milan *Erie County.* Platted by Ebenezer Merry following the War of 1812. Upon the town's incorporation in 1833, it is said, the Berlin-Milan Treaty was playing a prominent role in the news from Europe and may have inspired the citizens of this place to name it Milan. The first name of the site, in the early nineteenth century, was Beatty, for a minister who resided in the vicinity. Beatty had acquired the land and held it until about 1816, when Merry purchased it. For a time thereafter, it was known as Merry's Mill Pond; Merry had erected a grist and sawmill at the site. It was Merry who, in 1817, laid out the streets. The time of the name change to Milan coincided with the period when many American communities were adopting European names, such as Florence. In 1847, Milan was the birthplace of Thomas Alva Edison.

Milford *Clermont County.* Platted by John Hageman in 1806, this community was originally known as Hageman's Mills. Located on the Little Miami River, it constituted an important site for mills during the early years. The current name comes from "mill ford." Incorporation took place in 1836.

Milfordton *Knox County.* The community is in Milford Township. When early citizens submitted their preferences for a place-name, virtually all of them evoked some type of objection. The exception was Milford, offered by Judson Lamson, who favored it because he was a native of New Milford, Connecticut. Thus the Milfordton name can be construed as "the town of Milford Township."

Mill Grove *Morgan County.* A family named Patton operated a mill at this site. The "Grove" aspect of the name probably owed to a shady location.

Millbrook *Wayne County.* Powered by the current of a nearby stream, seven mills once operated here. Millbrook was founded in 1829.

Millbury *Wood County.* Surveyed, 1864, by R. B. Willison. When a name had to be selected in order to obtain a post office at the site, citizens were split between Millbury and Mark Lane as the choice. The former was for a town between Boston and Worcester, Massachusetts; the latter represented the English grain market. The decision was made with a coin toss, Millbury coming up the winner. In 1874, the community was incorporated.

Milledgeville *Fayette County.* Community authorities report that the historically accepted explanation is that the name was a direct reference to a "mill on the edge of the ville."

Miller *Lawrence County.* The cemetery inscriptions of twenty Millers in this township (Rome) are found in the record book. The earliest—of those whose birthdates could be ascertained—was Eliza, born 1862. Of the many other persons of this surname who sank their roots deep into this locality, one was Abraham Miller, a farmer, who settled in 1819. Another was A. Miller, who came here in 1830. The latter was described as a farmer and county commissioner. In 1859, H. M. Miller arrived, engaging in farming. E. R. Miller, described as a "general speculator," settled in 1864. If this is the Ohio River community that was once known as Millersport, it is believed to have been named for its first settler, Joseph Miller.

Miller City *Putnam County.* Platted, 1882, by Aaron Overbeck. First it was named Saint Nicholas to pay homage to two illustrious local frontiersmen, Nicholas Noriot and Nicholas Miller—who also happened to own the land at the site. In 1890 it was renamed Miller City, out of respect for Nicholas Miller.

Millersburg *Holmes County (seat).* Adam Johnson and Charles Miller moved to this site in 1824, putting down roots. The place was named after Miller. The community was incorporated in 1835.

Millersport *Fairfield County.* Laid out in 1825 by Matthias Miller. Located on the Ohio Canal, the place was named for Miller. Incorporation was in 1918.

Miller Station *Harrison County.* This designation probably leads back to one of the many early Millers living in this locality in 1816–1836. Included were David, Eli, Harrison, Jr., Asa, Stephen, Jacob, two Johns, Daniel (who came from Maryland and died in German Township in 1854), William, and James.

Millerstown *Champaign County.* Laid out in 1837. Casper Miller was the proprietor. Cousins John C. and Christ Miller are said to be the individuals honored in the naming of this hamlet. Christ was the son of Casper Miller.

Millersville *Sandusky County.* A landowner here, Peter Miller, laid out a portion of the town. He was named the first postmaster at Millersville.

Millertown *Perry County.* This town's name is readily explained by the fact that it was laid out by Jacob Miller, in 1834.

Millfield *Athens County.* Laid out, 1826, by John Pugsley. Pugsley became the first postmaster. The name resulted from a mill built at the site in 1802 by John Sweat.

Millport *Columbiana County.* Laid out, 1853, by Hugh Laughlin and Philip Willyard. Millport was once known as Franklin. It gets its current name from the fact that a grist mill and sawmill were prominent early establishments.

Millport *Pickaway County.* The town was laid out by Richard Stage. Stephen Short constructed a mill and distillery here as early as 1810. Later the site had access to the Ohio Canal.

Millrock *Columbiana County.* This name is also seen as Mill Rock. One theory is that stones cut at a local quarry were used in the mill here. In 1879, Peter Ulim operated the mill at this site.

Millsboro *Richland County.* Laid out, 1831, by John S. Marshall. As early as 1818, mills were being built at this location, which was spelled Millsborough. One or more were built by John Garretson of New York. The Purdy Mill, a sawmill, and several stills characterized the place.

Mills Station *Gallia County.* This train stop was erected on land owned by the Mills family. One listing of Ohio places refers to it as Mills.

Millville *Butler County.* Founded, 1815, by Joseph Van Horn. In 1805, Van Horn constructed a mill at this location, accounting for the site's name.

Millwood *Knox County.* The hamlet was laid out about 1825 by John Hann. Two theories regarding the naming of this town exist. One holds that it was so named because the first mill in the region was built in the woods at this location. Or it may have been named in recognition of a Mr. Millwood of Virginia, said to have been a friend of the town's founder.

Miltonsburg *Monroe County.* Laid out, 1836, by David Pierson. The community was named after David's son, Milton. Incorporation took place in 1859.

Miltonville *Butler County.* Platted, 1816, by Theophilus Egglesfield, George Bennett, and Richard Crane. Families of English descent settled the site, leading to speculation that it was named for the English poet John Milton.

Mineral *Athens County.* A profusion of various minerals occurred naturally in this village's surroundings, so it came by its name logically. The town was established in 1857.

Mineral City *Tuscarawas County.* Laid out, 1853, by George Lachner and Alfred David. The place derives its name from abundant mineral deposits in the vicinity. In 1882, Mineral City was incorporated.

Mineral Ridge *Trumbull County.* Incorporated in 1817, this village takes its name from the area's coal mines, the first of which began operation in 1835.

Minersville *Meigs County.* The village dates to before 1857. The primary occupation of the populace seems to have inspired the name. The Pittsburgh Coal Company had a bustling operation here, two salt works were nearby, and rock quarrying was a major endeavor. It is said that there are fourteen abandoned mines in the vicinity.

Minerton *Vinton County.* Never platted, this hamlet sprang up around 1880, with the coming of the Hocking Valley Railroad. At about the same time, coal-mining operations arose virtually overnight, accounting for the name of the community.

Minerva *Carroll and Stark counties.* John Whitacre is regarded as having founded this community, perhaps about 1818. Issac Craig was issued the first deed for land here, in 1813. The first child born in the fledgling settlement, and possibly its namesake, was Whitacre's niece, born July 14, 1828. Her name was Minerva Ann Taylor (or Thomas). An alternative explanation sometimes advanced is that the name traces back to Minerva, the Roman goddess of handicrafts and the arts. The place was platted and incorporated in 1833.

Minerva Park *Franklin County.* In 1895, the Minerva Amusement Park opened here and became popular. The village takes its name from that park, which closed in

1902. Although a likeness of the Roman goddess Minerva graced the entrance columns along Cleveland Avenue, the park took its name from the wife of the first developer, Minerva Shipherd. The village was incorporated in 1940.

Minford *Scioto County.* Platted in 1859 by Frank C. Gibbs. Prior to 1918, the town at this site was known as Harrisonville, while its post office was called Scioto. In 1918, both were changed to Minford in honor of Frank Minford (1866–1942). Frank had followed in the footsteps of his father, William J. Minford (1829–1908), as the town's blacksmith. The Harrisonville moniker had been the result of a friendship between the man who laid out the town and President William Henry Harrison.

Mingo *Champaign County.* The *History of Champaign County* recounts an anecdote regarding the genesis of this village. According to the story, Alexander Saint Clair Hunter met the Reverend B. W. Gehman along the road in 1844, and the former predicted that before long a railroad would bisect the valley and "right by that mulberry tree will be a village." In time, the Erie Railroad came through and a town site developed, much as Hunter had envisioned. The initial name of the place was Mulberry. It was later changed to Mingo, in all probability in honor of the Indian chieftain of that name. Thomas Hunter is said to have instituted the name change.

Mingo Junction *Jefferson County.* This site took on its name because it is situated where a Mingo Indian village once stood. The town was incorporated in 1882.

Minster *Auglaize County.* Founded, 1833, by Francis Joseph Stallo and originally referred to as Stallostown. The Minster name emanated from the Teutonic homeland of many of the settlers: Münster, Westphalia. Incorporation took place in 1839.

Misco *Perry County.* The original name of this coal-mining town was Prosper. J. G. and S. E. Underwood platted the community in 1894. The Misco post office commenced in 1903. It is thought that the place-name is connected to Paul Misco, who was killed in a mining accident in Guernsey County in 1902 or 1903 at age twenty-six. He was employed by the Wills (or Willis) Creek Coal Company, which owned land near Prosper.

Misner Corners *Mahoning County.* A great many Misners resided in this vicinity at the time of naming—twenty-four in the index of one Trumbull-Mahoning history alone. Some of them spelled it Mizener.

Mitchell's Mill *Geauga County.* In 1836, a mill was erected here on a branch of the Chagrin River by Martin Mitchell.

Mitiwanga *Erie County.* This locality is sometimes styled Mitiwanga Beach, fronting as it does on Lake Erie. However, this may be a redundancy, since at least one resident history buff claims that *mitiwanga* is an Erie Indian word meaning "sandy beach."

Moats *Defiance County.* The name probably traces back to Wallace Moats, a family physician in the 1870s at The Bend (Delaware Bend), just south of here, or to one of his ancestors.

Modoc *Athens County.* The Modoc War (1872–1873) spread this name far and wide, and it began to pop up in a number of states. The Modoc were a tribe of Native Americans in the Oregon-California region. There is a Modoc Road in Santa Barbara, California. It is unclear why the name was applied here in Athens County.

Moffitt *Hancock County.* This Blanchard Township location is near the site where the Moffitt brothers—Thomas, John, and William—established residence about 1826. Thomas later moved to Iowa, hoping that his health would improve.

Mogadore *Summit and Portage counties.* This name is said to have been imparted to the village by an Irishman named James Robinson. Upon finishing the chimney of a two-story dwelling for Martin Kent, Robinson swung his hat around in an arc and shouted, "Hurrah for Mogadore!" It is speculated that he had read of a town in Africa bearing that name, either in *Mungo Park's Travels* or *Riley's Narratives.* Mogador (no "e") is the former name of Essaouira, a city in Morocco founded in 1760. Mogadore, Ohio, was incorporated in 1900.

Mohawk Village *Coshocton County.* This name was inspired by the Mohawk tribe of Native Americans.

Mohicanville *Ashland County.* Laid out, 1833, by Simeon Beall and Henry Sherradden. The village took its name from Mohican Township, which was named for the Mohican Indians.

Monday Creek *Hocking County.* The community is on Monday Creek, which gained its name when it was reached by settlers on a Monday.

Monday Junction *Hocking County.* The site, also known simply as Monday, is on a branch of Monday Creek and was a railroad junction. (See the preceding entry.)

Monnette *Crawford County.* A number of Monnettes populated this area, beginning in settlement years. The Reverend T. J. Monnette is known to have been on the scene in 1873. Much earlier, in 1818, Catharine Monnette resided in the area. Oliver Monnette, born 1840, and M. J. Monnette, born 1847, were farmers. Two prominent area firms were A. Monnette & Co., and Monnette, Frazer & Co. An Abraham and a Jacob Monnette are known to have lived in the area as well.

Mononcue *Wyandot County.* It is believed that Mononcue was named for a Wyandot chief "who had become a fine preacher of the Wyandots." This is according to the volume *Mostly Ghosts: Stagecoach Inns, Hotels, Covered Bridges, Towns in Wyandot County, Ohio.*

Monroe *Butler County.* Laid out, 1817, by John H. Piatt and Nathan Sackett. The hamlet takes its name from President James Monroe (1758–1831).

Monroe Center *Ashtabula County.* This community at the center of Monroe Township was named for the fifth U.S. president, James Monroe.

Monroe Station *Jackson County.* Sometime after 1797 and before 1820, Aaron and Jesse Monroe settled near this site, accounting for the name. One source states, however, that the place was named for President James Monroe. The same correspondent places the site adjacent to the Monroe Furnace works and characterizes it as a stop on the Baltimore & Ohio Railorad.

Monroeville *Huron County.* Laid out, 1817, by John Sowers and Seth Brown. The city is named for President James Monroe, according to one source. A second source claims that Brown, having served in the War of 1812 under General William Henry Harrison, had reached as far north as Monroe, Michigan, during the campaign. At that juncture, he met and married Sarah Tuttle, a widow, bringing her to the Western Reserve following the war. Here he built a house and christened the area Monroe, in honor of the place where he had met his future wife. Later, to eliminate confusion in postal matters, "ville" was added to the name, there being another place called Monroe in Ohio.

Monroeville *Jefferson County.* Abraham Croxton laid off this town site and named it out of respect for President James Monroe.

Monterey *Clermont County.* Monterrey, Mexico, is the city that inspired this place-name. The hamlet was established at about the time of the Mexican War (1846–1848).

Montezuma *Mercer County.* In 1834, this place was founded by William Beauchamp. It is conjectured that the name stems from the one-time presence nearby of a Native American tribe, the Chickasaws, who were said to be descended from the Aztecs of Mexico. Some settlers referred to them as "Montezuma Indians."

Montgomery *Hamilton County.* Settled in 1795. The village was laid out in 1801 by Nathaniel Terwilliger. Families named Felton, Snider, Crist, Taulman, Weller, and Roosa (Rosa?) came to this place from Montgomery, Orange County, New York, and settled. (One source states that they came from Montgomery County, New York.) Many of them arrived in 1806–1807. Incorporation was accomplished in 1910.

Monticello *Van Wert County.* According to sources in the Brumbach Library in Van Wert, the early Swiss and German inhabitants of this locale were admirers of President Thomas Jefferson and named their home after Jefferson's mansion in Virginia.

Montpelier *Williams County.* Platted by Thomas Ogle in 1845. Two prominent places by this name exist in the United States. One is the capital of Vermont and the other is President James Madison's former home and final resting site in Virginia. It is not known whether one of them influenced the naming of this place. The word *Montpelier* is of French derivation. Incorporation of this village came in 1874.

Montra *Shelby County.* The Montra Tile Yards once operated here. The community became known by the name of the company.

Montrose *Summit County.* It is speculated that the name commemorates roses that grew high and wild here.

Montville *Geauga County.* The town may take its name from Montville, New London County, Connecticut. An alternative theory holds that the name is a result of the town's location at the highest elevation in the county. Settlement began about 1815.

Moorefield *Harrison County.* Gabriel Cane and Michael Moore platted this village in 1815. It took Moore's name.

Moore's Junction *Perry County.* This place-name is sometimes seen printed as Moore Junction. The rail junction was owned by Colonel T. W. Moore, entrepreneur and storekeeper. One source refers to a Moore family as "the major landowner in the area, who evidently first acquired land [here] around 1870." A printout from the United States Department of the Interior Geological Survey gives Moore's Junction's county as Washington, but this is thought to be in error. Maps show a Moore's Junction in Perry County.

Mooresville *Ross County.* Several Moores called this locale home. The place-name probably relates to one or more of them. Noah B. Moore was a grandson of Colonel Taylor W. Moore of Ross County. Born in 1871, Noah was a farmer and railroad employee. Joseph Moore was a local farmer and builder.

Moraine *Montgomery County.* From a city brochure comes the explanation that "the name . . . comes from the last glacier that deposited vast amounts of sand and gravel over the valley." The word *moraine* refers to the glacial deposits. The site's earliest known inhabitants were Native Americans of the Adena culture and Hopewell tradition. Shawnee, Delaware, Miami, and Iroquois people later frequented the place. Moraine became a township in 1953 and a village in 1957. In 1965, it was incorporated as a city. (A book published by the Ohio Secretary of State's Office gives the year of incorporation as a city as 1959.)

Moreland *Wayne County.* Moreland was founded in 1829 by George Morr, the landowner, and Jonathan Butler. The place adopted Morr's surname. A correspondent puts the year of founding at 1808, not 1829.

Moreland Hills *Cuyahoga County.* Moreland Hills was incorporated in 1929. The name's origin is vague, probably simply indicating a rolling and scenic topography.

Morgan Center *Gallia County.* It is said that the hamlet, which is near the center of Morgan Township, was named for Morgan's Raiders. John Hunt Morgan

(1825–1864) was a Confederate general in the Civil War who led a daring raid through Kentucky, Indiana, and Ohio in 1863.

Morgan Center *Knox County.* Morgan Center is near the center of Morgan Township.

Morganville *Morgan County.* Platted, 1833, by S. Short. Like the county, the village owes its name to a Revolutionary War commander, General Daniel Morgan (1736–1802).

Morges *Carroll County.* Morges was laid out in 1831 by John Waggoner and Samuel Oswalt. L. Vail did the surveying. The name was apparently appropriated from a commune on Lake Geneva in Switzerland.

Morning Sun *Preble County.* Founded, 1833, by James McQuiston. According to accounts, the founder and other local citizens got together one day to decide on a name for the community but could not come to an agreement. Upon awaking the next day, they beheld the rising sun and agreed to name the place Rising Sun—later altered to Morning Sun. It was listed as the latter as early as 1842.

Morning View *Belmont County.* Apparently the impressive vista afforded by the 1,265-foot elevation of this site inspired its name.

Morral *Marion County.* This town sprang up with the coming of the railroad. Thomas E. Berry, real estate agent and promoter, filed the plat plan with the county recorder in 1875. The name Morral was bestowed to honor Samuel Morral I, who owned land where the village is located.

Morristown *Belmont County.* Laid out, 1802, by William Chapline and John Zane. Chapline and Zane named the place for one of its first settlers, Duncan Morrison, who was its first postmaster and served as justice of the peace.

Morrisville *Clinton County.* The village was laid out and surveyed by Nathan Linton in 1840. The name comes from Isaac Morris, who owned a sizable adjoining tract of land.

Morrow *Warren County.* Laid out, 1844, by William H. Clement, George Keck, and Clark Williams. The town was named in honor of Governor Jeremiah Morrow (1771–1852).

Mortimer *Hancock County.* This place was once named Silverwood and later Stuartsville, after early settlers. The first post office was named Mortimer, probably for a family of that name. It is said that in 1947 the name was changed to North Findlay. However, it can still be found as Mortimer on current maps.

Morton *Monroe County.* In the 1850s, William L., Barzilla, and David Morton settled in Franklin Township in this county. All were born in the 1830s.

Moscow *Clermont County.* During the 1800s, it was popular to name towns after large cities in foreign countries. In all probability, this was the case with Moscow, Ohio.

Moss Run *Washington County.* This place was originally called Morse Run, for an early settler who manufactured shingles from chestnut wood. His was considered the first industry in Lawrence Township. The current place-name represents a corruption of Morse. A post office opened here in 1857.

Mount Blanchard *Hancock County.* Laid out, 1830, by Asa M. Lake. Incorporation took place in 1865. Mount Blanchard probably derives its name from the Blanchard River, which in turn probably traces back to a Frenchman named Blanchard who plied the waterways in this region.

Mount Carmel *Clermont and Hamilton counties.* Although the place was surveyed in 1788 for Major William Mosley of Virginia, Mount Carmel was never laid out. The first settlers, including John Rose in 1796, were from New Jersey, and it is thought that the place was named for Mount Carmel, New Jersey. Some of the settlers who came here from Mount Carmel, New Jersey, are believed to have moved on to Mount Carmel, Indiana. The name is biblical: Mount Carmel was the place in Palestine where Elijah addressed the issue of the worship of Yahweh or Baal. A convent is located there; the Carmelite monks take their name from it. *Carmel* indicates orchards or gardens that were cultivated on the slopes of the mountain.

Mount Carrick *Monroe County.* Sometimes styled simply as Carrick, this hamlet traces back its name to a postmaster at the site (1857), Thomas Carrick.

Mount Cory *Hancock County.* D. J. Cory founded the village in 1872, and it was named for him. The post office may have provided the "Mount" segment, as it was desired to avoid confusion with a Jefferson County place called Cora.

Mount Eaton *Wayne County.* The community was established on an elevation. "Eaton" probably refers to an officer in the Tripolitan War, Captain William Eaton (1764–1811; see also the Eaton entry). This community was platted in 1813 as Paintville. James Galbraith and William Vaughn laid it out. The name Mount Eaton was not applied until 1829. The village was incorporated in 1870.

Mount Ephraim *Noble County.* This village was christened for (and perhaps by) Ephraim Vorhies. The community was platted in 1838 on land owned by Vorhies, who also ran a tavern.

Mount Gilead *Morrow County (seat).* Settlement took place in 1817. Known between 1824 and 1832 as Youngstown, this community was laid out by Jacob Young in 1824. Sources state that earlier it had been known as Whetsom or Whetstone. It is said to have been incorporated by the Ohio legislature as Mount Gilead, the biblical name, in 1832, apparently honoring a similarly named town in Virginia. Incorporation, according to an alternate source, was accomplished in 1839.

Mount Healthy *Hamilton County.* First named Mount Pleasant, this place was required to change its name because of another town or towns identically named. The community had been spared during the 1850 cholera epidemic, so the locals adopted the name Mount Healthy.

Mount Holly *Warren County.* Platted in 1833 on land owned by Jacob Pearson. The place took its name from Mount Holly, New Jersey.

Mount Joy *Scioto County.* In the early years, a land speculator, Thomas Mount Joy, possessed approximately 3,000 acres in this vicinity. As a consequence, this place retained his name.

Mount Liberty *Knox County.* This town takes part of its name from its township (Liberty). The "Mount" is a result of its location in a hilly area near Mount Vernon.

Mount Nebo *Athens County.* This elevated site was acquired in 1870 by Eli Curtis. Curtis is quoted as declaring that the place was "dedicated . . . to the Lord of Hosts . . . to be used expressly for spiritual purposes and for a place to form the nucleus around which the City of the New Jerusalem (in time) is to be founded." Mount Nebo was the promontory from which Moses viewed the Promised Land (Deuteronomy 32 and 34).

Mount Olivett *Belmont County.* The second part of the name is sometimes spelled with one "t." And sometimes the word "mount" is dropped from the name. The place first had the name Fidelity and later Chaneytown for a man from Maryland, J. Chaney. The community was laid out in 1851 by James Rossell, a clergyman. In one New Testament mention (Acts 1:12), the Mount of Olives, a ridge east of Jerusalem frequented by Jesus, is called Olivet.

Mount Orab *Brown County.* The community was laid out by Daniel Keethler in 1850 and surveyed by William S. McLain. Keethler named the place after the Midianite prince Oreb and the rock where he was slain (Judges 7:25). At some point, the "e" was changed to "a." Other interpretations of Oreb include "crow" or "raven."

Mount Perry *Perry County.* The hamlet is in Perry County, named for Commodore Oliver Hazard Perry (1785–1819). The town was platted in 1828.

Mount Pisgah *Clermont County.* This highland community, never laid out, was settled by 1830. Because a cooperage once operated here, it formerly boasted the nickname Kegtown. The biblical Pisgah refers to the rugged headlands of the Abarim range between the Dead Sea and Jericho. It was from Mount Nebo in the Pisgah headlands that Moses looked out upon the Promised Land.

Mount Pleasant *Jefferson County.* Pennsylvanians Jesse Thomas and Robert Carothers settled this site in 1796 and laid out the village in 1803. The township (Mount Pleasant) was named for the village, not vice versa. Because the site was so attractive, twenty men were camped nearby to become early bidders when the government offered the land for sale. Lots were drawn, and Carothers won. Disgruntled losers were thought to have assigned the place the nickname Jesse-Bob Town.

Mount Sinai *Pike County.* This name apparently echoes the biblical Mount Sinai, where the Israelites camped after fleeing from Egypt. The precise location of their encampment is not known. It was on Mount Sinai that Moses received the Ten Commandments.

Mount Sterling *Madison County.* Surveyed and laid off, 1828, by John J. Smith. Smith, who was born in Kentucky, named this village after Mount Sterling, his favorite Kentucky town.

Mount Summit *Hamilton County.* The community is on a high elevation in upland eastern Hamilton County.

Mount Vernon *Knox County (seat).* Laid out, 1805, by Thomas B. Patterson, Benjamin Butler, and Joseph Walker. All three city fathers had journeyed from George Washington's home county in Virginia, and their new town was given the name of the first president's estate. Incorporation took place in 1830.

Mount Victory *Hardin County.* This name resulted from a legal dispute. Title to the land here was contested by Samuel McCulloch and Ezra Dille. The disagreement was resolved by the court at the county seat, which accepted bids for the sale of the land. When Dille outbid McCulloch, he considered it a "victory" and christened the place Mount Victory when the plat was recorded in 1851. The same year, the place was incorporated.

Mountville *Morgan County.* Mountville owes its name to Jacob Mount, a local figure in 1880. One source states that the community was laid out in 1837 and refers to it as Mountsville.

Mowrystown *Highland County.* Until 1829, this community was essentially a pioneer settlement. At that juncture, it was platted as a town by Samuel Bell, who named it in recognition of Squire Abe Mowry, a respected local citizen. One source gives the family name as Mowery.

Moxahala *Perry County.* The name of this hamlet is said by some to be a Delaware Indian term translating as "elk's horn" or "little falls." The site was laid out by A. S. Biddison in 1873.

Moxahala Park *Muskingum County.* An amusement park opened here during the first decade of the 1900s (perhaps in 1906), accounting for the "Park" in the name.

Financiers behind the Southern Ohio Interurban Line bankrolled the project. *Moxahala* is thought to be of Delaware Indian origin (see the preceding entry). Moxahala Creek trickles nearby.

Mudsock *Logan County.* Surveyed and laid out, 1847, by S. A. Harbison. The landowner was Henry Van Vheris. It is said that this site came by its name quite naturally, the mud having been four to five inches deep in its formative days. Horses and buggies regularly became bogged down in the sticky goo.

Muncie Hollow *Sandusky County.* This label is probably the result of the movements across Ohio of a tribe or subtribe of Native Americans, who traveled New Jersey and Pennsylvania before settling for a period in Indiana and Illinois. *American Place-Names* refers to them as Muncy or Muncie, while *Indiana Place-Names* cites additional spellings of Monsy, Monthee, Muncey, Min-si, and Min-thi-u. The latter source states that the Native Americans were a clan of the Delawares and advises that the name refers to "people of the stony country."

Munroe Falls *Summit County.* Settled, 1809, by a group of forty persons from Connecticut. The settlers were led by William Stow, Isaac Wilcox, Francis Kelsey, Thomas Gaylord, Jonathon and Samuel Gaylord, William M. McClelland, and Frederick Wolcott. At first this community was called Kelsey's Mills. Later the name was changed to Florence. In 1836, the Munroe brothers, Edmund and William, who had been merchants in Boston, purchased two hundred acres here, and the town was incorporated as Munroe Falls in 1838. Now a city, it celebrated its 150th anniversary in 1988. A falls on the Cuyahoga River lends a picturesque touch to the city's setting.

Munson Hill *Ashtabula County.* This hamlet derives its name from a New England place called Munsonville.

Murdoch *Warren County.* This place was the home of a Shakespearean actor and orator, Professor James E. Murdoch.

Murphy *Washington County.* Beginning in 1882, a post office was maintained here in the country store of William Murphy.

Murray City *Hocking County.* The plat for this village was recorded in 1873. It is said to have been named for an elderly Somerset, Ohio, gentleman who owned the land where Murray City reposes. The community was incorporated in 1892.

Museville *Muskingum County.* The site was named for R. W. P. Muse, a probate judge who assisted in securing the post office. Formerly the locale was known as Toadtown.

Muskingum *Washington County.* A post office served a small settlement here from 1881 to 1911. The place is near the Little Muskingum River, on Sackett Run. *Muskingum* means "elk's eye" in an Indian tongue.

Mutual *Champaign County.* In 1840, so the story goes, William Lafferty divested himself of some lots at this site, telling neighbors to whom he sold them that he intended to move to Texas. However, his only move was to a cabin nearby, which residents derisively referred to as "Lafferty's Texas." One source describes Lafferty as a "character from Mechanicsburg" who, after announcing his plans to move to Texas, erected a cabin at this site in 1814 (not 1840). This authority states that although the site at first was referred to as Lafferty's Texas, it soon became simply Texas. When the village was formally laid out in 1840 or 1846, it was named Mutual. One explanation for the change is that emigrants from Virginia who arrived in the 1840s realized that they needed to work together and christened the site Mutual. The place was incorporated in 1869.

Myers *Stark County.* Land was farmed in this township in the early years by William L. Myers, who was born in 1821. This map designation probably relates to him or his family.

Myersville *Summit County.* When a railroad was being built through the area about 1880, this spot was laid out on property belonging to John B. Myers.

Naceville *Pike County.* An early native of this township (Mifflin), John Nace, is the person after whom the hamlet was named.

Naomi *Henry County.* This community was known first as Freedom, which is the name of the township in which it is located. This name, however, was found to duplicate the name of one or more other Ohio towns. It is said that a local citizen, Mike Donnelly, offered a relative's name, Naomi, as a new name for the town. Apparently it appealed to the other residents, too.

Napier *Washington County.* George Napier, born in Scotland about 1795, resided here and gave the place this name. It is also sometimes known as Napier's Gap or Napier's Station.

Napoleon *Henry County (seat).* Initial settlers at this locality, of French derivation, named the place for Napoleon Bonaparte. Now a city, Napoleon was incorporated in 1863.

Nashport *Muskingum County.* Laid out in 1827. Situated on the Ohio Canal, this community was surveyed by Charles and John Roberts. The name recognizes Captain Thomas Nash, who is credited with founding the town.

Nashville *Darke County.* It is possible that General Francis Nash (1742–1777), a hero of the Revolutionary War, inspired the label that identifies this tiny hamlet.

Nashville *Holmes County.* The community is believed to be named after the city in Tennessee.

Navarre *Stark County.* Mrs. James Duncan, wife of the founder, was a French speaker; she gave the town the name of King Henry of Navarre (1553–1610), who became King Henry IV of France. James Duncan laid out Navarre in 1834. Incorporation was in 1872.

Naylor *Mahoning County.* Fourteen Naylors appear in the biographical index of a county history. One lived in Goshen Township, where this place is located. At least one other resided in nearby Smith Township.

Neapolis *Lucas County.* Founded, 1872, by J. O. Arnold, William A. Barnett, and Jackson Jordan. The name means "new city."

Nebraska *Pickaway County.* Postmaster D. F. Weaver changed the name of the post office here from Hedges' Store to Nebraska in 1859. His rationale for doing so is not documented. According to *American Place-Names*, the term *nebraska* is of Sioux origin, joining *ni* ("water") to *bthaska* ("flat"). The source advances the belief that this name referred to the Platte River, the course of which was wide, as opposed to being confined between high banks. Little Lick Run and Turkey Run flow through Nebraska, Ohio; perhaps these modest streams evoked Weaver's visions of the larger waterway. The spelling of Nebraska, the state, is credited to J. C. Frémont in 1844.

Neel *Brown County.* The site takes its designation from the family of early settlers Samuel and Mary Jane (Ousler) Neel. Their son, N. W. Neel, was born near here in 1827. A farmer and blacksmith, he also served as a county commissioner.

Neeleysville *Morgan County.* This town was first known as Newcastle. The change to Neeleysville was brought about by the Post Office Department to eliminate confusion with another Newcastle in Ohio. Robert Neeley founded the town.

Neff's *Belmont County.* Also known as Neff's Siding, this community was placed on the record in 1920. The name derives from Peter or Alexander Neff.

Negley *Columbiana County.* This community was named for James Scott Negley, born in 1824 in Pittsburgh. An avenue and a section of town in the Pennsylvania city bear the Negley name as well. A distinguished soldier, Negley served in the Mexican

War as a member of the Duquesne Grays. He also raised several regiments and fought in the Civil War. Later he served four terms in the U.S. House of Representatives and became an executive with the New York, Pittsburgh, & Chicago Railway. The first town plotted along the route of the line was named in his honor—Negley, Ohio. He died in 1901. At an earlier time, this community went by the name of Holly.

Nellie *Coshocton County.* This community was established on property owned by J. P. Darling. The name Darlington was put forth but was rejected owing to the existence of another Ohio Darlington. The name Maude was then suggested, being the given name of Darling's daughter. But there was also a Maude, Ohio, so that name, too, was rejected. Fortunately, Darling had another daughter—Nellie—and that name was accepted.

Nelson *Portage County.* A number of the early settlers at this spot arrived from the Nelson, New York, area, probably accounting for the name. The place is in Nelson Township. The area began to be settled in 1801.

Nelsonville *Athens County.* Platted in 1818; incorporated in 1871. The proprietor of the real estate here was Daniel Nelson, and the site assumed his name.

Netop *Washington County.* A post office was established here in 1897. A mail carrier reportedly told the Marietta postmaster that the place should be called "Knee Top" because that was the depth of the mud he had to wade through to make his deliveries. The result was the slightly knee-capitated Netop.

Nevada *Wyandot County.* Surveyed by J. H. Williams in 1852. The founders of this hamlet were George Garrett and Jonathan Ayers, who laid out the place. (Garrett is called Joel instead of George in one source.) It was named for the state of Nevada, which had recently been ceded by Mexico to the United States, or for the Sierra Nevada Mountains of California. The community was incorporated in 1866.

Neville *Clermont County.* This village was founded and laid out in 1808 by General Presley Neville. His father, Colonel John Presley, a Virginian who served in the Revolutionary War, had been rewarded for his service with 1,400 acres at this location. It was surveyed in 1788.

New Albany *Franklin County.* New Albany takes its name from the capital of New York State, Albany. It was laid out by William Yantis and Daniel Landon in 1837.

New Albany *Mahoning County.* Many of those who traveled to settle in the Western Reserve of Ohio began their journey in Albany, New York. This place takes its name from that state capital.

New Alexandria *Jefferson County.* Laid out, 1831, by Alexander Smith. The place was known initially as Tempo, as it featured a temperance hotel. The current name of the town is based on Smith's given name. Smith was born in 1791 and lived to age eighty-seven.

New Antioch *Clinton County.* Platted by Paul Hulls, Jr., Charles Underwood, and David Marbel, the community was named for the Antioch mentioned in the Bible.

Newark *Licking County (seat).* Laid out, 1802, by General William C. Schenck, who named the place after his native Newark, New Jersey. The city was incorporated in 1826.

New Baltimore *Hamilton County.* Platted, 1819, by Samuel Pottinger. The name may be explained by the arrival of Henry Sater and descendants (including Joseph and William Sater) from near Baltimore, Maryland.

New Bavaria *Henry County.* The place was settled by persons of German extraction, natives of the province of Bavaria.

New Bedford *Holmes and Coshocton counties.* Founded and surveyed in 1825. Having been laid out by John Gonser, who hailed from Bedford, Pennsylvania, this place owes its name to a Bedford Township in the Keystone State.

New Boston *Scioto County.* Platted, 1891, by Captain James and Mary Skelton, Anslem and Grace Holcomb, and Mike Stanton. A group of businessmen from the Boston, Massachusetts, area established a lumber mill here in 1887. New Boston takes its name from the larger Boston.

New Bremen *Auglaize County.* Located in German Township, this village was named for the German city of Bremen, where many of its early settlers were born.

Newburgh Heights *Cuyahoga County.* One of the earliest settlers here—if not the earliest—was William Wheeler. Wheeler erected a grist mill in 1799. The place-name probably traces back to Newburgh, New York, as several early settlers originated there. The village was incorporated in 1904.

New Burlington *Clinton County.* This village was founded in 1833 and settled largely by Quakers, many of whom had emigrated from the Burlington, North Carolina, area.

Newbury *Geauga County.* Settlement of this site occurred over a six-year period (1802–1808). The name was derived from that of a Massachusetts community. The place is sometimes referred to as Newbury Center, being located in Newbury Township.

New California *Union County.* According to a 1953 item in the *Columbus Dispatch*, the accepted belief is that a solitary traveler on his way to California pitched camp here and stayed for a time. Samuel B. Woodburn owned the property and retained William B. Irwin to plat the site in 1853.

New Carlisle *Clark County.* Laid out, 1818, by William Rayburn. This locale was settled by emigrants from the Carlisle, Pennsylvania, area. An earlier name for the place was Monroe.

Newcastle *Coshocton County.* One source states that both this town and the township in which it is located were named for New Castle, Delaware. However, a contrasting source advances the theory that this community may have taken its name from the Earl of Newcastle (a Royalist) or the city of Newcastle, England. Coal mining was practiced in this area, and the English city was considered synonymous with the coal industry.

Newcomerstown *Tuscarawas County.* When Chief Eagle Feather was found murdered, his second wife, called "the newcomer" by first wife Mary Harris, fled the encampment. She was tracked down by Eagle Feather's fellow Delaware tribesmen, captured, and executed. (Due to circumstantial evidence, "the newcomer" was thought to be guilty of the murder.) Newcomerstown is at the place where she was captured; this occurred about 1750. The town was settled by whites in 1815; the Neighbor brothers, from New Jersey, may have been the first. Incorporation took place in 1868.

Newell's Run *Washington County.* This entity became recognized about 1866 and takes its name from an early family of settlers. During the Indian skirmishes, 1791–1796, William Newell was a ranger stationed at Fort Frye.

New England *Athens County.* The first contingent of settlers at this place (circa 1853) had called New England home.

New Gottengen *Guernsey County.* Laid out, 1836, by Charles Heidelbach. This community was named in honor of Göttingen, Germany, the former home of Heidelbach.

New Guilford *Coshocton County.* This place was formed by a consolidation of hamlets known as East Union and Claysville. The community was laid out in 1825 by Dr. Elisha Guilford Lee, the first physician in the township.

New Haven *Hamilton County.* The village dates to 1815. The land on which it was laid out was purchased from Robert Benefield. The new proprietors, Joab Comstock, Sr., and Major Charles Cone, performed the laying out, while Joseph Sater did the surveying. New Haven, Connecticut, was Comstock's birthplace.

New Haven *Huron County.* Located in New Haven Township, this place owes its name to New Haven, Connecticut. The community dates to 1811.

New Holland *Fayette and Pickaway counties.* About 1818, this site was settled by Pennsylvanians who had come from Germany and Holland. A man named Fleming erected the first house in the village, and the community that sprang up became known as Flemingsburgh. Eventually it became New Holland. The property at the village site was originally owned by Levin Ross, Reese Young, and Wilkins Ogburn. The town was incorporated in 1835.

New Hope *Brown County.* This place got its start as a post office in 1828. It is said to have been named New Hope by early settlers who looked forward to that prospect.

New Lexington *Perry County (seat).* Founded by James Comley, this site became a settlement in 1817. Its name recognizes the Lexington in Massachusetts that gained fame in the Revolutionary War.

New Lexington *Preble County.* Lexington, Kentucky, inspired this village's original name of Lexington. Because there was another Lexington in Ohio, the "New" was added.

New London *Huron County.* Early settlers here came from New London, Connecticut. Earlier names included Merrifield, Kinsley's Corners, and King's Corners. Included among the initial group of settlers were Joseph C. Merrifield, Peter Kinsley, and John Carey. Settlement occurred not later than 1816.

New Lyme *Ashtabula County.* Emigrants from Old Lyme, Connecticut, settled this place. At first they called their new home Lebanon, but this name was in use elsewhere in Ohio and the postmaster general asked citizens to change it to avoid confusion. Thus the old Lebanon became New Lyme.

New Lyme Station *Ashtabula County.* This place is slightly southwest of New Lyme. (See New Lyme entry.)

New Madison *Darke County.* Laid out in 1817. Outgoing president James Madison (1751–1836) is the person to whom this village owes its name.

Newman *Stark County.* In the 1860s, John Newman built a mill on the Little Sandy River, half a county away from this site. That may account for this name. But a better guess is that the name comes from a chain carrier and axman on an early surveying party, Jacob Newman. Newman's Creek Bottom, a geographical feature of this locale, is thought to trace back to him.

New Market *Highland County.* Platted, 1799, by Joseph Kerr and Henry Massie. The town is named for a Shenandoah Valley town, New Market, Virginia. Ohio's New Market became the first platted town in present-day Highland County, which was then part of Ross County.

New Marshfield *Athens County.* New Marshfield was laid out by George Marsh in 1854.

New Martinsburg *Fayette County.* Martinsburg, Virginia (now West Virginia) conferred its name on this Ohio place. Some of the first citizens of this community came from that town.

New Matamoras *Washington County.* Laid out in 1847. The Mexican War being prominent in the news of the day, the place was named for Matamoras, Mexico. Names also in the running are said to have been Buena Vista, Corpus Christi, and Saltillo. When the post office was established here in 1851, "New" was prefixed to the name to avoid confusion with a Fulton County post office, Metamora.

New Miami *Butler County.* This community was previously known as Coke Otto and Kokotto. These appellations stemmed from the City of Hamilton's decision, in 1900, to install a new Otto Hoffman coke and gas plant here. The plant used three hundred tons of coal a day to run fifty ovens to produce gas sold to the Hamilton Gas & Electric Company. This in turn brought in the Hamilton Iron & Steel Company to produce pig iron. The place-name derives from the community's situation on the Great Miami River. Incorporation took place in 1928 or 1929.

New Middletown *Mahoning County.* Samuel Moore founded this town in 1825. The settlers came for the most part from Pennsylvania, lending credence to the theory that it is named for Middletown, Pennsylvania. One source, while agreeing that Moore laid out the town, gives the year as 1804.

New Milford *Portage County.* New Milford, Connecticut, is the place from which this hamlet takes its name.

New Moorefield *Clark County.* New Moorefield is in Moorefield Township. Apparently a number of early settlers came from Moorefield in what is now West Virginia.

New Paris *Preble County.* Laid out, 1817, by Andrew Ireland and James Fleming. Fleming desired to keep alive the memory of his former home, Paris, Kentucky.

New Petersburg *Highland County.* Platted in 1817. The place was named for the original proprietor of the land, Peter Maver.

New Philadelphia *Tuscarawas County (seat).* Founded, 1804, by John Knisely. The place takes its name from the City of Brotherly Love. It was incorporated in 1824.

New Plymouth *Vinton County.* New Plymouth sprang up about 1838. Its early settlers came from New England and named it for Plymouth, Massachusetts.

Newport *Shelby County.* This name is probably a result of the town's location on the Miami & Erie Canal. Newport was platted by Jonathan Counts in 1839 for Nicholas Wynant.

Newport *Tuscarawas County.* Philip Laffer planned this village in 1833. It became a significant shipping port for transporting materials by flatboat down Big Stillwater Creek to the Ohio & Erie Canal.

Newport *Washington County.* Laid out in 1839. The settlement took its name from the township, which had been named for Newport, Rhode Island. The township was established in 1798.

New Reading *Perry County.* Laid out in 1805. New Reading was originally called Obermeyersettle (or, in English, Overmeyertown), for Peter Overmeyer, one of the first settlers here. The current name traces to Reading, Pennsylvania, the previous home of many of New Reading's earliest citizens.

New Richmond *Clermont County.* Laid out, 1813, by Jacob Light. The name derives from Richmond, Virginia. The nearby town of Susanna, laid out in 1816 by Thomas Ashburn, was absorbed into New Richmond.

New Riegel *Seneca County.* Settled and laid out by Anthony Schindler, this town developed during the 1830s and 1840s. Former neighbors of Schindler's joined him here, coming from their former abode in Riegel, Germany.

New Rome *Franklin County.* An emigrant from Rome, New York, came to this site in an early year and set up residence. It is sometimes referred to and printed simply as Rome.

New Springfield *Mahoning County.* Located in Springfield Township, this community reposes in an area that had many natural springs.

New Stark *Hancock County.* No plat plan was ever recorded for this diminutive settlement. However, early residents reportedly came to the area from Stark County, Ohio, accounting for the name.

New Straitsville *Perry County.* The Straitsville Mining Company laid out the village in 1870.

New Strasburg *Fairfield County.* John Christy laid out the town in 1807. The Christys came from Germany, and that surname is still a common one in this vicinity. New Strasburg was named for the city of Strassburg in Germany (now in France).

Newton Falls *Trumbull County.* Located on the Mahoning River, this community initially was known simply as Falls. Sources disagree on the Newton portion of the name, which was added later. One believes that the designation was from Newtown,

Connecticut, while another claims that it honors Eben Newton, who taught school here about 1812. The village began to emerge around 1807. In 1872, it was incorporated. Today it carries the easy-to-remember ZIP code 44444.

Newtown *Hamilton County.* Newtown was settled by Aaron Mercer. It is said that several of his neighbors arrived from a Newtown in Virginia.

New Washington *Crawford County.* Settled, 1826, by George Myers. Myers owned the property where the village was to stand. In 1833, he obtained the services of surveyor T. C. Sweney and laid off lots for the community. According to the *History of Crawford County*, Myers is thought to have named the place, "possibly appending the adjective to prevent the world from confusing his protégé with a town of the same name on the Potomac." New Washington was incorporated in 1874.

New Waterford *Columbiana County.* Platted, 1851, by Robert and John Silliman. The site was known earlier as Bull Creek and Bull Creek Station. When the railroad came through in 1852, the name was changed to New Waterford. It is said that an immigrant family by the name of Taylor came to the site, having formerly lived in Waterford, Ireland.

New Weston *Darke County.* In 1871 or 1881, Washington A. Weston purchased land on both sides of the Cincinnati-Northern Railroad. When the land began to increase in value, he platted it and began selling lots for a place called Weston in 1883. Later, Martha J. Weston and Thomas S. Waring bought the land surrounding Weston and incorporated it into the village. The name was changed to New Weston to reflect the Waring addition. New Weston was incorporated in 1904.

New Westville *Preble County.* Before 1840, this site was referred to as McCowen Corner. The name was changed first to Westville, then to New Westville. It is the westernmost village in the county.

New Winchester *Crawford County.* This hamlet rose out of a weed lot about 1835. Its name is derived from Winchester, Virginia.

Ney *Defiance County.* The village was named in honor of the French military and revolutionary hero, Marshal Michel Ney (1769–1815).

Nicholsville *Clermont County.* "I know about Nicholsville, because it was named in honor of my great-grandfather's brother," a correspondent explains. "In 1825, Daniel Fee bought an acre of ground and built a home and a store. It was called Feetown. My ancestor, Nathan Nichols, bought the store from Mr. Fee. In 1847, he established a post office there and served as the first postmaster. The name was then changed to Nicholsville, in honor of Mr. Nichols."

Niles *Trumbull County.* James Heaton founded the city. A pioneer in the metals industry, Heaton constructed the state's first iron furnace, the Hopewell, in 1804. In 1809, near here, he built the Marie Furnace, which produced the first bar iron in

Ohio. The community that sprang up around the furnace was incorporated in 1834. It was dubbed Niles by Heaton; he took the name from a Baltimore weekly newspaper which he read avidly, the *Niles Register.* The nation's twenty-fifth president, William McKinley, was born here in 1843.

Norristown *Carroll County.* David Norris platted this community in 1832.

North Baltimore *Wood County.* Platted, 1874, for B. L. Peters, the proprietor, though the place was settled much earlier. Incorporation took place in 1876. The name is said to have been suggested by installation of the Baltimore & Ohio Railroad tracks.

North Bend *Hamilton County.* Judge Symmes had visions of this place as "the city of Miami" when he had it laid out in 1789 at the great northerly loop of the Ohio River. It was incorporated in 1845.

North Benton *Portage and Mahoning counties.* This location is sometimes referred to as North Benton Station. When a rail line was constructed through this area in the mid-nineteenth century, Thomas Hart Benton (1782–1858), a U.S. senator from Missouri, was prominently in the news. William Smith platted the site in 1834, and, an admirer of Benton, also named the community. The "North" sets this place apart from another Benton in Ohio.

North Berne *Fairfield County.* The town is in Berne Township, which is said to have been named by an early settler, Samuel Carpenter. The canton of Berne, Switzerland, had been the home of Carpenter's ancestors, and he wished to honor them in the naming of this place. Many other early citizens of this village are also thought to have been of Swiss ancestry.

North Bristol *Trumbull County.* This burg in Bristol Township possesses a name traceable to the same source as its neighbor to the south, Bristolville (see the Bristolville entry). It was settled about 1804, the same year that Alfred Wolcott surveyed it.

North Canton *Stark County.* The site is north of Canton, Ohio. The initial settlers, including Joseph Willaman (1806), were largely of German heritage and called the town New Berlin. Anti-German sentiment during World War I caused the name to be changed. North Canton is now a city, having been incorporated in 1905. (See also the Canton entry.)

North Fairfield *Huron County.* Now named for the township in which it is located (Fairfield), this community was first labeled Greenfield Corners in honor of William Greenfield. Early settlers arrived in this area about 1831 from Fairfield, Connecticut. North Fairfield was incorporated in 1939.

Northfield *Summit County.* The early settlers at this locality are thought to have come from Northfield, Massachusetts, accounting for the name here. Incorporation occurred in 1903.

North Georgetown *Columbiana County.* Laid out and platted in 1830 by George Stiger and John Whiteleather. It seems plausible to speculate that "Georgetown" came from Stiger's given name and "North" was added when the place was confused with the Georgetown in Brown County. At one time this community was incorporated, but it is currently unincorporated.

North Jackson *Mahoning County.* Located in Jackson Township, this community was settled in 1803 by explorers from Pennsylvania, including William Orr and Samuel Calhoun. A post office was introduced here in 1834, when Andrew Jackson ("Old Hickory") was president, thus accounting for the name designation. It is thought that both the early settlers and President Jackson were of Scotch-Irish heritage, but whether that contributed to the choice of name is not certain.

North Kingsville *Ashtabula County.* This community is north of Kingsville. (See Kingsville entry.) It was incorporated in 1913.

North Lawrence *Stark County.* See the Lawrence entry.

North Lewisburg *Champaign County.* Laid out, 1826, by Gray Gary. Incorporated in 1844. Lewisburg was the initial name of the community, after a General Lewis. There being another Ohio Lewisburg, "North" was prefixed to the designation.

North Liberty *Adams County.* The founder, whose name is unknown, is said to have been a zealous abolitionist who saw the North as a haven of liberty. He laid out the town in 1848. It is north of a stream named Cherry Fork.

North Liberty *Knox County.* Prefixing "North" to the Liberty name distinguished this community from a more southerly Knox County town known as Mount Liberty. Oddly, however, North Liberty is not in the county's Liberty Township.

North Lima *Mahoning County.* Laid out, 1826, by James Simpson. The "North" was apparently added to differentiate this Lima from others. The "Lima" (pronounced LIE-muh) is thought to have been borrowed from a Lima in New York State, which in turn is said to have taken the designation from Lima, Peru (pronounced LEE-muh).

North Madison *Lake County.* North Madison, as the name implies, is slightly north of Madison. Both were named for President James Madison.

North Monroeville *Huron County.* The town is north of Monroeville. Both were named for President James Monroe.

North Olmsted *Cuyahoga County.* The initial owner of the land in this area was Aaron Olmstead. Early names for the site included Lenox, for a Massachusetts village, and Kingston, for a place in New York State. In 1829, Aaron's son, Charles, offered town residents his personal collection of valuable books if they would rename the place in honor of his father. Not having a library, they accepted the proposal. (The "a" in Olmstead was lost at some point.) As the story goes, many of the books were damaged in transit and some rendered virtually useless, but the community kept its word. North Olmsted is in the northern section of Olmsted Township and north of Olmsted Falls. The city was incorporated in 1908.

North Perry *Lake County.* As the prefix indicates, this community is north of Perry. It is also in Perry Township. North Perry was incorporated in 1925. (See Perry entry.)

North Randall *Cuyahoga County.* When a post office went into service here in 1868, it was named after Postmaster General Alexander W. Randall, and his name remained with this place. North Randall was incorporated in 1908.

North Richmond *Ashtabula County.* Richmond Township is home to this community, a short distance north of Richmond Center. The "Richmond" aspect of these names is thought to lead back to a Richmond in Berkshire County, Connecticut.

North Ridgeville *Lorain County.* Sources differ slightly on credit for settling this place. One states that Joel Terrell put down roots here about 1810. A second says settlement was by Ichabod and Oliver Terrell and David Beebe, in 1809. The name was evoked by four ridges that jut across the township.

North Robinson *Crawford County.* Laid out, 1861, by Horace Martin, a surveyor for the county. The name derives from a Robinson family that arrived in the township in 1831.

North Royalton *Cuyahoga County.* This area was settled by several men, including John Coates, Knight Sprague, Robert Engle, and David Sprague. It is said that Knight Sprague built the town hall even though he was blind. He is also said to have called Royalton, Vermont, home, and persuaded the others here to name the place North Royalton. Settlers were here prior to 1818, but the town was not incorporated until 1927.

Northrup *Gallia County.* One source states that Northrup was laid out by John S. Northrup and bears his name. A newspaper article disputes this contention, stating that it was named for the founder, Daniel Northrup.

North Star *Darke County.* The name rationale becomes evident upon discovery that the place was founded by Heronimus Star and John Houston. The year was 1844.

Northwood *Wood County.* Ross Township incorporated into the village of Northwood in 1962. The Board of Trustees and other interested parties submitted suggestions for the village name at that time. Larry Brough, editor of the *Ross Township News,* suggested the name Northwood, owing to the location in the most northern portion of Wood County. Today Northwood is a city.

Norton *Summit County.* The village takes its name from Norton Township, which in turn received its name from Birdsey Norton of Connecticut. Norton was the principle property owner at this place, which was probably settled in 1810 by James Robinson of New York State. The township was organized in 1818. Birdsey Norton never moved here.

Norwalk *Huron County (seat).* Settled in 1815. Founded, 1816, by Platt Benedict, who laid out the community the following year. Benedict hailed from Danbury, Connecticut. Numerous citizens of Norwalk, Connecticut, took up residence on their Firelands grants here, bringing the name of their former home along. Another theory is that the place-name was a result of the site's orientation to some other place: "It's a nor' walk from here." Like its Connecticut counterpart, Norwalk, Ohio, is now a city. Incorporation took place in 1828.

Norwich *Muskingum County.* Laid out, 1827, by William Harper. At first, Harper dubbed the site Centerville, since it was the virtual halfway point between Cambridge and Zanesville. However, other places were using the Centerville designation, so he decided upon Norwich, the name of an English town. Reportedly the name appealed to Harper because his gun had been manufactured in the British community.

Norwood *Hamilton County.* This heavily wooded suburb of Cincinnati takes its name from its location north of the so-called North Woods. The words were joined to form Norwood. Today a city, it was incorporated in 1903.

Nova *Ashland County.* Nova means "new," and the place probably represented a new beginning for its settlers, or perhaps a new frontier.

Novelty *Geauga County.* An informational folder published by the Russell Women's Civic Club provides this explanation for the name: "It seemed a 'novelty' in 1898 to have the Interurban Railroad from Cleveland pick up milk, as well as passengers, from the . . . dairy farm, so the name 'Novelty' was given that stop."

Nutwood *Trumbull County.* At the root of this place-name is the fact that a great many hickory nut trees flourished at this site at the time it was named.

Oak Harbor *Ottawa County.* Platted in 1835. Oak Harbor was initially known as Hartford but took on its current name because of the wealth of oak timber shipped from this site for use in shipbuilding. The village was incorporated in 1871.

Oak Hill *Jackson County.* Carved out of the backwoods, Oak Hill takes its name from the stately white oak trees that dotted the surrounding hills. It was settled around 1817. A New Yorker, Julius Bingham, founded the community and laid it out. Bingham ran a trading post here and organized a Sunday school that is said to have met under the tall white oaks. One source states that the place was once known as Portland and began to take shape as early as 1799, during the township survey.

Oakland *Clinton County.* There was once a dense stand of giant oak trees at this site, inspiring its name. One source states that the community was originally laid out by James Birdsall, while another states that, in 1806, James Murray did so. Oakland was an established community as early as 1805. The current plat plan was filed by William Birdsall, but laid out later, about 1838.

Oakland *Fairfield County.* The town is named for its many magnificent oak trees. Charles Sager laid out the community, perhaps in 1839. An area historian believes that the 1839 date found in court records may be a misprint and should be 1869. His reasoning is that Sager left Stoudertown to found Oakland and Stoudertown was not founded until 1854.

Oakthorpe *Fairfield County.* This site was originally known as Slabtown, a name derived from the sawmill and slab piles here. A correspondent from the area writes: "I would think it was changed to Oakthorpe because of the many oak trees—many still standing—and the fact that 'thorpe' fit better than 'town.'" As Slabtown, it was established in 1827.

Oberlin *Lorain County.* This seat of learning (Oberlin College was established here in 1833) derives its name from an Alsatian Lutheran clergyman and advocate of humanitarian causes, Jean Frédéric Oberlin (1740–1826). Currently a city, Oberlin was incorporated in 1846.

Obetz *Franklin County.* Settled by Charles Obetz and his family in 1838, this village was initially known as Obetz Junction. The "Junction" referred to railroad routes that intersected here. Incorporation took place in 1928. Subsequent to 1879, nine descendants of Charles Obetz became medical doctors.

Octa *Fayette County.* This place was called Allentown at an early date, after a Revolutionary War soldier named Adam Allen. At some time the town name was changed to honor Miss Octa Barnes. Incorporation took place in 1896.

Odell *Guernsey County.* This community was named for the postmaster general at the time it was established.

Ogden *Clinton County.* Ogden was previously named Linden. Founded by railroad officials in 1854 or 1855, it takes its current name from the city of Ogden, Utah, on the Pacific rail route. That city took its name from a Hudson Bay Company operative who explored much of the western United States, Peter Skene Ogden.

Ohio City *Van Wert County.* Platted, 1876, by Butler, Patterson, & Company. The place's original name was Van Wert Junction. In 1882, town fathers voted 28–11 to dub it Enterprise. However, when it was discovered that another Ohio community used that name, Lewis J. Kiggins asked his fellow town council members if they liked the name Ohio City. It was put to a vote and was unopposed. Why Kiggins came up with the moniker is uncertain. The same night the name was voted upon, town fathers voted to incorporate.

Ohio Furnace *Scioto County.* The Ohio Furnace iron works and the surrounding community were named for the Ohio River, being located three miles from the waterway. The furnace was built in 1824.

Ohlton *Mahoning County.* Ohlton was laid out about 1815 by the first settler in the neighborhood, Michael Ohl, a native of Pennsylvania who came to Ohio in 1804 or 1805. He had a son, Charles, who was born in 1807 and resided in Ohlton. The name is also spelled Ohltown.

Okeana *Butler County.* The initial name here was Tariff Post Office. The post office opened about 1828 on a parcel belonging to Benjamin Lloyd, who also laid out a town. Some thirty years later, Okeana became the name of the community, in honor of the daughter of the Indian chief Kiatte. She was buried near the mouth of a stream adjacent to the town.

Okolona *Henry County.* This village formerly was known as Oakland, so named for the heavy timber present on the site. However, there being another Oakland in Ohio, the name was changed, retaining the "oak" sound. Where the "olona" originated is open to conjecture.

Old Fort *Seneca County.* This name stems from nearby Fort Seneca, which dates to 1813. Major General William Henry Harrison headquartered at Old Fort during the War of 1812. Old Fort was platted in 1882 by a Mr. Nighswander for R. R. Titus.

Oldham *Guernsey County.* This place–name probably stems from one or more of several Oldhams who were prominent in this area. Isaac G. Oldham farmed near here on Wills Creek, having arrived in the area in 1805. He reared a large family. Samuel Oldham was the father of I. A. Oldham. Marling Oldham was also well known in the area. In all, ten Oldhams are listed in the biographical index of a work that addresses Guernsey County's early years. A recently located source holds that the community was named for Thomas Oldham (born 1812), who lived on a farm north of Cambridge and in 1854 was elected to the Ohio General Assembly.

Olds *Washington County.* The railroad station, village, and post office here all used this name, drawn from Chauncey Newell Olds, solicitor for the Pittsburgh, Cincinnati, & Saint Louis Railroad.

Old Straitsville *Perry County.* Old Straitsville, referred to by some simply as Straitsville, is about a mile from New Straitsville. It was laid out in 1835 by Isaac and Jacob Strait. (See also the New Straitsville entry.)

Oldtown *Greene County.* Built on the site of an old Indian settlement, the town was once known as Chillicothe, then Old Chillicothe (there were about five Chillicothes in Ohio). After Native Americans were forced to vacate the area, residents called the place Oldtown, since it was on a stream called Oldtown Run. It was platted in 1838 or 1839 by Moses Collier. The place had been settled by William Thorn sometime between 1812 and 1815.

Old Washington *Guernsey County.* This place was platted in 1805 by George and Henry Beymer and dubbed New Washington. The Beymers being the major area landowners and the town's founders, the site became popularly known as Beymerstown. Upon incorporation, in 1829, it was christened simply Washington. (One source gives 1805 as the year of incorporation, but this is probably in error.) Two (a second source says five) years later, in Fayette County, Washington Court House was laid out as the county seat. Inevitably, mail intended for the Fayette County town was often missent to the Guernsey County village. Just as inevitably, the Post Office Department requested that Washington change its name. Reluctantly, it did so—to *Old* Washington, thus proclaiming its seniority over its "rival."

Olena *Huron County.* Settled, 1832, by William H. Burras. An earlier name for the location was Angell's Corners. For reasons not known, the name Olena was decided upon during a citizens' meeting.

Olentangy *Crawford County.* Experts disagree on whether this Indian word is of Shawnee or Delaware origin, and one authority calls it Algonquian. It translates roughly as "red-face-paint; from there; the river." This reference is to the red pigment, found at the location, which Indians applied to their faces. The source of the Olentangy River is not far from this village, which was laid out in 1840. George Sweney, William Snyder, and Paul J. Heddick were the moving forces.

Olivesburg *Richland County.* Laid out, 1816, by Benjamin Montgomery. Having a daughter named Olive, Montgomery decided to name the community in her honor.

Olmsted Falls *Cuyahoga County.* The place-name leads back to an early owner of large tracts in this area, Aaron Olmstead, and his son, Charles. (See North Olmsted entry.) At a falls here on the west branch of Rocky River, Watrous Ushere erected a sawmill about 1828. Shortly thereafter, Uriah Kilpatrick was operating a grist mill on the stream. Olmsted Falls was incorporated as a village in 1851. It is now a city.

Omal *Monroe County.* A newspaper report suggests that this town sprang up relatively recently when the Olin Mathieson Chemical Corporation built an aluminum plant here. "Omal" is probably an acronym (OMAL) derived from Olin Mathieson ALuminum.

Oneida *Carroll County.* George Hull, who started a grist mill here about 1840, named the village for Oneida County, New York, his previous home. The place received a stimulus from a railroad as well as from a canal.

Ontario *Richland County.* The Springfield Township real estate where this hamlet reposes was once owned by Hiram Cook. Cook had lived in Ontario County, New York, accounting for the name of this Richland County place, which was platted in 1834.

Opperman *Guernsey County.* Platted, 1903, by Thomas Moore. It is named in honor of a person who opened a coal mine here, J. H. Opperman.

Orange *Coshocton County.* The Burt family, from Orange County, New York, settled here about 1809. And, by apparent coincidence, so did families named Condit and Denman, from Orange, New Jersey, at about the same time. The town was laid out in 1839, with Hugh Maxwell erecting the first house.

Orange Village *Cuyahoga County.* Settlement of the site began in 1816. The township in which this village reposes was named Orange in 1820 by county commissioners. It was not until 1822 that Orange, Connecticut, took that name, so speculation is that this Ohio village may have been named for a community in another New England state, or even for William of Orange, since many of the local settlers had English ancestry. The village was incorporated in 1928.

Orangeville *Trumbull County.* Recent research by the local village historian, performed at the Mercer County, Pennsylvania, courthouse, is believed to reveal the name rationale. The account goes like this: "A neighboring town in Pennsylvania was settled by Irish Catholics, who were known for 'wearing of the green.' So that site was named Greenville. Orangeville, Ohio, was settled by Irish Protestants, known as 'Orangemen.'" Orangeville was incorporated in 1868. The Ohio-Pennsylvania line runs through the town.

Oregon *Lucas County.* Incorporated as a township in 1958, Oregon became a city in 1959. Oregon Township was organized by Isaac Street and others in 1837. When Street and his associates wished to lay out a town here, they wanted to call it Oregon. But Henry W. Hicks, a major landowner, devised the name Yondota, which was for a time used in certain official records. When Hicks's farm was transferred, however, this name was not accepted. Pierce Irving, a nephew of author Washington Irving, was in the area, and it was he who suggested the name Oregon. At the time, the Columbia River was also referred to as the Oregon River, which is said to mean "river of the West" in an Indian language. Some speculate that Pierce Irving got the idea for the name from the novel *Astoria*. John Jacob Astor had opened up the Northwest, and many travelers reached that area via the Oregon Trail.

Oreville *Hocking County.* Surveyed and platted, 1872, by James Davis for William H. Woodruff. The name came from the large quantities of iron ore present in the area.

Orland *Vinton County.* The ore industry was once the backbone of existence here.

Orpheus The community bears the name of the Greek mythological musician and poet of Thrace. Orpheus was also regarded as the founder of the Orphic Mysteries.

Orrville *Wayne County.* Orrville was named for Smith Orr (1797–1865), who courted the railroads on behalf of the area about 1852. (A correspondent refers to him as Judge Smith Orr.) Orr also began a sawmill operation, owned land nearby, and was active in developing the community. Today a city, Orrville was incorporated in 1864. One source gives 1814 as the year it was founded.

Orwell *Ashtabula County.* A resident whose former home was Orwell, Vermont, selected this name, sometime after organization of the township in 1826. Earlier it was known as Leffingwell, for Christopher Leffingwell. Orwell was incorporated in 1921.

Osborn *Greene County.* Laid out, 1850, by Samuel Stafford and John Cox. Surveying was done by Washington Galloway. The superintendent of the Mad River & Lake Erie Railroad, E. F. Osborn, Esquire, is the person for whom the town was named.

Osceola *Crawford County.* The name is frequently spelled Oceola. It was platted in 1837 or 1838. A Bucyrus, Ohio, surgeon, Dr. Andrew Hetich, Sr., suggested the name. One historical source described the rationale: "Its euphonious and poetical name [came from] the chivalrous and indomitable chief of the Seminoles."

Osceola *Warren County.* This community was started in 1838. Proprietors were Benjamin Baldwin and Lewis Fairchild. The site was named out of respect for the Indian leader Osceola (circa 1800–1838), who opposed the forced removal of the Seminoles from Florida in the 1830s and was betrayed and imprisoned by General Jesup.

Osgood *Darke County.* Part of the community was platted by the Winger family, possibly in the 1870s. It was incorporated as a village in August 1883, thanks to the efforts of Anne Brewer. It is said that a Civil War captain named Osgood entered the area late in the 1870s, became its first settler, and either named the town himself, or was honored by others. Osgood came from Versailles, Ohio.

Ostend *Washington County.* This name means "east end" in German, and the community was a German settlement in eastern Washington County, arising about 1842.

Ostrander *Delaware County.* Platted in 1852. This place-name is said to copy the surname of a civil engineer who surveyed the right-of-way here for the Big Four Railroad. Further details come from a local historian: "Most publicity says the town was named for Jacob Ostrander. I am positive that is wrong. He was listed as a stone mason. . . . The name of the person for whom the town was named [is] Shelmiah R. Ostrander." Shelmiah was a chief engineer for the Springfield, Mount Vernon, & Pittsburgh Railroad. Incorporation took place in 1875.

Otsego *Muskingum County.* Moses Abbott and Francis Wites were the proprietors of the land here. In 1838, a town was laid out for them by James Boyle. It was named for Otsego County (or Lake) in New York by Dr. Alonzo DeLamater.

Ottawa *Putnam County (seat).* Established in 1833 and incorporated the following year. This site had been an Ottawa Indian settlement and takes its current name from the tribe. Earlier it went by Tawa Town, for a chief of the Ottawas. The Ottawas are an Algonquian people whose earliest verifiabe location was on the north shore of Georgian Bay in the Province of Ontario, Canada. Tribal members also have inhabited Michigan, Wisconsin, Oklahoma, Kansas, and the western portion of Pennsylvania. The name comes from *adawe,* "to trade."

Ottawa Hills *Lucas County.* This village takes the first portion of its name from the Ottawa Indians, who once frequented this locale. "Ottawa" derives from *adawe,* "to trade." The "Hills" aspect of the name was inspired by the relatively rolling topography of this particular enclave, compared to the flatness of the surrounding countryside. Ottawa Hills was incorporated in 1924.

Ottokee *Fulton County.* The Indian chieftain Otosah had four sons, one of whom was the eloquent Ottokee. The town of Wauseon, Ohio, was named for one of Ottokee's brothers.

Ottoville *Putnam County.* Elias Everett, a surveyor, platted this site in 1845 for the Reverend John Otto Bredeick, whose given name it took. The initial survey was later abandoned, and Charles Wannemacher resurveyed the place in 1873. Incorporation was in 1890.

Otway *Scioto County.* The village of Otway is the namesake of Thomas Otway (1652–1685), an English dramatist. James Freeman, a respected citizen of the place, laid out the town and conferred the name. Otway, best known for his blank-verse tragedies, was one of Freeman's favorite poets. Otway was occupied before 1841 but not incorporated until 1890.

Outville *Licking County.* Outville is built on a 4,000-acre military grant given to Theodore Foster in 1800 by President John Adams in return for military service. Among the earliest settlers were Gina and Lucretia Sanford Beecher and a blacksmith, Mr. Oldaker. At first the site was known as Kirkersville Station; mail was put off the railroad here for delivery by spring wagon to Kirkersville. Lots were laid out about 1880 by Lyman Beecher on one side of the road and by Samuel Rugg on the other. It may have been in the 1850s when a station agent named Jim Outcalt renamed the community Outville.

Overpeck *Butler County.* This community bears the name of an early settler, Isaac Overpeck.

Owens *Marion County.* From this site, John D. Owen and his son operated quarries, shipping stone and lime. Also known as Owen Station, it was never platted.

Other Owens who lived in the vicinity included Emerson Owen, born 1905; Ivah D. Owen, born 1891; and Gayle H. Owens, born 1903. But the place-name is thought to be attributable to John D. and his son.

Owensville *Clermont County.* Laid out, 1836, by James McKinnie. This town was known in an earlier time as Boston. In 1833, a post office was opened here. William Owens, who kept the first store at the site, was postmaster. Owensville was incorporated in 1867.

Oxford *Butler County.* Platted in 1810. A year earlier, the establishment at this site of Miami University had been approved by the Ohio legislature. Aware that Oxford, England, was a renowned seat of learning, local officials thought Oxford would be a good name for this new center of academia. Now a city, Oxford was incorporated in 1830.

Padanaram *Ashtabula County.* Said by one source to be a "corrupted pop[ular] usage," this town name apparently traces back to the Paddan-Aram mentioned in Genesis. Paddan was a region around the city of Aram in northern Mesopotamia. Abraham resided there temporarily.

Padua *Mercer County.* Sometimes referred to as Saint Anthony, this site was settled in the 1830s by German immigrants and named in honor of Saint Anthony of Padua.

Pagetown *Morrow County.* This place has gone through a series of names—Morton's Corners (for Levi Morton), Nimmons' Corners (for John C. Nimmons), Olmsteadville (for Francis C. Olmstead), and finally Pagetown. It was surveyed and platted by James Eaton in 1838. Olmstead was the landowner. Jonas Vining had settled the site much earlier. A driving force behind developing a town was Dr. Samuel Page. When Isaac Page took possession of the site, he sold off seven acres to Marcus Page. It was Marcus who retained Eaton to lay off a town. Sources say it was called Pagetown in honor of the founder; presumably the reference is to Marcus Page.

Pageville *Meigs County.* Jesse Page, his wife, and three children arrived here in Scipio Township in 1816, coming from Maine. The name of this site probably traces back to the Page family. Jesse Page died in 1834.

Painesville *Lake County (seat).* During earlier times, this city was known as Oak Openings and Champion. The current name traces to Eleazer Paine, a developer in this region in the early 1800s. The place was incorporated in 1832. Paine and Abraham Skinner laid out New Market, a village. The Champion designation originated with General Henry Champion, who laid out the town of Painesville. Another source states that Painesville Township was created by an early settler, General Edward Paine, in 1800 and named after him. This source suggests that the city consequently may be said to trace its name to either the name of the township or General Paine.

Painters Creek *Darke County.* The first white settler here was Daniel Oakes in 1823. A name theory that sounds plausible is as follows: On some maps, the hamlet is identified as Panther Creek. The area was settled by German immigrants. And since early settlers are known to have been frightened by wildcats, one researcher believes the current name comes from "panther." One German dictionary defines *painter* as "a wildcat panther."

Paintersville *Greene County.* In 1840, Jesse Painter laid out this community on farmland that he owned.

Palermo *Carroll County.* The community utilizes the name of the Sicilian city. George K. McCaskey platted it in 1838.

Palestine *Darke County.* Laid out in 1833 by Samuel Loring. This biblical name is thought to have been suggested by the panoramic view that was available from the site of the village. One source claims the town was laid out in 1838.

Palmyra *Knox County.* Laid out in 1835. Although it is doubtful that any palms flourish here, the name means "palm city." In the Bible it was the name of an ancient Syrian city that now lies in ruins.

Palmyra *Portage County.* Landowners here initially included Elijah Boardman, Elijah Wadsworth, Homer Boardman, Jonathan Giddings, and David Boardman. Surveying got under way in 1797. Palmyra Township came into being in 1810. Ultimately from the Bible (see the preceding entry), the town's name probably was taken from a place in New York State.

Pancoastburg *Fayette County.* The land was owned by Isaiah Pancoast, who platted the town of Pancoastburg. For a time the name Waterloo was used to designate this place, but later the name was changed back to Pancoastburg. It was settled largely by former residents of New England.

Paradise *Mahoning County.* A church named Paradise (Evangelical Lutheran, Reformed, or perhaps both) may have stood here, leaving this name.

Paradise Hill *Ashland County.* Paradise Hill was so called because of its situation in a gorgeous natural setting.

Paris *Portage County.* It is debatable whether the place-name Paris should be included here as a town. The place is known by most as Wayland, with Paris being the name of the surrounding township. However, many use the labels interchangeably, calling the town Paris (or Parisville) as well. The landowners here were Henry Champion, Thomas Bull, Gideon Granger, and Lemuel G. Storrs. The place was first known as Storrsboro but the name was changed upon settlement, in approximately 1811, to Paris, after an upstate New York community. One of the first settlers was Richard Hudson. (See also the Wayland entry.)

Paris *Stark County.* Laid out, 1814, in the township of the same name. Frenchmen reportedly were among the early residents here, and they named the locality after the capital of France.

Parkertown *Erie County.* Sixty-two persons with the Parker surname appear in the biographical index of a county history. That is an intensive concentration, even for a surname as common as Parker. So the probability exists that the hamlet owes its name to one or more Parker families that resided here.

Parkman *Geauga County.* Parkman bears the same label as the township in which it is located. Joseph Williams and Samuel Parkman were proprietors of the place, which was named for Samuel and his nephew, Robert Breck Parkman. Moses Warren either surveyed the site or assisted in surveying it. One of the first settlers here was Samuel Ledyard.

Parkwood *Trumbull County.* In the 1920s, Marian Fleming, of Tod Woods, concocted this name, consolidating parts of Tod Woods and Arlington Park, both nearby.

Parma *Cuyahoga County.* The impetus for this name probably came from Parma, New York, but ultimately from Parma, Italy. The latter is a city in the north-central section of the country. Italian names were popular for a time as sources for names of new communities. The township in which Parma is located is also known as Parma. Parma was incorporated in 1924 and today is a city. The original label on the place was Greenbrier, owing to the profusion of a thorny vine whose tentacles virtually covered the area.

Parma Heights *Cuyahoga County.* Parma Heights is just west of Parma and was incorporated in 1912. (See Parma entry.)

Parral *Tuscarawas County.* The town was founded in 1900 as housing for workers with the nearby Robinson Clay Products Company. The president of the firm, John F. Townsend, held a share of silver mines in a Mexican town named Parral and gave that name to this place as well. Colonel Henry Boquet camped here in 1764 on his way to what is now Coshocton, where he was sent to negotiate freedom for eastern Pennsylvanian whites held captive by Indians.

Parrott's Station *Fayette County.* Located on a rail line, this hamlet received its name from George Parrott.

Pasco *Shelby County.* David Henry was the first settler here. Cedar Point was the original name of the community, but the name was changed in 1892 to avoid confusion with the northern Ohio place. The earlier name stemmed from a site where the road from Sidney forked toward Tawawa; the "point" was lined with cedar trees. A Judge Barnes is said to have reviewed U.S. maps, searching for a name that would minimize confusion with existing places. Pasco, Washington, and Pasco County, Florida—both quite distant—were the only other places bearing this label, so the judge selected Pasco for the name here.

Pataskala *Licking County.* Laid out in 1851 by Richard Conine, the town was first known as Conine. It is believed that the Delaware Indians referred to the Licking River as Pataskala. An article in the *Ohio Historical Quarterly* suggests that the antecedent of Pataskala may have been *Pt-aaps-'ku'-'l'u*, a conclusion arrived at by August Mahr, an expert. The same source suggests that to the Native Americans it meant "up to a point—always—a swell—exists," indicating the point to which the floodwaters of the Muskingum River caused the waters of the Licking River to back up and deepen. Pataskala was incorporated in 1892.

Patmos *Mahoning County.* The prime movers behind the emergence of this community were Levi Leyman, Benjamin Regle, and John Templin. The story is told that several town fathers were debating the name issue in a drawing room when a music book reposing nearby fell open to a song called "Patmos." Not ones to fly in the face of fate, those present interpreted this as a sign and adopted Patmos for the name of the town. The Old World Patmos is a rocky isle in a part of the Aegean known as the Icarian Sea. Although it affords magnificent scenery, the desolate, barren spot was once a place to which criminals were banished. It was there that the apostle John received the inspiration for the biblical Book of Revelation.

Patten's Mill *Washington County.* Richard Patten came to Palmer Township prior to 1812 and operated the first mill in the vicinity.

Patterson *Hardin County.* Laid out, 1846, by Peter C. Boslow and H. G. Harris. The surveyor on the project was Charles Arentschields. The name Petersburg was submitted, but Boslow was friendly with the secretary–treasurer of the Mad River Railroad (later to become the Big Four), Robert Patterson, and named the town in Patterson's honor.

Pattersonville *Carroll County.* The birth of this community occurred in 1907 when lots were laid off by George S. Patterson.

Pattonsville *Jackson County.* A record of burials in the immediate vicinity provides evidence that numerous Pattons resided here—twenty-two appear in one listing alone. The site was surveyed in the 1840s by Joseph Hanna.

Paulding *Paulding County (seat).* The Revolutionary War figure John Paulding was commemorated in the naming of this town, which was incorporated in 1872.

Pawnee *Medina County.* Although the reason is uncertain, this place was apparently named for the Native American tribe. It did not appear on an 1874 map, but by 1897 it was on a map. The Wheeling & Lake Erie Railroad (later to be the Norfolk & Western) was constructed through Pawnee.

Payne *Paulding County.* A United States senator from Ohio, Henry G. Payne, is the person for whom this community was named.

Payne's Corners *Trumbull County.* The Paines were an early family in this township. The place is spelled Payne on current maps. Also in an early year, Samuel Hutchins took deed to a hundred acres here.

Peebles *Adams County.* This village arose in 1881. According to the recorded history, a man named N. W. Evans suggested naming the town for John G. Peebles of Portsmouth, Ohio. Peebles was said to have "subscribed liberally toward furthering the railroad." Incorporation took place in 1886.

Pekin *Warren County.* Information supplied by the Warren County Historical Society states that this place-name appeared first in a printed program for a school exhibition. It seems that the school's geography textbook taught that Pekin (or Peking), China, was the largest city in the world. On the theory that their own community must be the smallest, residents applied the name to this Warren County hamlet. There was a post office here as early as 1874. Romanization of the name of the Chinese city has undergone an evolution, being at one time or another written as Peiping, Pekin, Peking, and now usually Beijing.

Pemberton *Shelby County.* Surveyed, 1852, by C. W. Wells. The town proprietors were John H. Elliot, Leonard T. Elliot, Benjamin C. Wilkinson, and George R. Forsythe. The plat was recorded the same year the survey was made. The town name honors a brother of General Pemberton, who became a Confederate rebel during the Civil War. The general's brother reportedly was a civil engineer on a railroad that was being constructed through the town site while it was being platted.

Pemberville *Wood County.* The village was surveyed in 1854 by S. H. Bell for James Pember. Settlers and a mill were here as early as the mid-1830s. Incorporation was in 1876.

Penfield *Lorain County.* This community, located in the township of the same name, derives its designation from a family that settled the area in an early year. Peter Penfield arrived from eastern New York in 1818. Other prominent Penfields were Truman, Amzi, and William Wirt.

Peninsula *Summit County.* This village takes its name from a landform created by the tortuous path of the Cuyahoga River. A rich bottomland site, Peninsula was incorporated in 1859.

Pennsville *Harrison County.* In 1851, Joseph H. Penn platted this hamlet, and it has been known by his name ever since.

Pennsville *Morgan County.* Founded, 1828, by Nathan Sidwell, Pennsville is in Penn Township. The name probably appealed to Sidwell, a Quaker, and may have referred to William Penn (1644–1718), the English Quaker who founded Pennsylvania.

Peoria *Union County.* This word, thought to have roots in French or Latin, was used to refer to the Illinois group of Native Americans. In French, it is *Peouarea.* The town was surveyed by Joseph K. Richey and B. A. Fay in 1870.

Pepper Pike *Cuyahoga County.* This city wears the name of the Pepper family of farmers who settled and worked land along Woodland Pike. Incorporation was accomplished in 1924.

Perintown *Clermont County.* Twenty-six Perins are indexed in a single county history, so it is probably fair to assume that one or several of them evoked the name of this community. Samuel Perin, who was born in Massachusetts in 1785, arrived in Clermont County in 1805 and established a grist mill and sawmill. He also served as a Clermont County commissioner. He was buried at Perin's Mills, now Perintown. A son, Ira (born 1807), was also prominent in this area, as was a grandson, Harvey Perin (born 1862).

Perkins' Corners *Mahoning County.* This site may derive its name from Enoch Perkins, one of the purchasers of land in the Western Reserve. One source suggests that George Perkins was associated in some way with this location.

Perry *Lake County.* This place-name is in remembrance of Commodore Oliver Hazard Perry's historic naval victory in 1813 near Put-in-Bay, Ohio. The town is in a township of the same name. Perry was incorporated in 1914.

Perry Heights *Stark County.* The place-name Perry, which is also the name of the township, is traceable (like many others in Ohio) to Great Lakes naval hero Oliver Hazard Perry (1785–1819). Shortly after Perry's victory near Put-in-Bay, Ohio, in 1813, county commissioners acted to establish and name Perry Township in his honor.

Perrysburg *Wood County.* This city derives its name from Commodore Oliver Hazard Perry, who put together and manned America's Lake Erie fleet during the War of 1812, ultimately defeating the British fleet. Incorporation was in 1833.

Perrysville *Ashland County.* Laid out, 1815, by Thomas Coulter. The name honors the victory in 1813 of Commodore Oliver Hazard Perry.

Perryton *Licking County.* Located in Perry Township, the town, like the township, takes its name from Commodore Oliver Hazard Perry.

Peru *Huron County.* The first settlers of this place arrived in 1815. Among them were Elihu Clary, Henry Adams, and William Smith. The site first went by the name Macksville. The Peru name is borrowed from the township, which in turn was probably named for Peru Township, Massachusetts.

Petersburg *Jackson County.* This community arose sometime after 1820—perhaps well after. Peter Weber was the individual honored in the naming of the town.

Petersburg *Mahoning County.* An early pioneer from Pennsylvania, Peter Musser, arrived at this spot about 1801. For a time it became known as Musser's Mill but later took Musser's given name as a prefix.

Petroleum *Trumbull County.* A village arose here about 1880. It is also referred to as Petroleum Village. It is said that this name resulted from the Indians' discovery of petroleum in one of the nearby springs.

Pettisville *Fulton County.* Laid out in 1857. Pettisville was founded by John Dyer. The name is said to trace back to a man of great favor, a Mr. Pettis, who was a grading subcontractor under the builder of the railroad here, Benjamin Folsom.

Pfeiffer *Hardin County.* Established in 1883 and sometimes known as Pfeiffer Station. In 1907, a post office was opened here. The current name traces to John Pfeiffer, once a postmaster at this place. Earlier still it was known as Wheeler, for a tavern owner named Portius Wheeler.

Phalanx *Trumbull County.* The site is also known as Phalanx Mills. According to historical documents, in 1884 a Fourier socialist colony was formed here. Members of such colonies were instructed to organize into phalanxes of four hundred families of four persons each according to the teachings of Charles Fourier (1772–1837). In these units, they would learn various skills and participate in an equal division of profits and labor.

Pharisburg *Union County.* In 1847, the place was surveyed by William B. Irvin. Allen Pharis was the proprietor and "administrator of Robert Pharis, deceased," according to records. A large house here was maintained by Samuel Pharis. The relationships between the Pharises are unclear.

Pherson *Pickaway County.* Business was conducted at a general store here by I. A. Pherson. His surname became affixed to the place. The year is uncertain.

Phillipsburg *Montgomery County.* Philip Studebaker was one of the landholders at this location, and the place was named after him. The reason for the spelling discrepancy is not certain. The town dates to 1836 and is said to have been named by James Hanks.

Phillipsburg *Tuscarawas County.* Philip Leonhart laid out this hamlet in 1854.

Philo *Muskingum County.* In 1830, a dam was erected here on the Muskingum River by James Taylor, who subsequently operated sawmills and flour mills at the location. The place became known as Taylorsville, and the village was laid out in 1833. Later, when a post office was sought for the place, it was found that that name was in use. When the post office opened in 1850, it used the first name of Philo Buckingham (1825–1853), whose family held title to generous portions of real estate on both sides of the river. Philo was incorporated in 1867. The place-name was not officially changed until 1952.

Philothea *Mercer County.* Bishop Purcell named this site in 1851. It is said to translate from the Greek as "God-loving."

Phoneton *Miami County.* Although there was a settlement here as early as 1875, it did not become known by this name until 1898 or after. At first it was spelled Phonetown. The name was the result of a large exchange facility constructed here between 1898 and 1901 by American Telephone & Telegraph. Forty persons staffed the building, twenty-five of whom were operators. That was a sizable undertaking in those days.

Pickerington *Fairfield County.* This city was laid out in 1815 by Abraham Pickering, who named the site. It was settled earlier by George Kirke. Incorporation took place in 1840.

Pickrelltown *Logan County.* This place was once known as Frogtown. Mahlon Pickrell, born 1810, farmed in this vicinity. The town, which was never formally laid out, is named for Mahlon's father, Henry. For the most part, it arose between 1825 and 1842.

Piedmont *Harrison County.* Platted, 1800, by Henry Butler. The Piedmont name was probably adopted because of the rolling, hilly contours above the valley in which the town reposes. The name succeeded the earlier designation of Butler.

Pierpont *Ashtabula County.* In 1798, the Connecticut Land Company sold a parcel of land at this location to Pierpont Edwards. The resultant hamlet became known by Edwards's given name.

Pigeon Town *Logan County.* In the early days, thousands of pigeons roosted in the trees at this place.

Piketon *Pike County.* Laid out about 1814. The town was named in honor of the explorer Zebulon Montgomery Pike (1779–1813); the county also was named for him.

Pine Grove *Lawrence County.* The Pine Grove Iron Furnace operated here, and the town took its name from the firm.

Pine Hill *Carroll County.* Pine Hill sat on a high hill covered with trees. A contributor recounts that her mother's farm home was nearby, "on the other side of the hill."

When she asked why everyone called the location Pine Hill, her mother pointed out that all the rural families nearby harvested their Christmas trees from the hill. Pine Hill also became the name of the tiny community at the site.

Pioneer *Williams County.* Surveyed, 1853, by James Thompson. Philetus Wilson Norris, who owned the site, was a true pioneer, entering the place when it was swampland and forest. He possessed a pioneering personality, and may in fact have named the place Pioneer himself. Not one to let moss grow under his feet, Norris also platted other villages, including one that is now part of Detroit, Michigan, and was the second administrator of Yellowstone National Park. He died in Kentucky and was buried in Michigan.

Pipesville *Knox County.* This place was known in an earlier time as Wolfe Post Office, for George Wolfe, the postmaster from 1842 to 1852. After Warren Pipes became the postmaster in 1852, the post office was referred to as Pipesville.

Piqua *Miami County.* This was the name of a Shawnee tribe. The name of an Ohio county, Pickaway, is the same word. An approximation of its meaning is "man risen from the ashes." Now a city, Piqua was incorporated in 1850.

Pisgah *Butler County.* Labeled with the Hebrew word for "peak," Pisgah is said to occupy the highest elevation in its township (Union). William Belch, who operated a hotel here in 1812, named the site, inspired by a church that stood on a nearby promontory.

Pisgah *Union County.* This biblical name refers to the vantage point (also called Mount Nebo) from which Moses beheld the Promised Land. Near the Dead Sea and Jericho, it constitutes the headland of the Abarim Range.

Pitchin *Clark County.* Founded, 1830, by George Hansborough. As the story is told, when a storekeeper here tapped a keg of beer one evening after all those present had put in a hard day's work, he invited everyone to "pitch in." Somehow this name took root and hung on. Hansborough operated a steam sawmill at the locality. A separate source credits Green Porter with starting the community in 1845 and points to David Bennett, in his capacity as storekeeper, as the person in charge of dispensing the firewater.

Pitsburg *Darke County.* Sometimes spelled Pittsburg. One historian speculates that "in days of yore" the town fathers had a dream of future greatness for this place, feeling that it would become a second Pittsburgh, Pennsylvania. At one time, areas of it were referred to as "New Pitsburg" and "Old Pitsburg." The village was incorporated in 1899. An earlier name for the site was Arnetsville.

Pittsfield *Lorain County.* Early settlers who arrived at this place in the 1820s from Pittsfield, Massachusetts, included Milton Whitney and William Matcham.

Plain City *Madison and Union counties.* Laid out, 1818, by Isaac Bigelow. Earlier names included Westminster and Pleasant Valley. In 1851, the name became Plain City, owing to its site on the Big Darby Plain.

Plainfield *Coshocton County.* Platted in 1816. The proprietors were Thomas Johnson and Edward Wiggins. The town derived its name from the plains on which it sat.

Plainville *Hamilton County.* Plainville's name is the result of its location on an attractive floodplain along the Little Miami River.

Planktown *Richland County.* Although there were numerous Planks in the area, John Plank is credited with founding this community. One of its leading citizens, he owned a hotel here in the early years.

Plants *Meigs County.* A number of prominent persons having this surname lived in the general area—sometimes using a variant spelling of the name. Among them were Wyatt Garfield Plantz, of the Pomeroy area; Tobias A. Plantz, Esquire; Mary E. Plants; and George Wyatt Plantz.

Plattsburg *Clark County.* It is said that in 1853 surveyors inscribed PLATSBURG across their site plat. This evolved into the village name when another "t" was inserted.

Plattsville *Shelby County.* The name of an early settler, John Platt, remained attached to this place.

Pleasant Bend *Henry County.* The name is said to have been put forth by Philip Burill, who made the suggestion to George Wolf, John Fraker, Fred Miller, Peter Desgranges, and other townsfolk. Burill reasoned that since the Toledo, Delphos, & Western Railroad made a bend here in its route through Pleasant Township, Pleasant Bend would be a fitting name. Apparently they agreed. The T.D.&W. was a narrow-gauge road.

Pleasant City *Guernsey County.* Benjamin Wilson platted the town in 1829. Point Pleasant was the name given to it by Squire Dyson, who considered it an eminently pleasant place in which to reside. It did have the advantage of being on the shoulder of a hill jutting into a valley. When the name became Pleasant City is uncertain. The community was incorporated in 1896.

Pleasant Grove *Belmont County.* Laid out, 1825, by John Anderson. The name is said to have been inspired by the pleasant orientation of the town, although earlier it was referred to as Hole in the Ground. In 1854, a post office was opened here and called Plankroad, a reference to the plank road coming through the place and connecting Cadiz and Bridgeport. At a later date, the post office name was changed to correspond with that of the community, Pleasant Grove.

Pleasant Hill *Miami County.* The hamlet was formerly known as Newton, in honor of Sir Isaac Newton. It was laid out by J. K. Teeter in 1843 after being surveyed by James Hauks. The post office was located at a singularly attractive spot, inspiring the Pleasant Hill name.

Pleasant Home *Wayne County.* Settled sometime before 1916, and possibly as early as 1883. In 1913, a gas well went into operation here. The name was applied simply because it seemed appropriate for this small cluster of well-kept homes with attractive lawns. At an earlier time, it was known as Pleasant Grove.

Pleasanton *Athens County.* Pleasanton earned its name by virtue of its commanding and pleasant view of the surrounding countryside.

Pleasant Plain *Warren County.* Originally referred to as New Columbia, this town was laid out by Samuel Craig in 1852. In 1860, for unknown reasons, the Ohio legislature changed the name to Pleasant Plain. This label was probably deemed to fit the community's situation.

Pleasant Run *Hamilton County.* The name probably flowed naturally, like the attractive upland creek that runs through this area.

Pleasantville *Fairfield County.* Laid out in 1828 by John Boston. Located in Pleasant Township, this village also owes its name to the area's fertile, gently rolling land. The village was incorporated in 1886.

Plumwood *Madison County.* A contributor writes: "My great uncle, C. F. Sanford, platted this town under the name of Sanford. When he applied for a post office, there was already a Sanford post office elsewhere in Ohio. So it was named Plumwood because there were so many wild plum trees in the area."

Plymouth *Richland and Huron counties.* Founded in 1825. Plymouth Rock and Plymouth, Massachusetts, inspired pioneers from New England to christen the place Plymouth. John Plank laid the place out. Its previous names included Planktown and Richland. Incorporation took place in 1835.

Plymouth Center *Ashtabula County.* Located in Plymouth Township, this hamlet derives its name from Plymouth Hollow, Connecticut. The site was settled about 1811. It is near the township's center.

Poast Town *Butler County.* The community was first known as West Liberty. When, in 1818, it was laid out by Peter Poast, it became known by his surname.

Poe *Medina County.* Poe occupies the proximate center of Montville Township. It was named for the Reverend Adam Poe when a post office was established here. The clergyman was the presiding elder of the district for the Methodist Episcopal Church.

Point Isabel *Clermont County.* The land here was owned by families named Smith and Swope. Michael E. Baum bought part of this property and founded a village. Pekin was the first label attached to the place, which Baum laid out in 1845. The "Point" segment of the name was suggested by the location in a triangle of land formed by intersecting roads. The reason for the "Isabel" is not clear.

Poland *Mahoning County.* This site was first named Fowler, after Jonathan Fowler, who first settled the location. The name was changed to Poland because many of the early settlers sympathized with the problems of the Polish people.

Polk *Ashland County.* Previously called Oak Hill, this town was laid out by John Kuhn in 1849, during the presidential administration of James K. Polk.

Pomeroy *Meigs County (seat).* Incorporated as a village in 1841; now a city. The name honors Samuel Wyllis Pomeroy, the original proprietor of the site, who moved here from near Boston, Massachusetts. His middle name is sometimes spelled Willys.

Pontiac *Huron County.* This hamlet bears the name of the Ottawa chieftain who made his presence felt just after the French and Indian Wars in the 1760s. Pontiac and other Native American leaders rose up against the English colonists.

Pool *Washington County.* A post office was located here from 1897 to 1903. The name traces back to Isaac Pool, who had a large farm here.

Portage *Wood County.* The community is in Portage Township on the Portage River and was settled in 1829 by Collister Haskins. Surveyed in part in 1836, it had a reputation as a bustling Indian trading settlement. From here it was probably a "portage" to another branch of the Portage River, the Maumee River to the west or other streams in the area. Portage was incorporated in 1857.

Port Clinton *Ottawa County (seat).* Platted, 1828, by General William Lytle and Ezekiel Haines. DeWitt Clinton, one-time governor of New York, inspired this city's name. He died the same year Port Clinton was platted. Incorporation occurred in 1852. It is on Lake Erie.

Porterfield *Washington County.* In 1790, Benjamin Tuck Ellenwood arrived here from Porterfield, York County, Maine. Thereafter this site was known as Porterfield.

Porter's Corners *Mahoning County.* Twenty-three Porters are listed in the index of an 1874 county atlas. David Porter was one who resided at this locality.

Porterville *Perry County.* This hamlet was once named Ruskville for a Jerry Rusk who, according to one source, "played there as a boy." A second source states that the name honored the family of John Rusk. The current name honors John Porter, who platted the town in 1848.

Port Homer *Jefferson County.* This Ohio River town was founded by W. H. Wallace, who in 1814 opened a store here and named the place for his son, Homer.

Port Jefferson *Shelby County.* The "Port" aspect of the name comes from the location of the place, on the Great Miami River. Jonathan Counts surveyed and platted it in 1836. Landowners were Abner Gerrard and Ezekiel Thomas. Colonel Counts also named the community, but it is uncertain why he chose the "Jefferson" segment. The most probable namesake is Thomas Jefferson, but this is undocumented. John Hathaway was the first person to settle at the site, before it was a town, in 1814 or 1815. Port Jefferson was incorporated in 1842.

Portland *Meigs County.* Laid out in the 1830s by the Wesley Browning family. The name is said to have been suggested by Portland, Maine, from which some of the Brownings emigrated.

Portsmouth *Scioto County (seat).* Laid out, 1803, by Henry Massie, a native of Virginia. According to accounts, Captain Josiah Shackford asked Massie to name the community in honor of Portsmouth, New Hampshire. In return, Shackford promised he would assist in its development. The city is a port on the Ohio River. Portsmouth, Virginia, and Portsmouth, England, are other notable cities with this name.

Port Union *Butler County.* Located in Union Township, this town takes the first part of its name from its former role as a port on the Miami-Erie Canal. The town was laid out by William Elliot. Its original name was McMaken's Bridge, in honor of the early settler who erected the first house (1827).

Port Washington *Tuscarawas County.* Colonel John Knight built a flour mill here on the Ohio Canal about 1827. The site was then referred to as Salisbury. Eventually it was renamed Port Washington—"Port" because of its situation on the canal and "Washington" for an unknown reason. Perhaps it honored General George Washington, who is known to have camped in eastern Ohio on at least one occasion.

Post Boy *Tuscarawas County.* Accounts state that a youthful post rider, William Cartmill, was murdered at this site in 1825 and that John Funston was convicted of the crime and subsequently executed. A nearby stream goes by the name Post Boy Creek.

Pottersburg *Union County.* In 1869, George F. Bennett and David A. Williams had this place laid out, employing Andrew Mowry as surveyor. At least two Potters lived in the general area: Nathaniel Potter and Elizabeth Reynolds Potter. It is not known whether their name relates to this place designation.

Poulton *Monroe County.* The source of this place-name is uncertain. John W. Poulton resided in this area at an early time. His father was from near Antioch, and his brother was W. Poulton.

Powell *Delaware County.* A Judge Powell assisted in acquiring a post office for this site. In gratitude, the community took his name. Powell was incorporated in 1947.

Powellsville *Scioto County.* John Irwin, Washington Irwin, and William Powell laid out this burg, which owes its name to Powell.

Powhatan Point *Belmont County.* Laid out in 1849 by Franklin W. Knox, this place had residents as early as 1819. It was named for Powhatan (died 1618), the Native American chief whose daughter, Pocahontas, married the English colonist John Rolfe in Virginia. Incorporation was in 1892.

Powhattan *Champaign County.* The founding of this place has become obscured over time, but it predates the 1850s. The name comes from the leader of the Powhatan Confederacy of Native American people.

Pratt's *Hancock County.* This place was probably named for the Pratt family. L. (probably Lowman) Pratt and E. Pratt owned land parcels on either side of the public thoroughfare at this point. An Amanda Township map dated 1875 confirms the ownership at that time. Other Pratts were also in the area. Harmon Pratt was in this township in 1859. He was a charter member of the IOOF chapter.

Pratt's Fork *Athens County.* It is difficult to attribute this place-name to one specific person. At least six Pratts were prominent in Athens County during its early years.

Prattsville *Vinton County.* A Massachusetts native and Revolutionary War veteran, Ephraim Pratt, is believed to be the patriarch of the family on whose land this community was established.

Prentiss *Putnam County.* This place-name in all probability relates to A. F. and Ruth E. Prentiss of West Leipsic, who came to the county in 1836. Their daughter was also named Ruth E. Prentiss. The hamlet appears to be about three miles from West Leipsic, in the same township.

Pricetown *Highland County.* Platted, 1847, by Jane Faris, David Faris, Alexander Murphy, and Elijah Faris. The name honors J. Winton Price, a Highland County judge.

Pricetown *Trumbull and Mahoning counties.* A mill operation here was bought by John Price. Judge Robert Price later took control of the business. At an early date, the place was known as Price's Mills. Jesse Holliday founded the community about 1803.

Princeton *Butler County.* The community likely took its name from Princeton, New Jersey, or the university located there. Perhaps some of the early settlers at this place arrived from that area of the Garden State. Princeton, Ohio, was laid out by Samuel Enyart in 1812. The initial name of the site was Maustown.

Proctorville *Lawrence County.* Laid out, 1875, by G. T. Shirky and incorporated the following year. Quaker Bottom was an earlier designation for this place. Its current name honors Jacob Proctor.

Prospect *Marion County.* Surveyed by Christian Gast in 1835. The inaugural name of this place was Middletown. But other communities in the state had that name, and in 1876 it was changed to Prospect on petition of the citizens. Why they chose Prospect is not known.

Provident *Belmont County.* The plat for this place was originally recorded as West Provident. The hamlet grew up around the Provident Mine. The plat was recorded in 1906.

Pulaski *Williams County.* This unincorporated community was at first called Lafayette. When it was learned that a number of Ohio places used that name, Pulaski was decided upon. Count Casimir Pulaski (circa 1748–1779), a Polish patriot, fought under General George Washington and General Lafayette during the Revolutionary War and was mortally wounded while leading his own cavalry unit during the siege of Savannah. The township is also Pulaski.

Pulaskiville *Morrow County.* Like Pulaski in Williams County, Pulaskiville was named in honor of Count Casimir Pulaski (see the preceding entry).

Pulse *Highland County.* With twenty-seven Pulses listed in an old Highland County history, this place-name undoubtedly derives from one of them or the family in general. In 1877, the Harwood Post Office opened here with F. O. Pulse as postmaster.

Pumpkin Center *Trumbull County.* Supposedly, two Halloweeners, Kenneth and Charles Swogger, painted "Pumpkin Center" on a bridge here about 1932. A second story states that Raymond King took pumpkins from his father's farm and smashed them on the road here in 1928, afterward inscribing "Pumpkin Center" on the bridge. Still a third version holds that the place-name came about simply because all the area farmers raised pumpkins.

Put–in–Bay *Ottawa County.* As the tale is told, when the American Commodore Oliver Hazard Perry was asked what to do with the British fleet, he replied, "Put them in the bay." It was from this bay that Perry's fleet sailed to victory over the British in the Battle of Lake Erie in 1813. The town was incorporated in 1877.

Pyrmont *Montgomery County.* The first house here was constructed by blacksmith Christopher Syler. In 1835, the community was laid out by Daniel Mundhenk and named in honor of his native town in Germany.

Quaker City *Guernsey County.* This village was once known as Millwood. In 1871, its largely Quaker citizenry chose the name Quaker City. The community incorporated a year later.

Qualey *Washington County.* A railroad station once stood here on the property of Mike and Bridget Qualey, Irish settlers. Later a post office operated here for twenty-seven years.

Quincy *Logan County.* Quincy was laid out in 1830 by James Baldwin and Manlove -Chambers. Records show that the village name was inspired by President John Quincy Adams (1767–1848).

Raab *Lucas County.* Also known as Raab's Corners, the site likely takes its name from a prominent early family in the county having the Raab surname.

Raccoon Island *Gallia County.* This community is at the mouth of Raccoon Creek, which empties into the Ohio River. According to the editor of the Gallia County Historical Society newsletter, an island once stood here, but "when the Gallipolis Locks and Dam were built, a reservoir of water was created and covered the island."

Radcliff *Vinton County.* About 1826 or 1827, Jonathan Radcliff arrived at this site in Vinton Township, and it is probably named for him.

Radnor *Delaware County.* David Pugh led other Welsh pioneers into this area to settle it, beginning about 1802. Pugh had purchased land warrants for 4,000 acres at this locality. The name traces back to Radnorshire, Wales, Pugh's former home. There is also a Radnor in Delaware County, Pennsylvania.

Ragersville *Tuscarawas County.* The hamlet was established about 1830. Conrad Rager was the proprietor of the site and it owes its name to him. Rager also platted the village in 1830.

Rainbow *Washington County.* A group of pioneers from Marietta started this settlement in 1795. The setting sun shining on a bend of the Muskingum River evoked the name.

Rainsboro *Highland County.* In 1830, this town site was platted by the landowner, George Rains, whose surname it retains.

Ramsey *Jefferson County.* The only known Ramsey connection in the area is Dr. R. M. Ramsey, who resided in nearby Smithfield about 1828.

Randles *Coshocton County.* Several Randleses settled in this general area. Abraham Randles, from Loudon County, Virginia, came to a bordering township in 1817 with his father and three brothers. It is thought that in the late 1800s, a foundry was operated in Jefferson Township by a Thomas Randles. This place likely was named for one of these Randleses.

Randolph *Portage County.* Settled, 1802, by Bela Hubbard and Salmon Wright of Connecticut. Randolph is named for Henry Randolph Storrs, son of Lemuel Storrs, the original owner of the land.

Rappsburg *Lawrence County.* In all probability, this village takes its name from John Rapp, an early settler in Mason Township, where the town is located. Township cemetery records reveal that several other persons with the surname Rapp died here, including Abner (1838–1910), Barbara, Daniel C., August, and Elizabeth B.

Rarden *Scioto County.* The hamlet keeps the surname of an early resident. Rarden Creek trickles nearby. Rarden was incorporated in 1886.

Ratcliffburg *Vinton County.* John Ratcliff settled in this township, probably between 1812 and 1820. Ratcliffburg is thought to have been named in his honor.

Ratliff Corners *Trumbull County.* Coming in 1811 from Pennsylvania, the Ratliff family became strongly identified with the history of Howland Township, in which Ratliff Corners is located. John R. Ratliff was the township clerk for eighteen years and justice of the peace for six.

Ravenna *Portage County (seat).* Settled in 1799. The first permanent arrival was Benjamin Tappan, Jr., an attorney from Massachusetts. A Mr. Starn and a Major Buell were discussing a name for the place with Tappan, and suggested Tappan as the name. But Tappan counterproposed Ravenna, and they acceded. Although Tappan had never been to Italy—let alone Ravenna, Italy—he either liked the sound of it or was persuaded by the fact that his fiancée favored it. In any event, the Ohio city is named for the one in Italy. The word is said to translate as "roots and flowers." Incorporation took place in 1852.

Rawson *Hancock County.* Founded, 1855, by J. G. Kelley and Frederick Keller. A newspaper account states that the place takes its name from L. Q. Rawson of Fremont, Ohio, president of the Lake Erie & Western Railway, which was expected to push a rail line through the community.

Ray *Vinton and Jackson counties.* This place is sometimes called Raysville. According to a descendant of the founder, Ray was laid out as Raysville in 1854 by Moses Ray.

Raymond *Union County.* The first resident here was Hezekiah Davis. The village, first known as Newton, was given the name Raymond in 1840 when the post office opened with John Raymond as postmaster.

Reading *Hamilton County.* Adam Voorhees platted the town (now a city) in 1798, and it was first called Vorheestown after him. The current name honors William Penn's son-in-law, Redingbo. Incorporation came in 1851.

Redbush *Washington County.* Located in Belpre Township near the Mildred Post Office, this hamlet was named because of the profusion of fiery-red bushes that grew wild here.

Redfield *Perry County.* One of the county's coal-mining communities, Redfield was platted in 1883 by Jacob C. Donaldson, agent for a group of Columbus investors including the Columbus & Eastern Railroad Company. A lawsuit over the mortgage named J. E. Redfield and others.

Red Haw *Ashland County.* This tiny hamlet was named because of the plethora of red hawthorne trees in the area.

Red Lion *Warren County.* Laid out in 1817 as Westfield by Abner Crane. Later a Mr. Holly opened a hotel at this spot. Holly had a red lion painted on his hotel sign, and the hamlet came to be known by that symbol.

Redoak *Brown County.* The hamlet is between two forks of Red Oak Creek, which presumably was lined with red oak trees.

Reedsburg *Wayne County.* A township trustee here in 1841 was William Reed. Sixteen Reeds are listed in the name index of an early county history. In all probability, this place-name traces back to William or one of the Reed families. One source gives the year founded as 1835.

Reed's Mills *Jefferson County.* It is not known whether the early Reeds in this area influenced the naming of this site. Robert Reed lived in the county during formative years. Another early resident, George W. Reed, is recorded as having possibly been descended from British royalty. Another local Reed, John W., son of Thomas and Jane Reed, was born in 1829. Joseph Reed was once a trustee of a college at Richmond, Jefferson County. Although the details are obscure, it is possible that a mill was operated here by a person named Reed. And at nearby Steubenville, there lived a Mary M. Reed, who married David McGowan.

Reedsville *Meigs County.* Laid out in 1855, Reedsville was named in honor of a Major Reed.

Reedtown *Seneca County.* Reedtown was once known as Cook's Gate because a man named Cook tended the toll gate here for the Columbus & Sandusky Turnpike. Other earlier names for this place included Kellytown, for a storekeeper at the site named Kelly, and Hanford's, after a tavern by that name. Reedtown is in Reed Township (organized in 1826), and the township was named for one of the earliest settlers, Seth Reed.

Reedurban *Stark County.* This may be the state's only town name decided by a contest advertised in a newspaper. Here is the wording of the ad, which ran in an 1893 edition of the Canton *Repository*: "Interurban town, situated at a passing point midway between Canton and Massillon on the Inter-Urban Electric Railroad. We will give to the one sending us the best name, the choice of one of our $200 lots with a warranty deed, free of cost. No names received after May 17, 1893. H. U. Reed & Co., YMCA Building, Canton, Ohio." The winning name was submitted by Charles Bayliss. H. U. Reed, of the Reed & Miller Real Estate firm, was the owner of the site. C. S. Miller surveyed it.

Reese *Franklin County.* On an early map, two parcels of property at this site appear to have been held by A. Rees and Amor Rees. The spelling of the place-name originally may have been Rees, too.

Reesville *Clinton County.* This location was once known simply as Cross Roads. After Moses Reese platted it in 1857, it became known as Reesville.

Rehobeth *Perry County.* Laid out, 1815, by Eli and John Gardner. The biblical name Rehoboth (with a second "o," not "e") means "roominess" or "broad place." Isaac gave the name to a well he dug (Genesis 26:22).

Reily *Butler County.* In 1820, John Reily laid out a town here on land that he owned. The township likewise is named Reily.

Reinersville *Morgan County.* Founded in 1848. A Pennsylvanian, Samuel Reiner, is the person for whom this community was named.

Reiss *Belmont County.* A small collection of homes grew up around the Reiss Coal Company mine here, taking its name from that enterprise.

Relief *Washington County.* This tiny hamlet, centered on a post office and a flag-stop station, acquired its unusual name through an offhand remark made when the post office opened in 1889. Someone commented that it was a relief not having to row across the Muskingum River anymore to pick up the mail.

Reminderville *Summit County.* Founded in 1955. This village takes its name from its first mayor, Clement L. Reminder. Incorporation also took place in 1955.

Remsen Corner *Medina County.* Sometimes seen in print as Remsen's Corners, this hamlet was named by its proprietor, who lived in upstate New York and possessed the Remsen surname.

Rendville *Perry County.* Rendville, platted in 1879 by Captain T. J. Smith and W. P. Rend, carries Rend's name.

Reno *Washington County.* In 1887, when a post office went into operation here, the place-name was Jericho. That duplicated other post office names, however, and could not be used. Little Muskingum was the second choice, but postal authorities turned it down as too long. The persons who had applied for the post office, Captain and Mrs. James R. Hyler, then decided on the name Reno to honor Major General Jesse Lee Reno (1823–1862) of Wheeling, the highest-ranking West Virginia soldier to lose his life in the Civil War. Captain Hyler had served with Reno during the second Battle of Bull Run in 1862. Reno, Nevada, was also named for him.

Renrock *Morgan County.* The post office at this site is said to have been named in 1850 by Judge Corner of Dye's Settlement. The judge reversed the spelling of his surname and added a "k" to form Renrock.

Renrock *Noble County.* This cognomen has the same explanation as the preceding entry.

Republic *Seneca County.* The previous name of this place was Scipio Center. A post office opened here in 1825. In 1841, the name was changed to Republic. According to one source, land here was purchased that year by Sidney Smith, who named it Republic, construing the meaning as "for the public good."

Resaca *Madison County.* This community was originally known as Stumptown because of the many stumps left after land-clearing efforts of early settlers. The current name was conferred by veterans returning from the Mexican War. They had participated in the Battle of Resaca de la Palma, the second battle of the war, which took place on May 9, 1846, between Brownsville, Texas, and the Rio Grande River.

Reynolds *Champaign County.* This place may have been named for John Reynolds, a pioneer in the area who became a judge.

Reynoldsburg *Franklin, Licking, and Fairfield counties.* Now a city, this place was originally dubbed Frenchtown for its founder, John French (1831). The current name probably honors John C. Reynolds, although one source suggests that it may have been named for early settler Jeremiah N. Reynolds. The community was incorporated in 1830.

Rialto *Butler County.* The origin of this town name is unclear. It is speculated to be a contraction of the Spanish words *rio* (river) and *alto* (high). The naming may have been connected to the Friend & Fox Paper Company, which owned most of the land here and had three mills at the site.

Rice *Putnam County.* This place is in Monroe Township. A. V. Rice, S. B. Rice, and C. H. Rice are shown on plat maps as having held property in this township in the 1800s. Other Rices shown on property maps from that period include Moses, who came to the county in 1833, and Myron, who arrived a year later. Peter Rice also was in the county in 1834. Moses was in Riley Township. A. V. Rice held land in Palmer Township.

Riceland *Wayne County.* A family named Rice is said to have resided at this crossroads hamlet.

Rice's Mills *Trumbull County.* This hamlet took its name from a family named Rice that moved from New England to western Pennsylvania and then to Trumbull County. Family members settled primarily in Greene Township and became influential. Ephraim Rice was one of them. David Rice arrived in 1818 and built a grist mill. R. C. Rice became county recorder. Myrtle Rice was a popular nonprofessional vocalist. David's grandson Fenelon became head of the Conservatory of Music at Oberlin. Rhoda Rice was a schoolteacher.

Richfield *Summit County.* Landowners of this site included Uriel Holmes, J. Wilcox, Benjamin Tallmadge, and John Smith. Settlement began in 1809. Some say the Richfield name comes from the rich agricultural soil present at the location. But in *Ohio's Western Reserve,* Lindsey asserts that a weed growing abundantly here, known as ox-balm or rich-feed, was beneficial to cattle. He goes on to say that upon organization of the township in 1816, Rich-feed was suggested as a name, but it quickly evolved into Richfield.

Richfield Center *Lucas County.* Some of the richest farmland in northwestern Ohio inspired the name of this site in Richfield Township.

Rich Hill *Knox County.* Although twelve Hills appear in the biographical index of a county history and this hamlet is situated on an elevation, the compiler suspects that its name was taken from a popular local figure, Dr. Richard Hilliar. The town is located in Hilliar Township, and Dr. Hilliar was the largest landholder in the vicinity.

Richland *Vinton County.* This site in Richland Township takes its name from the rich, loamy farmland in the area. There was never a platted town here.

Richmond *Jefferson County.* The land proprietors here were Joseph and Mary Talbott, who bought the land in 1808. Joseph employed Isaac Jenkinson to survey and plat a town, a process completed in 1815. Why the town was named Richmond is uncertain. At least three possibilities have been advanced. It may have been named for Richard Richmond, an African American who worked for Joseph Talbott. Many early residents came from Virginia, however, so it may have been named for the capital of that state. In 1804, several years before the town was platted, a church existed five miles from this site, and it was called Richmond Church. It belonged to the Presbyterian Society and was organized by the Reverend George Scott.

Richmondale *Ross County.* Platted, 1811, by Joshua and John Moffitt. At first this community was called Moffitt's Town, but later it was renamed Richmond, after Richmond, Virginia, the previous home of the Moffitts. However, there being another Richmond in Ohio, the post office was called Richmondale (sometimes seen printed as Richmond Dale).

Richmond Center *Ashtabula County.* Richmond Center is at the virtual center of Richmond Township. (See North Richmond entry.)

Richmond Heights *Cuyahoga County.* The Richmond family, with Elihu Richmond the patriarch, bought land and put down roots at this place. The town was incorporated in 1917.

Rich Valley *Noble County.* The hamlet may take its name from Abraham Rich, Sr., son of Jacob Rich. Jacob may have arrived in the United States as early as 1740. A conflicting account states that the site's rich soil inspired the name and that the hamlet dates to about 1884.

Richville *Crawford County.* It was in 1840 that Nathan Rich laid out and platted this hamlet. He may have named it for himself, or the place may have assumed his name in the natural course of events.

Richwood *Union County.* The location was surveyed and platted in 1832 by Thomas G. Plummer on a tract of forest termed "the Richwoods." There is said to have been a multiplicity of tree species here, with rich, black soil conducive to plant and crop growth. Dr. John P. Brookins and his family built the first cabin.

Ridgeville *Warren County.* The community, which dates to 1814, is at the summit of a ridge. The original proprietor was Fergus McLean.

Ridgeville Corners *Henry County.* An Indian trail gave way to a road running along the top of Belmore Ridge here, and when tavernkeeper Barton Palmer laid out the town in 1839, he projected that someday such a thoroughfare would connect the towns of Bryan and Napoleon.

Ridgeway *Hardin and Logan counties.* Samuel McCulloch laid out this village in 1851 and later purchased it. It was named for the original proprietor of the land, the Ridgeway Company.

Rimer *Putnam County.* The hamlet was platted in 1881 for Daniel P. Rimer by James W. Rimer.

Rinard's Mills *Monroe County.* The first grist mill here was developed in 1818 by Isaac Rinard (1770–1865), according to one reference. Another source claims that Isaac did not settle here until about 1830 and states that he built a sawmill and grist mill on the Little Muskingum River. Another early settler in this township (Washington) was James Rinard.

Ringgold *Morgan County.* Platted in 1846. The name of this town honors a soldier who died in a battle of the Mexican War, Major Samuel Ringgold.

Ringgold *Pickaway County.* The explanation of this place-name is probably the same as for the town of the same name in Morgan County (see the preceding entry). Major Ringgold was the first American officer to lose his life in the Mexican War.

Ring's Mill *Monroe County.* This name traces back to the family of Walter and Margaret Ring. In the 1840s, Walter built a sawmill and grist mill at this location. A correspondent, whose maiden name was Ring, writes: "And on down the creek . . . you come to Ring's Mill, named after my Great-grandfather Ring, and the stone house is still standing."

Rio Grande *Gallia County.* The first name chosen for this place, Adamsville, had to be changed when it turned out that it duplicated the name of another town in the state. It is said that the current name comes from the river in the Southwest. When it was chosen, the Mexican War was being waged along the stream and the name was in the news regularly. It is said to have been selected by Sylvester Wood, who was unfamiliar with Spanish pronunciations; the Ohio town is pronounced RYE-o (not REE-o) Grande. Incorporation came in 1935.

Ripley *Brown County.* Ripley was laid out in 1812 by a Virginian and named for Staunton, Virginia. The current name honors General Eleazer Wheelock Ripley. Incorporation came in 1826.

Risingsun *Wood County.* This village went through a succession of names. First it was called Saint Elms, a name suggested by first settler David Woolam, who bought a tract here in 1834. Many citizens thought that the name was "too refined" for such an untamed area, however, and some preferred to call it Coon Town. Later it was called Stony Battery, a name evoked by a limestone outcropping at this location. By 1874, citizens had become unhappy with Stony Battery, and they called a meeting to settle on a new name. David Earl is credited with nominating Risingsun, which has been the name ever since. The place was incorporated in 1879.

Risley *Medina County.* Abraham and Persis Jameyson purchased sixty-five acres here in 1874 from Ansel and Narcysee Jenne. Five acres were taken from the farm by the railroad, and a siding and depot were built. When the first train came through, the only passenger aboard was a Mr. Risley, so the place was named in his honor.

Rittman *Wayne County.* A correspondent puts the year of founding at 1832. The community was named for the one-time treasurer of the Atlantic & Great Western Railroad, Frederick B. Rittman. The railroad later became the Erie-Lackawanna. Now a city, Rittman was incorporated in 1911.

River Corners *Medina County.* Settlers congregated here at a point along River Road now called River Corners. Originally it was termed River Mills or Spencer Mills (being in Spencer Township). The east branch of the Black River flowed past, providing water power for the mills that arose along its banks.

Riverdale *Pike County.* Riverdale derives its name from its location on a tributary near where it feeds into the Scioto River.

Riverlea *Franklin County.* Riverlea is on the Olentangy River. The village was incorporated in 1940.

River Styx *Medina County.* Settled, 1816, by John and David Wilson. The place was called Wilson's Corners, but when a post office was authorized, it was discovered that this name was taken, so it was named River Styx. In Greek mythology, Styx was the river of Hades that the souls of the dead had to cross. This name was thought appropriate, since the region had been covered by great "dismal swamps" identified on prepioneer maps as "the infernal regions." It was also home to reported incidents of "hauntings" and other mysterious activities.

Rix Mills *Muskingum County.* A mill at this site was owned by Edmond Rix, a native of England.

Roachester *Warren County.* Founded circa 1816. The first plat for this community was owned by Mahlon and James Roach, so it must have seemed logical to call the place Roachester.

Roads *Jackson County.* Founded, 1845, by Charles Kinnison. Oliver Tyson was the surveyor. Kinnison was proprietor of the farm out of which the town was carved. It was long known as Berlin Crossroads or simply Berlin. Sometimes it was written Berlin X-Roads. But a newspaper account reveals that "during the First World War, in a burst of patriotic fervor, its name was shortened to Roads." This was done because of the wave of anti-German sentiment.

Roaming Shores *Ashtabula County.* Located in Rome Township, this community sprang up on the shore of Roaming Rock Lake when the lake was developed. One source lists the town's name as Roaming Rock. It was incorporated in 1979.

Robertsville *Carroll County.* Esay Roberts laid off the plot for this town in 1877. His memory lives on in the name of the town.

Robertsville *Stark County.* Platted in 1841. The community was founded by a Frenchman, Joseph Robard (or Robart). Originally Robartsville, the name was subsequently Americanized.

Robins *Guernsey County.* This place formerly bore the name of a nearby creek and a local Indian trail, Trail Run. Later a gentleman named Robins kept a store at the site, which took on his name.

Robtown *Pickaway County.* Isaac Robison, a Pennsylvania native, and his father, Michael, arrived here in 1822. They settled this point in the southern sector of Scioto Township, and it became known as Robtown. Isaac reared a large family.

Robyville *Harrison County.* Fourteen Robys are listed in the biographical index of an old county history. Lesly Roby is mentioned as having resided in Monroe Township; however, that township is at the opposite corner of the county from this hamlet. Lesly Roby probably passed away in 1838, as records reveal that his will was probated that year.

Rochester *Lorain County.* The township of the same name was formalized here in 1835, with the village being incorporated in 1849. Land agent Benjamin Perkins's hometown had been Rochester, New York.

Rockbridge *Hocking County.* Rockbridge was initially known as Millville Station. The inspiration for the current name was a natural rock bridge of solid sandstone a stone's throw from the townsite.

Rock Creek *Ashtabula County.* Incorporated in 1849. Rock Creek is named for the stony, winding creek on which it is located.

Rockford *Mercer County.* The village was laid out about 1820 as Shanesville. The post office went by Shane's Crossing. A French-Indian, Anthony Shane, was a scout for General Anthony Wayne and in exchange received a land grant here. Even earlier, Anthony Madore ran a trading post here; Madore died in 1815. Shane stayed until 1832, when he accompanied the Shawnees to Kansas. It is not known whether he ever returned to this area. In 1890, town fathers decided to change place-names and selected the name Lacine. But while the matter was pending, the Post Office Department decreed that the name would be Rockford, and Rockford it has been ever since.

Rockport *Allen County.* This village was platted by Samuel Rockhill in 1836. In all probability, the place took the first syllable of its name from that of its founder and joined it to "port."

Rockville *Adams County.* Laid out in 1830. The place functioned as a shipping point for stone quarries in the region.

Rocky Fork *Licking County.* This stream-side community gets its name from the waterway, the banks of which are lined with large rocks and boulders.

Rocky Hill *Jackson County.* A correspondent from this locality writes: "Rocky Hill was just that—in Bloomfield Township on [Route] 35 between Jackson and Centerville."

Rocky Ridge *Ottawa County.* Platted in 1874. It is believed that this hamlet owes its name to a nearby outcropping of limestone.

Rocky River *Cuyahoga County.* This community arose about 1815 on the shores of a stream named Rocky River, which is descriptive of its boulder-strewn course. Rocky River today is a city. The year of original incorporation was 1892.

Rogers *Columbiana County.* Laid out in 1883. Incorporated in 1895. The plat for this village was made by T. G. Rogers, after whom the place is named.

Rokeby Lock *Morgan County.* A Rokeby post office was installed in 1839, when the village was known as Unity. Scotland's Rokeby Castle is the town's namesake.

Rollersville *Sandusky County.* About 1832, a senior local land proprietor and one of the earliest settlers at the place which bears his name was Henry Roller. Wilson Teeter assisted Roller in laying out the town, while James Evans proposed the name, to pay homage to the elder of the landowners who contributed to the site.

Rome *Adams County.* The home of the Rome Beauty apple, this town was founded and laid out by William Stout. He is described by the Adams County Historical Society as "an ambitious young dreamer and history buff" who rode along the river bank near his home, staking out lots. He is said to have dubbed the place Rome after "the once-grand shipping port of the Roman Empire." The town is still referred to as Stout by some local residents.

Rome *Ashtabula County.* Located in Rome Township, which name it acquired in 1828, this town owes its own name to either Rome, Italy, or Rome, New York. Local historians are uncertain which place inspired the designation.

Rome *Delaware County.* Founded by Almon Price, this location was also once known as Rome Corners. Nicknamed "the Pope of Rome," Price had been a student of Roman history. The community was incorporated in 1838.

Rome *Richland County.* Rome, New York, is thought to be the place for which this hamlet was named.

Rootstown *Portage County.* John Wyles and Ephraim Root were the first non-Native Americans to visit the place, in 1800. Subsequently they had it surveyed. David Root arrived in 1801, settling the place in 1802 and becoming the town's first permanent resident.

Roscoe *Coshocton County.* The hamlet is said to be named for the English historian and author William Roscoe (1753–1831). It was laid out in 1816 by James Calder and initially called Caldersburg.

Rosedale *Madison County.* Considerable land here was purchased by a Captain Andrews, who built and opened a store. He dubbed his estate Rosedale Farm, after the post office which he had obtained in 1832. Andrews also became the postmaster. His store was the first in the township. Darius Burnham surveyed the community and chose Liverpool as its name. But when the post office was relocated from its rural setting to Liverpool, the Rosedale name became reestablished.

Rose Farm *Morgan County.* Surveyed, 1892, by J. F. Dougan for Jacob Rose. The place was laid out by R. D. Brown and named for the Rose family.

Roseville *Muskingum County.* John Rose platted this small community in 1812 and built a cabin at this location in 1814. Known as New Milford until 1830, the place was incorporated in 1840.

Rossburg *Darke County.* Laid out in 1868. John G. Ross and Robert Ross had adjacent lots here. Probably John, or both Rosses, laid out the community. It was incorporated in 1888.

Rossburg *Warren County.* The name emanates from Enoch A. Ross, who about 1820 started a tannery operation here.

Rosseau *Morgan County.* Laid out, 1834 or 1835, by Joshua Davis. A post office of the same designation opened in 1837. This community was named for Jean-Jacques Rousseau (1712–1788), the French philosopher and author of *The Social Contract,* the *Confessions,* and other works.

Rossford *Wood County.* Rossford was founded in 1898 by Edward Ford. Ford selected this site on the Maumee River for his plate-glass manufacturing plant. Needing to bring in a work force from Pennsylvania and Europe, Ford built the village using his own finances. He named it for his wife, Carrie Ross Ford. The village of Rossford was created in 1940, when Rossford took in the adjoining development of Eagle Point Colony. City status was achieved in 1970.

Rossville *Knox County.* This place was laid out by and takes its name from Jacob Ross.

Roundhead *Hardin County.* This village, like the township in which it is located, takes its name from the Wyandot chief who had a village at this site. Roundhead's Indian name was Stiahta.

Rowsburg *Ashland County.* Laid out by Michael D. Row in 1835, the town bears his name.

Roxanna *Greene County.* Roxanna traces back to 1845 and takes its name from the postmistress, Roxanna Clark. It was once known as Claysville.

Roxbury *Morgan County.* The community's name was inspired by that of Roxbury, Massachusetts. Most of the area's earliest settlers came from New England. The original spelling was Rocksbury, indicating a boulder-strewn or rocky setting.

Royalton *Fairfield County.* Forty persons set out in 1800 from Royalton County, Vermont, with their destination the Mississippi River or beyond. They included Dr. Silas Allen and his four sons, Abner Burnat and family, and John Searle and family. The Allen family took a liking to this Fairfield County region and decided to abort their westward trek, putting down roots here. The town was laid out by its proprietors, Jedediah and Lemuel Allen, in 1810. William Hamilton performed the survey. Dr. Allen died in 1822.

Royersville *Lawrence County.* A Pennsylvania native named Alexander Royer arrived in the county in 1846, securing employment as a bookkeeper. He or his relatives may be the namesake for this place.

Rudolph *Wood County.* Surveyed, 1890, for Daniel Mercer by W. H. Wood. This hamlet formerly went by the name Mercer's. Later the name was changed in honor of a principal merchant of the town, H. J. Rudolph.

Ruggles *Ashland County.* Situated in Ruggles Township, this village and the township derive their name from Almon Ruggles. Ruggles settled in Huron County in 1808 and in 1815 laid out the city of Norwalk.

Ruggles Beach *Erie County.* Initially referred to as Ruggles Grove, this site owes its name to the surveyor of Huron and Erie counties, Almon Ruggles. Ruggles arrived here in 1810, residing on the lakeshore between Huron and Vermilion. He later distinguished himself as a judge. Ruggles Beach was settled about 1805.

Rupert *Madison County.* This place bears the name of an early Union Township family. Andrew, David, and Margaret Truit Rupert resided here. In 1882, Andrew and David were township trustees. Margaret was the wife of David.

Ruraldale *Muskingum County.* Laid out, 1854, by J. B. Millhouse. This locality was settled as early as 1816 and at one time was known as Rockville. The site belonged to Samuel Millhouse. The current name probably comes from its countrified setting. Sometimes the name is written Rural Dale.

Rush Run *Jefferson County.* An early settler near the Ohio River in this township was David Rush. He is probably the person to whom this place-name may be attributed.

Rushsylvania *Logan County.* Laid out, 1834, by James Clagg. The community was first known as Claggstown. The Rush River passes through town, and the current place-name comes from the name of the stream.

Rushtown *Scioto County.* Formerly known as Falls of Scioto Brush Creek and as Lucas Ferry, Rushtown takes its name from Rush Township. It is believed that the township took its name from Dr. Benjamin Rush, an early physician in the settlement days. It is unclear whether there is any relationship between this individual and the Dr. Benjamin Rush (1745?–1813) who was a signer of the Declaration of Independence.

Rushville *Fairfield County.* The place is sometimes referred to as East Rushville, as Rush Creek separates two parts of the village. First known as Clinton, Rushville was laid out by Joseph Turner in 1808. Nine Rushes are mentioned in one Fairfield County history, so this place-name is probably attributable to one or more of those families.

Russell *Geauga County.* The first settlers in this area were members of the Gideon Russell family who arrived in 1818. Russell is at the center of Russell Township and is also known as Russell Center. The township took the Russell name in 1827.

Russell *Highland County.* Because of the railroad, this site is also called Russell's Station. It was platted in 1853 or 1854. The name leads back to William Russell, who may have platted the town. In an early county history, eleven Russells appear in a listing. In 1868, Samuel Russell was a county commissioner. The father of Elizabeth B. Russell was an officer during the Revolutionary War.

Russell's Point *Logan County.* This village was named for John Russell, who reared his family and worked a farm near this site.

Russellville *Brown County.* This place was founded by and named after Russell Shaw. The year was 1817.

Russia *Shelby County.* Surveyed, 1853, by Dave Pampel for Lewis Philip. It is thought that the name was inspired by some resemblance that the land here bore to the section of the Russian empire from which some of the settlers came.

Rutland *Meigs County.* Settled 1799. One account claims that two of the original settlers came from two different Rutlands—John Miles from Rutland, Massachusetts, and Abel Larkin from Rutland, Maine. It is said that the two asked that this place also be so named. The township is named Rutland as well. Another source claims that early settlers came from Rutland, Vermont. The village was incorporated in 1913.

Ryansville *Lawrence County.* Farmer and merchant John J. Ryan settled in this township in 1857. The site designation probably traces to him or his family. Another county person with this surname during the early years was M. B. Ryan.

S

Sabina *Clinton County.* The first settler here is believed to have been Andrew Love. Warren Sabin platted the town in 1830 and named it for himself. Sabin was proprietor of the real estate. In 1860, Sabina was incorporated.

Sagamore Hills *Summit County.* The terrain of this community is marked by hills. *Sagamore* is a Native American term for a tribal chief.

Saint Bernard *Hamilton County.* One of the first settlers here (if not the first) was John Ludlow. He came to the Cincinnati area in 1789 and to the portion of Saint Bernard once known as Ludlow Grove in 1794. After a German native, locksmith John Bernard Schroeder, invested in a subdivision here, the area was given the name of one of his favorite saints, Saint Bernard (1090–1153), the French Cistercian abbot of Clairvaux. Some claim the name stems from the place's similarity to the Alpine hills named for Saint Bernard de Menthon. Saint Bernard was incorporated as a village in 1878 and as a city in 1912.

Saint Charles *Butler County.* The community is thought to have taken its name from an early religious leader in the town, Charles Stewart.

Saint Clairsville *Belmont County (seat).* Settled, approximately 1801, by David Newell. This village was initially labeled Newellstown in honor of the first settler. Eventually, however, the name evolved to the current one, which recognizes General Arthur St. Clair (1734–1818), who was governor of the Northwest Territory. Incorporation took place in 1807.

Saint Henry *Mercer County.* Settled in 1836. By 1839, enough settlers inhabited Saint Henry that Bishop Purcell granted permission to form a parish here. At first using the home of Henry Beckman, mass was celebrated once a month by the Reverends Henry Herzog and Francis Bartels. The Reverend Louis Navarron, a French priest from the settlement of Versailles, directed the construction of the first church. In 1842, the Most Reverend Archbishop Purcell dedicated this edifice to the honor of Saint Henry, "the pious Emperor Henry II of Germany." By coincidence, this name choice also honored four of the first six church wardens—Henry Bruns, Henry Romer, Henry Wimmers, and Henry Hemmelgarnn. The first baptism at the church took place in 1841. The village of Saint Henry was incorporated in 1901.

Most of the information in this entry apparently was published in a booklet authored by Joyce L. Alig, an excerpt from which was furnished by the Mercer County Historical Society.

Saint Joe *Belmont County.* This community was recorded in 1888 by Joseph Hutchinson and referred to by some as Saint Joseph. It is unclear whether Hutchinson was a much-revered individual or whether there was some religious rationale behind the place-name.

Saint John's *Auglaize County.* Platted, 1835, by John and Mary Rogers and Daniel and Elizabeth Bitler. According to historical accounts, there was some contention among the proprietors over a name for the place and the question was settled by casting lots. A Shawnee village called Blackhoof Town formerly occupied this site.

Saint Joseph *Portage County.* This community takes its name from the Catholic church erected here in the 1830s. The church still has an outdoor grotto patterned after the one in Lourdes, France.

Saint Martin *Brown County.* In 1830, Father Martin Kundig was sent to this place to offer the sacrament of mass. A native of Lucerne, Switzerland, he founded the first Catholic church in Brown County and dedicated it in honor of his patron, Saint Martin (circa 316–397), the Christian convert who became bishop of Tours.

Saint Paris *Champaign County.* Laid out, 1831, by David Huffman. New Paris was the name Huffman gave the village, out of admiration for Paris, France. However, due to some confusion in the mails, a request was made to change it to Saint Paris, and the town complied.

Saint Patrick's *Shelby County.* Settlement by persons of Irish descent is believed to have provided the motivation for the town's naming. Patrick, a fifth-century apostle, is the patron saint of Ireland.

Saint Rose *Mercer County.* A native of the town and descendant of those who settled this place tells this version of its naming: "About 150 or 160 years ago, a small group of German Catholics settled in a spot now called Saint Rose. . . . It slowly grew and in a few years, there was a need for a Catholic church, which was soon built. Then came the problem of a name. . . . There was a swamp [nearby], which was full of wild rose bushes, so they named it Rosengoren. The place continued to grow, and in 1911 a bigger Catholic church was needed, [as well as] a name for the parish. Someone came up with the patron saint name of Saint Rose."

Saint Stephen's *Seneca County.* The community derives its name from the founding here of Saint Stephen's Roman Catholic Church (1842). The church's first priest was the Reverend Salesius Brunner.

Salem *Columbiana County.* Laid out in 1806. Zadok Street and John Straughan platted the town, which today is a city. The Street family had come to this area from Salem, New Jersey, and named it for that place. Incorporation was in 1830.

Salem Hall *Washington County.* It is speculated that the site derives its name from Salem, Massachusetts.

Salesville *Guernsey County.* The following account is set forth in the book *Names for a New Land*: "There is a legend about the naming of [the] village of Salesville . . . which is strange and unbelievable but has been passed down for generations. Seth Sales, for whom [according to legend] the town was named, was a shipwrecked sailor on a pirate ship. One morning land was sighted and inland the remaining crew found a freshwater spring. They dropped to all fours and drank voraciously. In an instant, Seth Sales realized he had swallowed more than water. Whatever it was, it stuck in his throat, and as days went by his throat began to swell, getting larger and larger, and Sales realized he was a sick man. He made his way to a friendly port and finally to the only place . . . where he had relatives. That spot was [near] Salesville. . . . This story . . . has been handed through . . . generations . . . beginning with the great-great-grandmother, who said she was present when an autopsy was performed on the body. They opened the ex-pirate's throat to determine the nature of his ailment. Inside they found a live lizard. Fanciful as it is, this is the only known story of the naming of Salesville." Charles Brill is credited with having laid out the community in 1835. The village was incorporated in 1878.

Salina *Athens County.* Located on the Hocking River in Dover Township, this community was named Salina because of an early salt manufacturing enterprise here. A salina is a salt lake or salt works.

Salineville *Columbiana County.* This community in Saline Township was laid out in 1839 by James and John Farmer. The place-name was inspired by salt wells at this locality. (*Saline* means "salt" or "salty.") Workers employed in the salt wells were dubbed "salt-boilers." This industry was succeeded by the mining of coal. One source speculates that the place may have been founded about 1809.

Saltair *Clermont County.* Saltair was settled by 1859. The name stems from the Salt family, which possessed a good deal of real estate in the vicinity during the formative years of the site.

Saltillo *Holmes County.* During the Mexican War (1846–1848), the Mexican city of Saltillo was occupied by U.S. troops, and the Holmes County burg is thought to have taken its name from the city south of the border. A version of how this may have come about centers on the frequent fights that used to break out in a store at the site. A former soldier, observing one of these events, stated that it reminded him of the fighting he had experienced during the war at Saltillo, Mexico. An optional version, seemingly far-fetched, holds that Spanish infiltrators arrived to mitigate additional German and English settlement in the area. One such person got a mail delivery job and took a lunch break near this place. Asked how he liked the area, he replied, "Saltillo," referring not to the area but to the lack of salt on his food. *Sal* is Spanish for "salt," while *illo* refers to a lack or scarcity. (It was believed most Spaniards preferred their food highly seasoned; salt was in short supply at the time.)

Saltillo *Perry County.* The place arose in 1849. F. Bradshaw owned the site. The name is believed to derive from Saltillo, Mexico, now a resort city and capital of Coahuila state.

Salt Run *Jefferson County.* The hamlet derived its name from a nearby saltwater spring that fed a yellowish, saline stream.

Samantha *Highland County.* The initial label on this place was Beeson's Crossroads, for local storekeeper Edward Beeson. In 1842, David Kinzer bought property here to establish a community, which he also platted. About 1845, Kinzer and others desired to change the name of the village. Possibly on a whim, they agreed to name it for the first maiden to cross the store's threshold. Presently a lass on horseback arrived, dismounted, and entered the store. Reportedly they asked her name and she replied, "Samantha."

Sand Beach *Ottawa County.* Platted in 1922. This name was probably the first, most logical designation that popped into the originator's mind; Sand Beach has Lake Erie frontage.

Sand Hill *Washington County.* The sandy soil at this site gave the place its name.

Sandusky *Erie County (seat).* Wyandots had an encampment here as early as 1740. John Garrison and his family are credited with founding present-day Sandusky in 1810. Previously the site was known as Ogontz, Ogontz Place, or Ogontz's Place, after an Ottawa chief residing here. Later still, the name became Portland. During one period, traders maintained a post here that went by the name of Fort Sandoski. In August 1816, Zalmon Wildman conferred upon the place the name Sandusky City. This was adapted from a name given to it by the French and perpetuated by the Indians, Lac Sandouske. "City" was later dropped. Scholars interpret the name as meaning "at the cold water." A Native American form of it indicating a supply of pure water was *ot-san-doos-ke*. Sandusky was incorporated in 1824.

Sandyville *Tuscarawas County.* Henry Laffer laid out the town along Sandy Creek in 1815. It is in Sandy Township at the head of the Sandy-Beaver Canal.

Santa Fe *Auglaize and Logan counties.* This community may have been named for the capital of New Mexico, perhaps when that place was in the news. *Santa Fe* is Spanish for "holy faith."

San Toy *Perry County.* This once-booming coal town arose around 1900 and enjoyed some years of productivity. Conflicting accounts attempt to explain the place-name; all of them are vague or suspect. One holds that "it is a Chinese name."

Another states that the town was named after a character in *The Mikado,* the Gilbert and Sullivan operetta. However, a search of the libretto for such a character, or one with a similar name, fails to lend credence to this theory. Still a third account advances the notion that the community was named for a Saint Thois.

Sarahsville *Noble County.* Surveyed and platted, 1829, by Benjamin Thorla. Sarahsville was named in honor of the wife of one of the landowners, John Devolld. Sarahsville was incorporated in 1860.

Sardis *Monroe County.* The site was laid out in 1843 by James Patton, described as a man with a veneration of the past. It is speculated that Patton had read of ancient Sardis, the city in Asia Minor, and conferred the name upon this Monroe County site. The surveyor was Frank Mason.

Savannah *Ashland County.* A swale, or low-lying wet area, here must have evoked the name, which suggests a meadow or grassland.

Savona *Darke County.* Speculation might lead one to believe that persons from New York State settled in this area, since there is a town of Savona, New York. The one in New York may have been named for a city in Italy. A previous name of Savona, Ohio, was Tecumseh, in honor of the noted Indian chief.

Sawyerwood *Summit County.* Local native William T. Sawyer spawned this community, which was intended to be little more than a development. Sawyer's ancestors, according to historical records, settled in this township about 1829.

Saybrook *Ashtabula County.* One of the original proprietors of this site was Samuel Mather. It is understood that the place was named for the town of Saybrook, Connecticut.

Sayre *Perry County.* This village was platted by Daniel Sayre in 1884, although he had been selling plots for several years prior to that. It was located in a coal-mining region.

Schley *Washington County.* A small collection of homes grew up around a post office that first opened here in 1899. The name honors Winfield Scott Schley (1839–1911), an admiral in the Spanish-American War and deposed hero of the Battle of Santiago de Cuba.

Schooley's Station *Ross County.* Founded circa 1861. A train station was created here when the Marietta & Cincinnati Railroad went through the site. John Schooley was postmaster and railroad agent.

Schumm *Van Wert County.* This place-name is linked closely with the history of the Schumm family. A native of Germany, John George Schumm purchased eight hundred acres of government land for a thousand dollars. The property was in the vicinity of this village. The year was 1838. In 1846, the family patriarch passed away, but not before dividing his land among five children, with each receiving 160 acres. When the Cloverleaf Railroad was being built through the area in 1878, Schumm family members were asked for a right-of-way. This was given, but with the following provisions: a station would be erected where the railroad crossed the north-south road; it would be named Schumm; it would stop to pick up and drop off passengers; and it would not divide any of the existing Schumm land parcels. These conditions were met. One of these parcels remained in the Schumm family through 1992, and the data for this entry were contributed by a Schumm family member. Henry M., Henry G., Louis J., and six other Schumms are profiled in the biographical section of a county history.

Science Hill *Mahoning County.* The community also answers to the name Science-ville. The place was settled about 1840. The only explanation that could be found for the name is that its inhabitants exhibited an avid interest in science.

Scioto Furnace *Scioto County.* Erected in 1828, the blast furnace here was the work of county pioneer General William Kendall. A community comprised mostly of employees and their families grew up around it. It is widely accepted that Scioto means "deer" in the Iroquois tongue. However, one source claims that it means "good hunting."

Sciotoville *Scioto County.* Laid out and surveyed, 1841, by J. Riggs for Charles Moore and James Taylor, Jr. The village owes its name to the nearby Little Scioto River. *Scioto* means "deer" in one of the Native American tongues.

Scipio Siding *Seneca County.* The hamlet is in Scipio Township and was settled in 1821. William Anway chose the name, inspired by a village in New York's Cayuga County.

Scotch Ridge *Wood County.* The site was known as Ten Mile House when a post office opened here. Immigrants from Scotland colonized the place, accounting for adoption of the name Scotch Ridge.

Scott *Paulding and Van Wert counties.* J. T. Scott (born 1851) laid out the village sometime after 1872. It was named after him and for some time was referred to as Scott-town. Scott, who owned a great deal of land here, is said to have retained the surveyor and "parcelled out" the site. (One source identifies him as John J. Scott.) Incorporation took place in 1887.

Scott's Crossing *Adams County.* The community was first known (about 1812) as Auglaize, after the Auglaize River. About midcentury, most of the land here was owned by a family named Scott. The site is where the Pennsylvania Railroad and old State Route 305 met the Auglaize River.

Scottown *Washington County.* This tiny hamlet takes its identity from the man who ran the first store here, Isaac Scott. The year was 1865.

Scroggsfield *Carroll County.* A pioneer missionary who saw this place as "a good field" for his ministry, the Reverend Scroggs, was the person for whom this place was named.

Seaman *Adams County.* The name leads back to the surname of one of the village's founding families.

Sebastian *Mercer County.* This community probably takes its name from the Saint Sebastian Catholic Church here. Saint Sebastian, a third-century Roman officer who became a Christian martyr, is the patron saint of sports.

Sebring *Mahoning County.* George Sebring founded this community, which is named after him. The community was incorporated in 1899.

Seceders' Corners *Trumbull County.* For brevity, the site was sometimes referred to as Cedars Corners. The name was applied as the result of a schism between factions of a church not far away. When the rift developed over church beliefs and practices, one segment of the congregation splintered off, or seceded, and established a church at this site. The place became known as Seceders' Corners.

Sedan *Scioto County.* Daniel S. Bondurant, in 1871 the first postmaster at this community, named the place. In 1870, the Germans had taken Sedan, France, in the Franco-Prussian War. Bondurant was of German descent, and the name appealed to him.

Seeleyville *Morgan County.* Seeleyville is estimated to have sprung up around 1828. John Seeley kept the first store here.

Sego *Perry County.* This community reportedly started when William Curry, a blacksmith, established his shop here in 1846. The name of the town is said to be taken from a similarly named place in Africa, probably Ségou (or Segu) in southern Mali.

Selig *Adams County.* The community was named for a one-time merchant here, Hugo Selig.

Selma *Clark County.* This community, which served as a prominent stop on the underground railroad, had a sizable African American population. Its name is probably attributable to Selma, Alabama.

Senecaville *Guernsey County.* This "ville" takes its name from the Seneca Indians.

Senior *Warren County.* Gunpowder apparently was manufactured here during World War I by a firm known as the Senior Powder Mills.

Sentinel *Ashtabula County.* This community derives its name from a newspaper, the Ashtabula County *Sentinel.*

Seven Hills *Cuyahoga County.* This descriptive place-name was apparently conferred because the area called to someone's mind the famous seven hills of Rome.

Seven Mile *Butler County.* After General Anthony Wayne, commander of the American army in the Northwest Territory, set out with his troops from Fort Hamilton, Ohio, circa 1793, they made camp at several sites on their way north to engage the Native Americans. The going was slow; they had to build a crude road as they progressed in order to move all their equipment. One of their camps was called Seven Mile Camp because it was seven miles from Fort Hamilton. The village that took shape here much later was first called Utica, but that name had to be changed because there was another Utica in Ohio. It is said that the name was changed to Seven Mile not only because of the relation to Seven Mile Camp but also because the village was seven miles from the Butler County Courthouse in Hamilton. The earliest known proprietor of the village site was Samuel Brand (one source says Robert Brand). He sold it to John Walter (or Walters), who laid out the town in 1841. The plat plan was drawn up in 1851 by John L. Ritter. Incorporation came in 1857 or 1874, depending upon which source is to be believed.

Seventeen *Tuscarawas County.* Seventeen dates from 1829, the year Lock 17 of the Ohio & Erie Canal was constructed here.

Seville *Medina County.* Surveyed and platted by Nathaniel Bell. Laid out, 1828, by Henry Hosmer. Named for the city of Seville, Spain, this village is said to have reminded the author Washington Irving of the better-known Spanish city because of similarities in climate and situation. It is believed that Irving, who had served as a diplomat in Spain in 1826, was a guest at the town's hotel when he made the observation that resulted in adoption of the name.

Seward *Fulton County.* Seward was formerly known as Phillips Corners, after the Eli Phillips family, initial settlers of Fulton County. A Seward family built and operated the Seward Store here. Another village building was known as the Seward Inn. Charlie was one of the better-known members of the Seward family. A relative of this family, William Seward, was secretary of state under Presidents Lincoln and Johnson. He purchased the future state of Alaska for the United States from Russia. An unpopular move at the time because Alaska was considered nothing but a wasteland, the transaction became known as "Seward's Folly."

Sewellsville *Belmont County.* Settled as early as 1807, this place until 1831 was known as Union. From then on, it was called Sewellsville, in recognition of Peter Sewell, first postmaster at the local post office.

Shade *Athens County.* First known as Pleasant Valley, this site was designated Jerseyville about 1880 because most of its early residents had come from New Jersey. The local post office assumed Shade as its name, after the Shade River. Then, sometime between 1922 and the early 1930s, the state erected a town sign bearing the name Shade. After that, previous names for the site passed out of use.

Shadesville *Franklin County.* A. G. Hibbs laid out and founded the town in 1853. The name is sometimes styled Shadeville. Shade was the maiden name of the founder's wife.

Shadyside *Belmont County.* When a narrow-gauge railroad was laid through this locale in 1879, a small hamlet grew up around the stop. It was termed Shadyside, after a farm of that name adjacent to the railroad. The farm belonged to James Leasure, who had planted a fringe of evergreens along his roadfront, inspiring him to call his estate Shadyside Farm.

Shaker Heights *Cuyahoga County.* From the early years of the nineteenth century until 1889, Shakers resided here in a religious colony. Incorporation took place in 1912.

Shaker Village *Warren County.* Of the several Shaker settlements in Warren County, one was here.

Shalersville *Portage County.* The proprietor of the land here was General Nathaniel Shaler, whose surname was adopted by the place in 1812. It had previously been known as Middletown.

Shane *Jefferson County.* The hamlet of Shane owes its name to a person or persons of that surname who resided nearby in pioneer days. James Shane came in 1798 from the Keystone State, while Isaac Shane was among the first permanent settlers to arrive in the township, coming in 1803. John Shane and Benjamin Shane were others with ties to this area.

Shanesville *Tuscarawas County.* The name of this community honors Lieutenant Abraham Shane, who planned the village. Shane was a recruiting officer during the War of 1812.

Shannon *Sandusky County.* The name of this place in all probability traces back to one of the Shannons who were prominent in this area at an early time. George Shannon, born in 1787, came to the area in 1809. One of his eight children, John, lived here, near the Sandusky River. John was born in 1813 and was prominent at this site about 1877.

Sharon *Noble County.* Located in Sharon Township, the village was platted by Edward Parrish and Robert Rutherford in 1831 and named for a community in Connecticut.

Sharon Center *Medina County.* Hart & Mather, or Hart & Mather Town, was the original name of this Sharon Township location. William Hart and Samuel Mather were founding partners in the Connecticut Land Company. Both were deceased when this area was primed for settlement, but the place-name persisted until 1829, when the township surveyor, Peter A. Moore, suggested it be renamed Gash, for his native Scottish county. (It should be noted that a search of current Scottish place-names failed to turn up a county named Gash.) People thought the name too harsh, however, and Mrs. Samuel Hayden suggested Sharon, which was accepted. Because of Sharon's proximity to the place called River Styx, also in Medina County, it is widely believed that the name stems from Charon, the mythical ferryman whose job it was to transport dead souls to the other side of the Styx River in Hades. Local historians, however, place no credence in this explanation.

Sharonville *Hamilton County.* Sharonville traces its history to 1788. It was originally called Sharon or Village of Sharon, for the profusion of rose of Sharon bushes that flourished in the area. Older residents repeat an unconfirmed tale about the place's renaming. One day, it seems, the remains of a deceased person arrived at the Village of Sharon train station that should have been shipped to another Ohio place named Sharon. "As a result of the wayward corpse," a source states, "the Village of Sharon became the Village of Sharonville" in hopes of avoiding another such incident. The city prepared a two-hundred-year history of the place in 1988.

Sharpeye *Darke County.* One source states that when C. M. Sharp operated a store here, one of his offerings was whiskey. It is said that he advertised it under the "Sharp Eye" brand, in competition with a libation marketed by another individual in the area.

Sharpsburgh *Athens County.* Sometimes seen printed as Sharpsburg, this Bern Township site attributes its name to an early settler, Abraham Sharp.

Shawnee *Perry County.* Shawnee takes its name from the Native American tribe. The community was founded in 1872 by T. J. Davis.

Shawnee Hills *Delaware County.* Shawnee Hills derives its name from the Native American tribe. The town was incorporated in 1941.

Shawtown *Hancock County.* It is believed by some that this town was named for the Honorable O. P. Shaw, a farmer and veteran of the Civil War, who served on the local draft board in 1917. However, a good possibility exists that it was named for one of two earlier Shaws to appear on the scene: George, an early county commissioner, or Robert, who entered Madison Township in 1834. The town was laid out in 1882 by E. T. Cummins.

Shay *Washington County.* In the late 1800s, a drilling firm named Shay & McMullen, headquartered in Pittsburgh, set up operations here in Independence Township. John Shay was so popular and well liked that his name was given to the post office that went into service here in 1899.

Sheffield *Ashtabula County.* Settled, 1811, by Major Moore. The land proprietor was Samuel Mather, and the hamlet was first known as East Matherstown. Nine years after the place was settled, John Gregg, township justice of the peace, lobbied to have the name changed to that of his former Massachusetts hometown, Sheffield. Both the community and the township were so named.

Sheffield *Lorain County.* The township is also named Sheffield. In 1815, the township land was purchased by Captain Jabez Burrell and Captain John Day of Sheffield, Berkshire County, Massachusetts. They bought the parcel or parcels from William Hart of Saybrook, Connecticut.

Sheffield Lake *Lorain County.* The "Sheffield" portion of the name traces back to Massachusetts and from there to Sheffield, England. *Shaef* is interpreted as denoting "separation," and the Shaef River separated Yorkshire from Lancashire at the English city. Sheffield Lake is on Lake Erie, north of Sheffield. Now a city, it was incorporated in 1921.

Shelby *Richland County.* Laid out, 1834, by John Gamble. First known as Gamble's Mills, the site was later redesignated Shelby in honor of the first governor of Kentucky, Isaac Shelby (1750–1826), who distinguished himself during the Revolutionary War and the War of 1812. An Ohio county is also named in his honor. C. C. Post submitted the name suggestion for this city, which was incorporated in 1853.

Sheldon Corners *Trumbull County.* This place-name undoubtedly traces to one or more Sheldon families who lived in the neighborhood. Flavel Sheldon lived in Trumbull County, although not in this township (Fowler).

Shenandoah *Richland County.* George and William Altorfer laid out the town in 1844. The Altorfers hailed from the Shenandoah Valley of Virginia, resulting in importation of the name for this Richland County locality. A number of possible interpretations of this Algonquian word, or parts of it, have been advanced, including "great plains," "beautiful daughter of the stars" (*schind-nan-dowi*), and "spruce-stream."

Shepherdstown *Belmont County.* This place was named by Nathan Shepherd after himself when he placed the plot layout on the county record in 1816.

Sheridan *Lawrence County.* Early maps show that the Sheridan Coal Works and the Sheridan Mining Company owned large parcels here. Thus the industries may have predated the place-name.

Sherrodsville *Carroll County.* Founded, 1882, by Allan and John Pearch. Charles Sherrod was proprietor of the land, and the community was named for him.

Sherwood *Defiance County.* Isaac Sherwood, who rose to the rank of general during the Civil War, is the individual for whom the community was named.

Shilling's Mill *Mahoning County.* H. E. Shilling is shown in an 1874 atlas to have resided at this site on the Mahoning River. Chances are that he operated a mill here. George Shilling had land just southeast of this spot.

Shiloh *Montgomery County.* This biblical name implies a place of sanctuary or shelter. It refers to a site north of Bethel (Judges 21:19) where the tabernacle was set up (Joshua 18) by the Israelites.

Shiloh *Richland County.* The name of this hamlet, first called Salem, was changed to Shiloh, from a Hebrew word meaning "a place of rest." (See the preceding entry.)

Shively's Corners *Mahoning County.* Frederick Shively settled in this area in 1812. His son, George, also called this vicinity home. The map designation of Shively's Corners probably leads back to Frederick or later members of the family.

Shreve *Wayne County.* Permanently settled in 1821. Shreve was first known as Clinton's (or Clinton) Station. Later, when it was incorporated, the name Shreve was bestowed upon it to honor Thomas Shreve, a village benefactor and its first settler. At the time of the last name change, according to one account, the other contender was Jones, for a well-known local family. Shreve got the nod by one vote. A differing version states that the alternative name was Foltz, for another early resident, David Foltz. Still a third source states that the community was named for early landowner Fred Shreve and gives the year founded as 1853. The village was incorporated in 1859.

Shunk *Henry County.* Old-timers relate that a post office and trading post were operated at this site before 1870 by John Shunk, thus accounting for the place-name.

Siam *Seneca County.* This place was initially called Attica Station, then Attica Junction. At the time residents decided to apply for a post office, they submitted the name Detroit. However, because of the prominence of Detroit, Michigan, the postal authorities would not approve it and told local citizens to call it Siam instead.

Sidney *Shelby County (seat).* Established in 1820. Charles Sidney Starrett donated the land as a site for the community and named it for his namesake, the English author and courtier Sir Philip Sidney (1554–1586). The future city was incorporated in 1834.

Signal *Columbiana County.* This site was settled about 1800. The name origin is uncertain. The best speculation seems to be that it was railroad related.

Silver Creek *Hardin County.* From 1846 to 1867, the hamlet was referred to as Hudsonville and was little more than a railroad stop. Frederick Hanger then expanded the stop into a town and named it Silver Creek, after a stream running along the east side of the community. The creek took its name from the impression it gave as the sun shone off it.

Silver Lake *Summit County.* In 1874, Ralph H. Lodge purchased the lake here and proceeded to develop a large amusement park, which became a mecca for thousands, who reached it via the railroad and other forms of transportation. In 1912, the railroads discontinued their excursion service, which proved detrimental to the park. In 1917, the park was sold and subdivided for residential development. Incorporation took place in 1918. The Silver Lake name was inspired by its clarity. In the *Will Lodge Manuscripts,* the tale is told of a law student returning from a concert at what was then the Western Reserve College, in Hudson. The year was about 1855, and the hour was late; a full moon was glaring down. When the student beheld the body of water in the light of the moon, he called it "a bit of paradise," and later, when he learned it was called Wetmore's Pond, he vowed that it would ever after be known as Silver Lake. It is claimed that Lodge knew of this story upon purchasing the tract and made the Silver Lake name official.

Silverton *Hamilton County.* It was not long after the Revolutionary War when this site began to be settled. First known as Enterprise, it was later called Mosner, after David Mosner, who opened a country store here in 1809. Much later, in 1884, a town plat was filed by Robert J. Cresap and Seth S. Haines. Maxwell Brown owned the property. The place was dubbed Silverton in honor of Haines's wife, whose maiden name was Elizabeth Silver. A city today, it was incorporated in 1904.

Sinking Spring *Highland County.* The place was platted in 1815 as Middletown by Jacob Hiestand. However, the Middletown name was found to be already in use in Ohio. The spring, a local landmark, evoked the current name.

Sioux *Pike County.* The name comes from the Indian people also known as the Dakota. According to the *Illustrated Dictionary of Place-Names,* the word comes from the Ojibway *nadouessioux,* "snakes" or "enemies," terms tribes often applied to their rivals.

Sitka *Washington County.* A post office opened here in 1890. The hamlet was named Sitka to commemorate the death of Joseph S. Bukey, who drowned at Sitka, Alaska, on May 12, 1872, while serving with the 22nd U.S. Infantry. Bukey's mother, Eliza Hill, was a member of a family that first settled this locale.

Sixteen-Mile Stand *Hamilton County.* Located on an old toll road, this site is said to have been sixteen miles from downtown Cincinnati as measured from Fountain Square or the Ohio River.

Skeels' Crossroads *Mercer County.* The name derives from Sephas Skeels and applies to a high point of land surrounded by a curve in the Wabash River. One source states that this place "had to be forded by travelers going in any of the four directions." It is sometimes seen styled Skeels' Crossing. A stone in a local cemetery marks the resting place of Milo Skeels, son of H. and A. Skeels, who died in 1850 or 1856 (the date on the stone is unclear).

Slate Mills *Ross County.* To construct the race for a grist mill here, workmen had to blast out a formidable layer of slate.

Slater *Auglaize County.* The Slater name probably became attached to this hamlet as a result of one of the several persons in the county who had that surname. In 1852, Robert Slater was a landowner in Logan Township. Phebe Slater resided in Union Township in 1835. In 1895, William Slater ran for county treasurer.

Sligo *Clinton County.* Settled about 1838 by a hatter named George Taylor. The community name traces to a brand of iron manufactured at the Sligo Mill in Pittsburgh and used in the blacksmith's shop here during the early years. The mill probably was named for a town in western Ireland.

Slocum *Scioto County.* This locality is also referred to by some as Slocum's Station. The name came from an early Slocum family that resided here. Among those with that surname buried at Slocum's Cemetery are Mary, Cyrus, Archibald, and Lydia. One local history buff believes the name of the site refers to Cyrus Slocum (1816–1851).

Smith's Corners *Mahoning County.* In 1803, Robert Smith came to this township. Probably this settlement took on his or his family's name.

Smithville *Wayne County.* The first house in the village was erected by Thomas Smith in 1818. It is after him that the place was named. Smithville was incorporated in 1888.

Smyrna *Harrison County.* This is one of the many Ohio towns that were given names of places mentioned in the Bible. The biblical Smyrna was a principal city of Asia Minor. During Roman times it was known for its beauty and its promotion of emperor worship. Its Christian congregation was one of seven mentioned in Revelation (1:11).

Snively *Wayne County.* A family of doctors named Snively resided here in the early years.

Snode's *Mahoning County.* This place carries the name of a family that pioneered at this site—probably the family of William Snode. In 1824, Joseph Snode and family arrived by covered wagon.

Snow Hill *Clinton County.* Several persons with the Snow surname were in this area at an early time, including more than one with unlikely given names. Granville H. Snow was a North Carolina native, while Frost and Mary Snow came from Virginia. Ice A. Snow also resided in this vicinity. The community was platted and laid out in 1817 for the proprietor, Charles Harris. A second source agrees that Harris originated the hamlet but puts the year at 1806 and adds that he "named [it] for his native home in Maryland."

Snyder *Mahoning County.* In all probability, this name traces to a landholder shown in an 1874 county atlas, John J. Snyder, or his predecessors. Both his land and this place were just southeast of East Lewistown.

Snyder's Mill *Clark County.* D. L. and J. Snyder operated a distillery and flour mills at this site. The mills were destroyed by fire in 1854 but later rebuilt.

Soaptown *Trumbull County.* It is widely thought that a soap works operated at this place at an early date, inspiring the name. This assumption is unsubstantiated, however.

Socialville *Warren County.* Two Mormon missionaries from Illinois—a father and son named Lamaree—arrived here in 1840, and the place became known as Mormontown. Subsequently a Methodist church was built on land owned by Henry Hageman, and at his suggestion the name of the community became Socialville.

Sodom *Trumbull County.* The community got its name in this manner: About 1840, the temperance issue was being hotly discussed. Nearby, at Church Hill (or Churchill), a Dr. Fisher lectured to locals on the topic, his message being quite well received. So the residents asked him to deliver a similar message down the road, at the schoolhouse where Sodom is now located. He did so, but the message was received much more coolly than at Church Hill. In his next message at Church Hill, Dr. Fisher reported that the message he delivered "down the road" did not meet with anywhere near the embrace he had hoped for, and added humorously that he "feared that locality was a perfect Sodom." This word got around, and the name was adopted, prevailing to this day.

Solon *Cuyahoga County.* The city was named for Solon Bull (1800–1850), a prominent early settler of the place. Incorporation took place in 1927.

Somerdale *Tuscarawas County.* The hamlet of Somerdale sprang up around coal mines. The first mine was opened in 1886 by Joseph H. Somers, inspiring the name of the place.

Somerset *Perry County.* Settled, 1804, by persons named Miller and Fink. The town proper dates to about 1810. Midway between Lancaster and Zanesville, it was initially known as Middletown. Later it was renamed Somerset, for Somerset, Pennsylvania.

Somerton *Belmont County.* A place in Somersetshire, England, is said to have evoked the name of this community.

Sonora *Muskingum County.* Laid out, 1852, by Isaac Stiers. The proprietor was John Brown. The community may have been named for the state in northern Mexico. However, an alternative explanation exists that makes a better story. According to local lore, a farmer was milking a cow here when a traveler stopped and asked him the name of the place. The cow was startled by the unfamiliar voice of the stranger, and to soothe her, the farmer said, "So, Nora." And the traveler nodded and repeated, "Sonora," believing it to be the name of the town.

South Amherst *Lorain County.* The community is south of Amherst. (See Amherst entry.) At various times it was known as Podunk, the Little Whig Hole, and Amherstville (chartered in 1873). And either Amherst or South Amherst was at one time referred to as Plato and The Corners. South Amherst was incorporated in 1918.

South Bloomfield *Pickaway County.* The belief is that this name stems from the south-of-Columbus location of the place and the vast fields of blooming yellow wildflowers that flourished here.

South Delta *Fulton County.* South Delta is slightly south of Delta. (See Delta entry.)

South Euclid *Cuyahoga County.* South Euclid is slightly south of Euclid. (See Euclid entry.) The city was incorporated in 1917.

Southington *Trumbull County.* Located in Southington Township. The two entities trace their name to that of a town in Connecticut.

South Lebanon *Warren County.* South Lebanon is about four miles south of Lebanon, the county seat. (See Lebanon entry.) At one time the town was called Deerfield; the township is still known as Deerfield. Dating to 1795, this is the oldest community in the county. Owners of the townsite were Benjamin Stites, Sr. and Jr., and John S. Gano. The village was incorporated in 1847.

South New Lyme *Ashtabula County.* This community is in the southern portion of New Lyme Township, south of New Lyme village. Many of the early settlers here arrived from East Lyme, Connecticut.

South Olive *Noble County.* This place sprang up about 1851. The name is a result of its location, south of Olive Township.

South Point *Lawrence County.* This name stems from the fact that the Ohio River town is Ohio's southernmost point.

South Russell *Geauga County.* South Russell, logically, is south of Russell. (See Russell entry.)

South Webster *Scioto County.* South Webster was formed and incorporated in 1887 from the platted towns of Bloomfield (1837) and Webster (1853). The village is named for Daniel Webster, the "South" being added to distinguish it from a place known as Webster in Darke County.

South Woodbury *Morrow County.* Laid out, 1830, by Daniel Wood. The first edifice here was a log cabin constructed by Joseph Horr. The name in all probability results from Wood's name and the fact that there is a North Woodbury located farther north in the county.

Southworth *Allen County.* This place-name more than likely traces back to one of the Southworths who at an early time resided in this county. One pioneer land buyer was B. P. Southworth, about 1834. In 1837, Constant Southworth taught school near here.

South Zanesville *Muskingum County.* This community is just south of Zanesville. (See Zanesville entry.)

Spanker *Montgomery County.* There was a post office here in 1880, but the place probably was settled earlier. This was the location of Branston Hutchins's carriage shop, where Spanker wagons were produced. The community was also referred to as Spankertown.

Spargursville *Ross County.* This hamlet is about four miles from Bainbridge. Apparently, some of the Spargurs of the county were identified with the place. Elizabeth Spargur, the daughter of A. N. Spargur, married Dr. W. W. Davis. In 1878, a bank was established locally by Spargur, Head, & Company. Involved in that enterprise were J. B. W. Spargur, Asa W. Spargur, and others.

Speidel *Belmont County.* As early as 1856, this site was known as Pugh. Speidel served as the post office and railroad stop for what was termed Burton's Station. However, other places going by the name Burton were confused with this location. In 1898, Sidney Burton contributed an acre of land for a new Methodist Church and solicited a substantial donation from Joseph Speidel, a wholesale grocer in Wheeling, West Virginia, across the river. In exchange, Burton offered to have the station and post office renamed Speidel. The changes took place in 1899.

Spencer *Medina County.* The village is in the township of the same name. According to historians, about 1832, Calvin Spencer, owner of the Spencer Mills, offered fifty dollars' worth of lumber toward construction of a schoolhouse if the town fathers would name the township for him.

Spencerville *Allen County.* Platted, 1845–1846, by Conover, McConnell, and Tyler of Dayton. The village takes its name from Colonel William Spencer, who was a member of the State Board of Public Works.

Spiller *Meigs County.* A person named T. Spiller resided in this township at an early date. It is supposed that the place-name traces back to that individual.

Spore *Crawford County.* This place-name likely is traceable to the family of Sidney L. Spore, a Holmes Township farmer whose parents settled in nearby Chatfield Township in 1837.

Sprague *Monroe County.* Forty-eight Spragues appear in the biographical index of a county history tome. The place-name is thought to lead back to Benjamin Sprague, born 1768 in New Jersey. He came to Monroe County in 1827. His brother, Samuel M. Sprague, also migrated to this general area.

Spreng *Ashland County.* The diminutive hamlet of Spreng takes its name from John Spreng, born 1845. A farmer and auctioneer, Spreng worked the land here in the latter part of the 1800s. After he sold the Ashland & Western Railroad a right-of-way, the railroad put in a switch siding and Spreng established a grain elevator. For a time, he handled grain, coal, and other goods, later opening a general store at the site.

Springboro *Warren County.* Jonathan Wright laid out this village in 1816. When it came time to select a name for the community, some residents suggested Wrights-town, but Wright protested and suggested Springboro, which was then adopted.

Springdale *Hamilton County.* Platted, 1806, by John Baldwin. Located in Spring-field Township and itself long known as Springfield, this community was asked by the Post Office Department to alter its name. The "Spring" was retained, but "field" was changed to "dale." The village was incorporated in 1839. As a city, it was incorporated in 1959.

Springfield *Clark County (seat).* Settled circa 1803. Surveyed in 1801. Local sources concur that the Springfield name was inspired by a spring from which water overflowed a cliff and fed into Buck Creek. Early names for the city included Gillis-town and Post Town. Incorporation took place in 1827.

Springhills *Champaign County.* Laid out, 1832, by Joseph Woods. The name is also spelled Spring Hills. The hamlet was surveyed by J. L. Morgan. It was first named Middleburg. The Honorable J. C. Phillips rechristened the site, which is at the base of some hills and surrounded by several natural springs.

Spring Mountain *Coshocton County.* At 1,110 feet above sea level, this community is the highest in the county, located on the summit of a hill. It was founded in 1836 by Thomas Gillam. Previously it had been dubbed Van Buren, for President Martin Van Buren. The name Spring Mountain is said to have been suggested in 1856 by a local teacher, Mrs. George Conant, who admired the many springs issuing forth from the bottom of the hill.

Spring Valley *Greene County.* Located on the edge of a valley at the foot of some hills, Spring Valley is in a township of the same name. The moniker is descriptive and euphonious. The place was laid out in 1842.

Springville *Seneca County.* Surveyed, 1834, by David Risdon. Located in Big Springs Township, the town gets its name from a high-volume spring at a small lake here.

Springville *Wayne County.* Founded in 1850. This was a place of several springs, inspiring the place-name.

Squirreltown *Adams County.* Also written Squirrel Town. The community in 1992 consisted of about four houses and a mobile home, a church, a firehouse, and an abandoned school. It obtained its name from the large number of squirrels found here.

Stafford *Monroe County.* Stafford—first dubbed Bethel—was founded in 1835 by an Irishman, John Jones, on his farm. About 1845, it was renamed by a Scotchman, William Steel. One historian conjectured that he did so to associate the site with a Stafford "on the other side of the Atlantic" that he recalled with fondness from his youth.

Stanhope *Ashtabula County.* This name traces to a flamboyant, salty Scotchman, Captain Stanhope, who, during the Gold Rush, sailed ships between Panama and New York.

Stanhope *Trumbull County.* John R. Stanhope and Charles R. Stanhope were active in the Grace Episcopal Church in this locale during settlement times. It is likely the place was named for one of them or for the family.

Stanley *Henry County.* This community sprang up solely because the railroad came through the area. Strangely enough, verbal history passed down from those times states that the name derived from the fact that potential passengers had to stand on the platform to flag down the train because the place was not a regular stop on the route. Possibly the label was intended to be "Standly," but through popular usage became Stanley.

Stanleyville *Washington County.* In 1878, the area around Fearing Post Office was named Stanleyville in honor of Thomas Stanley, who settled the locale in 1800.

Starr *Hocking County.* Located in Starr Township. It is said that Joseph Starr wrote to Henry O'Neill in 1811, entreating O'Neill to petition the Ohio legislature to recognize a town at this site and to name it Starr. Apparently that is what occurred. The name Starr was applied to the township as early as 1812.

Star's Center *Mahoning County.* Shortly after 1800, a family named Starr moved to this place. More than likely, it was named for them and later mapmakers dropped the second "r."

Staunton *Fayette County.* Laid out, 1845, by Willis Rowe. According to a newspaper published nearby, there was considerable contention over a name for the location. One citizen, Stephen Evans, finally reminded his neighbors that most of them had come from Staunton, Virginia, and suggested adoption of that name. The others agreed.

Staunton *Miami County.* Laid out, 1806, by James Smith. The town is in Staunton Township. Smith hailed from Staunton, Virginia.

Steamburg *Ashtabula County.* Abel Meade decided that the west branch of the Ashtabula River could be used by steamboats all the way to Lake Erie. His dream never materialized, but the name stayed with the site.

Steam Corners *Morrow County.* In the early years, a steam sawmill was operated here by Hall, Allen, & Company. The town was never laid out. The first store here was opened by C. W. Rowalt in 1865.

Steel Run *Washington County.* Henry Steel had an eighty-acre farm here as early as 1858. The site derives its name from him.

Steinersville *Belmont County.* John Steiner laid out the community in 1831.

Steinersville *Seneca County.* Steinersville was platted for Henry H. Steiner in 1852.

Stelvideo *Darke County.* This village was laid out in 1851 by Solomon Farmer and platted by George Hartell, Jr. "Stel" was derived from *stella* or *stellar* and means "star," while *video* means "view." Thus the name means "star view."

Stemple's *Carroll County.* Stemple was a common name in early Carroll County. Twenty-four persons with this surname are listed in an early biographical index. David Stemple was born in Washington Township, where this hamlet is located. A son, John M. Stemple, a merchant, was born in 1848. In an early business directory of nearby Dellroy, a Stemple is listed as operating a hardware store there. It is not known if this hardware operator was John M. Stemple or not. A second source advances the notion that the town's likely namesake was Levi Stemple, farmer and hotelkeeper, born in this township in 1839.

Sterling *Wayne County.* Portions of this community were platted by Joseph Ross in 1880. Settlers were here as early as 1824, however, and one source gives 1830 as the year founded. Various names that the place went by included Johnson's Corners and Russell Station. In 1861, the place became known as Amwell after Adnah Bessey told neighbors that he had had a life-threatening illness, "but now I am well." In the post-1880 era, Ross, a silversmith, chose the name Sterling in admiration of fine silverware.

Steuben *Huron County.* Settled by immigrants of German descent, this community was named in honor of Baron von Steuben, the Prussian general who came to the aid of George Washington's army during the Revolutionary War.

Steubenville *Jefferson County (seat).* Laid out, 1797, by Bazaleel Wells and the Honorable James Ross. The latter was a Pittsburgh attorney and political figure; Ross County, Ohio, was named after him. Steubenville takes its name from Fort Steuben, which in turn was named for the Prussian military officer Friedrich Wilhelm, Baron von Steuben (1730–1794). Steuben enlisted in the American army and helped train George Washington's men during the Revolutionary War. Steubenville was incorporated in 1805.

Stewart *Athens County.* Born here in 1812, Daniel B. Stewart laid out the village in 1874. It was named for Daniel or for Archelaus Stewart, another early citizen of Rome Township, where the tiny hamlet is located.

Stewartsville *Belmont County.* This village grew up around a mining industry that began in 1868. It takes its name from John Stewart of the Stewart & Mehan mining firm.

Stillwater *Miami County.* The community's name was inspired by the sluggish current of the Stillwater River.

Stockport *Morgan County.* One authority claims that the name results from the fact that the place was at the heart of a stock-raising region and on a navigable portion of the Muskingum River. Another source gives the original name of the site as Windsor (it is in Windsor Township) but claims that it was renamed for Stockport, England. Incorporation was in 1867.

Stone Creek *Tuscarawas County.* Laid out, 1854, by Phillip Leonard and formerly called Phillipsburg. Leonard designed the town alongside the rocky, narrow bed of Stone Creek.

Stone Ridge *Wood County.* Surveyed, 1872, for landowner Caleb Bean. The physical characteristics of the locale suggested the name.

Storm's *Ross County.* This site also is known as Storm's Station. The Peter Storm family arrived in 1802 from Martinsburg, Virginia (now West Virginia), and settled in the vicinity of Twin Township. John Storm, a member of the large family, served in the War of 1812. Another source states that a John Storms was proprietor of the land when a railroad stop was secured for the site.

Stoudertown *Fairfield County.* The Stouder family once ran the only commercial enterprise in town. It is said to have provided many services and commodities—harness shop, post office, groceries, dry goods, gas pumps (as they became needed), hitchracks, hay, oats, corn, and a stable.

Stoutsville *Fairfield County.* Laid out, 1854, by an early settler, Benjamin Stout. George Stout settled in the vicinity as early as 1804, coming from Bucks County, Pennsylvania. Simon Stout operated a dry goods store in the town. In 1906, A. E. Stout served as township clerk. In 1968, Stoutsville was incorporated. At one time it was known as Stout's Station.

Stovertown *Muskingum County.* Laid out in 1832. This hamlet name honors Samuel Stover, who built a dam and sawmill at the site in 1813, then added a grist mill, and later was found murdered. At an unknown early year, David Stover also came here to Brush Creek Township.

Stow *Summit County.* Joshua Stow, from Middletown, Connecticut, founded this place in 1804. Incorporated in 1956, the community now has city status.

Strasburg *Tuscarawas County.* Laid out, 1828, by Jonathan Palck. The village attributes its name to the city of Strasbourg in France.

Stratford *Delaware County.* The town was once referred to as Stratford-on-the-Olentangy owing to its situation on the Olentangy River. The appellation was inspired by Shakespeare's Stratford-on-Avon.

Stratton *Jefferson County.* Several prominent Strattons lived in this vicinity. The First National Bank of Toronto (Ohio), organized in 1907, was presided over by W. B. Stratton. At nearby Empire, H. S. Stratton was superintendent of the Great Northern Sewer Pipe Company and Stratton Fire Clay. H. E. Stratton was a mine superintendent in the area.

Streetsboro *Portage County.* Settled in 1832. The original owner of the land in the township, Titus Street, gave his name to the community, which today is a city. One source disagrees on the year of settlement, putting it at 1822. Incorporation took place in 1972.

Stringtown *Pickaway County.* This sobriquet came about, it is said, because of the manner in which the place is strung out along what is now State Route 56.

Strong's Ridge *Huron County.* This place is probably named in recognition of Francis and Mary Curtis Strong, who in 1817 became parents of the first child born to settlers in Lyme Township.

Strongsville *Cuyahoga County.* Acting as agent for landowner Governor Caleb Strong of Massachusetts, John Strong and associates arrived here in 1816, organizing the township in 1818. The city is named for both of the Strongs. Strongsville was incorporated in 1927.

Stroup *Trumbull County.* This place takes its name from the Stroup family, respected citizens of Southington Township and descendants of a Pennsylvania Dutch family. Samuel Stroup arrived here about 1834 or 1835.

Struthers *Mahoning County.* In 1799, Turhand Kirtland sold four hundred acres at this locality to Captain John Struthers of Pennsylvania. Now a city, Struthers was incorporated in 1902.

Stryker *Williams County.* The site proprietors were E. L. Barber and J. N. Sargent. James Thompson did the surveying in 1853. John Stryker of New York, a prominent official with the Air Line Railroad, is the man for whom this place was named. In 1854, when the village plat was recorded, the first railroad was being laid into Williams County. The year of incorporation was 1853.

Stubbs' Mill *Warren County.* A mill was constructed here early on, about 1798–1801. At some point it came under the operation of Isaac Stubbs, Sr. Later it was known as Zimri Stubbs' Mill. Zimri was Isaac's son.

Suffield *Portage County.* Founded in 1802. Previously known as Peasetown, this community was renamed Suffield in 1818. The German immigrants who settled the site and founded a United Church of Christ here had lived in Suffield, Connecticut.

Sugar Bush Knolls *Portage County.* One of the younger and smallest geopolitical entities in the state, Sugar Bush Knolls was so named because it was developed in a sugar bush (a stand of sugar maples). It was incorporated in 1964 (one source says 1965) and was developed on land formerly owned by the Davey Tree Expert Company. The prime movers behind creating the village were Cy Porthouse and Wendell Binkley.

Sugar Creek *Tuscarawas County.* German and Swiss settlers came here as early as 1810. The town takes its name from a creek that meanders down the valley. The creek was so named because of the abundance of sugar maples lining its banks.

Sugar Grove *Fairfield County.* Sugar Grove was laid out by Elizabeth Rudolph. The first house in town was constructed by Samuel White in 1835. In the earlier years, an impressive stand of sugar timber stood here, inspiring the name.

Sugar Tree Ridge *Highland County.* The proprietor of the site was John Bunn. The village was established in 1844. The name was a natural consequence of its location, on a ridge bedecked by a great profusion of maple trees.

Sugar Valley *Preble County.* In all probability, this place was named because of a dense coverage of sugar maples in the area and a sugar camp located here.

Suiter *Lawrence County.* A number of persons named Suiter lived in the county during its early years, though none can be traced to this site. Alexander J. Suiter, born 1819, came to this area in 1828. Israel L. Suiter, born 1840, was Alexander's son. Two other Lawrence County Suiters were W. M. and William J.

Sullivan *Ashland County.* Once a part of Huron County and the original Firelands grant, Sullivan takes its name from an early settler.

Sulphur Springs *Crawford County.* Platted, 1833, by John Slifer. At one point this community was dubbed Annapolis. Its current name stems from a large sulphur spring not far from the town.

Sulphur Springs *Perry County.* A sort of mineral water was discovered here coming forth naturally from the earth.

Summerfield *Noble County.* Founded by Moses Horton. Laid out in 1827. A Methodist preacher, the Reverend John Summerfield, was honored by the naming of the town.

Summerford *Madison County.* In 1813, John Summers, a blacksmith from Virginia, emigrated to this locality. There may be some connection between him and the naming of the site, which lies in a township whose name is pronounced the same but spelled Somerford. Another possibility is that a link exists between the place-name and a Daniel and Rachel Sommers, who helped organize a Christian church at the location. Joseph Chrisman surveyed and laid off lots for the town in 1836.

Summerside *Clermont County.* Surveyed, 1788, for General George Mathews of Virginia. The former name of the site was East Mount Carmel. In 1885, officials of the Cincinnati, Georgetown, & Portsmouth Railroad who held a contest to rename the community chose the euphonious label of Summerside.

Summersville *Union County.* This site was surveyed and the plat was recorded in 1835. Proprietors included John Johnson, William Summers, and James R. Smith. The village was named for Summers.

Summit Station *Licking County.* On the railroad line between Newark and Columbus, this site was at the highest elevation. A tiny hamlet grew up around the station.

Summitville *Columbiana County.* Platted by Peter Friedt in 1853, the site took this name as a result of its altitude. Reportedly it was at the summit of the steepest grade on the C & P Railroad.

Sunbury *Delaware County.* Sunbury was platted by William and Lawrence Myers in 1816. The Myerses, who also named the town, came from the Wyoming Valley of Luzerne County, Pennsylvania, and purchased the land here. There was a Sunbury in their home state, and the Sunbury name has a long history. In 1768, two sons of William Penn—Richard and John—established the Manor of Sunbury in the Wyoming Valley on a branch of the Susquehanna River. In 1772, Governor Richard Penn and the Provincial Council ordered John Lukens and William McClay to lay out a town in Northumberland County, Pennsylvania, "to be called by the name of Sunbury." It is believed that Governor Penn imported the name from Sunbury-on-Thames, England, fifteen miles southwest of London. Despite the apparent link between the Ohio and Pennsylvania Sunburys, some historians doubt that there is any connection. According to one historical source, in England the Saxons are considered the true founders of Sunbury, as reflected in a document known as the Sunbury Charter, dating to the period 959–980 A.D. Versions of the name include *Sunnan-*

byrig, *Sunna's Burh*, *Sunna's Haw*, and *Sunberie*. There are several other Sunburys, in other states, Canada, and Australia.

Swander's *Shelby County.* The hamlet was once named Swander's Crossing in honor of an agent for the Dayton & Michigan Railroad, which placed a flag station at the site in 1867. The agent, James Swander, also became the first postmaster and operated a store at this location. A direct descendant states that Frederick Schwander of Berne, Switzerland, was the progenitor of the family, arriving in Philadelphia in 1732. He later moved to Lehigh County, Pennsylvania. Another descendant, also named Frederick, settled with his wife, Eva, in Fairfield County, Ohio. They dropped the "ch" from the surname. Three sons—James, David, and Philip—owned farmland here in Shelby County.

Swankton *Montgomery County.* A number of Swanks settled in this area, including the Reverend Jacob Swank, the Reverend John Swank, and Noah Swank. They were active in the Swankite sect, which predated the United Brethren Church.

Swanton *Fulton County.* Swanton reposes on the banks of Swan Creek, from which it takes its name. Speculation has it that the creek was named after early settlers mistook a gaggle of cranes on the stream for swans. Swanton was mostly uninhabited forest as late as 1845. The Swanton of today replaces incipient communities known variously as Centerville, East Swanton, West Swanton, and South Swanton. The current Swanton was incorporated in 1883.

Swartz Mill *Fairfield County.* In all probability, this place was named for Henry Swartz, one of the earliest settlers at the site.

Swazey *Monroe County.* This venue was settled by European Americans about 1820–1822. Later a church that was built here was dedicated by the Reverend John Swazey. In his honor, it was named Swazey Chapel, and from this set of circumstances the community took its name.

Sweetwine *Hamilton County.* A settlement predominantly of Germans here in the southwestern sector of Anderson Township grew grapes and produced wine. Some gossips say they were their own best customers.

Swift's *Washington County.* Charles Swift settled the Muskingum River bottomland here.

Switzer *Monroe County.* Switzer is in Switzerland Township, to which most of the settlers came from Switzerland.

Sycamore *Wyandot County.* The community is in Sycamore Township, which was named for Sycamore Creek. It was laid out in 1842, although George Harper had opened a store at the site even earlier, in 1836. One early scribe maintains that the so-called sycamore trees in the vicinity, from which the places take their name, are actually plane trees. Such trees are often called buttonwoods or sycamores. Incorporation took place in 1884.

Sylvania *Lucas County.* A newspaper article states that General David White, who settled Sylvania Township about 1832, began a village near this site in 1833, calling it Whiteford. When the Erie & Kalamazoo Railroad entered the area, it bypassed Whiteford, dealing that village a fatal blow. After a local judge named Wilson moved to a spot nearer the railroad depot, others followed, and the new place was called Sylvania, probably for the sylvan nature of its surroundings. Sylvania was incorporated in 1867.

Symmes *Butler County.* Although this site was settled around 1795 by Celadon Symmes, it bore little resemblance to a town until the 1830s. John Cleves Symmes held the deed to a great deal of land in this sector during the early years.

Syracuse *Meigs County.* Why this place was named Syracuse is not known. It may have been named by settlers from the Syracuse, New York, area. But more likely it was named simply because it evoked the romanticism of a faraway place. The ancient Syracuse, a seaport on Sicily's eastern coast, was the birthplace of Archimedes. The apostle Paul spent three days there (Acts 28:12).

Taborville *Geauga County.* *Tabor* reportedly means "camp" in Czech, but it is not known why the word was applied here. Mount Tabor is a biblical name (Joshua 19:22 and elsewhere).

Tacoma *Belmont County.* This name comes from an Algonquian term of obscure meaning. In the state of Washington, its application was generally associated with snow-capped peaks or gods. Perhaps this place was named in wintertime, when the forested hills in this vicinity were blanketed with a fresh layer of snow. The previous label was Olney; the change was made in 1877.

Tallmadge *Summit County.* Founded, 1807, by David Bacon. The city is named for Colonel Benjamin Tallmadge of Connecticut, who owned a good deal of land where the community is now situated (in addition to other holdings in the Western Reserve). Tallmadge was a lieutenant colonel during the Revolutionary War and later a churchman, business promoter, and U.S. congressman. Incorporation of this city was in 1951.

Tappan *Harrison County.* The community takes its name from the presiding judge of the county court, Benjamin Tappan, who served from 1816 to 1823. The hamlet arose about 1840.

Tarlton *Pickaway County.* Incorporated in 1835. It is conjectured that the place was named for the British cavalry commander Sir Banastre Tarleton (or Tarlton, 1754–1833), who served on the wrong side during the Revolutionary War. The story is that early settlers here were considered "a nest of Tories" by their neighbors.

Tawawa *Shelby County.* Tawawa was a name for the Ottawa Indians, as well as the name of a creek near this village in Green Township.

Taylor Station *Franklin County.* Surveyed and platted, 1853, by David Taylor (1801–1889). Once known as Grahamsville, this hamlet has also been known simply as Taylor, Taylorstown, and Taylor's Station.

Taylorsville *Highland County.* Platted in 1846. The proprietor was Isaiah Roberts. The place was named for an early family of settlers, the Taylors.

Taylorsville *Muskingum County.* Laid out in 1833. Founded by James Taylor, this community bears his name. Taylor built a dam and grist mill at the site.

Taylortown *Richland County.* A number of Taylors played prominent roles in this county during its early years, though none have been pinpointed here. Charles, D. A., John, R. M., and Johnson Taylor could have had ties to this hamlet.

Tedrow *Fulton County.* This place-name possibly is connected to Isaac Tedrow, who with his wife was active in the Methodist Episcopal Society here about 1842. County histories mention several other Tedrows as well.

Teegarden *Columbiana County.* This place-name is probably connected to one of several persons with the Teegarden surname who resided in the vicinity. About 1830, Uriah Teegarden established a carding machine one township south of here. At a site known as Teegarden Station, he served (1868) as the first postmaster. Others in the index of a county history include J. A., the Reverend William, and S. B. Teegarden.

Temperanceville *Belmont County.* Laid out, 1837, by Robert Gallagher. A vigorous advocate of temperance, Gallagher named his community after that cause.

Terrace Park *Hamilton County.* The community reposes in a beautifully forested area of the Little Miami River valley characterized by an elevated, terraced topography. Incorporation took place in 1893.

Terre Haute *Champaign County.* Laid out in 1836. David Miller and David Loudenback were the surveyors on the project. The plot was owned by George Craig. It was apparently located on a relatively high elevation, since the name translates from Latin as "high ground." It is unclear when this hamlet arose. The name may have been inspired by the larger city of Terre Haute, Indiana, if indeed that city predated this community.

Texas *Henry County.* The Native Americans known as the Teyas ("friends") are the source of the name of the state of Texas. Why the designation was transplanted to this Ohio site is uncertain.

Thackery *Champaign County.* A locally prominent man named Thackery who owned real estate here also founded the hamlet and left the legacy of his name with it. Thackery laid out the town about 1893.

The Bend *Defiance County.* This place may have been known as Delaware Bend at one time. It was laid out in 1874 by W. D. Hill & Company. The village lies within a large loop of the Maumee River, which runs along the easterly and southerly fringes of the community.

The Plains *Athens County.* True to its designation, this place, dating to 1908, is on a flat plain.

Thivener *Gallia County.* This tiny hamlet takes its name from a pioneer Thivener family that settled in this area.

Thomas *Meigs County.* It is unclear which Thomas this hamlet's name leads back to. In this township (Salisbury), an elector in 1805 was Cornelius Thomas. In the next township west (Rutland), Jason Thomas resided in an early year.

Thompson *Geauga County.* According to one history, this place was named "by and for" Matthew Thompson, who is said to have been a resident of Suffield, Connecticut.

Thornport *Perry County.* Laid out in 1839. The Licking Reservoir and Ohio Canal were being created nearby, stimulating the idea for the founding of a village at this site. Area farmers who saw an opportunity to ship their grain via water instead of over land convinced authorities to cut a channel between the canal and reservoir for this purpose. Thornport is in Thorn Township.

Thornville *Perry County.* First known as Lebanon, this burg was laid out about 1811 by Joseph McMullen. Owing to the existence of at least one other Lebanon in Ohio, the designation was changed. The place is in Thorn Township, and both town and township were so named because of the numerous thorn bushes in the area.

Thorps *Clark County.* This name may originate with Thomas Thorps or one of his eleven children. Thomas settled at nearby South Charleston.

Thurman *Gallia County.* United States Senator Allen Thurman (1813–1895) is the person for whom this community was named.

Tick Ridge *Washington County.* This designation was earned thanks to the large number of wood ticks thriving in the area.

Tiffin *Seneca County (seat).* Founded, 1821, by Josiah Hedges. Ohio's first governor, Dr. Edward Tiffin (1766?–1829), an acquaintance of the founder, became the city's namesake. The city was incorporated in 1835.

Tiltonville *Jefferson County.* Several members of the Tilton family are buried here. In 1776, Joseph Tilton journeyed from Pennsylvania to Ohio and settled at this site. Caleb Tilton, a grandson, was born in 1784. Susannah Tilton was Joseph's wife.

Timberlake *Lake County.* Located on Lake Erie, the village takes the first part of its name from the lovely trees that dot the area. Incorporation took place in 1947.

Tinney *Sandusky County.* The Tinneys resided in Michigan, but when their locality became too populous for their liking, possibly in the 1860s, they traded their land sight unseen for property here in Jackson Township. The name traces back to four brothers, including Darwin, Andrew, and Jackson Tinney (the name of the fourth could not be ascertained). The brothers held most of the property at this location, which earlier was known as Greensburg. Other Tinneys identified with this site were Sarah, Cora, Dan, and Ida. For many years, Alfred Tinney, a son of one of the original settlers, lived in the family home on County Road 41; the house still stands. Alfred taught school in one room of the farmhouse.

Tipp City *Miami County.* The landowner here, John Clark, set out to form a village, platting it in 1840. As a great admirer of William Henry Harrison, Clark dubbed the place Tippecanoe. Harrison had campaigned for the presidency using the slogan "Tippecanoe and Tyler, too." Citizens of the burg added "City" to the name a few years afterward. It was not until 1938 that the town formally shortened its name to Tipp City. Incorporation dates to 1851.

Tippecanoe *Harrison County.* Founded in 1840. William Henry Harrison, hero of the Battle of Tippecanoe, became the first president from Ohio. The same year this hamlet was founded, "Tippecanoe and Tyler, too" was the slogan of the successful Harrison-Tyler campaign. "Tippecanoe" took office on March 4, 1841, but died a month later.

Tiro *Crawford County.* According to *American Place-Names,* the name Tiro (sometimes Tyro) may have been given to some newly founded sites because it translates from the Latin as "novice."

Tiverton Center *Coshocton County.* Tiverton Center is in Tiverton Township. Both owe their name to a township in Newport County, Rhode Island, from which early settlers had come.

Toboso *Licking County.* Laid out in 1852. A newspaper article speculates that, there being a Quixote Street in the town, Toboso was named after a place in Spain.

William Stanberry laid out the community. (At least one source spells his name Stanbery.) Crumel Fairbanks may have been the initial settler, occupying a place on Stanberry's land.

Todds *Morgan County.* A family named Todd (possibly Todds) gave its name to this speck on the map.

Toledo *Lucas County (seat).* Toledo takes its name from a major city in Spain. The suggestion to so name this city was made by William J. Daniels in 1833. The earlier towns of Vistula (founded 1832) and Port Lawrence (founded 1817) were consolidated to form Toledo. Incorporation took place in 1836.

Tontogany *Wood County.* Settled, 1830, by Samuel Hamilton. The place had been surveyed in 1815 and given the name of a Native American chief, Tontogany. Tontogany Creek runs nearby. Incorporation took place in 1874. Hamilton had come from New York State.

Toot's Corners *Mahoning County.* Persons with the Toot surname may have settled here about 1830. In an 1874 county atlas, Jacob and Levi Toot are listed as landowners.

Torch *Athens County.* The place was first known as Torchtown, later shortened to Torch. It is said that in pioneer days, in order to light the way to the church, residents would gather pine boughs from the forest and hoist the lighted torches to illuminate the path.

Toronto *Jefferson County.* Laid out, 1818, by John Depuy. Earlier names included Newburg and Sloan's Station. The current name came about in 1881 because a prominent citizen hailed from the metropolis of Ontario, Canada. One authority claims that the new name honored a man named Dunspaugh, said to have been responsible for stimulating the local clay industry, who hailed from the Canadian city. The *Illustrated Dictionary of Place-Names* delves into some of the possible translations of the word from its Indian origins: "lake (onto)" and "to open," from the Seneca *kanitare*; *thorontohen,* from the Iroquoian, meaning "timber in the water," or *deondo,* indicating "logs floating on the water." However, many citizens of the Canadian city prefer the Huron translation of "much" or "many," relating to a meeting place of many, which may have referred originally to a crossroads where many animals passed.

Townsend *Huron County.* This community is in Townsend Township, where the majority of land was once owned by Kneeland Townsend. Elmer E. Town send and his father, John T. Townsend, were early residents of the Fitchville-New London area.

Trail *Holmes County.* Indian Trail Creek, a nearby stream, conferred its name upon this hamlet. The site was likely on an Indian trail.

Tranquility *Adams County.* In 1832, the Honorable John T. Wilson opened a store at this site, effectively founding the town. Soon others were building their homes here. Wilson suggested the name Tranquility to the Post Office Department when it opened an office here in 1848. The place was described as "a sleepy community on George's Creek."

Trebein *Greene County.* Known earlier as Frost Station, Pickeneyville, and Beaver Station, the place is near what was then the Xenia & Dayton Railroad stop. F. C. Trebine owned a mill nearby. In time the spelling of the town's name evolved from Trebine to Trebein.

Tremainesville *Lucas County.* This community is thought to be named for Calvin Tremaine (circa 1832).

Tremont City *Clark County.* Settled, 1800, by John Ross and others from Kentucky. The community was first known as Clarksburg. When a post office was authorized, the name was changed to Tree Mount, a name inspired by the town's location at the foot of a heavily forested hill. The form of the name was altered by postal authorities. Incorporation took place in 1918.

Trenton *Butler County.* Incorporated, 1896. Many early settlers at this place arrived from New Jersey. At first (circa 1815) they called the spot Bloomfield in honor of a New Jersey governor. However, it was necessary to change that name in order to acquire a post office, so the name of the New Jersey capital was selected in 1831.

Triadelphia *Morgan County.* The village was founded by three brothers—Joseph, Nathan, and Samuel Roberts. The year platted was 1838. The name is said to have been inspired by the brothers' memories of Philadelphia; they linked "Tri," for the three brothers, and *adelphos* (Greek for "brothers").

Trimble *Athens County.* The name honors Ohio Governor Allen Trimble (1786–1821). The hamlet was known earlier as Oxford, a name said to have been applied after an ox thief and his new acquisition reached the swollen Sunday Creek near here and neither he nor his ox was able to ford the torrent.

Trinway *Muskingum County.* Nowhere in historical documents is it clearly spelled out why Trinway was so named. Local speculation is that the name comes from Trinity, meaning "three," and refers to the fact that in the village's early days, it could be reached three ways—by railroad, canal, and highway. The east-west rail line eventually became the Pennsylvania Railroad's main line between New York and Saint Louis, and a north-south branch connected this route to Zanesville. Trinway previously was known as Dresden Junction, springing up about 1860.

Trombley *Wood County.* Formerly Blake. Surveyed in 1885. In that year, the only business in the hamlet was Trombley's sawmill, from which the place took its name.

Trotwood *Montgomery County.* Laid out in 1854. Betsey Trotwood, a *David Copperfield* character, is believed to have been the inspiration for this place-name. Louis R. Pfoutz, one-time storekeeper and postmaster here, was a Charles Dickens enthusiast and gave the site this name. It was formerly known as Higgins Station, for one of its first settlers, Amos Higgins. Trotwood today is a city, having been incorporated in 1901.

Troy *Miami County (seat).* Laid out in 1808. Incorporated in 1814. The surveyor was Andrew Wallace. Early citizens recorded memories of persons here who could recite lengthy excerpts from Homer's *Iliad*, in which the ancient Greek city of Troy plays a prominent role. This place is thought, as a result, to have been named for the classical Troy.

Troyton *Delaware County.* One might dissect the name of this hamlet as "the town of Troy." It is in Troy Township.

Trumbull *Ashtabula County.* Like Trumbull County, this hamlet traces its name back to Jonathan Trumbull, who was governor of Connecticut. The township in which it is located is also named Trumbull.

Truro *Franklin County.* Settled after 1806 primarily by refugees from Canada, this village was named by David Taylor, an early immigrant. The site was reserved for Canadians sympathetic to the colonists' cause during the American Revolution. Taylor's former home had been Truro, Nova Scotia.

Tunnel *Washington County.* The Marietta & Cincinnati Railroad built a tunnel at this location, replacing a long and tedious switchback system for getting trains over the hill. A post office opened in 1855; the tunnel was completed in 1863.

Tunnel Hill *Coshocton County.* This town dates from about the time that a post office was obtained (1873). The office was secured largely through the influence of railroad officials, who were undertaking the construction of a tunnel a mile to the northeast.

Tupper's Plains *Meigs County.* Truman Hecox entered this place in 1800. The first settlers may have been Ashley Gibbs and Sylvester, his son, shortly thereafter. The village was not laid out until 1840, by James Martin. Although much of the surrounding region is upland in nature, at this site it is level and probably was reminiscent of a plain. Although Martin called his community Martinsville, another Ohio town was already so named. Postal authorities suggested Tupper's Plains, for Edward Tupper, who was said to have surveyed the locality in 1802. The name was adopted, giving the community a name unique among U.S. places. Edward Tupper was probably descended from General Benjamin Tupper (1738–1792), also a surveyor, who may have been with the Ohio Company at Marietta. Benjamin had a son, Major Anselm Tupper (1763–1808), who was also a surveyor.

Tuscarawas *Tuscarawas County.* This is a Native American word said to translate as "open mouth." The place is on the Tuscarawas River in Tuscarawas County.

Twenty-Mile Stand *Warren County.* Stagecoach stops with tollhouses were sometimes designated as stands. This community was four miles from Sixteen-Mile Stand in Hamilton County and about twenty miles from Cincinnati. The measurements are thought to have used Fountain Square in Cincinnati as a reference point. A tavern (or stand) operated here, and a post office opened in 1824.

Twin Lakes *Portage County.* This small residential community and its lakes stand on two sides of State Route 43. The lakes are called East Twin Lake and West Twin Lake. They are about the same size.

Twinsburg *Summit County.* This city was founded in 1817 by Moses and Aaron Wilcox, identical twin brothers. The Wilcoxes, who worked as business partners, died on the same day. Today the city is noted for its "Twins Days" festival, held annually. Incorporation occurred in 1954.

Tycoon *Gallia County.* According to a newspaper article authored by James Sands, "the name Tycoon Lake can . . . be indirectly attributed to the Wood family, as it was probably William Wood who named the mill at Wood's Mills the Tycoon Mill. . . . The lake was named after the community of Tycoon that grew up around the mill of William and Sylvester Wood." Sylvester Wood built a house here in 1852. He was the son of William Wood of Virginia. Sylvester's sons, Luther and Elmer, became prominent in Gallia County.

Tylersville *Butler County.* Laid out, 1842, by Daniel Pocock. The village is sometimes known locally, for an unknown reason, as Pug Muncy. It was named Tylersville for the tenth U.S. president, John Tyler (1790–1862), by John Sullivan.

Tymochtee *Wyandot County.* This name is said to be a Wyandot word for "the creek or river around the plains."

Tyrell *Trumbull County.* Two early settlers at this juncture were Ebijah and Elijah Tyrell, twin brothers whose surname remained with the hamlet.

Tyrone *Coshocton County.* A post office was established here in 1850, with John Alexander the moving force behind its acquisition. At least one early settler at this place came from Tyrone County, Ireland; that is thought to be how this community got its name.

Uhrichsville *Tuscarawas County.* A newspaper in the county reports that a Pennsylvanian, Michael Urich, arrived here in 1804 and erected a mill on Little Stillwater Creek. Urich reportedly was able to obtain 1,500 acres here at a dollar an acre. The construction of a dam furnished water power for his mill at this site, first called Waterford. Locals termed the place Urich's Mills, which in 1839 became Urichsville. It was incorporated the same year. At some point the place-name gained a second "h."

Unionport *Jefferson County.* Laid out, 1859, by William Harvey. A previous name was Mount Moriah. However, there was some discontent with this label, and at least four other names were submitted for consideration as a permanent one: Exchange, Kossuth, Unionport, and Harveysburg. When the matter was left to Harvey to resolve, he chose Unionport. The place is on a stream, but it is uncertain whether the stream was navigable enough to justify the "port" segment of the name.

Union Ridge *Columbiana County.* The "Ridge" aspect of the name is a result of the high elevation of this site. The "Union" portion is more obscure. It could come from the "union" nearby of Pennsylvania and Ohio, from intersecting roads, or from a religious gathering spot. The community has a rich religious history: a United Brethren in Christ church was meeting here as early as 1864. There was also a Quaker meetinghouse here.

Union Station *Licking County.* The "Union" aspect of the name is the result of the place's situation in Union Township, while the "Station" portion comes from its location on a railroad.

Uniontown *Stark County.* Founded in 1816. It is believed that the primary reason for naming the site Uniontown is that it was a transfer point from one stagecoach line to another. In addition, it was at the union (junction) of the Cleveland-Pittsburgh and Canton-Middlebury pikes. Thomas Albert and Elias Brenner were the fathers of the village.

Unionville *Lake County.* This name came about as a result of the town's position, virtually on the Lake-Ashtabula county line. It thus represents the union of the two counties.

Unionville *Union County.* Laid out, 1847, by William B. Irwin for David, John, and Frederick Sager. It is said that M. P. Rice and forty others petitioned in 1879 for the place to be named Unionville. It is not known why they favored this name; perhaps they felt that it helped identify the place with Union County and as a community of importance.

Uniopolis *Auglaize County.* Platted and organized by John Huffman in 1837, Uniopolis is in Union Township. It is reasonable to assume that the namers joined part of "Union" to a portion of "metropolis" in the hope that the community might become a thriving city.

University Heights *Cuyahoga County.* The current label came into being in the mid-1920s as a result of the site's proximity to John Carroll University. The city was incorporated in 1907 as Idlewood.

Upper Arlington *Franklin County.* This site was granted to several Revolutionary War veterans in 1800. But modern-day Upper Arlington did not begin to take shape until 1913, when brothers Ben and King Thompson purchased 840 acres from James Miller. In 1918, the village was incorporated. The name seems logical, since the site is north of the village once known as Arlington (now Marblecliff). Upper Arlington became a city in 1941.

Upper Fivemile *Brown County.* Named for Fivemile Creek, Upper Fivemile is just north of the community of Fivemile.

Upper Sandusky *Wyandot County (seat).* Laid out in 1843. The city was designated Upper Sandusky by virtue of its position toward the upper reaches of the Sandusky River. Incorporation took place in 1848.

Upton *Sandusky County.* This place was sometimes referred to as Upton's Landing. Located on a waterway leading to the Sandusky River, it consisted of a small cluster of homes near a dock and boat rental place operated by the Joe Upton family.

Urbana *Champaign County (seat).* Laid out, 1805, by Colonel William Ward. The Latin word for "city" is behind the name of this place. Incorporation was in 1814.

Urbancrest *Franklin County.* Incorporated in 1948, this village employs a name that was probably suggested by its position in an urban area on the brink (or "crest") of nearby Columbus.

Utica *Licking County.* A number of the early residents of this site came from New York State and other eastern venues, so it seems likely that the name traces back to Utica, New York. In earlier times the place was known as Wilmington, but it was called Robertson's Mills when it was laid out in 1815. A second source puts the founding date at 1810 and gives the founder as William Robertson of Franklin County, Pennsylvania. The Utica name came into vogue in 1821 upon application for a post office—there already being another Wilmington in Ohio. Incorporation came in 1841.

Utley *Athens County.* This hamlet was begun by William R. Utley, described as a "capitalist and promoter" from New York City. Utley was the prime mover in getting a rail line extended up the Federal Valley to a coal mine he operated at Stewart.

Utopia *Clermont County.* Out of the dissolution of the Fourierite Association emerged this community, which was founded on utopian principles, resulting in the place-name. Henry Jernegan laid the settlement out in 1847.

Vadis *Belmont County.* One historian speculated that this town name was inspired by the title of a popular book published in 1895, *Quo Vadis.*

Vale's Mills *Vinton County.* J. Q. A. Vale, the nephew of pioneer Samuel Vale, owned and operated a mill near this site for many years.

Valley City *Medina County.* This community lies in the valley of the west branch of Rocky River. Thus its location determined the name.

Valley Hi *Logan County.* This sobriquet was first applied to a ski slope at this locality. Later it was generalized to apply to a community that grew up in the area. It is one of the highest points in Ohio.

Valley Junction *Hamilton County.* This place was never surveyed. Two railroads formed a junction here, and several dwellings sprang up. Located in the valley of the Great Miami River, the place was an important stop on the Indianapolis & Cincinnati and Whitewater Valley rail lines.

Valley View *Cuyahoga County.* The name must have seemed natural, since the place is on the brink of the vast Cuyahoga River valley. Valley View was incorporated as a village in 1919.

Valley View *Scioto County.* "I would say Valley View is just what the name implies," states a long-time area resident. "If you have ever been to our county, . . . we have long rows of hills running north and south from the river with . . . very narrow valleys between, giving the idea of 'Valley View.'"

Vanatta *Licking County.* This village owes its name to William Vanatta, who came to the area in 1833 and was a prominent citizen for years thereafter.

Van Buren *Hancock County.* Laid out, 1833, by George Ensminger and John Trout. The place was incorporated in 1866. The name honors President Martin Van Buren (1782–1862).

Vandalia *Montgomery County.* Laid out, 1838, by Benjamin Wilhelm. At the time of the town's founding, the National Road was under construction, inching its way toward Vandalia, Illinois. The town was named for that city. Wilhelm became the first postmaster when an office opened here in 1843. Vandalia was incorporated in 1848.

Vanlue *Hancock County.* William Vanlue laid out this town in 1847. In 1867, it was incorporated. It is unclear whether the village was named by Vanlue or simply in honor of him.

Van Wert *Van Wert County (seat).* Founded 1837 by James Watson Riley. A newspaper account related that the city takes its name from the county, which was named for Isaac Van Wart. The spelling was corrupted over time. Van Wart, David Williams, and John Paulding captured the English spy Major John André near Tarrytown, New York, in 1780. Like Van Wart, Paulding and Williams have Ohio counties named after them. Van Wert was incorporated in 1848.

Vaughansville *Putnam County.* The place was laid out by Daniel C. Vaughan (or Vaughn). The year was 1847 (or 1843).

Vega *Jackson County.* The supposition is that Vega was named for the brightest star in the constellation Lyra. This theory is set forth by Charles P. Harkins in *Out of the Past.* However, the Spanish word *vega* means "fertile plain" and could have been the source of the name. Joseph Hanna performed the survey in the 1840s.

Venedocia *Van Wert County.* Venedocia is said by some to have been named for a place in Wales. In his *History of Van Wert County,* Floyd O'Daffer holds that *Venedocias* was "a variant form of Venedocia . . . used in Latin in the Dark . . . and Middle Ages for the Welsh *Gwynedd* . . . [representing] the name of the Anglesey, Caernarvon, Merioneth, and Denbigh tribes inhabiting this region"—that is, the ancient region of Gwynedd (or Gwyneth) in northern Wales. Descendants of early settlers at this place tell a different story. They maintain that the name means "to this place I came." Initial settlement was by the William Bebb family, which left Wales in mid-1847 and found its way here later the same year. Once in Ohio, the family was guided by Governor William Bebb, a cousin.

Venice *Butler County.* Laid out, 1817, by Dr. Benjamin Clark. Because of its attractive site, Clark dubbed the place Venus. The change to Venice may have been a corruption of his original intent.

Venice *Erie County.* Town fathers selected this name because of the aquatic location of the place, on Sandusky Bay. Venice, Italy, sits in a lagoon and is known for its many canals.

Vermilion *Erie County.* The city's name is said to have originated with the local red clay. The Ottawa Indians reportedly used the clay as war paint. It is thought that the first white settler here may have been William Hoddy, in 1808. Incorporation took place in 1838.

Vernon *Lawrence County.* The Mount Vernon Iron Furnace, which operated here, gave the site its name.

Vernon *Trumbull County.* This community bears the same name as the township in which it lies. Both trace the name to Vernon, Connecticut. The area was settled no later than 1806.

Vernon Junction *Richland County.* Founded in 1872. The community, at the junction of the Big Four and Toledo, Walhonding Valley, & Ohio railroads, was first dubbed Junction City. The current name is said to have been appropriated from Vernon Township in Crawford County.

Verona *Montgomery County.* This Verona is thought to have been named after the city in Italy.

Versailles *Darke County.* Incorporated in 1855. This place-name, echoing the name of the place outside Paris where Louis XIV had his royal palace, was conferred when France was popular owing to its support of the American Revolution. Previously (as early as 1819), the name was Jacksonville (in honor of Andrew Jackson), but residents became disenchanted with Jacksonian politics and caused the name to be changed. Across the creek, a community called North Jacksonville emerged around 1842; it was later absorbed into Versailles.

Vesuvius *Lawrence County.* An iron works named Vesuvius was located here. Given the nature of the business—pouring molten metal—the works and the community that grew up around it were probably aptly named after the fiery volcano in the Bay of Naples, Italy.

Veto *Washington County.* There was a post office at this country crossroads from 1850 to 1902, when it was put out of business by rural free delivery. It was named in recognition of Judge Ephraim Cutler's successful 1802 veto of a clause that would have allowed slavery in Ohio.

Vickery *Sandusky County.* In 1881, 1882, or 1883, this village was platted by Robert Vickery, becoming known by his surname. It is on what was the Lake Erie & Western Railroad, where it met the Sandusky, Fremont, & Southern Electric Railroad. One source states that the community was named not for Robert but for John Vickery, an Erie County native born in 1861. However, Robert Vickery owned the land adjoining the railroad, which came through in 1881. He was one of four brothers who came from England in 1854. One of the brothers was named William. Others with the surname Vickery mentioned in an early history of Sandusky County include James P., John H., Fred A., and Richard.

Victoria *Mercer County.* The place was once known as Saint Joseph's, but because of another Ohio place with that name, it was changed to Victoria. It is thought that Victoria was the name of the postmaster's wife or daughter. As Saint Joseph, the place was platted in 1861.

Vienna *Trumbull County.* No one knows why this place was so named; apparently there was no connection to Vienna, Austria. The name is pronounced locally as VYenna. A number of other towns in the United States use the same name. The Vienna in Illinois is said to have taken its name from a local Native American chief named Vienna-Cocosimmon. Other Viennas are in South Dakota, Maine, Georgia, and Maryland. One recent summer, Michael Freund, of the Austrian capital, visited Ohio's Vienna to take photographs and gather information. Freund's trip through the United States was funded by his home city and the Mobil Corporation for the purpose of sending him to all or most of the Viennas in the country. With the resultant data, he was to compile an article for the company's magazine, to be published both in English and German.

Vigo *Ross County.* The hamlet may have been named for Colonel Francis Vigo, also known as Joseph Maria Francesco Vigo, a trader of Italian ancestry. Vigo journeyed to Spain, became a citizen there, and joined the Spanish army. Later he sailed to America and became a financial backer of George Rogers Clark before and during the Revolutionary War. He lived for many years in Vincennes (now in Indiana) and became an American citizen. When he died in 1836, he was nearly a hundred years old.

Vincent *Washington County.* Henry Earle Vincent owned the property where the village is situated. When he donated a parcel of land for railroad purposes, the railroad company became the first to designate the place with the Vincent name. After H. E. laid out the town in 1853, he installed Rollin C. Vincent, his son, as postmaster, in 1857.

Vinton *Gallia County.* Samuel F. Vinton is the person who gave his name to this hamlet, which he laid out in 1832 with General Samuel R. Holcomb. Incorporation took place in 1882. Samuel Vinton served in the U.S. Congress. One source uses "G" as his middle initial.

Vinton *Vinton County.* The village takes its name from the county, which, like the hamlet in Gallia County, was named for the early Ohio political figure Samuel Finley Vinton.

Virgin *Washington County.* The designation honors the Virgin Mary. The place was settled by Irish immigrants who came to help build the Marietta & Cincinnati Railroad in the 1850s.

Wabash *Mercer County.* Formerly called Wabash City, this community is at the mouth of the Beaver River, which empties into the Wabash River not far distant.

Wade *Washington County.* Formerly identified with Ostend Post Office, this place became Wade in 1864 when Postmaster Squire D. Riggs had the name changed. The name honors a Civil War–era U.S. senator from Ohio, Benjamin Franklin Wade (1800–1878). A strong abolitionist and radical reconstructionist, Wade was president pro tempore of the Senate and next in line to become president if Andrew Johnson had been convicted on impeachment charges.

Wadsworth *Medina County.* This general area was settled in 1814 by the Durhams—Dean, Oliver, and Daniel. Frederick Brown constructed the first house in the village in 1816. The city takes its name from General Elijah Wadsworth of Litchfield, Connecticut, who in 1799 purchased the majority of the township. A Revolutionary War veteran, Wadsworth settled out of the county, in Canfield, Ohio. Wadsworth achieved city status in 1911.

Wahlsburg *Brown County.* This place-name traces back to the Christian Wahl family. Christian was born in Germany. His son Peter was at various times a farmer and merchant, running a general store at the intersection in Wahlsburg. Another son, Christian Wahl, Jr., was deeded seventy-four acres at the southwest quadrant of the intersection by his father, and two of this son's daughters—Gussie and Lillie May—operated a store diagonally across from Peter's, in competition with Peter's son and successor, Jesse (called Jack).

Wainwright *Tuscarawas County.* In 1894, a coal mine was opened here by R. W. Wainwright. The resultant community took on his name.

Waite Hill *Lake County.* This place-name stems from the Waite family. William Waite settled on a promontory here in 1821. His son had arrived a year earlier and cleared the land. Waite Hill was incorporated in 1928.

Wakeman *Huron County.* This place is in Wakeman Township, and the village and township take their name from the early land proprietor, Jesup Wakeman. The township was formalized in 1824.

Walhonding *Coshocton County.* Platted, 1841, by T. S. Humrickson, William K. Johnson, and G. W. Sullivan. The name is thought to come from a Delaware Indian word for a ditchlike section of river or a ravine. The village grew up around the Walhonding Canal.

Walnut Creek *Holmes County.* This community was originally known as New Carlisle. The original town lots were laid out by George Kaser, Daniel Funk, and J. B. Schrock. When citizens applied for a post office, the name Walnut Creek was adopted owing to the profusion of walnut trees nearby and the stream meandering through the site. The town was platted in 1827.

Walton Hills *Cuyahoga County.* A family of Waltons settled in the southwest corner of Bedford Township in the mid-1830s. A Quaker from Pennsylvania, Joseph Walton was the first to come here. His children were Abner, Benjamin, Betsy, Rebecca, and Abigail. The village was incorporated in 1951.

Wapakoneta *Auglaize County (seat).* This name once identified a Shawnee encampment here and was the name of a Shawnee chief. The village was incorporated in 1849.

Warfield *Washington County.* The post office that began service here in 1882, like the surrounding area, was called Warfield, after a family of that name that settled here. The post office, it is said, closed in 1885 when the postmaster was sentenced to prison for five years.

Warner *Washington County.* A post office was established nearby in 1871, along the line of the Marietta & Pittsburgh Railroad. The contract for building the road was held by General Adoniram Judson Warner, so, fittingly, the place was named for him.

Warren *Trumbull County (seat).* Laid out, 1800, by Ephraim Quimby. Incorporated in 1834. The name honors the surveyor, Moses Warren.

Warrensville Heights *Cuyahoga County.* The city was initially settled around 1808 by Mrs. David Warren, her husband, and eight children. The family walked from their previous home in New Hampshire. Warrensville Heights was incorporated in 1957.

Warsaw *Coshocton County.* William Cartwright laid out Warsaw in 1834. The name refers to Poland's capital city. It was inspired by settlers' empathy with that nation's efforts to secure freedom and independence.

Washington *Richland County.* Washington was laid out by Wesley Barnes, James Sirpliss, and John Conwell. It is in Washington Township, which was named for George Washington.

Washington Court House *Fayette County (seat).* This Virginia Military Tract city was laid out, according to one source, about 1807. A second source states that it was laid out in 1810 or 1811. One of the veterans of the Revolution who received a land grant here was Colonel Benjamin Temple, whose agent, Thomas Hinde, was the city's first settler, constructing a cabin in 1807. According to a newspaper account, Temple asked Hinde to name the site Washington, which he did. But when the first court of common pleas was convened here in 1810 and a log courthouse was erected three years later, the words "Court House" were added to the place-name. It then became distinguishable from other Ohio sites using Washington in their names. Incorporation occurred in 1831.

Washingtonville *Columbiana County.* Frontiersmen were moving westward from Pennsylvania when this place was settled and named in the first president's honor. George Washington's presidency had been from 1789 to 1797; he died in 1799. Some of the settlers, reaching relatively level land after crossing the Alleghenies, were satisfied to remain in this locality. Washingtonville was incorporated in 1848.

Waterford *Knox County.* Laid out in 1841. The village was surveyed by Merrit Beam, while the land was owned by Noah L. Levering and Josiah Fawcett. Perhaps the name describes the situation of the place, on the north branch of the Kokosing River (Owl Creek). Before bridges were in place, it would have been necessary for travelers here to "ford water." A grist mill was among the early businesses here. Daniel Levering is believed to have been one of the earliest settlers in this vicinity, arriving before 1812.

Waterford *Washington County.* Waterford Township was organized in 1790. This small community is just south of Beverly, at a spot on the Muskingum River where the water level was usually low. As a result, early travelers were able to ford the water readily, and the place became known as Waterford.

Watertown *Washington County.* Sherman Waterman was killed here, on the south branch of Wolf Creek, in 1795. The town, the township, and eventually the post office were named in his honor.

Waterville *Lucas County.* Platted, 1818, by John Pray. Incorporated in 1882. Waterville's name, in all probability, was inspired by its situation on the banks of the Maumee River.

Wathey's *Carroll County.* On a farm in Augusta Township, Zachary Wathey was born in 1822. He became a county commissioner and gave his name to this place.

Watkins *Union County.* William Conklin and Thomas P. Watkins were the real estate owners. Joseph S. Watkins, deputy surveyor, did the survey in 1838.

Watson *Sandusky County.* It is thought that this hamlet owes its name to Cooper K. Watson, born in Kentucky in 1810, who became an Ohio judge and congressman.

Watson *Seneca County.* The genesis of this place-name is not clear. However, six Watsons were prominent in the early years of the county and are listed in the index of the *History of Seneca County, Ohio.* Chances are that the name of this site relates to one or more of the family members.

Wattsville *Carroll County.* David Watts is the person after whom the place was named.

Wauseon *Fulton County (seat).* Wauseon was a prominent Potawatomi Indian chief and brother of Ottokee, who also is the namesake of an Ohio town. In 1838, the land which about sixteen years later was to become the site of the community was ceded to the U.S. government by Wauseon. J. H. Sargent and E. L. Barber, surveyors with the New York Central Railroad, founded the town in 1854. It was incorporated in 1857 and is now a city.

Waverly *Pike County (seat).* The city was named by Captain Francis Cleveland, an uncle of President Grover Cleveland. Francis may have come here as an engineer to work on the Ohio Canal. A devotee of Sir Walter Scott's Waverley novels, he is believed to have suggested Waverly as the name of the community, which previously had been known as Uniontown. Waverly was laid out in 1829 and incorporated in 1842.

Wayland *Portage County.* In 1850, when a canal was being constructed, this spot was known as Newport. It had also been known as Parisville (it is in Paris Township). In the 1870s, when it acquired a somewhat wild reputation, it was known as Cyclone. It is said that the Cyclone name caused too much apprehension among passengers on the Baltimore & Ohio Railroad when the conductor would walk down the aisle shouting, "Cyclone, Cyclone!" About 1900, the name Wayland took hold. According to one version, about 90 percent of the settlers were Welsh, and in referring to them, others said they came from "Wale Land." However, a dissenting explanation in one source states that the Wayland name memorializes a Baptist minister who had preached at the site, the Reverend Wayland D. Hoyt.

Wayne *Wood County.* This community traces back its label to General Anthony Wayne (1745-1796), who defeated Native Americans at the Battle of Fallen Timbers not far from here in August 1794. Previous names of the town included Prairie Depot and Freeport. Wayne was incorporated in 1865.

Wayne Center *Ashtabula County.* This hamlet is sometimes referred to simply as Wayne. It is in Wayne Township, named, like a great many other Ohio sites, after General Anthony Wayne.

Waynesburg *Crawford County.* Laid out and platted in 1833. The proprietors were Richard Millar (or Millard) and Aaron Cory. The name honors General Anthony Wayne.

Waynesburg *Stark County.* Laid out, 1814, by Joseph Handlon. The place-name traces back directly to General Anthony Wayne, whose fame was great in Ohio.

Waynesville *Warren County.* A senior Ohio settlement, Waynesville dates back to 1796. The landowners were John Smith, Evan Banes, and Samuel Heighway. General Anthony Wayne is the town's namesake.

Weaver's *Darke County.* Arriving in 1819, Peter Weaver erected the first house in Weaver's Station.

Weaver's Corners *Huron County.* The place-name probably has a connection to David Weaver, who resided in this area early on.

Webster *Darke County.* Jacob C. Carlock held title to the land here and named the place, presumably out of admiration for Daniel Webster (1782–1852), the statesman and orator.

Wegee *Belmont County.* Sometimes styled Weegee, this label originates with nearby Wegee Creek. The belief is that *wegee* was the European Americans' spelling of a Native American word meaning "winding" or "crooked."

Weilersville *Wayne County.* Several Weilers, probably closely related, were associated with this locality. Joseph Weiler served as township trustee in 1842–1844. J. J. Weiler, possibly Joseph's son, served as a trustee for the same venue in 1872–1873. An A. Weiler is also mentioned in a biographical index covering Wayne County.

Weimer's Mills *Darke County.* One of the county's earliest mills was erected here by a Mr. Weimer.

Wellington *Lorain County.* Both city and township trace back their name to William T. Welling, who came here from Montgomery County, New York. It is also said that some residents favored the name out of a deep respect for the Duke of Wellington (1769–1852), the British soldier and statesman. Organization of the village as a municipality took place in 1855.

Wellston *Jackson County.* A member of the Constitutional Convention, the Honorable Harvey Wells, gave his name to the village. The city was incorporated in 1876.

Wellsville *Columbiana County.* Wellsville was named in honor of the person who platted the community, William Wells, Wells laid off the lots in 1824.

Welshfield *Geauga County.* Jacob Welsh and Anna, his daughter, were the earliest settlers in this township, arriving in 1810. As the tale is told, the name of the township was changed from Welshfield to Troy in 1834 after Welsh welshed on a vow to sign over fifty acres.

Wendelin *Mercer County.* The Church of Saint Wendelin was organized here in 1856, with the local community taking on the name Wendelin as a result. The town appears on some maps as Saint Wendelin.

West Alexandria *Preble County.* Laid out in 1818. William Alexander laid off the lots in one township and Henry Kiesling the lots overlapping into an adjoining township. Alexander is the person for whom the village was named. Incorporation took place in 1836.

West Andover *Ashtabula County.* Located in Andover Township, West Andover is west of Andover. (See Andover entry.)

West Austintown *Mahoning County.* The community is just west of Austintown. (See Austintown entry.)

West Bedford *Coshocton County.* A number of pioneer families settling at this point came from Bedford County, Pennsylvania. Included was Micajah Heaton, who laid out this site in 1817. For some years it was known as Heaton's Town. The township in which West Bedford is located also is named Bedford.

Westboro *Clinton County.* The name of this community may be related to a pioneer surveyor in the township, Peyton West.

West Brookfield *Stark County.* This moniker was bestowed in remembrance of a Brookfield in Clinton County, New York.

West Carlisle *Coshocton County.* Platted, 1817, by John Perkins and John McNabb, owners of the land at this site. Perkins had come to the area from Carlisle, Pennsylvania, resulting in this place-name.

West Carrollton *Montgomery County.* Alexander Grimes, Moses Smith, and H. G. Phillips platted the town in 1830, although the locality was settled much earlier. It was initially dubbed Carrollton. But after it was discovered that Carroll County also had a Carrollton, the name here was changed to West Carrollton. It is possible that Charles Carroll, who inspired the name of the Carroll County community, also was the namesake for this town. (See Carrollton entry.) West Carrollton was incorporated in 1887.

West Charleston *Miami County.* Previously known as Friendtown, this place later adopted the given name of its founder, Charles Friend, who laid out the town in 1807.

West Elkton *Preble County.* Laid out, 1847, by J. L. Street. The landholders were R. W. Swain, Nathan Hornaday, J. N. Gift, Jesse Stubbs, Walter Wheeler, J. H. Stubbs, Stephen Leas, P. S. Patton, Henry Maddock, J. P. Brown, James Smith, and Isaac Wright. Originally the locale was known simply as Elk, probably because elk were a common sight in the area in those days. A quarterly meeting of the Society of Friends was held at Elk. It is said that a Mr. Dix, a storekeeper, ordered some merchandise sent to him at Elk. It arrived, but was addressed to Elkton, so locals adopted that name for the community. Later still, when it was learned that another Ohio town used the Elkton label, "West" was prefixed to distinguish this place from the other. West Elkton was incorporated in 1848.

Western Star *Summit and Medina counties.* This locality has gone by other names: Starr's Corners; Griswold's Corners, or simply Griswold, after the five sons of Alexander Griswold; and Jedburg, for the partriarch of a local family, Jedediah Richards. The "Western" aspect of the current designation may be a result of the place's location, on the western boundary of Norton Township. The "Star" probably comes from Nathan Starr, a Connecticut man who held deed to the land here. In 1842, Western Star was incorporated.

Westfall *Pickaway County.* The hamlet was laid out by Abel Westfall.

West Farmington *Trumbull County.* The name stems, in all probability, from Farmington, Connecticut, just west of Hartford. Some early settlers of this place set out from that one. Ohio's West Farmington is in Farmington Township, slightly west of the crossroads called Farmington. It was incorporated in 1887.

Westfield *Medina County.* Westfield was settled in 1817 by Joseph Winston, Hammer Palmer, Richard, John, and Benjamin Morton, Timothy Nye, and Henry Thorndike. The name is taken from Westfield, Massachusetts, which was the hometown of the owner of the land at this site, James Fowler. It is also known as Westfield Center. The community was incorporated in 1908.

West Independence *Hancock County.* This place-name has its roots in feelings of patriotism. The "West" was added to distinguish the place from at least one other Ohio place named Independence.

West Lancaster *Fayette County.* A significant number of the early immigrants to this place arrived from Lancaster, Pennsylvania, accounting for the adoption of the West Lancaster name.

West Lebanon *Wayne County.* The Reverend William S. Butts and Philip Groff became the inaugural settlers at this site, arriving in 1808. Groff had come from a Lebanon County, Pennsylvania, town named West Lebanon and transported that name to this place. One authority puts West Lebanon's year of founding at 1833.

West Leipsic *Putnam County.* West Leipsic is immediately west of Leipsic, virtually adjoining it. (See Leipsic entry.) West Leipsic was incorporated in 1882. It had been laid out in 1852 by John W. Peckenpaugh.

West Mecca *Trumbull County.* Located in Mecca Township, West Mecca is just west of Mecca. (See Mecca entry.)

West Middletown *Butler County.* West Middletown is separated from the city of Middletown by the Great Miami River. Most locals today disavow the existence of West Middletown, considering it absorbed into Middletown proper. However, in the 1800s, the Baltimore & Ohio Railroad constructed a line from Dayton to Cincinnati, passing Middletown on the west side of the river. There the railroad established a stop and named it West Middletown.

West Millgrove *Wood County.* According to a correspondent in this community, originally there were two Millgroves; one was a mile east of this town. Both had a post office, causing confusion in mail distribution. The railroad, which brought the mail, took it upon itself to rename the towns, calling this one West Millgrove and the one to the east Hatton. Town fathers here resisted, but the new names stuck. The "Mill" portion of the name is explained thusly by the correspondent: "Our town had many mills. There were wood mills, grist mills, and most small factories here that produced anything were called a mill. There was [also] a glove mill." West Millgrove was incorporated in 1875.

West Milton *Miami County.* Founded about 1805 by Joseph Evans. The story is that the founder's eldest daughter had read *Paradise Lost* and was so taken with John Milton's work that she influenced her father to christen the village for the English poet (1608–1674). In 1835, the town was incorporated.

West Point *Columbiana County.* The origin of the name is uncertain, although the "West" portion may be traceable to the place's location on the west fork of Little Beaver Creek. Henry Bough settled the place.

West Richfield *Summit County.* This community is immediately west of Richfield. (See Richfield entry.)

West Rushville *Fairfield County.* This hamlet is just west of Rushville. (See Rushville entry.)

West Salem *Wayne County.* Founded in 1834. Early settlers are said to have located here after having been residents of a place called Salem. Whether it was Salem, Massachusetts, or another Salem is unclear. West Salem was incorporated in 1865.

West Unity *Williams County.* The town site was owned by William L. Smith and John Rings. The place was named for Unity, Pennsylvania. Miller Arrowsmith was the surveyor. It was laid out in 1842 by Rings, and incorporated in 1866.

West Wheeling *Belmont County.* Martin S. Todd laid out the community in 1838. It is an Ohio suburb of Wheeling, its West Virginia neighbor across the bridge. Many workers in Wheeling's factories and mills have made their homes in West Wheeling.

Weymouth *Medina County.* When a post office went into service here, it was named by Judge Bronson for Weymouth, Massachusetts, which in turn had been named for Weymouth in southern England.

Wharton *Wyandot County.* Founded in 1846. Once known as Whartensburgh, the village was named out of respect for a Mr. Wharton. Sources state that the town was surveyed in 1846 and laid out in 1848. The latter date may be in error. Incorporation took place in 1878. The name requested at that time was Maple City, but for some reason, the Wharton, or Whartensburgh, name prevailed. Some speculate that the surveyor, Samuel Rathborn, married a woman with the surname Wharten, and it was he who suggested the place-name. The difference in spelling is not accounted for.

Wheelersburg *Scioto County.* Settled in 1820. Laid out, 1824, by the Reverend Dan Young. One source states that the town at first was called Concord. In 1826, the name was changed to its current form to honor an early settler, Major Porter Wheeler, who had served during the War of 1812 and was known as an Indian fighter. A second source points out that William Harrison Wheeler was born here in 1841, a son of Isaac Hastings Wheeler. And William Henry Wheeler is said to have toiled on a farm here until 1861, when he enlisted in military service.

Whigville *Noble County.* Dating to 1851, this hamlet took its name as a result of being a stronghold of the Whig political party.

Whisler *Pickaway County.* William and Elizabeth Whisler donated a parcel of real estate on which to build a church, and the community was named for the donors. At one time this hamlet was referred to by some as Pinchgut.

White Cottage *Muskingum County.* Major Lewis Nye of Connecticut opened a tavern in a white cottage at this locality in 1809. Matthew Gillespie later ran the tavern after marrying Nye's widow. It is said that many important persons patronized the tavern, including Henry Clay and Andrew Jackson. Colonel George Rankin, Nye's son-in-law, eventually acquired the business. In 1839, a town called Newtonville was laid out here by A. Ensminger, and Rankin became the first postmaster. The post office was dubbed White Cottage. Eventually it was discovered that another Newtonville existed in Ohio, so in the 1880s the railroad station here was named White Cottage—and eventually the community as a whole.

Whiteford *Lucas County.* In 1835, General David White laid out the plat for the town that arose here.

Whitehouse *Lucas County.* Laid out in 1864. A director of the Wabash Railroad Company, Edward Whitehouse, acquired this property in 1855.

White Oak *Brown County.* The hamlet stands at the intersection of White Oak Creek and White Oak Valley. It is known both as White Oak and as White Oak Valley, taking its name from the profusion of white oak trees in the neighborhood.

White Sulphur *Delaware County.* This diminutive collection of houses takes its label from nearby sulphur springs.

Whiteville *Fulton County.* The name must relate to one or more of the Whites who resided locally in an early year. A likely candidate is David White, born 1818, who settled near here in 1834. Jay White and Elmer White were also citizens of this area.

Wick *Ashtabula County.* The hamlet takes the name of the Presbyterian missionary who established the first Presbyterian church in the Western Reserve, the Reverend William Wick. The First Presbyterian Church of Youngstown was organized by him. A dissenting view comes from another source, stating that the community bears the name of C. C. Wick, a storekeeper at the site who went bankrupt in 1865 for his overextension of credit.

Wiertemburg *Carroll County.* Germans who settled here named Wiertemburg for the former German state that is now part of Baden-Württemberg. The town was platted in 1836 by John G. Hudelmeyer (or Huddlemyer).

Wigginsville *Clermont County.* Interestingly, there were individuals in the area at about the time this hamlet arose named J. R. Wiggins, J. R. Wiggans, J. D. Wiggans, Ben Wiggins, and J. W. Wiggins. Note the variations in spelling. However, a U.S. Geological Survey printout spells the town's name Wiggonsville. But stranger still is this passage from Aileen M. Whitt's atlas of Clermont County: "The [town's] name was a nickname of Benjamin South, who was a hatter in the area. Friends called him Ben 'Wiggins.'"

Wightman's Grove *Sandusky County.* The name emanates from Thelismer O. Wightman, owner of River Side Park (or Wightman's Grove) on the Sandusky River north of Fremont. Wightman, who was born in Ottawa County in 1847, developed and improved the site, laying off lots in 1924. The work was performed by a civil engineer, J. R. Kuns. The place subsequently became a popular summer resort.

Wilhelm Corners *Trumbull County.* Three Wilhelms are listed in the surname index of an old county history, associated with Bazetta Township, not far from this site. There is probably a relationship between the place-name and the family or families.

Wilkens' Corners *Licking County.* By 1811, a farm was being worked here by Daniel Wilkens. A few years later, Henry Wilkens arrived and ran a grist mill at the location.

Wilkshire Hills *Tuscarawas County.* The name of this relatively young community is an adaptation of that of its founder, Roger Wilkins, who laid out the place.

Willard *Huron County.* Founded in 1875. The place was first called Chicago or Chicago Junction because of the meeting here of the Sandusky, Mansfield, & Newark Railroad with the Baltimore & Ohio. But because names using "Chicago" caused a good deal of confusion, a label was chosen that honored the president of the B&O, Daniel Willard.

Williamsburg *Clermont County.* This small town is named for the city in Virginia.

Williamsfield *Ashtabula County.* The deed holders here were Joseph W. Brown, John Allen, and Samuel Parkman. Settlement took place about 1804. After the trio sold their holdings to General Joseph Williams, the place became known as Williamsfield.

Williamsport *Morrow County.* Laid out in 1836. Enoch Hart was perhaps the earliest settler here, but he divested his landholdings to Jerry Freeland. Freeland in turn sold out to William Dakan, who laid out the town and named it for himself.

Williamsport *Pickaway County.* Platted in 1818. Incorporated in 1842 or 1844. One theory is that the first postmaster here (from 1816 to 1820), John Williams, gave his name to the hamlet. A second possibility is that the place was named by Joshua Reynolds, who emigrated from Williamsport, Pennsylvania, and had an affinity for that name. A third possible explanation is that the name traces back to William B. Davis, who was postmaster off and on for fifty years. Williamsport is about ten miles from the old Erie Canal.

Williamstown *Hancock County.* The post office that was established here in 1835 was called Eagle, possibly after nearby Eagle Creek. There is also an Eagle Township in the county. The proprietor of the town site was John W. Williams, from whom the place took its name. He laid out the community in 1834.

Willoughby *Lake County.* This name traces back to Professor Westel Willoughby, a prominent educator who hailed from Herkimer County, New York. The place was settled about 1799, and in 1815 it was known as Chagrin, after the Chagrin River, which flowed through the site. The Willoughby name was affixed in 1834. The city was incorporated in 1883.

Willoughby Hills *Lake County.* Willoughby Hills sits on rolling land southwest of Willoughby. (See Willoughby entry.) It was incorporated in 1954 and is now a city.

Willowdell *Darke County.* This name is sometimes spelled Willodell. At one time, the place was referred to as Woodland, but postal authorities pointed to a Woodland, Michigan, and requested a name change for this locality. Bernard Littman, who was to be the first postmaster here, renamed it in 1890. A descendant states that Littman spotted a willow tree standing in a water-filled hole in a field and dubbed the spot Willowdell. The sharpshooter Annie Oakley was born here in 1860.

Willowick *Lake County.* William A. Flood was the moving force behind the formation of this entity in 1924. The name was formed by borrowing portions of the names of two nearby cities, Willoughby and Wickliffe. Willowick became a city in 1957.

Willowville *Clermont County.* Union volunteers mustered here before marching off to the Civil War; it was known then as Camp Lucas. The current name probably comes from the many willow trees in the vicinity.

Willowwood *Lawrence County. The History of Symmes Creek* states that Jacob Holschuh arrived here from nearby Washington County in 1870, married, and purchased the mill and general store. In 1880, he constructed a new store building (which still stands), and the U.S. Post Office Department opened a post office within it, making Holschuh postmaster. One day a visiting postal inspector asked residents to offer a name for the new office. A Mr. Wilson was chopping wood nearby. The inspector asked Wilson what he was doing and Wilson replied, "I'm chopping willow wood." According to the account, those present immediately agreed to name the post office Willowwood. (It is sometimes seen printed Willow Wood.) The site was known in an earlier age as Millville, owing to the presence here of John Brammer's mill, built in 1830.

Wills Creek *Coshocton County.* In *Names for a New Land,* by F. A. Morgan, the tale is told of George Washington having been sent to this area by the British governor of Virginia in 1754 to push back the French and their Native American allies. Washington's supply base was located near Maryland's Wills Creek, where a fortified warehouse was maintained at the point where the creek enters the Potomac. When Ebenezer Zane, coming from the same area, arrived at a point in Guernsey County, he encountered a sluggish stream that reminded him of his Maryland home. It became known as Wills Creek, and this Coshocton County settlement took its name from the waterway.

Willshire *Van Wert County.* Laid out, 1820 or 1821, by the landowner and surveyor, Captain James Riley. According to a newspaper item, Riley, an Irish sea captain, had been shipwrecked off Cape Bojador, northwest Africa, in 1815 and taken hostage by pirates. William Willshire, a British consul stationed at Mogador, Morocco, ransomed Riley, who never forgot the deed. After quitting his sea career, Riley entered the northwest Ohio wilderness, becoming a deputy surveyor under the surveyor-general of the United States, Edward Tiffin. When Riley settled in this area, he named his town in remembrance of the man who had rescued him from pirates. Riley was elected to the state legislature in 1823, but by 1826, in ill health, he had returned to the sea. He died there in 1840.

Wilmington *Clinton County (seat).* Incorporated in 1828, the city probably takes its name from Wilmington, North Carolina. Most places bearing this name, including the Wilmingtons in Delaware and Massachusetts, owe it ultimately to the Earl of Wilmington, Spencer Compton (1673?–1743), a British politician.

Wilson *Monroe and Belmont counties.* This relatively new town was begun by Wilson & Wells land developers in 1956. It was platted by Keith Harper, Robert W. Wells, and J. O. Wilson and named for Wilson.

Winameg *Fulton County.* Winameg is said to be named for a Native American chief.

Winchester *Adams County.* Laid out, 1815, by Joseph Darlinton. The village was incorporated in 1865. Darlinton was born near Winchester, Virginia, and gave this place the name of that town.

Windfall *Medina County.* It is said that a mighty wind—possibly a tornado—once struck here, felling all the large trees and possibly inspiring this name. By 1888, Windfall was an active hamlet.

Windham *Portage County.* The early holder of the real estate here was Caleb Strong, who in 1811 divested himself of the property. It was purchased by a group that named the place Strongsburg. Strong, however, was a Federalist who had opposed the War of 1812, a popular cause in the Western Reserve, so the village name grated on many residents as time wore on. In 1820, Strong's declining popularity prompted citizens to change the village name to honor a Connecticut town, Windham.

Windsor *Ashtabula County.* Settled, 1799, by Solomon Griswold and George Phelps. Windsor is also the name of the township here, formalized in 1811 and named by the original settlers for their embarkation point, Windsor, Connecticut.

Windsor *Richland County.* Initially dubbed West Windsor, this hamlet was laid out by A. T. Page, Joseph Page, Roger Moses, and Henry Page in 1837. Hailing from Windsor County, Vermont, the Pages imported the name to this locality.

Windsor Mills *Ashtabula County.* Just west of Windsor in Windsor Township, this hamlet is on Phelps Creek—a clue that at one time there was probably a mill at the site.

Winesburg *Holmes County.* The vicinity was settled as early as 1815, but it was not until about twelve years later that the first permanent home was established here. The village was laid out in 1832. Four bachelors from Philadelphia founded the town: the Reverend William Smith, Frederick Happold, John Michael Smith, and Dr. August Scheurer. Christian Smith, the reverend's brother, is given credit for laying out Winesburg. The name was suggested as Weinsberg by Dr. Scheurer for a German city remembered for its heroic women. It is related that when the German city was being besieged, its women pleaded with the enemy for one wish to be granted: that they be able to take their costly treasures with them. The request granted, they proceeded to carry their husbands out of Weinsberg. In 1833, the U.S. Post Office Department altered the Ohio town's spelling to Winesburg. Ohio-born writer Sherwood Anderson made the place famous in 1919 by entitling a collection of his stories *Winesburg, Ohio.*

Winfield *Tuscarawas County.* This hamlet was named for Winfield Correll, the deceased son of C. C. Correll, the town's first postmaster. The community was once known as Mechanicsburg and had the nickname "Pinchie." The latter came about when a blacksmith who was building his cabin refused to feed his helpers and one of them whooped "Pinchgut!" "Pinchie" was a shortened version that persisted for many years thereafter.

Wingert's Corners *Crawford County.* The post office here went by the name Brokensword. The hamlet takes its name from William Wingert.

Wingett Run *Washington County.* The community was once known as Scottown. But after Joseph Wingett established residence here at the mouth of a stream and called it Wingett's Run, the place became known by that moniker, or simply Wingett.

Winkler's Mills *Monroe County.* Godfrey Winkler owned and operated a mill at this location.

Winona *Columbiana County.* When locals desired to secure a post office for the site, this name, from Henry Wadsworth Longfellow's poem *The Song of Hiawatha* (1855), was adopted at a public meeting. The village had been established in the early 1800s. Among the first citizens were John, Thomas, Robert, and Zimri Whinnery, John Johnson, and James Burson.

Winters' Station *Sandusky County.* F. W. Clapp surveyed lots here in 1860 for Jacob Winters. He also surveyed lots for Meshac Frest and Carper Kollopp. (There may be errors in the spelling of these names, as they were taken from handwriting.) The "Station" portion of the name probably comes from the place's location on the Fremont & Indiana Railroad.

Wintersville *Jefferson County.* This city was laid out by and named for John D. Winters, who served as a Jefferson County commissioner. Incorporation took place in 1947.

Wisterman *Putnam County.* This diminutive place was named in recognition of David Wisterman of this county. He was born in Kalida, Putnam County, in 1838. A history of Putnam County lists twenty-five Wistermans.

Withamsville *Clermont County.* The Witham family founded and settled this hamlet. A Maine native, Morris Witham, purchased a thousand-acre tract, brought his children here, and settled the site in 1800.

Wolf *Tuscarawas County.* Laid out on the Cleveland & Marietta Railroad in 1874 by Enoch G. Wolf, this place was better known in an earlier time as Wolf's Station. Today it contains a small cluster of homes.

Wolf Creek *Washington County.* Wolf Creek, from which the place takes its name, was so designated because of the many wolves that roamed the area during settlement times. The last ones disappeared about 1832.

Wolfhurst *Belmont County.* It was 1910 when Charles J. Wolf recorded the plat of this village.

Wolf's Corners *Mahoning County.* Sometimes known simply as Wolf, this southern Milton Township site probably traces back to J. W. Wolf. Eleven others with the Wolf surname appear in the 1874 index of a county atlas.

Woodington *Darke County.* An early resident at this location was John Woodington. The place probably traces its name to him. Woodington was platted in 1871.

Woodland *Union County.* Woodland was never surveyed or platted. Its name was inspired by the same vast forest that suggested the name of nearby Richwood.

Woodmere Village *Cuyahoga County.* Incorporated in 1945 and sometimes referred to simply as Woodmere, this entity covers less than a square mile. The "mere" suffix may indicate a boundary line or a part or segment. The name as a whole was probably adopted because it sounded good or seemed promotional.

Woodsfield *Monroe County (seat).* Archibald Woods, from Wheeling, West Virginia, founded this village in 1815. It was incorporated in 1835.

Woodside *Wood County.* Surveyed, 1883, for Seymour W. Owen by D. D. Ames. Two factors may have combined to inspire the name—the town is in Wood County and there was a sawmill here in settlement days, suggesting an ample supply of timber nearby.

Woods' Station *Butler County.* This locale was once referred to as Rogersville and as Wood. The current name derives from the first president of what was referred to as the "Junction Railroad," John Woods. Hiram Pierson, its first citizen, is said to have conferred the name, which is sometimes truncated to Woods. The place was a stop on the CH&I division of the Cincinnati, Hamilton, & Dayton Railroad. The town itself dates to about 1858.

Woodstock *Champaign County.* Platted in 1834. Woodstock was settled as early as 1820 and before receiving its current name was known as Smithville and Hartford. The Woodstock designation is thought to have been attached about 1834; however, it is also said that pioneers from Woodstock, Vermont, arrived in 1837 or 1838.

Woodville *Clermont County.* Laid out, 1828, by Jesse Wood. The first house here was constructed by Adam Bobs. The community took on the name of the man who laid it out.

Woodville *Sandusky County.* Laid out in 1838. Some say this town was named for Ephraim Wood, a Vermont native who arrived here in 1832. One source, however, credits an Amos Wood with laying out the town in 1833 and claims that the name commemorates him. Still another source claims that the place was laid out in 1836 but agrees that it was named after Amos Wood, adding that Wood and George H. Price were the landowners.

Woodworth *Mahoning County.* Known at an early date as The Crossroads, this place after 1842 assumed the name Steamtown. By 1900, some local citizens considered this name degrading—especially when printed on Youngstown & Suburban Railroad tickets. Reportedly they renamed it in recognition of a local attorney who had performed legal services for the community, Lawrence Woodworth.

Woodyard's *Athens County.* James Woodyard emigrated to this area from Virginia sometime between 1805 and 1810.

Wooster *Wayne County (seat).* Founded in 1807 by the Larwills, who were the first settlers. The city's name honors the Revolutionary War general David Wooster (1711–1777). Now a city, Wooster was first incorporated in 1808.

Worstville *Paulding County.* Platted in 1882. Lying hard against the New York, Chicago, & Saint Louis Railroad, this community took the name of one of its founders, John W. Worst. With M. J. Patterson, C. D. Patterson, and others, Worst designed the town and filed the plat plan with the county recorder.

Worthington *Franklin County.* The Reverend James Kilbourne founded the city in 1803, laying it out in 1804. He gave it the name of an Ohio governor and member of Congress, Thomas Worthington (1773–1827). This name was confirmed in 1835 by an act of the Ohio legislature when the place was incorporated. As a city, it was incorporated in 1956.

Wren *Van Wert County.* The name was changed from Greenwood in 1883. The townspeople submitted the name Wren owing to the presence of a great many of the songbirds in the vicinity. Wren was incorporated in 1898.

Wrightsville *Morgan County.* This locality was laid out in 1838 by H. Wright and named for (perhaps also by) him.

Wrightview Heights *Greene County.* Laid out in 1953. At a meeting to select a name, Wrightview Heights was chosen; the place is close to Wright-Patterson Air Force Base. The base was named in part to honor the Wright brothers, Orville and Wilbur, of Dayton, inventors of the airplane.

Wyandot *Wyandot County.* It is recorded that when the first 160 acres were platted here, the site was named Wyandot "to honor the tribe whose reservation this land had been." The Wyandot tribe departed this area in 1842.

Wyoming *Hamilton County.* The place was named for Wyoming County, Pennsylvania, according to one source. A second source notes that "pleasant valley" is the interpretation of the Indian word *wyoming*. This community was founded in 1861 by Colonel Robert Reily of Butler County. Reily was killed in the Civil War Battle of Chancellorsville in 1863. Incorporation took place in 1874.

Xenia *Greene County (seat).* One day in 1803, several interested citizens—John Paul, William Beatty, General Benjamin Whiteman, his father-in-law and mother-in-law, and others—gathered to name their community. Greenville, Washington, and Wayne were among the names discussed. Eventually a scholarly looking gentleman stepped forward and, so the tale goes, said, "Gentlemen, allow me to suggest a name for your . . . town. In view of the kind and hospitable manner in which I have been treated whilst a stranger to most of you, allow me to suggest the name Xenia, taken from the Greek, and signifying hospitality." The others accepted the name among the nominations and voted on them. Xenia and another name received the same number of votes. General Whiteman's mother-in-law, Laticia Davis, was given the honor of casting the deciding vote, and she opted for Xenia. The scholarly gentleman was identified as the Reverend Robert Armstrong. Incorporation occurred in 1814.

Yale *Portage County.* Some historians speculate that a Yale alumnus here persuaded his fellow pioneers to name the place after his alma mater.

Yankeeburgh *Washington County.* Strong Yankee sentiment among the citizens gave this place its name. It was known as Yankeeburgh as early as 1865.

Yankee Lake *Trumbull County.* One source states that this name was probably influenced by New Englanders, or Yankees, who settled the locale. A source close to the community, however, points out that the site was known earlier as Lingermore

Lake. When a ballroom was opened here in 1927 replete with bands and beauty queens, a contest was held to name the ballroom. Because the place was virtually surrounded by Yankee Creek, it was decided to drop Lingermore and call the body of water Yankee Lake. Subsequently the village also came to be called Yankee Lake. The lake no longer exists; an informant states that "the dam broke and cost too much to repair, so the lake was drained." Yankee Lake Village was incorporated in 1934.

Yatesville *Fayette County.* This community is thought to have been established by M. L. Yates, whose name remained attached to the place.

Yellow Bud *Ross County.* Founded in 1800 or shortly thereafter, Yellow Bud is named for the stream here, Yellow Bud Creek.

Yellow House *Washington County.* George West, Jr., a huge, good-natured man, opened the West post office here in 1881 in his house and store. Situated on a hill, the yellow frame house became a landmark, and a small community known as Yellow House surrounded it.

Yellow Springs *Greene County.* Founded in 1804. For several decades, visitors were attracted to this place to partake of water from the local springs. The yellow discharges contained high concentrations of iron that were believed to be health-enhancing. Yellow Springs was incorporated in 1856.

Yelverton *Hardin County.* This town is the namesake of John Yelverton, who held a good deal of the equity in the Mad River & Lake Erie Railroad. Reportedly, persons named Goss and Harris conferred the honor in 1858.

Yoder *Allen County.* This community sprang up after oil was discovered locally. The name honors the family of a congressman of the time, S. S. Yoder (1841–1921).

York Center *Union County.* York Center is centrally located in York Township. The community was platted in 1841.

Yorkshire *Darke County.* Once a busy railroad town, this village was founded by Richard York in 1879.

Yorkville *Jefferson and Belmont counties.* Many of the early settlers came here from around York, Pennsylvania. They dubbed the village Yorkville; it is in York Township. The ultimate antecedent is probably York, England.

Yost *Perry County.* A German Catholic settler with the Yost surname resided here at an early time. It is believed that the Yost post office dates to 1897.

Youba *Athens County.* Although some citizens wanted to call the post office Morrison for the first postmaster, John Morrison, and his assistant and wife, Nettie Garrison Morrison, the postmaster himself preferred the name Yuba. That central

California town (now known as Yuba City) had been Morrison's headquarters from 1851 to 1857, when he was a horseshoer and blacksmith for a stagecoach line operating between San Francisco and Nevada City, California. Morrison often reminisced about Yuba Dam, Yuba Pass, and Yuba Mine. When the name was submitted to Washington, a mixup resulted in the addition of an "o," yielding Youba instead of Yuba.

Youngstown *Mahoning County (seat).* In 1797, John Young, a surveyor newly arrived with a party of settlers from Whitestown, New York, laid out this city with the assistance of Turhand Kirtland. It is believed that Young applied his own name to the site. The city's incorporated status was recognized in 1849.

Youngsville *Adams County.* David Young founded this hamlet and in 1840 opened a store at the site. Also toiling here as a merchant was J. F. Young.

Z

Zaleski *Vinton County.* Laid out in 1856. Peter Zaleski, a Pole of considerable means residing in Spain, established a mining company that operated locally. His company also laid out and named the town, which was incorporated in 1880.

Zanesfield *Logan County.* An early landowner at this locale was Isaac Zane. The town takes its name from him. It was settled in 1819.

Zanesville *Muskingum County (seat).* Ebenezer Zane (1747–1812), the architect of Zane's Trace, a congressionally sanctioned path blazed through the wilderness of southeastern and southern Ohio, and his brother Jonathan are the persons commemorated in this place-name. They were assisted in their pathfinding efforts by Ebenezer's son-in-law, John McIntire. McIntire and Jonathan laid out a town here in 1799. It was first called Westbourne, but the Post Office Department started referring to the place as Zane's Town. It may have been 1801 when the name underwent its final change to Zanesville. Incorporation as a village came in 1814 and as a city in 1850.

Zenz City *Mercer County.* In 1898, the Zenz family kept a store here in a large, two-story brick building. In 1904, the place ceased to have a post office. Previously it was known as Violet. It is seen on at least one popular current map as Zens City. The latter style may have validity, as one source claims that the town was founded by a John Zen. This source also states that the previous name of the location was Sharpsburg.

Zimmerman *Greene County.* Jacob Zimmerman was the first settler here.

Zoar *Tuscarawas County.* Settled, 1817, by Separatists led by Joseph M. Bimeler. The name stems from the biblical city to which Lot fled after leaving Sodom. Ohio's Zoar was incorporated in 1846.

Zoar *Warren County.* This biblical name suggests "smallness." Zoar was one of five cities spaced along the floor of the Jordan Valley. To provide refuge for Lot, it was spared the destruction that befell Sodom.

Zoarville *Tuscarawas County.* Laid out in 1882. A previous name of this community was Valley City, which duplicated the name of another Ohio place. The change to Zoarville was appropriate, for the place was founded by members of the Zoarite sect.

County Names

Adams. Named for John Adams, second president of the United States.

Allen. Named in honor of Ethan Allen, leader of the Green Mountain Boys during the Revolutionary War.

Ashland. Named for the estate maintained near Lexington, Kentucky, by the famous political figure Henry Clay.

Ashtabula. The word *ashtabula* derives from an Indian term for "fish." The county is the largest of Ohio's eighty-eight counties.

Athens. Athens, Greece, the ancient center of classical learning, is the place for which this county is named.

Auglaize. "Fallen timbers" is the accepted translation of this Shawnee word.

Belmont. The French word signifies "beautiful mountain." It was probably inspired by the awesome views available from the county's higher elevations, which look out over the Ohio River.

Brown. The namesake, General Jacob Brown, defeated the British in the Battle of Lundy's Lane during the War of 1812.

Butler. General Richard Butler, for whom this county was named, was killed in General Arthur St. Clair's defeat by the Indians in 1791.

Carroll. The name comes from the last surviving signer of the Declaration of Independence, Charles Carroll.

Champaign. The name comes from the French word *champ* and refers to a broad stretch of level land.

Clark. Named for General George Rogers Clark, active during the Indian wars.

Clermont. The French word suggests "clear mountain."

Clinton. Named for the vice president of the county's organizational body, George Clinton, who had also been a delegate to the second Continental Congress. Clinton County was established in 1810.

Columbiana. The name joins the names of Christopher Columbus and Queen Anne.

Coshocton. The Anglicized Indian word has come to be translated as "black bear town."

Crawford. Colonel William Crawford, for whom the county was named, was a close friend of George Washington and a soldier during the Indian Wars and the Revolutionary War.

Cuyahoga. This Indian word, which translates as "crooked," was inspired by the Cuyahoga River. The river wends a tortuous course through the county and beyond.

Darke. Named for Colonel William Darke, a Revolutionary War soldier who led the retreat from the disastrous American defeat at Fort Recovery in 1791. This is the only Darke County in the United States.

Defiance. Carved out of the wilderness, the county found itself a hotbed of conflict during the Indian Wars. Its people were said to have defied the Indians, thus inspiring the name. Fort Defiance was here.

Delaware. The Delawares who lived in this vicinity inspired the name. The Native American tribe took its name from the Delaware River of Pennsylvania and Delaware, along which it had formerly lived.

Erie. The name comes from the Erie Indians. *Erie* is said to translate as "cat" or "the nation of the cats." In the Huron tongue, *eriche* or *erige* is thought to signify "lake of the cats." The reference to cats is believed to refer to a species of wildcat that frequented the region occupied by the Erie Indians.

Fairfield. According to historians, Arthur St. Clair, the first governor of the Northwest Territory, conferred the name. It is thought that he was impressed by the region's "fair fields," some of the richest agricultural land in the state.

Fayette. Named out of respect for the Marquis de Lafayette, the Frenchman who distinguished himself by fighting on the side of the Americans during the Revolution.

Franklin. Named in honor of Benjamin Franklin.

Fulton. Named for the man who pioneered the steamboat, Robert Fulton.

Gallia. Settled by the French Five Hundred, this county takes its name from the ancient Latin name of France, *Gallia*.

Geauga. "Raccoon" is said to be the English equivalent of the Native American word *geauga*.

Greene. Named for a hero of the American Revolution, Nathaniel Greene.

Guernsey. The name stems from the Isle of Guernsey, from which many early settlers of this county came.

Hamilton. It is believed that the name honors Alexander Hamilton.

Hancock. Named out of respect and admiration for a signer of the Declaration of Independence, John Hancock. Hancock presided over the Continental Congress.

Hardin. Named for General John Hardin, a Revolutionary War veteran who was sent on a peace mission by President George Washington. Hardin was slain here by Miami Indians.

Harrison. Named for General William Henry Harrison, who distinguished himself in the War of 1812 and was the first citizen of Ohio to be elected president.

Henry. The county took the name of Patrick Henry, a Virginian who was noted for his oratorical skills and patriotism ("Give me liberty, or give me death").

Highland. The name stems from the county's location in a hilly, upland region between the Little Miami and Scioto rivers.

Hocking. The Native American term *hockhocking* is the basis for this name. It translates roughly as "bottle." The shorter version came about as a result of Anglicization.

Holmes. Named for a daring young officer, Major Holmes, who lost his life in the ill-fated attack on Mackinac during the War of 1812.

Huron. The Wyandot Indians of this area were referred to as Hurons by the French.

Jackson. Named for Andrew Jackson, "Old Hickory," who led the victory over the British at New Orleans during the War of 1812 and became the seventh U.S. president in 1829.

Jefferson. The name comes from that of the man who was president at the time the county was formed, Thomas Jefferson.

Knox. Henry Knox, George Washington's chief of artillery during the Revolutionary War, was honored in the naming of this county.

Lake. The name comes from the county's location on the south shore of Lake Erie. Lake is the smallest county in Ohio.

Lawrence. During the War of 1812, Captain James Lawrence of the U.S. Navy commanded the frigate *Chesapeake*. Although he was defeated and killed by the British, the daring young officer was considered a hero after telling his men, "Don't give up the ship!"

Licking. The Licking River flows through the county and suggested the county's name. Salt licks in the vicinity inspired the name of the waterway.

Logan. Named for an officer in the Indian Wars, General Benjamin Logan. In 1796, he led soldiers who destroyed several Native American encampments in the area.

Lorain. Named for the Lorraine region of France at the request of Heman Ely, founder of the city of Elyria.

Lucas. Named for Robert Lucas, an early governor of Ohio. The county is at the border with Michigan, and Governor Lucas in 1835 declared war against Michigan in a disagreement over the location of the state line.

Madison. The fourth president, James Madison, was serving at the time this county was formed.

Mahoning. "At the lick" or "at the licks" is thought to be the meaning of this word, which is said to be French.

Marion. The "Swamp Fox" of the Revolutionary War, General Francis Marion, is the person for whom the county was named. He is remembered for his effective tactics against the British.

Medina. The name traces back to the burial city of Muhammad in Saudi Arabia.

Meigs. The name comes from an early governor of Ohio, Return Jonathan Meigs.

Mercer. General Hugh Mercer, who gained fame during the Revolutionary War, is the person after whom the county was named.

Miami. *Miami* is believed to be an Ottawa Indian term for "mother."

Monroe. James Monroe was a candidate for the highest office in the land when the county was formed. He became the fifth U.S. president.

Montgomery. Named for General Richard Montgomery, who died in the American assault on Quebec in 1775.

Morgan. General Daniel Morgan was honored with the christening of this county. He earned fame during the Revolutionary War.

Morrow. At the time of the formation of this county, Jeremiah Morrow was Ohio governor. He also served in the U.S. Senate and House.

Muskingum. "A town by the river" is reported to be the rough translation of this Delaware Indian term.

Noble. When the county was being organized, Warren Noble chaired the state's committee on additional counties, and he became the county's namesake.

Ottawa. The Ottawa Indians were noted for their trading culture, and the word is said to mean "trader."

Paulding. Named for John Paulding, a hero during the Revolutionary War.

Perry. Named for the hero of the Battle of Lake Erie (1813), Commodore Oliver Hazard Perry.

Pickaway. This label derives from the Indian term *piqua* and translates as "man risen from the ashes."

Pike. This name comes from the discoverer of Pike's Peak, Zebulon Pike.

Portage. Indians once traversed this area, using it as a portage between two rivers, the Tuscarawas and the Cuyahoga.

Preble. Named for Captain Edward Preble, a naval commander in the Revolutionary and Tripolitan wars.

Putnam. The name comes from a prominent Revolutionary War figure, General Israel Putnam, a Massachusetts native.

Richland. This name was inspired by the county's agriculturally rich farmlands.

Ross. A Federalist political figure, James A. Ross, was recognized in the naming of the county. Ross is said to have been a close friend of the first governor of the Northwest Territory, Arthur St. Clair.

Sandusky. Most interpreters believe that the Native American word *sandusky* means "at the cold water."

Scioto. "Deer" is said to be the meaning of the Native American term *scioto* (or *scionto*).

Seneca. Named for the Seneca tribe of Native Americans who once resided in the area.

Shelby. Named for Kentucky's first governor, General Isaac Shelby, who served during the American Revolution.

Stark. Remembered as the "Hero of Bennington," General John Stark, for whom the county was named, distinguished himself during the Revolutionary War.

Summit. Relative to surrounding areas, this county possesses a high elevation, which suggested the name.

Trumbull. This entity is named in honor of an early Connecticut governor, Jonathan (or Johnathon) Trumbull. George Washington, whom he served in the American Revolution, is said to have nicknamed him Brother Jonathan, a term that later became a common way of referring to any American. Governor Trumbull (1740–1809) at other times served as a U.S. congressman and senator. Connecting Trumbull County to Connecticut is the fact that the area lies within the Connecticut Western Reserve.

Tuscarawas. "Open mouth" is considered to be the translation of this Indian term.

Union. This county was formed from parts of four other counties, thus creating a "union."

Van Wert. Named after the Revolutionary War hero Isaac Van Wart. The spelling of Wart was corrupted to Wert.

Vinton. The county owes its name to an early Ohio political figure, Samuel Finley Vinton.

Warren. Named for General Joseph Warren, who lost his life during the Revolutionary War in the Battle of Bunker Hill.

Washington. When this county was formally created, George Washington was heading the Constitutional Convention.

Wayne. Named in honor of General Anthony Wayne.

Williams. Named in remembrance of a hero of the Revolutionary War, David Williams.

Wood. Named in honor of an officer in the War of 1812, Colonel Wood. The colonel is said to have been the engineer who built Fort Meigs, a compound that repelled numerous attacks by the British and Native Americans.

Wyandot. The name recognizes the Wyandot Indians, who remained in the area until about 1842.

Acknowledgments

The compiler is grateful to the following for submitting information that was helpful in composing the entries.

Nancy Abels
Leah Arbaugh
Vera Arthur
Ashtabula County Historical Society
Mark Baer
Marilyn H. Bagby
Amy Baker
Lois A. Baker
Mark A. Baker
Patricia Baumann
Richard E. Baumbach
Mary Nichols Bettle
David Blair
Jim Blount
Don Bogosian
Laura Boltz
Elaine Borkosky

Charles W. Boso, Jr.

Margaret Bouic

Peg Breitweg

John W. Bricker

Betty Brooks

Isabel B. Brothers

Thea Murray Burns

James Caccamo

Floyd W. Call, Jr.

Sarah Calvin

Ruth Carper

Marcella Cartwright

Eleanor Carver

Crawford C. Childers

Pauline Cline

Bernard E. Clinehens

Clifton C. Cook

Denise Cook

Richard L. Cooley

Ona Fay Coons

Beverly Cowles

Norma Craven

George Crout

John Crusey

Michael P. Dansack, Jr.

Sheila Darrow

Debbie Davidson

Bekkie J. Davis

Jack Davis

Don Dean

Audrey DeBolt

Edgar W. Dennis

Patti DeVaughn

Jerry B. Devol

Edward Dickey

Judy Dillon

Joseph A. Dubyak

Walter F. Dymond

Gary Edwards

Arlene J. Egelsky

Carl Thomas Engel

Carl Erchenbrecher

Robert E. Ervin
Franklin Etter
Victor Evers
Joyce Falinski
Lou Farmer
Bette Fetters
Kimberley D. Fields
Judith Davidson Fisher
Norma L. Flannery
Mary Fleming
Walter T. Florence
Paul M. Frankart
Shirley W. Fletcher
David L. Forgatsch
Isabelle Fourman
Franklin County Genealogical Society
Kathryn Gardner
Daryl G. Garrison
Linda M. Gieser
Audrey Gilbert
Madelene Gilmore
Leland V. Girton
Nina Glass
Ruth Gove
Atha Gray
Dwight Greer
Esther Gregg
Velma S. Griffin
Julia L. Hach
Brian Hackett
Zoe Hannum
Barbara Hart
Ruth Hart
Jane S. Havens
Dallas Haydon
Gerri Heck
Dorothy Helton
Joyce Hintz
Janice Holm
Jean Holt
James R. Hopkins
Louisene Hoy

Jerry Hughes
Beth Ann Hummel
Grace Jackson
Charles M. Jacobs
Barbara Jewell
James Michael Johnson
Ethel Jones
Dennis Jordan
Mrs. Herman Kaltenbach
Della S. Kaple
Frances Kluter
Dave Knapke
Myra Studer Koop
Rita Kopp
K. Kubb
Marilyn Kuntz
Gladys Lafontaine
Lula Bell Lash
Mary Louise Leslie
Will H. Lewis
Bevan Linn
Dr. Kenneth Lloyd
Harriet Loar
Christine Long
Walter Martin
Dorothy L. Mattox
Marcus Maxwell
Richard B. McClimans
Eloise Mechling
Pat Medert
Tom Mehling
Miami Historical Society of Whitewater Township
H. Dale Michael
Mary W. Miller
M. LaVerne Mitchell
Zelma L. Morgan
J. Gordon Morrow
Alice Morton
Warren Motts
Helen Mowrey
Woody L. Mullenhour
Fran Murphey

Charles A. Murray
Howard R. Nutter
James C. Oda
Wilma Osborn
Marie Osborne
Ilena Palmer
S. Pascual
Peggy Patterson
Eileen Pleiman
Ernestine Polsley
Dwight E. Price
Linda K. Queen
Rita Ray
Thomas B. Rentschler
Jack Rhea
Perma Jean Rice
Ettie E. Rieman
Mrs. Don Rininger
Adrian E. Roberts
Virginia B. Robinson
David Rodich
Edna Romick
Evelyn B. Rothgeb
Helen Omwake Rouser
Kim Roush
Donna Ruse
John L. Sanford
Beecher Saunders
Jackie Sautter
Mary Louise Sayre
Cathy J. M. Schaefer
Milton Schumm
Carl H. Shamhart
Shelby County Genealogical Society
M. Shultz
Lois A. Shumway
Jo Anne Slaymaker
Alma Aicholtz Smith
Greg Smith
Mrs. Thomas E. Smith
Virginia Smith
Nyle Stateler

George F. Stilwell
Mary L. Strait
Joe Strotman
James Sturgeon
Norm Swaisgood
Frances Swartz
Elinor M. Taylor
June Thayer
Eulalia M. Thompson
Stephen A. Tilley
Sandra Tracy
Genie Ulp
Edward Valentine
Mrs. Don Vandemark
Eugene Van Voorhis
Grandon E. Wade
Marion Watson
Darlene F. Weaver
Walter C. Weigel
Paulette J. Weiser
Clarissa Went
Alden White
Joan White
Joan G. Will
Willard F. Willson
Catherine Wilson
Dorothy E. Wingard
Margaret Zeller